# REDISCOVERING SAINT PATRICK

THIS BOOK IS DEDICATED TO
JOHN VICTOR LUCE
(1921–2011)

Marcus Losack

# Rediscovering
# Saint Patrick

the columba press

First published in 2013 by
## the columba press
55A Spruce Avenue,
Stillorgan Industrial Park,
Blackrock, Co. Dublin

Origination by The Columba Press
Cover design by Shaun Gallagher
Printed by Bell & Bain Limited

ISBN 9781 78218 017 3

The publishers are grateful for permission to use the following materials in the publication of this book: Translations of St Patrick's *Confession* and *Letter to Coroticus* are by John Luce (2009), revised by Marcus Losack (2011) incorporating elements from N. J. White (1905), Ludwig Bieler (1962), Daniel Conneely (1979), Pádraig McCarthy (2001), © John Luce and Marcus Losack, 2011. Passages from Dom Morice *Histoire de Bretagne* are translated by Francine Bernier; extracts from Joseph Viel *La Gouesnière et Bonaban* (Dinan, 1912) translated by Francine Bernier and Christophe Saint-Eloi. Maps of Roman Britain and the settlement in Brittany at the time of the rebellion of Magnus Maximus (385 CE) and the Bay of Mont St Michel including the ancient Forest of Quokelunde are by Kevin O'Kelly, Alan Oram and Marcus Losack, based on the work of L'Abbé Manet and René Henry. The map of La Forêt de Quokelunde and coastline before the inundation of the Bay of Mont St Michel by the sea in 709 CE is by René Henry, *Au Peril de la Mer*, © Éditions Découvrance, La Rochelle, 2006. The aerial photograph on page 250 is reproduced with the kind permission of Château de Bonaban. Genealogical tables for the early kings of Brittany are from Pierre Le Baude, Dom Morice and M. Daru. A number of other charts have been adapted from various genealogical tables compiled by Laurence Gardner and published in *The Bloodline of the Holy Grail* (New York, 2001). These have been greatly simplified, showing only the main lines of descent and succession that are relevant to the origins of St Patrick. If we have failed to acknowledge or trace any copyright material, we offer our sincere apologies.

# Contents

The personality, birthplace and mission of Saint Patrick constitute a link between ourselves and our sister island, appealing to the deepest sympathies of religion and consanguinity, which I should be loath to see dissevered, and which I hope, therefore, may resist the rudest assaults of sceptical criticism, although this and every other consideration must give way to the voice of truth. It is impossible that all of which has been handed down to us as to the existence and actions of such a personage should be a mere fiction – that a nation should have been deceived as to the most important event of its history – the introduction of Christianity, and the man who was the principal instrument in the work; or that it should have made itself, either voluntarily or involuntarily, the agent of deception.

St Patrick has an abiding presence, whose memory is in the hearts of millions … And with his spirit we may still hold communion through the literary remains, scanty as they are, which he has bequeathed to us.

*J. H. Tukner, MA,*
*Scotland, 1872*

# KEY GEOGRAPHICAL REFERENCES

*Alba:* An ancient name for Scotland.

*Britannia:* (Latin, singular) The Roman name for Britain.

*Britanniis:* (Latin, plural) The name given for St Patrick's homeland. Trans: 'in the Britains' or 'in Brittany'.

*Britannias:* (Latin, plural) Also recorded as Patrick's homeland.

*Bannavem Tiburniae:* The place where Calpurnius (Patrick's father) owned the estate from which St Patrick was taken captive.

*Caledonia:* The Roman name for the northern region of the island of Britain, now Scotland.

*Gaul:* A region of Empire on the continent.

*Galliis:* (Latin, plural) Trans: 'the Gauls'. Mentioned by St Patrick as the place that he longed to visit to see the religious friends for whom he held great affection.

*Silua Uoclut/Vocluti:* (Latin) Known in Irish as 'Fochlad'. Wood of Foclut. A place that St Patrick remembered in a disturbing dream when he heard the 'Voice of the Irish' calling him to return to them.

*Tyrrhene Sea:* Refers to the Bay of St Malo between the Isles de Chaussey, Tombelaine and Mont St Michel.

*Isles of the Tyrrhene Sea:* Islands where there were early forms of monastic community in the Bay of Mont St Michel.

*Nemthor (Naem Tor/Tours/Nemturris):* Recorded in later documents as the place where St Patrick was born.

*Sabhall:* (Gaelic) Trans: 'Barn'. The place where St Patrick founded his first church in Ireland. Now known as Saul, near Downpatrick, County Down.

*Armorica:* The name applied by the Romans to Brittany.

*Armoric Letha:* A coastal region of Armorica. Identified in some of the ancient sources as the place where St Patrick was taken captive. Also known as 'Letha' or 'Lethania Britannia'.

*La Forêt de Quokelunde:* (French) An ancient forest in Brittany. Local traditions record that Irish pirates crept up through this forest before they attacked the Calpurnius estate at Bannavem Tiburniae and took St Patrick captive.

# HISTORICAL BACKGROUND

307 Constantine Chlorus becomes Emperor in Britain.

314 Constantine the Great, son of Contantine Chlorus, becomes Emperor of Rome.

323 Birth of St Martin.

336 Athanasius, exiled in Gaul, founds monastery at Trier.

357 Publication of St Athanasius' *Life of Antony*.

360 Hilary helps Martin (aged 37) found monastery at Liguge.

380 Maximus invited to marry Helen or Ellen, daughter of Eudes (Eudav Hen) a king of the ancient Britons.

383 Maximus declared 'king' and Emperor by the Roman Legions in Britain under his command.

383 Rebellion of Magnus Maximus. British Legions cross to Gaul landing at Aleth (St Malo) and the mouth of the Rhine, attacking on two fronts. Maximus takes over the imperial palace at Trier as a centre for his command. Valentinian flees, Gratian killed in Paris.

383 Maximus becomes Emperor of the West, in a treaty with Theodosius, Emperor of the East and is recognised by Sulpitius Severus as 'king'. Martin lobbies Maximus in support of the Priscillians.

383 Calpurnius leaves Strathclyde in Northern Britain and follows Conan to Brittany as part of the settlement under the new Emperor, Magnus Maximus.

384 Possible birth of St Patrick.

385 Queen Helen (Ellen) develops a close relationship with St Martin and becomes a devoted servant.

385 St Augustine converts to Christianity.

385 Conan made king of Bretagne, Duke of Armorica.

388 Martin warns Maximus that Valentinian is plotting to kill him. Maximus allows Priscillian to be executed.

389 In Brittany, Conan marries St Patrick's sister, Darerca.

393 Paulinas of Nola and his wife take vow of continence.

393 Conversion of Sulpicius Severus to asceticism.

394  Sulpicius Severus visits Martin (aged 70) at Marmoutier.

395  St Augustine writes the 'Confessions'. Severus writes a Life of Martin (but delays publication).

397  Death of St Martin. 11 November.

398  Irish King Niall of the Nine Hostages raids Brittany. The raids continue for the next five years.

400  Patrick, aged 16, taken captive from Bannavem Tiburniae.

401   Given as date for St Martin's death. Also given as 405.

405  Pelagius travels to Rome and North Africa to challenge St Augustine's Doctrine of 'Original Sin'.

405  Roman troops leave Britain, enter Gaul to defend Rome.

406  On 31 December the River Rhine freezes again at Mainz. Barbarians cross in vast numbers and rampage through Gaul. Thousands killed. Parts of Gaul become a 'wasteland'.

407  Patrick escapes from Ireland, returns by ship to Brittany.

407  Patrick joins St Martin's community at Marmoutier for four years and is trained and tonsured there.

410  August 29th, Alaric enters the Salesian Gates in Rome.

411  Patrick leaves St Martin's monastery on the Loire. Joins a community of 'barefoot hermits' in the 'isles of the Tyrrhene Sea' located off the coast of northwest Brittany. Undertakes spiritual formation there for nine years.

420  Augustine and Jerome write and campaign strongly against the 'heresies' of Pelagius and Priscillian.

421  Death of Conan in Brittany. Pelagius condemned. Disappears, possibly killed.

421? Patrick 'sells his nobility'. Commissioned by St Senior on Mont St Michel. Patrick returns to Ireland as an apostle.

423  Darerca (Conan's widow) goes to Ireland to help her brother St Patrick in his mission. Grallon appointed king in Brittany. He marries St Patrick's sister, Tigris.

429  St Germanus sent by Pope Celestine to Britain to combat 'the Pelagian Heresy'.

431  Palladius sent to Ireland by Pope Celestine as 'the first bishop to the Irish believing in Christ' (Prosper).

432  Traditional date given for St Patrick's arrival in Ireland.

459? St Patrick writes his *Letter to Coroticus* of Strathclyde.

460? St Patrick writes the '*Confession*'.

461  Traditional date given for St Patrick's death. Patrick disappears from all known historical and ecclesiastical records for the next two hundred years.

664  The Synod of Whitby. Wilfrid acts as spokesperson for Rome. The Kingdom of Northumbria accepts the authority of the Roman Church, regarding tonsure and the Easter cycle.

672  Wilfrid arranges for Dagobert II to marry Gizeles, Comptes de Razés. With Wilfrid's support, Dagobert is restored to the Merovingian throne in Gaul.

678  Dagobert's assassination. Wilfrid's God-daughter marries Gizeles de Razés (according to Lobineau's genealogy).

680  Anglo-Saxons take the Kingdom of Strathclyde and pose a real military threat to Ireland.

681  Muirchú writes a 'biography' of St Patrick. Civil war in Ireland between Romani and Hibernensi.

695? 'The Donation of Constantine' is published in Rome.

697  Synod of Birr in Ireland. Roman Reforms accepted.

697  St Patrick is accepted as patron saint of all Ireland, founder of the Church in Armagh and is now officially recognised as Ireland's apostle.

720  King Nechtan of the Picts evicts Irish monks and declares his kingdom to be conformed with Rome.

780  Welsh Church conforms to Rome.

795  Vikings attack Ireland and Scotland.

800  Charlemagne crowned in Rome as the new Emperor.

1066 Battle of Hastings, the Normans takeover Britain.

1156 Norman Invasion of Ireland. The 'Romanisation' of Western Christendom is secured until the Reformation.

# A POSSIBLE CHRONOLOGY FOR SAINT PATRICK

384:    St Patrick's family move from Scotland to Brittany.

385:    Patrick is born in Brittany (possibly at Tours or on his father's estate at Bannavem Tiburniae).

401:    Patrick is taken captive from Brittany.

407:    He escapes from slavery in Ireland.

407–411:    Patrick is trained at the monastery of St Martin of Tours.

411–420:    Patrick undertakes religious formation with 'barefoot hermits' in the isles of Tyrrhene Sea (near Mont St Michel).

420–428:    Patrick continues religious formation in these islands.

428:    St Patrick is ordained as a bishop by St Senior on Mont St Michel and commissioned for the mission to Ireland.

428:    Patrick returns to Ireland as an apostle.

429:    St Germanus sent to Britain by Pope Celestine.

431:    Palladius sent to Ireland by Pope Celestine as part of the first official mission from Rome.

432:    Traditional date given in the Irish annals for the beginning of St Patrick's mission in Ireland.

461:    Traditional date given for St Patrick's death.

CHAPTER ONE

# Rediscovering Patrice

Sometimes the meaning of a journey
Is unknown to the traveller[1]

As we drove through the old wrought-iron gates along a tree-lined avenue towards the front entrance of the hotel there was a moment of sudden anxiety and disappointment. We expect French châteaus to be luxurious, extravagant and well kept but this one seemed strangely neglected. First impressions are notoriously unreliable.

I had travelled to Brittany with a colleague and close friend to research some of the sacred sites associated with the Celtic tradition in Brittany. The hotel had been booked online at the last minute, simply to provide a break from work and celebrate a jubilee birthday.

All the tower rooms at the château have high ceilings and spectacular views of the grounds and surrounding forest. I noticed a coat of arms at the top of a sheet of headed note paper which had been left on the table. Written in French with an English translation, it provided basic information for guests about the château's history and local significance, as follows:

> The first castle or rather fortress that was built here dates from the Roman period, during the fourth century. At that time, this place was called Bonavenna (or Bonabes) de Tiberio. It belonged to a Scottish prince, Calpurnius, who had come here to avoid Saxon forces who were invading Britain … One night, Irish pirates arrived in nearby Cancale. They spread through the Wood of Quokelunde, which stretched under Gouesnière-Bonaban as far as Plerguèr. Armed with pikes and axes, they slaughtered the prince and all his family. His property was looted and the castle burned to the ground … Only his young son, Patrice, survived from this slaughter. He was taken captive to Ireland. There he looked after sheep and learned the language of the country of which he became the oracle and the disciple.
>
> *Historical Information, Château Bonaban, St Malo*

I have read a lot of books about the Irish saints and have visited many of the ancient, sacred sites associated with St Patrick in Ireland, but before arriving at this hotel I had no idea whatsoever that Patrick had any connections with Brittany.

I had to read Château Bonaban's historical information for guests again to process the enormity of what was being said. Could this really be the place where St Patrick once lived, before he was taken captive and sold as a slave in Ireland?

The only reliable historical information we have about St Patrick is contained in his own writings. Patrick wrote two letters, dated to the fifth century.[2] In his *Confession*, he mentions the name of a place where his father owned an estate, which he called 'Bannavem Tiburniae' in Latin.[3] One day, when St Patrick was only sixteen years old, the estate was attacked by pirates. Patrick was taken captive to Ireland, where he was sold as a slave. These are St Patrick's words, based on the oldest surviving copy of his *Confession* found in the *Book of Armagh*, a tenth-century Irish manuscript now preserved in Trinity College, Dublin:

> I am Patrick, a sinner, without a formal education, the least of all the faithful and utterly despised by many. My father was Calpurnius (a Decurion) the son of Potitus, an elder from the village of Bannavem Tiburniae; he had a small estate nearby from where I was taken captive. I was then about sixteen years of age.[4]

Old Irish and Breton sources say his father and mother, Calpurnius and Conchessa (who is said to have been 'French' and a close relative of St Martin of Tours), were both killed during the attack, together with many others.[5] Bannavem Tiburniae has never been identified, its precise location lost to historical memory in the years after St Patrick's death. Countless books have been written about St Patrick over the centuries but we still don't know where he came from and, therefore, who he really was. Most scholars insist he came from somewhere in Britain, either Strathclyde in Scotland, Wales, Cumbria, the Bristol Channel or even Glastonbury in England.

Almost two hundred years ago an Irish scholar claimed to have identified Patrick's homeland and birthplace on the continent in what is now north-west France but he could not provide the necessary detailed local evidence to convince the majority.[6]

The uncertainty about St Patrick's place of origins has never been resolved. It is one of the great unsolved mysteries surrounding his life and the unknown origins of the early Irish church.

I had to look closely again at the names, in English and French. The historical information provided for guests of Château Bonaban was intriguing not least because of the way the names were spelled. 'Bonaban' and its older form 'Bonavenna' or 'Bonabes de Tiberio' was clearly recognisable as another form of the name for Patrick's home which he called 'Bannavem Tiburniae' in Latin but there was something even more intriguing about the information provided by the hotel. Could the French Forest of Quokelunde be the same as the Irish Wood of Foclut that St Patrick remembered in his dream when he heard the 'Voice of the Irish' calling him to return? This is how Patrick described the dream he had about this wood:

> One night in a dream, I saw a man whose name was Victor, dressed as if coming from Ireland and carrying many letters. He gave me one of them to read and as I did, I heard the *Voice of the Irish*.
>
> In that same moment as I was reading I thought I could hear the voice of those around the Wood of Foclut, which is close beside the Western Sea. It was as if they were crying out to me with one voice, 'We beg you, O holy youth, to come and walk once more among us.' I woke up suddenly feeling that my heart was broken and I could read no further.[7]

Suddenly, there was a feeling of being drawn into a tangled web of history and touched by the hidden hand of destiny. Could it be possible that both these places were right here under our feet, in the grounds of the château? The names looked the same except for slight variations in spelling but this can be accounted for. When names were copied in ancient manuscripts, letters were often changed to reflect the way language was spoken and written in different countries. The most common practice was to change a 'v' into a 'b' or a 'd' into a 't'. This tendency to change letters affected place names especially.[8]

The linguistic principle is fairly simple. The letter 't' is difficult to pronounce whilst 'd', its correlative, is easier for the mouth to grasp. 'D' is often used when the tongue intended 't' or 'th'. The Welsh say 'Tafyd' when the English is 'David'. Germans say 'dank' and the English 'thanks' or 'durst' rather than 'thirst'. The conversion of a 'b' into a 'v' is very common. The name 'Foclut' or 'Foclud', for example, appears as 'Fochlad' in Old Irish and 'Voclut' or 'Uirclut' in Latin. Could this explain the difference in spellings between 'Foclut' and 'Quokelunde' and 'Bannavem' or 'Bonaban'?

According to linguistics expert Christine Mohrman, who made a detailed study of St Patrick's Latin, there are definite Gaulish influences in Patrick's writings; influences that in her opinion, could not have come from Scotland, Wales or anywhere else in Britain.[9] If the local tradition provided for guests staying at Château Bonaban was true, it would have enormous implications for our traditional understanding of St Patrick.

Any plans we might have had for the next day now had to be cancelled. Local research was required in the hope of finding some historical evidence to support the château's claim to fame. After breakfast the next morning we decided to visit St Malo, the nearest large town, hoping to find a book or perhaps an old map to verify the names. Imagine our surprise when we saw the sign on the roadside. The name 'Quokelunde' appeared again, not as a forest this time but as part of an advertisement for local tourist accommodation.

In *Macbeth*, Shakespeare asks the question, 'What's in a name?' It was as if someone had just dropped a billboard from the skies saying *Trust this sign – The quest is on.*

'Quokelunde' was obviously a name with local significance in Brittany. In Ireland, historical sites can often be identified from the original Irish or Gaelic name, usually included on maps but also on local road signs. For example, the name 'Kildare' comes from the Irish *Cill Dara* which means 'the church of oak' (*cill* = church and *dar* = oak).

The village called Saul, near Downpatrick, County Down in Northern Ireland comes from the Gaelic *Sabhall* which means 'a barn'. According to an ancient tradition, when St Patrick returned to Ireland as an apostle the first church he founded was in a barn given to him by a local chieftain. This is preserved in the ancient Irish (Gaelic) name of the village. Place names can sometimes provide the oldest reliable evidence, preserving the location of an ancient, historical site. Perhaps the forest called 'Quokelunde' also had an ancient pedigree.

As we followed the coast road towards St Malo, the ocean was visible most of the way, stretching out beyond the horizon to the west. Ireland was out there somewhere, buried in the mist. Passing through one of the gates that lead into the old, walled city we knew it was like looking for a needle in a haystack. Just as we were about to leave empty-handed and disappointed from a shop that specialised in old maps, the owner recommended a bookshop called Bibliothèque Le Môle, which appeared a few minutes later, tucked neatly away among old alleyways and narrow, cobbled streets. This shop was dark inside, like Aladdin's cave. Books were strewn all over tables and floors.

Having explained in very inadequate French what we were looking for, the owner, M. Duquesnoy, checked his computer for titles. He made a telephone call and then beckoned us to follow him outside before leading us through a labyrinth of back alleys to the local municipal library, Le Bibliothèque de St Malo, on the Rue D'Alsace.[10] He whisked us upstairs to meet the assistant librarian, Mme Sophie Ellvard. After more brave attempts at conversation (a little French goes a long way in Brittany) she returned with five or six books saying, 'I think you might find what you need in here.' We sat down at a reading desk and started taking notes. It did not take long to find what we were looking for.

St Malo had been almost completely destroyed by bombs during the Second World War but the town and surrounding countryside has an ancient history. In Roman times it was called 'Aleth', the strategic site of a military base or *tiburnia* for the Legion of Mars.[11] This might explain why St Patrick linked the two words *Bannavem* and *Tiburniae*. In Celtic languages the word *Bannavem* or *Bonaban* can be interpreted etymologically as the 'foot of a river'. In Gaelic, *bun* means 'sole' or 'foot' and *am, aven* or *avon* is a river. At the time of St Patrick, a tributary of the River Rance flowed from Aleth towards the present site of Château Bonaban. It could, therefore, be correctly understood as existing near 'the foot' of this river, the last point accessible by ship from the coast, and, therefore, vulnerable to an attack by pirates.

Such etymological derivations have been used to support the claims of Strathclyde, the Bristol Channel and even Boulogne as the place St Patrick came from, but it can also be applied to Aleth and the ancient site of Château de Bonaban as both are close to the mouth of the River Rance. *Tiburnia* is a Latin name applied by the Romans to a military base in Gaul and could perhaps be a reference to the camp for the Legion of Mars, which was stationed at Aleth.[12]

Etymology can be intriguing. In Greek, for example, the name 'Aleth' means 'true, nothing concealed, real'. In classical mythology, Lethe was a river in Hades whose water caused forgetfulness of the past for those who drank from it. In Greek, *lethe* means forgetfulness, oblivion, morbid drowsiness or a continued and profound sleep, from which a person finds it difficult to be awakened; a state of inaction or indifference.[13] What a great omen and such an appropriate one for the quest to recover the truth about St Patrick!

The next discovery suggested that local traditions about St Patrick presented to guests at Château Bonaban could have more than a shamrock of truth.

In Roman times a large oak forest that was sacred to the Druids and early Christian monastic communities stretched along the coast from St Malo to Mont St Michel. An ancient forest called 'Quokelunde' definitely existed here in the fifth century. It was part of a more extensive and well-known forest called the 'Desert of Scissy', taking its name from the large number of hermits who lived there.[14] One French writer described it as a *Thébaid Celtique* or 'Celtic Desert', referring to a place in Egypt where desert monasticism originated in the fourth century.

Then we found the source which had been used to inform guests at the château. It was tucked away on page fifty-five of a wonderful book called *Histoire et Panorama d'un Beau Pays (The History and Panorama of a Beautiful Country)* by the French historian Robidue. The author gives credit to a Breton antiquarian for being the first to identify Bonaban as the place from which St Patrick was taken captive.[15]

Scottish historians hold Dumbarton to be the birthplace of St Patrick. M. de Gerville identified Bannavem Tiburniae, the geographical designation given in Latin in St Patrick's *Confession*, as Bonaban, and the place of his birth. He believed this to be so without doubt, a view which is shared with unanimity by all the local Breton historians, except Lobineau.[16]

Having given credit to M. de Gerville, Robidue continues his account. The following passage has been translated and paraphrased from the original French. This text provides more detailed information about St Patrick's family and their connections with Brittany, providing an historical context for the local tradition preserved at Château Bonaban.

It was in 388 AD, when the Roman general Magnus Maximus withdrew his legions from Britain, that St Patrick's family moved here from Scotland. Maximus was hoping to become Emperor and came to Brittany with many soldiers under his command …

As Britain was left without protection, St Patrick's father, Calpurnius, who was a Scottish Prince, also came here with his family. He was cousin to Conan-Meriadec, the legendary king of Wales, who gave him a large fertile estate on lands next to the sea. Local tradition claims it was from here St Patrick was taken captive to Ireland, when pirates attacked the family estate at Bonaban.[17]

We thanked the librarian for her helpfulness and walked outside to the busy streets, knowing that enough had been achieved for one day. It was definitely time for coffee and a visit to the local crêperie! We needed some time to reflect on the strange experiences which had occurred over the previous twenty-four hours. The situation we found ourselves in was impossible to explain rationally. Surely, these events could not have happened by chance? What had drawn us to this place at this time and why us?

Having found the historical source for a local tradition that St Patrick was taken captive from Brittany, there was a strong sense of what can only be described as 'historical intuition' that an even greater story was going to be revealed.

As experienced pilgrimage leaders and spiritual guides we knew it was important not to leave without giving thanks and honouring the stories associated with this place and memories sacred to its past; so the following morning, after loading suitcases into the car in preparation for an early departure, we took a short walk through the grounds of the château, past the beautiful lake, into the forest, looking for an appropriate place simply to pray. We lit two small votive candles, then gathered some wild flowers and placed them under the boughs of two inviting old oak trees that were growing so close together they could have been one.

Among all the trees of the forest, the oak was especially sacred to the Celts, who believed it contained memories of the past and the wisdom of the ancestors. Had these particular oak trees grown from the seeds of others, the ancestors of older trees that existed in this forest at the time of St Patrick?

The thought that St Patrick had been here before had touched our hearts deeply, not least because of what he may have suffered in this forest as a teenager if this really was the place where he was taken captive. We gave thanks for the lives of St Patrick and his family and prayed for the healing of memories.

There was an almost tangible, mystical sense of God's presence as if St Patrick had appeared through the trees and was praying beside us as we savoured these moments in deep, peaceful silence.

As we walked back through the forest the sun broke through in majesty with golden rays, illuminating the path with bright light and the trees with halos of amber. The weekend stay at Château Bonaban had been magnificent after all the initial anxiety and disappointment.

Driving back through those beautiful old wrought-iron gates, feeling a mixture of joy and yet sorrow for having to leave this sacred and mysterious place, we talked philosophically about the dangers of jumping to conclusions, making rash judgements and how first impressions can be so unreliable. As St Patrick knew from his own experience, sometimes we never can tell where destiny and the hand of providence may be leading us.

---

*Notes*

1. Dietrich Bonhoeffer, *Letters and Papers from Prison* (Minneapolis, 2010).

2. The arguments for authenticity and dating to the fifth century include the mention of decurions (employees in the Roman administration) use of the word 'Britanniis' or 'Britanniae', quotes from the ante-Jerome bible and also Patrick's reference to the practice of the Christians in Roman Gaul, of sending ransom to the pagan Franks to free Christians held captive as slaves (LC 10). This must have been written after they crossed the Rhine and settled in Gaul in 428 CE but while the Franks were still pagan before 496 CE when they followed their king, Clovis, into the Church. See N. J. White, *Introduction to: A Translation of the Latin Writings of St Patrick* (London, 1918).

3. Copies of St Patrick's writings have survived in various manuscripts. For a full description and history of the texts, see Ludwig Bieler, *Libri Epistolarum Sancti Patricii Episcopi* (Dublin, 1993), p. 7 ff.

4. C 1: English translations of St Patrick's writings can be found in Ludwig Bieler, *The Works of St Patrick* (New York, 1952) and Daniel Conneely, *The Letters of St Patrick* (Maynooth, 1993), edited posthumously by Patrick Bastible. A radical new translation into English of St Patrick's *Confession* and *Letter to Coroticus* can be found in Marcus Losack, *Rediscovering Saint Patrick* (Annamoe, Wicklow, 2012).

5. See Whitley Stokes, *Tripartite Life of St Patrick* (Dublin, 1887), ii, p. 415 ff. Conchessa was 'of the Franks'.

6. Dr John Lanigan, *Ecclesiastical History of Ireland*, 4 Vols (Dublin, 1829), i: ch. 3, p. 80 ff.

7. C 23.

8. John O'Hanlon, *Lives of the Irish Saints* (Dublin, 1875), iii, p. 458, n. 272.

9. Christine Mohrmann, *The Latin of St Patrick: Four Lectures* (Dublin, 1961).

10. Bibliothèque Municipale de St Malo, 16 Rue d'Alsace, St Malo.

11. 'La ville d'Aleth vit fuir son prefet militaire, sa garnisons celèbre, ses magistrats aux longues tôges.' Bertrand Robidue, *Histoire et Panorama d'un Beau Pays* (Rennes, 1953), p. 60. See also *Cambridge Ancient History, XII: The Crisis of Empire, AD 193–337* (Cambridge, 2005), p. 259.

12. See Irish/English online Dictionary and Buillet, *Dictionary Celtique.*

13. Online Etymological Dictionary <http://www.etymonline.com/>

14. Bertrand Robidue, *Histoire et Panorama d'un Beau Pays* (Rennes, 1953), ch. 1, pp. 14–22. Robidue quotes other sources for the information about Patrick and Calpurnius including P. H. Morice, *Histoire de Bretagne* (Paris, 1742), i, pp. 284–386, n. 30. See also *Les Memoires de Gallet*, ch. 1, no 15 and M. Trebutien, *Le Mont St Michel: au Peril de la Mer* (Caen, 1841).

15. Robidue, *Histoire*, p. 22.

16. Robidue, *Histoire*, p. 54, n. 1. See Charles de Gerville, *Lettres sur la communication entre les Deux Bretagnes* (Valognes, 1844). Charles de Gerville 1769–1854) was an archaeologist and antiquarian who published prolifically. He is famous for being the first to apply the name 'Roman' or 'Romanesque' as an architectural term. For information about him and a list of publications, see Gerville, Charles (de), Institut National d'Histoire de l'Art: INHA @ www.inha.fr. M. de Gerville not only identified the site of Château Bonaban as Patrick's 'Bannavem Tiburniae', he also claims St Patrick was born there.

17. *Les archaéographes écossaise font naitre Saint Patrice aux portes de Dumbarton M. de Gerville traduit 'Bonvenna de Tiburniae', désignation geographique prise dans les Confessions du saint, par 'Bonaban', et place la son berceau: Il s'appuie, sans doute, sur le temoignage a peu pres unanime des historiens Breton, moins Lobineau.* Robidue, *Histoire*, p. 56.

18. Robidue, *Histoire*, p. 54 ff.

CHAPTER TWO

# A Doorway in Time

Sometimes the present creates the future by
Breaking the shackles of the past; but it is equally
True that sometimes the past creates the future by
Breaking the shackles of the present[1]

After the strange and unexpected events that took place in Brittany the search for evidence to substantiate Château Bonaban's claim to fame quickly turned into a Grail-like quest. Could evidence be found elsewhere to support the local traditions about St Patrick preserved at Château Bonaban? There was a feeling of compulsion to investigate this matter further and try to establish the truth. What could never have been imagined back home in Ireland is how challenging the quest would be and how many more intriguing surprises would slowly but surely be revealed.

In his own writings, St Patrick provides very little information about his place of origins or family background. Those places he does mention have never been securely identified. Despite the huge number of books written about him – enough to fill a whole library – we still did not know where he came from and, therefore, who he really was, until now.

The fifth century has been called 'the lost century' because there are very few historical records for this period. This has always presented great difficulties for those seeking the truth about St Patrick. Serious historical uncertainties surround most of the traditional claims made about him. At the same time, this is what makes the study of Patrick so challenging. If St Patrick came from Britain as most writers insist, or from Brittany as many of the early Breton historians claim, the first step is to find out what was happening in those regions at that time.

What were the historical circumstances that may have shaped his life? Only by entering St Patrick's world can we begin to appreciate the context in which his letters were written, which in turn might help to disentangle the threads of legend and tradition which have been woven together in so many of the claims that have been made about him.

To further our inquiry, it is necessary to step back through a doorway in time and explore some of the key historical events that were taking place around the time of St Patrick.

This beckons a return to the late fourth century and the Roman world into which St Patrick was born, probably around 385 CE. A series of events were about to unfold that would not only have a dramatic impact on St Patrick's life and destiny, they would change the whole future course of European history.[2]

*Europe and the fall of Rome*
In the closing decades of the fourth century, the Roman Empire was on the brink of collapse. From the time of St Patrick's birth and for several decades afterwards, the coastal regions of Britain and north-west Gaul descended into military chaos through local rebellions, barbarian invasions, political instability and piracy. Military and economic resources were stretched beyond their limits and security was deteriorating rapidly. Ireland stood on the margins of Europe and therefore was not subject to such attacks, apart from occasional raids from Britain. For the seven years St Patrick was held captive as a slave in Ireland, this was probably a safer place to be than his homeland.

Around the middle of the fourth century, when Patrick's parents were probably still teenagers, Germanic tribes had intensified attacks on the northern frontier of the Empire. Incursions were frequent. National security was undermined by local rebellions. Roman generals hungry for power plotted with their enemies, the Barbarians. Regional uprisings were common, especially in Britain and Gaul. In 350 CE, Julian was appointed by the Emperor Constantius II as Caesar over the Western Provinces in efforts by the imperial authorities to restore security.[3] Known as Julian 'the Apostate', he reigned as Emperor from 361–363 CE and was a member of the Constantine dynasty.

Magnus Maximus (340–388 CE) was commander of the Roman legions in Britain. He must have been concerned about the rapidly deteriorating military situation and the soldiers under his command observed with increasing alarm, various developments taking place on the continent, including security issues and Julian's support for a return to the 'pagan' traditions. Magnus was related to the Imperial House of Constantine, a powerful dynasty which had ruled the Empire only a few years before when the Empire was more secure and prosperous. This family had already produced several emperors including Constantius Chlorus (306 CE) and Constantine the Great (312–337 CE), whose official recognition and acceptance of Christianity generated great wealth and prestige for the Church.

Constantine was succeeded by his son Constans (337–350 CE), followed by two more Emperors carrying the same name.[4] Under Constantine, the Empire was divided into four 'dioceses', to correspond with two Emperors and two Caesars. Each was placed under a senior officer, called the Praetorian Prefect.[5]

As Barbarian attacks became more frequent and severe, memories of those 'golden days' of Constantine the Great must have been forefront in many minds, not least those in Britain who held to an ancient belief that members of this particular family had a divine right to imperial rule. When security deteriorated even further, the legions in Britain decided the Empire would be better served under the leadership of Magnus Maximus and acted swiftly to secure their ambitions. Britain was one of the strongest, wealthiest regions of the Roman Empire. Perhaps the British felt they alone could save it from impending disaster? Other factors may also have been significant.

According to a Welsh legend known as the 'Dream of Macsen Wledig', a deliberate plan to further the claims of Britain to imperial rule had been orchestrated when Maximus was invited by the British aristocracy to marry Helen or Ellen, daughter of the high king of Britain, Eudes (Eudaf Hen).[6] This is said to have been an arranged marriage through which Britain hoped to provide an Emperor in the west.[7] Through this marriage, Maximus inherited a place within a British royal family, related to the House of Constantine.[8]

Such actions would not have been viewed as abnormal. There had been a long history of rebellion and 'usurpation' in Britain and Gaul against the ruling Emperors. Magnus was only the latest in a long line of Roman commanders encouraged by supporters in Britain to challenge the established authorities.[9]

In 383 CE, Maximus was clothed with imperial purple by the soldiers under his command before they crossed the Channel into Gaul, determined to seize power.[10] His name alone carried power. In Latin, Magnus Maximus means 'the greatest of the great'. In the context of these imperial ambitions Magnus had much to live up to because of this name and the noble blood that flowed through his veins.

The British appear to have believed they had God on their side. This can be confirmed from a reliable contemporary source, the *Life of St Martin of Tours* by Sulpitius Severus. According to Severus, Maximus told St Martin that 'he had not of his own accord assumed the sovereignty'. He had simply 'defended by arms the sovereign necessities of the Empire'.[11]

The Latin phrase *regni necessitatem* is significant. It implies a tradition of sacred kingship in Britain linked, at least in part, to the House of Constantine. It can be translated as the sovereign necessities (or requirements for divine rule) within the Empire.

Severus confirms this when he tells us that Maximus had to pay regard to this expectation 'which had been imposed on him by the soldiers according to the divine appointment'.[12] Maximus is often referred to as a 'usurper' just as rivals in a disputed papacy are called 'antipopes'. The reality of political, military and religious life within the Empire at this time was far too complex for stereotypes.

The rebellion came to a head when Gratian, one of the incumbent Emperors in the west, was executed by soldiers loyal to Maximus. Gratian's brother Valentinian had to flee for his life but managed to return with the support of Theodosius, Emperor in the East. In an effort to make peace, Theodosius brokered a treaty with Maximus from 383–388 CE.

The British had set their sights on imperial rule and through rapid, success-ful military advances they had now achieved it. As the newly installed Emperor of the West, Magnus Maximus quickly established his centre of command at the Royal Palace in Trier, the former residence of the Emperors Gratian and Valentinian. In many ways, Trier was more important than Rome at this time. Strategically, it was the capitol for imperial administration. From there, the Romans monitored operations along the Rhine, guarding the northern fron-tiers against the Barbarians.[13]

Maximus had gained a reputation for ruthlessness, which gave Theodosius no reason to trust him. The decisive moment came at Aquileia in Italy, in Sep-tember 388 CE. If Maximus had won this battle he would have been crowned Emperor of Rome. As the 'First Lady' of Empire, his wife, Ellen, would have become one of the richest and most powerful women on the planet. But this particular period of British imperialism was to be short lived. Less than five years after crossing from Britain into Gaul to initiate this rebellion, the British were defeated. Magnus was arrested and executed immediately by soldiers loyal to Theodosius, beheaded at the third milestone from Aquileia.[14] This marked the end of an era for the House of Constantine. Imperial rulers would think twice before ever trusting the British again.

In relation to the origins of St Patrick, it is important to note that when the rebellion was launched, forces loyal to Maximus appear to have attacked on two fronts. Some British forces landed at the mouth of the Rhine. According to sev-eral early Breton historians, others landed in Brittany at the mouth of the River Rance, using the strategic and heavily fortified Roman port at Aleth (St Malo) where they enlisted local support and consolidated the rebellion. This is a sig-nificant issue for Patrick's biography, to which we will return.

The political and religious situation which existed from 385–432 CE in the north-western coastal regions of the Empire created a series of events which probably had a significant influence on Patrick's life and destiny. After the legions crossed into Gaul with Maximus, Britain was left without military defence, vulnerable to attacks from the Picts in the north and Irish to the west.

Rebellions had been taking place in Britain and Gaul for a long time before Magnus Maximus came to power and they did not end with his death. Gibbon records that, after Maximus, Marcus was placed on the throne as lawful Emperor of Britain and the West although 'the Latins' were ignorant of this fact.[15] This is not surprising; Nennius describes the situation which existed between Britain and Rome at this time as a war. The breakdown in communi-cations with Rome also resulted in a lack of reliable historical records.

After the execution of Maximus, chaos ruled throughout the western Empire. Britain was left in a vulnerable state for the next forty years, denuded of its soldiers and military defences. This is confirmed by Gildas, who speaks of those left in Britain as a 'wretched remnant' who made a desperate appeal to the Roman Consul, Aetius, for support.[16]

From 390–405 CE Rome had tried to bolster its defences in Britain and Gaul but the Roman navy was struggling to contain piracy in the Iccian Sea, the name given to the stretch of water between what is now Ireland, the south-west coast of England and France. In 405 CE the situation was so serious that the Roman legions in Gaul were withdrawn to defend Italy, the heartland of the Empire. The legions in Britain, strengthened after the execution of Maximus, were also withdrawn in 406 CE in a final effort to save Rome. This left Britain and Gaul with no defence. Constantine took control of power in 407 CE and subdued Spain in 408 CE but the military situation was very unstable and security deteriorated rapidly. Britain and Brittany became more 'independent' at this time. Gibbon mentions another revolt in 409 CE and says 'the independence of Britain and Armorica was soon confirmed by Honorious, the lawful Emperor of the West'. Unrest continued from 409–413 CE. Both regions took responsibility for their own security in the face of increasing attacks from the Barbarians.[17]

Whether St Patrick came from Britain or Brittany, both places were dramatically affected by these historical events. The period between Magnus's push to become Emperor from 383–388 CE, the Barbarian invasions of 405 CE and the fall of Rome in 409 CE must have been a critical time for St Patrick and his family.[18] For some, it must have seemed as though the end of the world was nigh. That which could never have been imagined now became reality.

In his book, *How the Irish Saved Civilization*, Thomas Cahill describes very dramatically how events unfolded on the night of 31 December 406 CE when the River Rhine froze in Germany.[19] It was not the first time this great river had frozen. Attacks from Germanic tribes had been taking place for years. The Rhine provided a natural barrier between the Roman Empire to the south and barbarians to the north and west, bordered by Roman forts along the Limas line. Several legions had been stationed along the river at the northern frontiers of the Empire around what is now Frankfurt and Mainz, in the region of Hessen.

In the winter of 406 CE the Rhine froze at Mainz. After an extended period with sub-zero temperatures, it turned into an autobahn of ice. Roman defences along the northern frontier were breached by hoards of Barbarians desperate for food and hungry for land. Various tribes including Huns, Vandals, Arans and Sueves, poured across the bridge that nature herself had built. It has been estimated that as many as one hundred thousand barbarians crossed the river at this time. For the next three years the Empire would be plundered by marauding tribes. When Alaric and his warriors entered the Salesian Gates in Rome on 24 August 409 CE, Rome's defences were breached for the first time in a thousand years. The 'eternal city' had fallen into the hands of the enemy. Germanic tribes rampaged through Gaul and Spain and did not stop before crossing into North Africa.

North Americans in general and New Yorkers in particular will understand what it must have felt like to be Roman on that day. As O'Driscoll remarks, in many ways this was Rome's 9/11. The unthinkable had become reality and the military and cultural power that had conquered and controlled most of the western world was suddenly struck to its own heart's core.[20] The strongest, most wealthy Empire in the world was forced to submit and negotiate agreements previously intolerable. Nothing would ever be the same again. Like the twin towers in New York, the Empire fell rapidly; within twenty years of Alaric's triumphal entry into Rome, the western Empire consisted essentially of the city of Rome and its original territories in Latium, central Italy.[21]

What took place on land was mirrored on the high seas. After Julius Caesar defeated uprisings in Gaul and the Romans had conquered the south of Britain in 47–50 CE, the Empire maintained a sophisticated and powerful naval force capable of defending incursions from various barbarian seafaring tribes including the Irish. The *Classis Britannica* was a major Roman military fleet stationed at the Port of Iccius in north-west Gaul, now Boulogne-sur-Mer, in France. Roman military strength had been unequalled since then, although there were signs of weakness and impending decline.

Fiscal corruption and political decadence were apparent many years before the final crash. These are the kind of 'unforeseen' disasters we neglect to prepare for, ignoring signs which may be there but are never taken seriously, until it is too late.

As Roman power collapsed in the early fifth century, so went the Roman navy.[22] In 429 CE, Vandals embarked on ships from southern Gaul and landed in North Africa, establishing their own dominion in the breadbasket of the Roman Empire. The Vandals were not just sword wielding horseback riders as we imagine Attila the Hun to have been. They had a powerful navy which contributed to the fall of the Western Empire when their pirate king, Gaiseric, eliminated Roman shipping on the Mediterranean.

By the middle of the fifth century, the Vandals were masters of the sea and by 476 CE 'Old Rome' had fallen completely from power in Western Europe. The Barbarian invasions in many ways marked the end of the classical civilisations of Greece and Rome. Europe entered the so-called Dark Ages which would last for the next five hundred years, from 400–900 CE.

The devastation is vividly described by Gildas, who could have been speaking about the situation in Britain or Brittany when he writes with dejection:

The more we try to push Barbarians to the sea the more barbaric things we see. If we want to avoid having our throats cut, the rising flood tide swallows us. To whichever side of the coast we turn, we meet death.[23]

Before we start to imagine the whole world imploding, it is important to remember that only the western Empire fell to the Barbarians. The eastern Empire was not so radically affected and continued to thrive, based at the ancient crossroads between east and west in the Imperial City of Constantinople, now Istanbul in Turkey. When the west collapsed the east flowered as 'Nova Roma' or 'New Rome' – Byzantium. In the west, things began to unfold in a different way.

As Barbarian tribes flooded into Gaul, massive changes were taking place in Britain, especially after the legions were recalled to defend Rome in 405 CE. Germanic tribes including Angles, Saxons and Jutes attacked Britain from the North Sea. The Picts (the name means 'painted ones' because of tattoos on their bodies and their use of war paint) invaded southwards from Caledonia (Scotland). Irish chieftains began raiding the coasts of Britain and Brittany. After the fall of Rome security once provided by the Roman army was gone and the whole country was ripe for plunder. Britain was trapped by invasions on three sides.

Around 450 CE, Germanic tribes invaded Britain in greater force. The ancient Britons became the victims of what is now called 'ethnic cleansing'. The island the Romans had called 'Britannia' was renamed Angle-land or England. Before these invasions the Britons were a Celtic speaking people steeped in the cultural traditions of their Gallic ancestors. Finding itself pushed towards the western margins of Britain, Celtic culture managed to survived only in Ireland, Scotland, Wales and parts of the south west. Celtic place names were eradicated from south-east England as far north as the border with Scotland.

Somewhere, either in Britain or on the northwest coast of Brittany, St Patrick was born into this cauldron of social uncertainty and unrestrained, physical violence. As we listen to St Patrick's story, as recorded in his *Confession*, special attention will be given to the geographical references that are crucial to identify where he came from and who he really was. Patrick wrote this letter when he was an older man, reflecting on some of the key events that shaped his life and destiny and conscious that death, his own death, was probably immanent. In the following chapter are some of the treasured memories St Patrick wanted to share with us.

*Notes*

1. Fred Turner, Professor of Arts and Humanities, Texas University.

2. The dates of St Patrick's birth and death are uncertain. Patrick does not mention specific dates. 385 CE can be given as the approximate date for his birth. 461 CE is traditionally remembered as the year of his death. The ancient Irish Annals mention various dates, with inherent contradictions and uncertainties.

3. W. F. Skene, *Celtic Scotland: A History of Ancient Alban* (Edinburgh, 1886).

4. For his account of events in Gaul, see Edward Gibbon, *Decline and Fall of the Roman Empire*, 8 vols (London, 1862), iv, pp. 52–5; James O'Donnell, *The Ruin of the Roman Empire* (US, 2009).

5. Skene, *Celtic Scotland*, p. 92 ff.

6. 'Eudda', a wealthy Lord in North Wales. See Gibbon, *DFRE*, iii, p. 359, n. 10.

7. Macsen Wledig is the Welsh name given for Magnus Maximus. The title 'Wledig' means ruling leader or imperator. For an account of this dream, see David Nash Ford, *Early British Kingdoms* [website] <www.earlybritishkingdoms.com/bios/maximus.html>. Helen's identity is controversial. Carrying the same name as Helena, the mother of Constantine the Great, she was related to the House of Constantine. It is not unreasonable to think of this as a sacred or 'holy' bloodline. Roman Emperors were considered divine, even when they were Christians.

8. See M. Thierry, *Norman Conquest* (London, 1819); Bill Gunn, *Historia Brittonum by Mark the Anchorite* (London, 1819) p. 143 ff., n. 55–8. Also Robert Williams, 'The British Origin of Helena' in *Enwogion Cymru: Biographical Dictionary of Eminent Welsh* (South Carolina, 2009).

9. For an excellent study of this period see Peter Heather, *The Fall of the Roman Empire: A New History* (London, 2005).

10. Gibbon acknowledged how complex the political situation was at this time, especially the conflict and rivalry between Maximus and Theodosius, the Emperor in the East who had been appointed by Gratian and Valentinius. Gratian was only twenty years old and caused public scandal and great offence to the army because he dressed as a barbarian. He 'frequently showed himself to the soldiers and people with the dress and arms, the long bow, sounding quiver and the fur garments of a Scythian warrior.' Gibbon, *DFRE*, iii, p. 358.

11. Sulpicius Severus, 'Life of St Martin' in *The Nicene and Post Nicene Fathers*, eds Philip Schaff and Henry Wace (New York, 1894), xi, p. 13, n. 1.

12. *Ibid.*

13. St Ambrose was born in Trier, son of a Pretorian Prefect in Gaul. St Augustine tells us, in his *Confessions*, of a friend's contact in the Roman Secret Police who had been converted to asceticism after finding a document about St Antony at a cottage used by hermits outside the walls of the Palace at Trier, at the time of the rebellion of Maximus. St Jerome came to this city as a young man in the 370s. See St Augustine, *Confessions*, p. 160; Gerald Bonner, *St Augustine of Hippo* (Norwich, 2002), p. 89, n. 2; James O'Donnell, *The Ruin of the Roman Empire*, p. 306.

14. In the same year his son Victor was killed in Gaul. Nennius, 'History of the Britons: Historia Brittonum' in *Six Old English Chronicles*, ed. J. A. Giles (London, 1858), p. 29.

15. Gibbon, *DFRE*, iv, p. 54, n. 95.

16. 'The Works of Gildas' in *Six Old English Chronicles*, ed. J. A. Giles (London, 1868) p. 307.

17. Gibbon, *DFRE*, iv, p. 131.

18. For details of Maximus in Gaul and Brittany, see P. H. Morice, *Histoire de Bretagne* (Paris, 1707); also *Memoires Pour Server de Preuves a l'histoire de Bretagne*, 3 vols (in folio) (Paris, 1742–6). Morice was drawing on earlier sources including Bertrand d'Argentré, *Abrégé de*

*l'Histoire de Bretagne* (Paris, 1695). Also see Commission Histoire de Skol Vreizh, *L'Histoire de la Bretagne et des Payes Celtique* (Morlaix, 1966).

19. Thomas Cahill, *How the Irish Saved Civilization* (New York, 1995).

20. Herb O'Driscoll, teachings given on pilgrimages with Céile Dé in Ireland, Wales and Brittany from 2000–2011.

21. See Peter Heather, *The Fall of the Roman Empire* (London, 2005).

22. See 'Roman Navy', *UNRV History* [website] <www.unrv.com/military/roman-navy.php.>

23. See Gildas, ch. 20.

# CHAPTER THREE

# *Saint Patrick's Confession*

> My name is Patrick, a sinful person without any formal education, least among all the Christians and greatly despised in the eyes of many. I am the son of Calpurnius (a Decurion) as he was the son of an elder, Potitus, who belonged to the village of Bannavem Tiburniae. Near this village he had a small estate from where I was taken captive, when I was about sixteen years old. I was not aware of God's presence at that time and I was taken as a slave to Ireland, along with thousands of others.[1]

When St Patrick sat down to write about his life, he began by telling us his name; *Ego Patricius* in Latin, meaning 'I am Patrick' or 'My name is Patrick'. He also mentions the names of his father and grandfather, Calpurnius and Potitus. The family belonged as citizens to the Roman Empire as can be seen from the Latin form of their names. In his first letter, to the Soldiers of Coroticus, Patrick says his father was a Decurion. This title applied to a senior official in local government whose duty was to provide a cavalry of at least ten horsemen to support the Roman army.[2] It was only possible for those who owned sufficient land and resources.

Patrick tells us that his family owned a villa or small estate near a place called 'Bannavem Tiburniae'.[3] The location is uncertain and was lost to historical memory in the years after St Patrick's death. Despite the countless books written about him and extensive research by scholars, neither the location of St Patrick's homeland nor the village from which he was taken captive have ever been securely identified.

Frustrated by the lack of geographical detail given in St Patrick's own writings and confused by contradictory accounts in the ancient sources, most writers have given up the quest.

Scholars assume that St Patrick came from Britain but there is no agreement as to the precise location. Despite the view taken by the majority of scholars, the identification of Patrick's homeland within the island of Roman Britain, whether in the north at Strathclyde or anywhere else, has not been supported with any reliable evidence and therefore remains uncertain.

Ludwig Bieler, one of the foremost authorities on St Patrick, said, 'The search for Bannavem Tiburniae is quite hopeless.'[4]

This is what made the discoveries in France so exciting and challenging. Despite what some claim, St Patrick's place of origins is one of the great unsolved mysteries surrounding his life and the origins of the Irish and early European church.

In his *Confession*, St Patrick did not say he was born at Bannavem Tiburniae. Neither does he say how long he had lived there or been there before he was taken captive. He does not mention another home, which might suggest that he had grown up on his father's estate during those years before the age of sixteen, when he was taken captive.

There is not enough specific geographical detail to make any assumptions. All we can know for certain is that Bannavem Tiburniae existed close to where his father, Calpurnius, owned an estate. Patrick remembered this place and what happened there when he was a teenager. This is where he was taken captive when Irish pirates attacked the estate before he was sold as a slave in Ireland. It was a traumatic experience and one that St Patrick would remember for the rest of his life.[5]

Let's try and imagine what it may have been like for him.

The family's home was being attacked by pirates. Patrick may have witnessed friends or neighbours being killed. Wrenched away in the flower of his youth, he was dragged across the seas to a foreign country outside the territory of the Roman Empire.

Ireland at that time had a fearful reputation as a pagan, barbaric nation located 'at the ends of the earth'. Irish pirates in the fifth century did not operate with the ethics of the Salvation Army. Old Irish and Breton sources say Patrick's mother and father were both killed during the frenzy. Patrick may have witnessed their deaths.

Those who were taken with him from the village that day would have known each other and some may have been friends. Slave traders took only the girls and boys who were saleable. Adults were usually killed or had to flee. An orgy of rape, murder and gratuitous violence was probably the order of the day. It was a case of kill or be killed. The Celts often severed the heads of their victims, which were then displayed either on their belts, bridles of horses and the masts of their ships or on poles outside their villages when they returned.

This horrific and tragic event must have had a huge impact on Patrick as a young teenager. The inner and outer landscapes, the light and the dark, were woven together in his life and experience from an early age as they are for us. Both must be appreciated if we are to come to a deeper understanding of his story.

However painful it was, Patrick managed to triumph over adversity and find peace within himself and with God. Reflecting on these events as an older man, he tells us that he bore no grudge or malice about what happened even against those who had taken him captive. This is one of the most enduring qualities of his personality and shows a degree of spiritual and psychological maturity which provided the foundations for his teachings and legacy.

Patrick had experienced God's forgiveness in his own heart and wished to extend that forgiveness and love towards others. His deeply personal and profound faith in God deepened through these experiences. A sense of spiritual direction came to fruition in his life despite these events, perhaps even because of them.

St Patrick was held captive as a slave in Ireland for six or seven years. He does not tell us where he was enslaved or the name of his slave master. Instead he chose to describe the personal transformation which began when he was suffering.

In the midst of these difficulties between the ages of sixteen and twenty-three, Patrick began to have a series of mystical or religious experiences which changed the course of his life. It was during this time of exile from homeland and family that he came to embrace a deeper faith. He sensed the presence of God through this spiritual awakening and left us an extraordinary account of his experience. Patrick describes how his heart turned towards God and became more aware of God's presence in the midst of loneliness and the hardship of slavery, tending animals in all weathers on a remote and deserted hillside. In these moments when he had lost everything, he found God. We can let St Patrick's words speak for themselves:

> There the Lord opened my unbelieving mind so that at that late hour I should remember my sins and turn with all my heart to the Lord my God. He kept me safe as a father would comfort his son …
>
> After I came to Ireland I was herding cattle and I used to pray many times a day; more and more the love of God and awareness of God's presence came to me, my faith increased and my spirit was moved so that in one day I would pray as many as a hundred times and in the night nearly as often, even while I was staying in the woods and on the mountain …
>
> Before daylight I used to be stirred to prayer in snow, frost and rain and I felt no ill effects from it because the spirit was fervent within me.[6]

Patrick escaped from Ireland during the seventh year of his captivity. In his *Confession* we hear nothing about the people he worked for or what relationships he may have had. He probably spent much of this time in isolation. He practised asceticism through a discipline of regular prayer and fasting.[7] It was during this time of renunciation, constantly exposed to the elements of nature that he began to hear voices and see 'visions'. Divine intervention and encouragement was about to turn the wheel of fortune in his favour.

This is the second time in his *Confession* that St Patrick provides a clue to his place of origins. Patrick describes how one night in a dream he heard a voice saying it was time to return to his homeland. It told Patrick that a ship was waiting and ready to take him there:

> And there, as it happens one night I heard in my sleep a voice say to me; 'it is good that you fast, you are soon to go to back to your homeland'.[8] And after a while again I heard a voice say to me, 'Look your ship is ready.' It was not nearby but at a distance of perhaps two hundred miles. And I had never been there nor did I know anybody there …
>
> Shortly after that I took flight, left the man with whom I had been for six years and journeyed by the power of God, who directed my way unto my good. And I feared nothing until I reached that ship.[9]

Patrick describes in detail how he escaped. He had to walk a long way from the place of his captivity to a ship that was waiting, which he boarded almost immediately. The captain was not sure about taking him at first but changed his mind suddenly, allowing Patrick to sail with them. The crew members were not Christian.

They invited Patrick to 'suck their breasts' – an old Celtic ritual which was a sign of loyalty, friendship and commitment for the journey.[10] Patrick says he refused to do this because of his religious beliefs but they took him on board anyway. The ship sailed and they were three days at sea before they reached land. St Patrick does not tell us where the ship sailed from, which port it was sailing to or where it landed. The narrative suggests he was planning to return home.

Scholars are divided in their opinions about where the ship landed. Those convinced that St Patrick was born in Britain and was taken captive from Britain usually accept that he was planning to return home after his escape and, therefore, sailed from Ireland to Britain. Others say the ship landed in Gaul.[11]

Wherever it sailed to, St Patrick was aware of God's guidance and support throughout this daring escape and bid for freedom.

Patrick's account of this journey provides a few descriptive details which allow for speculation as to where he escaped from and where the ship may have landed. If he was held captive in County Antrim in the north of Ireland as most of the ancient sources claim, such a long walk could have taken him to one of the ports on the south east coast of Ireland, including Wicklow or Arklow.[12] In the fifth century these ports were used for trading on the continent. The ship was probably a trading vessel large enough to carry cargo and a small crew.

Where is the ship likely to have landed after a three-day journey? Members of the Wicklow Sailing Club helped shed light on St Patrick's journey from a maritime perspective. The distance between Wicklow Harbour and St Malo in

Brittany, the nearest port to Château Bonaban, is about 365 nautical miles. This allows for some interesting calculations. In a vessel that would travel at 5-knots-per-hour (about average in those days for a medium sized boat carrying cargo) with light prevailing westerly winds, the journey would take three days ($365/5 = 73$ divided by 24 hrs = 3.04 days). These calculations are based on a 24-hour clock, since the ship would have continued sailing through the day and night with no landings before the coast of Brittany.[13]

Another possibility is that it landed further down the coast. The journey from Wicklow to Carantec would have been even shorter, only 340 nautical miles, and it would have taken less than three days sailing to reach this port.[14]

On the other hand, Ireland to Holyhead in Wales is only about 70 nautical miles. Even at 3-knots-per-hour such a journey would have taken only about 18 hours ($70/3= 23.3$ divided by 24) less than one day's sailing. Journey times are ultimately dependent on weather conditions, prevailing winds and other crucial factors, such as the size of the boat and the experience of the crew.

The reason for including these calculations is simply to show that from the evidence given in his own writings it is certainly possible that when St Patrick escaped from Ireland he could have travelled as far as Brittany. If his intention was to return home, as seems clear from his *Confession*, then it is also possible that the home to which Patrick sought to return was in Brittany and not Wales, or northern Britain.

This allows for the possibility that the family estate where St Patrick was taken captive was not located in Britain but on the continent.

Wherever the ship landed, the situation encountered there was very dangerous. The ship's crew had to walk through a deserted landscape, wandering for twenty-eight days without seeing other human beings during which time they almost starved to death. This was not the place to be with a cargo of dogs.[15]

In desperation, the sailors asked Patrick for help. Even though they were Gentiles or 'pagans' and not Christians, they suggested he pray to 'his God' for them. The word pagan derives from the Latin *pagus*, which refers to a Celtic tribal area. The *pagani* were literally 'the country people' outside the Roman *civitas*. Paganism was originally, therefore, a reference to the old religion, practised especially in the countryside, before the adoption of Christianity.

After miraculously finding food in a herd of wild pigs which kept the crew from starvation, St Patrick's reputation increased among the sailors but he refused to eat the wild honey when they invited him to share in a ritual of thanksgiving.

The narrative suggests that Patrick was trying to return to his homeland but that he did not reach 'home' for many years. Much depends on how we interpret the text, which could be taken to mean he was reunited with his extended family again after 'many years' in captivity.[16] This is one of two passages where 'Britanniis' is identified as his homeland.[17] More than any other geographical reference in his writings, this name provides the key to knowing where St Patrick came from. As the meaning of 'Britanniis' is uncertain, the original Latin form from the *Book of Armagh* will be retained in the following passage, without committing to any specific translation:

> After many years [of captivity] I was *in Britanniis* again with my [extended] family who received me like a son and sincerely begged of me, that after all the troubles I endured, I should not leave them to go anywhere else.[18]

Most scholars have identified Britanniis exclusively with Britain but it is important to note, the original word in Latin is recorded in a plural form. The question is, does it refer to the island of Britain, to Brittany or perhaps to both these regions at the same time? Some writers have suggested that when St Patrick spoke about his homeland, he was referring to a region on the continent that was also known as 'Britain'.

It is possible that a coastal region in Armorica had adopted this name during or perhaps even before the rebellion of Magnus Maximus in 383 CE. Most of the early Breton historians insist without doubt that a British colony was established there at that time and called 'Britain' from which the name 'Brittany' or 'Bretagne' is derived. This is a controversial subject with widely differing views among historians, but one which is crucial to recovering the truth about St Patrick.

Even though it appears in plural form in the earliest surviving manuscript, most English translations usually give the singular form 'in Britain' despite the fact that this is potentially misleading. Critical editions of St Patrick's *Confession* in Latin were published by N. J. White in 1905, followed by Ludwig Bieler in 1950. These are now the accepted texts for academic study. In their translations, White and Bieler both render the Latin name for St Patrick's homeland as 'Britain'.[19]

The implications of this matter for understanding St Patrick's origins cannot be underestimated. As a consequence of decisions made with regard to translation, widespread credibility was given to the established, traditional view which identifies St Patrick's homeland and place of origins, exclusively with the island of Britain. Almost the full weight of established and current academic opinion is strongly in favour of the theory of Britain. After the unexpected discoveries made at Château Bonaban, there appeared to be equally strong grounds to question this. M. de Gerville considered the established tradition to be a gross historical error. Could the truth about where St Patrick came from have been lost simply because of the way one single Latin word has been interpreted and translated?

Following more detailed research, it became increasingly obvious that historical evidence given to support the theory of Britain was far from conclusive and probably based on unsafe foundations. This matter is of great historical importance and it will be explored fully in due course. At this stage, it is important simply to focus on the evidence, as it appears in St Patrick's writings.

### Homeland

After finding his way back home, Patrick tells us that members of his extended family welcomed him back with love and affection 'as if' he was their son. They begged him, after all the troubles he had endured, never to leave them again. Then, at the very moment when he was reunited with his closest surviving relatives after many years of separation, suddenly the unexpected happened. Patrick experienced another powerful dream in which he felt called to return to Ireland.

This is one of the most moving passages in St Patrick's *Confession* and one of the most impressive and evocative accounts of a spiritual calling in the whole of Christian literature. St Patrick's account of his dream has touched the hearts of millions, not least those who have recognised in these words a lasting testimony of God's call for Patrick to return to Ireland as an apostle and fulfill the command of Jesus to carry the gospel 'to the ends of the earth'.

> And there, in a vision of the night, I saw a man coming as it were from Ireland, whose name was Victor, carrying many letters. He gave me one of them to read and as I did so, I heard the *Voice of the Irish*.
> In that same moment as I was reading from the beginning of the letter, I thought I could hear the voice of those around the Wood of Foclut – which is close beside the Western Sea. It was as if they spoke with one voice, 'we beg you, holy youth, to come and walk once more among us.' When I woke up my heart was broken and I had to stop reading. Thank God that after all these years the Lord has granted them what they cried out for.[20]

St Patrick's account of this dream is not only great literature, that continues to hold deep religious and spiritual significance for others, it includes some very significant geographical references which have influenced our traditional understanding of his place of origins. Just as most books written about St Patrick claim that he came from Britain, so there has been a traditional assumption that the Wood of Foclut existed in Ireland.

The origins of this assumption date back to the seventh century. An influential Bishop in Ireland called Tirechán claimed that St Patrick's 'Wood of Foclut' existed in his own diocese near Killala, in County Mayo.

This claim became enshrined in one of Ireland's most ancient ecclesiastical records when Tirechán's narrative was included with other Patrician documents in the *Book of Armagh*, still preserved in Trinity College, Dublin. Since then, it has formed part of an established tradition that has never been seriously questioned. Ever since Tirechán made this claim, it has been widely accepted that the Wood of Foclut existed in the west of Ireland.

> 'Wood of Fochlad' *Caill Foclaid* [Old Irish] is the name of the district which is in Tirawley, in the north-east of Connaught, and there is a church there to day.[21]

The question is, was Tirechán telling the truth?

An interesting conversation that took place at a special St Patrick's Day celebration in Washington DC helped to address this question. I met someone there who said he worked for 'the intelligence community'. His expertise involved analysing reports in the hope of teaching intelligence agents how to write better reports.

The formula he advocates is this: 'Always remember that just because somebody says something is true does not mean it necessarily is true, unless sufficient and reliable evidence is given to support it.' The same principle can fruitfully be applied to any claims made about St Patrick.

Tirechán wrote his narrative more than two hundred years after St Patrick's death. He insisted that the Wood of Foclut existed in his own diocese in the west of Ireland. Understandably for a bishop of his time, he did not provide historical evidence to support this. Medieval hagiographers were not constrained by the same standards which are supposed to apply to modern historical analysis.

Despite these uncertainties, Tirechán's claim has always been given a high degree of historical credibility.[22] It has been suggested that 'Foclut' or 'Foclud' is the only genuine Irish name in the whole of St Patrick's *Confession*. This too is based on an assumption that Tirechán was telling the truth and that 'Caille Foclaid' was the name of an Irish wood that could be identified with the place St Patrick recalled in a dream.

The existence of a forest called 'Quokelunde' in Brittany and a local tradition that claims that this wood is the place from which Patrick was taken captive, gives a reason to doubt the Tirechán tradition. If the claim preserved at Château Bonaban was true, then the name of the wood recalled by St Patrick in his dream may have had Breton or Gallic rather than Irish origins. In various surviving copies of St Patrick's *Confession*, the name 'Foclut' appears with different spellings. These are clearly recognisable as different forms of the same name. In Latin manuscripts, it begins with a 'v' or 'u' and usually ends with an 'i', 'e' or 'q'.[23]

In Old Irish manuscripts, it begins with an 'f' and ends with an 'i', 't' or 'th' (e.g. 'Focluti', 'Foclut', 'Focluth'). In English translations the usual rendering is 'Foclut' or 'Foclud'. The diversity of spellings passed down through the centuries is surprising and suggests the origin of this name is uncertain. If there is any truth in the local tradition preserved in Brittany, it has to be considered possible that both the Irish and Latin forms could be derived from an original Breton name, a forest called 'Quokelunde' that existed close to the present site of Château Bonaban.[24] In Brittany, this name appears as 'Quokelunde', 'Qokelunde' or 'Cokelunde'. The second part of the name 'lunde' or 'lande' (from which we have the English word land) is probably a later addition reflecting Anglo-Saxon or Frankish influence.

David Parris, a specialist in Old French at Trinity College, Dublin, has suggested that 'Quokelunde' may have originally derived from a name that sounded something like 'Kwokle' which would have been recorded in Latin as 'Uirclut' or 'Uirglut' and 'Foclud' in Irish; this change of spelling would have taken place following recognised and well established laws of language change when words in Old French were recorded in Latin.

When St Patrick recalled this powerful dream, he said a man called 'Victor' appeared before him carrying many letters and looking 'as if' he came from Ireland. There is no justification on the basis of a particular interpretation of this dream to assume that the Wood of Foclut must have existed in Ireland. This assumption has often been made on the grounds that because Patrick heard the 'Voice of the Irish' calling from the Wood of Foclut for him to return to them, these voices must have been voices coming from Ireland and from people he must have known, perhaps from a place near where he was held captive or somewhere in Ireland with which he was familiar.[25]

As with other geographical references in St Patrick's *Confession*, however, it is possible that the true location of the Wood of Foclut may have been lost to historical memory in the years after St Patrick's death, disappearing in the twilight zone between the claims of Irish hagiography and an imaginative but mistaken form of dream analysis.

Jeremy Taylor, a Jungian analyst and expert in group spiritual direction through dreams, identifies issues which must be taken into account when trying to understand or interpret the images and symbols we experience in dreams. He warns against the dangers of 'mistaken literalism'. This can happen when we try to interpret a dream in a specific way and he advises caution because 'only the dreamer knows the meaning of a dream'.[26]

St Patrick's description sounds more like a nightmare than a dream. When he heard these voices calling him, Patrick says he woke up suddenly, feeling heartbroken. He was so disturbed by the dream that he could 'read no more'.[27] If we heed Taylor's advice, we should not make any historical or geographical assumptions based on what was experienced in a dream or nightmare. However significant it may be, his dream should not be interpreted to support a particular geographical location, unless there is real evidence elsewhere to make an alternative interpretation impossible.

Having said that, because St Patrick left so few geographical references concerning his place of origins, it is important to consider the possibility as most writers have always done, that even though Patrick remembered this wood in the context of a dream, it was a real place with a historical and geographical reality and was not simply part of his subconscious dream world.

When historical facts are uncertain, sometimes speculation or 'historical intuition' is the only resource left. So what was it about those voices and what may have happened in the Wood of Foclut to cause St Patrick such heartbreak? One possibility is that his distress can be understood in the context of the traumatic experience of being taken captive. This thought had first occurred to me during a walk through what is probably a remnant of the old forest that surrounds Château Bonaban, the day our prayers were offered under those old oak trees. For whatever reason, there was a sense that St Patrick may have suffered there.

If Patrick's 'Wood of Foclut' could be identified with the Forest of Quokelunde, which existed close beside the location of the family's home on the northwest coast of Brittany, then could it also be possible that St Patrick may have been experiencing in his dream the memory of the traumatic events which took place in that forest the day he was taken captive? Perhaps the voices that he associated with this wood were the cries of friends and family who had been killed or taken captive to Ireland? Perhaps those cries still haunted him.

If St Patrick was remembering the trauma of abduction, could the 'Voice of the Irish' have been the cry of those taken captive with him on that fateful day and the 'thousands of others' he said were removed from their homeland, including those who were still living in Ireland as they had not yet managed to escape from slavery as Patrick had recently done? Was St Patrick being called in his dream to go back to them?

The voices that St Patrick heard calling to him from the Wood of Foclut could have been associated not with the place where he was held captive, but the place where he was taken captive. What makes St Patrick's account doubly significant is that it is the first occasion in his writings where he mentions two place names in conjunction which is a rare coupling of geographical references.

St Patrick describes the Wood of Foclut as being 'close beside the Western Sea'.[28] Those who accept Tírechán's claim, that Foclut existed in the west of Ireland, have usually gone one stage further in a speculative form of dream interpretation, claiming that when St Patrick mentions the 'Western Sea' ('Mare Occidentale' in Latin) he must have been referring to the Atlantic Ocean off the west coast of Ireland. Again there is no historical evidence to support such an exclusive interpretation. The 'Mare Occidentale' was a name given by the Romans to the ocean which existed to the west of the Roman Empire. It could have referred to the west coast of Spain or France, including the coast of Brittany.

Despite this traumatic and powerful dream, St Patrick tells us that he did not return to Ireland immediately. He ends his account by simply saying, 'Thanks be to God that after all these years the Lord has granted them according to their cries.' Perhaps he was referring to the 'many years' his friends were held in captivity in Ireland, before he could return again to care for them?

### The Missing Years

St Patrick tells us nothing about what happened next, from the time of his escape from Ireland at the age of twenty-three to his return as an apostle, traditionally dated 432 CE. These are sometimes called the 'missing years', a period clouded with more legend and uncertainty than any other part of his biography. Most accounts of what happened during this time are contained in later sources providing an abundance of fascinating detail much of which is spurious but including some traditions that are possibly authentic. The question as to where St Patrick went for religious training and spiritual formation will be discussed later.

Wherever it was, St Patrick eventually returned to Ireland as a self-proclaimed apostle.[29] He went back to the land of his captivity, this time not as a slave to human beings but as a servant of Christ and a hostage to God.[30]

As St Patrick draws towards the end of his *Confession*, some final geographical clues are given which may help to identify his homeland. These are contained in a few short passages in which Patrick describes difficulties he experienced with his 'seniors'. We are left wondering what exactly may have caused or motivated him to write his *Confession*.

It appears to have been prompted by a particular situation of difficulty. The religious community or church which may have initially supported his mission in Ireland had turned against him. Unidentified Church leaders (Patrick calls them his seniors) were seeking his removal.

This is the first time readers are made aware of an issue that would have a very significant influence on St Patrick's biography in the centuries after his death – Church politics. It is possible that St Patrick may have written the *Confession* not only as a response to accusations of personal misconduct but as a defence against potential charges of heresy.[31]

Patrick may have been in Ireland for some time before his suitability for this ministry was questioned. It appears from the description given of these events that he was rejected by leaders in the Church, possibly clerics or Church elders who held a position of authority over him. They challenged his suitability for the Irish mission, convened a meeting to discuss his case and were now seeking his removal.

Perhaps out of respect, St Patrick does not name these shadowy figures who were resident in a country outside Ireland. Neither does he tell us which church or religious group they represented.[32]

When he describes his rejection by these 'seniors', Patrick provides clues about where he came from and where a religious community that he closely identified with was based.

He explains how the attack made on his own character and integrity had arisen because of the public report of a 'sin' which he admitted committing when he was about fifteen years old, before he was taken captive to Ireland.[33] St Patrick had found himself in a difficult situation because of this inquiry. He strongly argues that the accusations made against him were unjust. Depending on the nature of these charges and how serious they were, his reputation could have been damaged beyond repair and his life may even have been threatened. It is best to let St Patrick tell us the story in his own words:

> I was tested by some of my seniors, who came and cast up my sins as unfitting me for my laborious episcopate, and on that day I was surely tried, to the point where I could have fallen here and forever ...[34]
> They found an occasion for their charge against me after thirty years, in a deed I had confessed before I became a deacon. In my anxiety I confided to my best friend, my mind full of sorrow, what I had done one day in my youth, indeed in one hour, because I was not yet in control of myself. I know not, God knows, if I was then fifteen years old ...
> I did not believe in the living God, nor had I believed in Him from childhood, but remained in death and unbelief until I was severely chastised and truly humbled by hunger and nakedness, and that daily.[35]

Many years before, Patrick had confessed this 'sin' to a close friend, who had betrayed him by disclosing it to others. Patrick tells us that he had been 'corrected by the Lord' before he went to Ireland and therefore had a clear conscience about the work he was doing and his suitability for this ministry. Now he had greater spiritual maturity and felt the past should not be held against him.

As Patrick tries to explain the complexities of a situation that led to his estrangement from the religious leaders who may or may not have initially supported him, he provides more clues about where he came from and where these 'seniors' were based:

> I feel very sad to talk about one of my closest friends, with whom I had trusted the secrets of my soul. I found out from some of the brethren at the gathering that was held about me; *I was not present at it nor was I 'in Britanniis'* – nor did it originate from me – that he would stand up for

me in my absence ... he even told me to my face with his own words
'Look, you are going to be recognised as a bishop' – something for which
I was completely unworthy.

So why did he change and then decide to disgrace me in public, in the
presence of everyone, concerning that personal matter which he had
granted me forgiveness for earlier, out of the depths of his own heart, as
God who is greater than all had forgiven me? I will not say more than
this.[36]

The familiar phrase *in Britanniis* which occurs in this passage, is usually
translated as 'in Britain', as before, but could Patrick have been referring to
Brittany? If so, the meeting held to discuss his position might have been held
not far from Brittany, perhaps in neighbouring Gaul. An appropriate translation of the text might be:

And I had learned from some of the brethren before that gathering at
which my defence came up – I was not present at it nor was I in Brittany[37] nor did the matter originate from me – that he would argue for
my defence.

A clue which might reveal the truth can be found shortly afterward. Having
dealt with his defence, St Patrick switches attention away from his problems
with Church leaders to focus on his ministry in Ireland.

After describing the success of his work, as well as the difficulties he experienced, Patrick explains how attached and committed he was to the Irish
mission, which as far as he was concerned was not negotiable. It had been
ordained and supported by God.

It appears there may have been a complete breakdown in relations between
Patrick and those who had been seeking his dismissal. In response to criticisms
and attempts to remove him from office he does not mention being absolved,
at least not by his seniors. Patrick gives the impression he decided to 'go it
alone' and stay where he was, without bowing to these external pressures. He
describes how, even though he might have wished to leave Ireland to make a
journey *in Britanniis* he could not do so because he had made a vow to God
that he would remain in Ireland for the rest of his life, to serve the flock
entrusted to him, in exile from homeland and family:

The Lord has given grace to many of his female disciples, because even
though they are forbidden they continue steadfast in their following of
him ... As a result, even if I would wish to leave them and make a journey *in Britanniis* – and I would most dearly love to make that journey,
so as to see my homeland and family; not only that but also to proceed
further in to the Gauls to visit the brethren and see the faces of the saints
of my Lord ...[38]

God knows I greatly desired it; still I am bound by the Spirit who testi-
fied to me that if I do this he will pronounce me guilty; and I am afraid
of losing the labour I began, and not I but Christ the Lord who ordered
that I should come and be with those people for the rest of my life.[39]

St Patrick's description of his longing to make this journey is very significant
from a geographical point of view. Most scholars insist the word 'Britanniis'
should again be translated as Britain. This would make sense if St Patrick's family was in Britain and his church or religious community was based in Gaul.
Exactly the same could be said about Brittany, however, if St Patrick's homeland
was located there this passage would still have a sense of geographical integrity,
perhaps even more so. As an experiment which might help shed light on this
matter, a revised translation can be offered to see whether it makes geographical
and literary sense. If St Patrick was actually referring to Brittany, then the geographical references in the passage above could be translated as follows:

> As a result, even if I would wish to leave them and make a journey to Brit-
> tany and I would most dearly love to make that journey to see my
> homeland and family not only that but also to proceed further into the
> Gauls to visit the brethren and see the faces of the saints of my Lord.[40]

The journey St Patrick was contemplating would make perfect sense from
a geographical point of view, if it can be shown that Brittany and 'the Gauls'
were considered separate regions on the continent at the time of St Patrick. If
so, this passage reflects a genuine consistency in St Patrick's mental geography.
This would be the case, for example, if St Patrick's homeland was on the coast
of north-west Brittany, but the religious friends he longed to see were based at
St Martin's Monastery on the banks of the River Loire, which was in Gaul.

Later in this study, evidence will be presented to suggest that a coastal region
in North-west Brittany was distinguished from Gaul at the time of St Patrick.[41]
This region retained its sense of cultural and political independence from the
rest of Gaul right up to the time of Pippin and Charlemagne in the eighth and
early ninth century.

The division of Gaul into separate regions is confirmed by Sulpitius Severus
probably caused by the civil wars raging at that time. 'Britanniis' may have been
a familiar term in local ethnic geography, distinguished from other parts of
Gaul.

The area where St Martin of Tours was based, in a monastery on the banks
of the River Loire, was within Gaul. The area around Aleth (St Malo) and the
coastal region as far north as Mont St Michel was considered part of Brittany.
This region was known to the ancient Irish writers as 'Armoric Letha' or 'Lethania Brittaniae'. The Romans may have called the north-west coastal region of

Gaul 'Armorica' but this is not the only name by which it was known to ancient writers, who have recorded a local ethnic view of geography. The name 'Britain' was therefore applied to two separate regions occupied by the ancient Britons, one on either side of what is now the English Channel. Brittany is often referred to as 'La Petite Bretagne' or 'Little Britain', to distinguish it from 'Grande Bretagne' or 'Greater Britain'.

As St Patrick draws his *Confession* to a close, he reflects deeply on the significance of his life, the good and bad, the light and dark and the many blessings he had received despite all the dangers and difficulties he experienced. Patrick had found peace and healing within himself despite countless adversities. His steadfast faith and trust in God led him to experience a profound sense of intimacy with God, the gift of wisdom and a truly loving and compassionate heart which had carried him to the threshold of a deeper, steadfast joy.

He was now ready to face death, in gratitude for everything that had happened and the many gifts from God he had received. This is the way St Patrick chose to end his *Confession*:

> Wherefore I give un-wearying thanks to my God, who kept me faithful in the day of my trial. I give un-wearying thanks to my God who delivered me from all my troubles and so helped my work with such divine power. I steadfastly exalt and glorify your name where ever I am, not only when circumstances favour me but when I am afflicted, so that whatever happens to me, good or bad I must accept with an even mind and thank God always ...
>
> God showed me that I should believe and that God is endlessly to be trusted. And who so helped me, that I, a man ignorant of God's ways, in the last days should dare to undertake this work so holy and so wonderful. And as we have seen it written so we have now seen it fulfilled, we are the witnesses that the gospel has been preached to the limit beyond which no one dwells ...
>
> None shall ever assert that the credit is due to my own uneducated self, but regard it rather as a true fact to be firmly believed, that it was all the gift of God. And this is my Confession before I die.[42]

There is no record of what happened to St Patrick after this letter was published. From the way his *Confession* ends, he appears to have sensed that his own death was immanent.

It is possible that St Patrick was killed shortly after it was written, and that he died *persona non grata* rejected and despised as an outlaw or 'heretic' as far as the emerging church was concerned.[43] This alone explains what happened next.

Patrick disappeared from the Church's radar after his death, like a ship gone down in the Bermuda Triangle. He simply vanishes from all known ecclesiastical and historical records in Ireland, Britain or the continent for the next two hundred years. St Patrick's writings seem to have disappeared with him as if they went out of print or were quickly taken off the shelves in the ecclesiastical bookshops of that time.

It was not only St Patrick's place of origins that became lost to historical memory in the centuries after his death. Any clear record of his mission to Ireland was also forgotten. His complete disappearance from all surviving official documents for the next two centuries is astonishing. In the historical and ecclesiastical records for this period, it appears that as far as Church leaders, writers and the most respected chronicles were concerned St Patrick never existed.

---

*Notes*

1. *Confessio:* 1 (C 1)

2. Decurion (Latin: *decurione*) has been included because of St Patrick's statement in his Letter to Coroticus 10, *decurione patre nascor* – meaning 'I am the son of a Decurion'. The word deacon (Latin: *diaconum*), which can be found in the Book of Armagh copy of St Patrick's *Confession*, appears to be an interpolation reflecting later ecclesiastical influences. MacNeill said, 'It is not unlikely that he wrote decurion in both places.' See Eoin MacNeill, *Saint Patrick, Apostle of Ireland* (London, 1934), p. 6.

3. This name appears with a variety of spellings which are clearly recognisable, e.g. Banuem Thaburniae, Banauem Taberniae, etc. See Ludwig Bieler, *Clavis Patricii II: Libri Epistolarum Sancti Patricii Episcopi* (Dublin, 1993), p. 56, 118.

4. For a summary of efforts to identify 'Bannavem Tiburniae' see Bieler, *The Life and Legend of St Patrick* (Dublin, 1949), pp. 51–3, 133 ff.

5. Slave trading was a common practice amongst the Celts in Ireland, as it was across the whole of Europe and North Africa at the end of the fourth century.

6. C 16. John Luce suggested the animals were cattle. Other writers have suggested sheep or pigs.

7. Asceticism derives from the Greek *askesis*, a self-imposed discipline of spiritual exercises involving some form of renunciation. These practices were associated with Egyptian Desert Monasticism, a tradition which influenced early European monasticism.

8. C 17: *Bene ieiunas cito iterus ad patriam tuam.* Bieler, *Libri*, p. 65. *patriam* means 'homeland' similar to the Germanic *heimat*.

9. C 17.

10. *Sugere mammellas eorum:* C 18. The sucking of breasts was a pre-Christian rite of protection, well attested in ancient Ireland. M. A. O'Brien, *Miscellanea Hibernica, Etudes Celtiques,* 3 (1938), p. 372 ff.

11. Bury said 'the ship made for the coast of Gaul'; J. B. Bury, *The Life of St Patrick, His Place in History* (London, 1905), p. 33 ff. Despite claiming the ship landed in Gaul, Bury held firmly to the established tradition that St Patrick's homeland was in Britain.

12. The Latin phrase given is *ducenta milia passus* (C 17); Bieler, *Libri*, p. 66. This distance is not precise and there were variant readings in the early manuscripts, which allow for a journey from Dalriada (Antrim) in the north, to the south-east coast. In notes attached to *Fiacc's Hymn* (n. 9) the Scholiast makes the distance sixty miles 'or as others say, a hundred' which underlines the uncertainty of the precise distance. See J. H. Todd, *St Patrick, Apostle of Ireland* (Dublin, 1864), p. 367, n. 3.

13. Assistance with the initial calculations was given by J. B. S., Ashford, Co. Wicklow. Mark Mills (Mills Design) calculated the distances in nautical miles, from charts. He suggested there is no upper limit to the journey time, only a lower feasible limit of three days. Alan Rountree built a vessel similar in size to that which St Patrick may have used and was able to confirm the accuracy of these calculations, based on his experience of sailing these routes.

14. Fred Rountree kindly calculated the journey time to Carantec, an ancient port in Brittany, where the ship could have landed.

15. C 19. Bury suggested the cargo of dogs was Irish wolfhounds for sale on the continent. See J. B. Bury, *The Life of St Patrick, His Place in History* (London, 1905), p. 31.

16. *Et iterum post paucos annos in Brittanniis eram cum parentibus meis.* C 23. Bieler, *Libri*, p. 70. Some accounts claim St Patrick's mother and father were both killed during the attack the day Patrick was taken captive. If so then when St Patrick returned to his homeland *in Britanniis* after escaping from slavery in Ireland, he would have met his closest surviving relatives. See Stokes, 'Notes on *St Fiacc's Hymn*', *Tripartite Life*, ii (London, 1887), p. 415.

17. A variety of spellings are recorded in the original manuscripts, including: Britanniis, Brittanniis, Brictanniis, and Brittannia. See Bieler, *Libri*, p. 70.

18. C 23.

19. 'And again, after a few years, I was in Britain with my kindred.' C 23. See N. J. White, *Translation of the Latin Writings of St Patrick* (London, 1918); Ludwig Bieler, *The Works of St Patrick* (New York, 1952), p. 28.

20. C 23.

21. Stokes, *Tripartite Life*, ii (London, 1887), p. 421.

22. Binchy warned students not to trust anything Tirechán said, just because Tirechán had said it. See D. A. Binchy, 'Patrick and his Biographers', *Studia Hibernica*, 2 (1962).

23. Bieler lists all the various spellings including: Vocluti, Focluti, Foclut, Focluth, Uoluti, Ueluti, Uirgluti, Uirgulti, Uelutique, Uirgultiq, Uolutiq, Uoluti. See Bieler, *Libri*, p. 71. In translation, he gives 'Wood of Voclut'. Bieler, *The Works of St Patrick*, 1934.

24. See Robidue, *Histoire*, p. 55.

25. 'Silua Focluti', *Proceedings of the Royal Irish Academy, Section C: Archaeology, Celtic Studies, History, Linguistics, Literature*, 36 (1923), pp. 249–55. See also Patrick O'Neill, 'The Identification of Foclut', *Journal of the Galway Archaeological and Historical Society*, 22/4 (1947).

26. Jeremy Taylor, *Dreamwork* (New York, 1983).

27. *Et ualde compunctus sum corde.* C 23: Bieler, *Libri*, p. 71. In his writings, St Patrick often speaks about the heart and this is a particularly strong statement.

28. *Quae est prope mare occidentale.* C 23.

29. 'In proportion to the faith I have received ... it is my duty to make this choice; without thought of the risk of censure I incur, to make known the gift of God and his everlasting consolation, fearlessly and confidently to spread God's Name everywhere, so that even after my death I may leave a legacy to my brethren and sons whom I have baptised in the Lord.' C 14.

30. In his *Letter to Coroticus*, St Patrick reveals the depth of his commitment to the mission in Ireland when he says, 'I am a slave in Christ to a foreign people' – *denique seruus sum in Christo.* LC 10.

31. For the model of a *Confessio* as an autobiography written to justify a spiritual calling and as a defence against possible charges of heresy see Nora Chadwick, *Age of the Saints in the Celtic Church* (Durham, 1960; facs. edn, Llanerch, 2006), p. 24 ff.

32. Patrick says, 'I was attacked by a number of my seniors (Latin: *senioribus meis*) who came forward and brought up my sins.' C 26; Bieler, *Libri*, p. 72.

33. There has been speculation as to what this 'sin' might have been. It may have been at the higher end of the scale, such as participation in pagan worship, taking life or some form of personal misconduct.

34. C 26.

35. C 27.

36. C 32. *Emphasis added.

37. *Nec in Brittanniis eram.* C 32: Bieler, *Libri*, p. 75.

38. C 19.

39. *Pergens in Britannias et libentissime paratus eram, quasi ad patriam et parentes; non id solum, sed eram usque Gallias vistare fraters, et ut viderum faciem sanctorum Domini mei.* C 43.

40. C 43.

41. Dr Lanigan proposed the existence of a region called 'Britain' on the continent but he did not identify this with modern Brittany, saying, 'this Gallican or rather Aremoric Britain must not be confounded with the country now called Brittany; for it lay much further to the north.' In fact, Lanigan's 'Britain' was about 350 km north of modern Brittany. See John Lanigan, *Ecclesiastical History of Ireland* (Dublin, 1823), pp 98–119.

42. C 62.

43. *Indignum est illis Hiberionaci summs.* It seems they do not believe in one baptism, or that we have one and the same God who is father to us all. In their eyes, it is a disgrace that we are Irish. See Bieler, *Libri*, p. 99.

# CHAPTER FOUR

# The Unknown Apostle

Mark: (about to receive the injection) 'Is this going to hurt?'
Therapist: (moving towards him) 'Truth always does, a little.'[1]

In the two hundred years following St Patrick's death in 461 CE, until the closing decades of the seventh century, it is impossible to find any clear historical
references to him or his writings. The St Patrick we know today fails to appear
in any surviving historical records from this period. This remains an enigma
and one of the great unsolved mysteries of his life and legacy.

After Patrick's death, Ireland developed a sophisticated and creative monastic culture. Christianity was embraced by increasing numbers. From the
beginning of the sixth century, the Irish church entered a 'Golden Age' which
would last for another five hundred years. Celtic Christianity blossomed in Ireland, Wales and other regions on the margins of Western Europe, where
indigenous religious and cultural traditions were strong.[2] The Irish tradition
became rooted in Scotland through St Columba's foundation on Iona, then
spread to Northumbria and as far south as Glastonbury in England before
being carried even further into France, Belgium, Germany and the heartlands
of Europe.

Before the arrival of Augustine in Canterbury in 597 CE, the influence of
Irish and Welsh monastic traditions in Britain was pervasive and stronger than
anything Rome had to offer in these regions at this time. Irish monastic foundations developed on many of the sites where hermitages had been established
by early Irish saints. The largest monasteries became centres of learning and
some acted as proto-universities.[3] With a dynamic combination of education
and spiritual formation, students flocked to Ireland's 'monastic cities' from
across Ireland, Britain and the continent. The significance of Celtic monasticism within the Christian spiritual tradition and the development of European
culture during the so-called Dark Ages after the fall of Rome, has yet to be fully
understood or appreciated.[4]

Following the example of the Egyptian Desert Tradition, an early form of
Christian monasticism was encouraged by the pioneering efforts in Ireland of
St Martin of Tours, St David of Wales, St Declan of Ardmore, St Brigid of Kildare and St Enda of Aran, among many others. Irish monastic teachers
including St Finian of Clonard and St Finian of Moville, attracted thousands
of students, as did the famous monasteries at Bangor in County Down,

Northern Ireland and Bangor, north Wales. Much to our surprise, there are no references to St Patrick within the literature that emerged from any of these monasteries during this period.

In the sixth century, a large monastic federation developed around St Columba, who left Derry in 563 CE to found a monastery on the island of Iona.[5] Columba was born in Donegal in 521 CE, only fifty years after St Patrick's death. Tradition closely associates St Patrick's mission with Columba's native stronghold in the north of Ireland. Slieve Mis (Mount Slemish) in County Antrim is said to be the place where St Patrick was held captive as a slave and County Down was the location of Patrick's first church in the Barn at Saul, not far from Downpatrick. Strangely, there is no record of St Patrick in any of the writings which emerged from St Columba's monasteries, or from the monasteries in Down or Armagh before the seventh century.

*The Book of Durrow*, preserved in Trinity College, Dublin is one of the earliest ecclesiastical documents to have survived in Ireland, dated to the sixth century. It has a brief entry for *sancta praesbiter Patrici* (a holy elder called Patrick) which is somewhat vague and could be a reference to anyone. The title presbyter or elder was an early form of Christian leadership before the development of diocesan organisation with its characteristic order of deacons, priests and bishops.[6]

Likewise, there is a brief mention of 'Abba Patrick' in Adamnan's *Life of St Columba* which was first published in 688 CE but as scholars have noted, this is an isolated reference, too vague again to justify any claim that St Patrick was remembered with any special form of veneration within the early Irish church.[7]

It is very strange and more than surprising that Patrick is not mentioned in the earliest hagiography of an Irish saint, Cogitosus's seventh-century *Life of St Brigid* and not a word of significance about him can be found in any of the important Hiberno-Latin manuscripts written during this period, including the Penitentials of Finnian, Cummian and Fota. When the lack of recorded information is compared with claims that he makes in his own writings and the prominence given to him in later documents and Church traditions, this silence is not simply astonishing, it is completely bewildering.[8]

Cummian's letter *De Controversia Paschali* (Concerning the Easter Controversy) is dated around 630 CE. It was addressed to Segene, fifth abbot of Iona (632–652 CE). Cummian cites ten Easter cycles which he says were known in Ireland, beginning with 'that which holy Patrick, our bishop, brought and followed' (II: 208–209). Cummian states that all of these ten disagreed with the eighty-four-year cycle practised on Iona. He says St Patrick brought and composed the first Easter Cycle 'with Easter on moon 15 to 21, and equinox March 21'.

This was not true. St Patrick could not have used this cycle, known as the Dionysian Cycle, which was not introduced even in Rome until the sixth century. It therefore appears that even Cummian (who was one of the most highly educated and best informed scholars of his day) was possibly unsure concerning the truth about St Patrick.

If St Patrick was the founder of Irish Christianity and the apostle of Ireland as he is acknowledged today, why was he not mentioned by the saints who came after him, especially in the sixth and seventh centuries when Irish Christianity must have gained some inspiration from his mission and legacy? If the seeds of the gospel had been planted by Patrick in Ireland and those he converted to the faith, why was his presence not recorded or his achievements honoured?

Most alarming of all, there are no references to St Patrick in the writings of St Columbanus (540–615 CE), who left Bangor in 595 CE, and established several Irish monasteries on the continent, including Luxeil in France and Bobbio in Italy. Here we have one of the most highly educated and probably best informed monks in the early Irish church, many of whose writings have survived, yet Columbanus appears to be unaware of Patrick's existence and shows no knowledge of his writings. Columbanus appears never to have read or even heard of St Patrick's *Confession* or *Letter to Coroticus* and makes no reference to them.

In one of his own letters, written to Pope Boniface IV in 613 CE, Columbanus refers to the origins of the Church in Ireland, about which he claims to speak with authority. There is no mention of St Patrick, as if Patrick had no part to play.[9] In this letter, Columbanus acknowledges to the Pope that Ireland had received Christianity from Rome, saying, 'Our possession of the Catholic faith is unshaken: we hold it just as it was first handed to us by you.' But he makes no reference to Patrick. St Columbanus may have been referring either to the mission of Palladius, who was sent to Ireland by Pope Celestine in 431 CE according to the *Chronicle of Prosper of Aquitaine*, or perhaps to the monasticism of St Martin of Tours, who is often associated with the origins of Irish, Welsh, Scots and Breton monasticism.

St Ninian is alleged to have visited St Martin and named his first church 'Candida Casa' or the 'The White House', following Martin's foundation at Tours. When he was about to be deported from France, St Columbanus went to Tours for an all-night vigil at St Martin's tomb. This suggests there was an established veneration of St Martin in the early Irish Church. A copy of Severus's *Life of St Martin* was preserved alongside other important Patrician documents in the *Book of Armagh*, suggesting there was a significant link between St Martin and St Patrick. If so, Columbanus appears not to have known about it or perhaps for some reason, he chose not to mention it.

Why does St Columbanus not mention him, especially if St Patrick had been ordained in Rome by Pope Celestine or if Rome had supported St Patrick's mission and was responsible for the form of Christianity introduced to Ireland, as many later sources claim?[10]

St Patrick's absence from ecclesiastical records in Ireland is compounded by a similar omission from historical documents of Britain and the continent from the fifth, sixth and seventh centuries. Patrick fails to make an appearance in Bede's *Ecclesiastical History*, even though the most famous saints trained in the Irish tradition, including Columba, Colman, Aidan, Cuthbert and Hilda, are given extensive coverage.

Some writers have suggested this silence is because Bede was dealing specifically with the history of the Church in England and Britain but if his mission had been commissioned by the Papacy and St Patrick had introduced the ecclesiastical customs and traditions of Rome to Ireland, as later tradition claims, we would have expected Bede to mention this somewhere in his prolific writings.

No excuse is credible in relation to Prosper of Aquitaine, the most reliable and best informed Roman Chronicler of his day.

Prosper never mentions St Patrick or his ministry in Ireland, even though they were contemporaries. Neither does Sulpitius Severus, another well informed, very influential writer at the turn of the fourth century who was a contemporary of St Patrick. Severus records detailed information which is very significant in relation to claims found in several ancient documents that St Patrick was trained in the community of St Martin at Tours, but he never mentions St Patrick by name in any of his writings.

If Patrick's mother, Conchessa was a close relative of St Martin of Tours and Patrick spent four years in spiritual formation with his community and was tonsured there, as later documents claim, it is strange that Severus also fails to mention him. Some scholars have taken all this deafening silence to even question St Patrick's existence.

The reality is, a person called Patrick wrote two significant letters and definitely existed. His writings are not forgeries. They are genuine historical documents from the fifth century, proven to be so from internal evidence. So what happened to any information that did survive during the two centuries after his death? What caused his contribution to the origins of early Irish Christianity to be so neglected for these first two centuries and go unrecognised? This is certainly fertile ground for conspiracy theorists.

Later traditions associate St Patrick very closely with St Germanus of Auxerre, an influential Church leader in Gaul who was well connected to the authorities in Rome.

If Patrick had prepared for his mission to Ireland with St Germanus, we would expect Prosper and Bede to have known about it. This suggests we may not have been told the truth about St Patrick.

The best source we have for information about Germanus can be found in a *Life of St Germanus* written by Constantius of Lyon in 480 CE, only a few years after Patrick's death. This document does not mention anyone called Patrick as a student of St Germanus in Auxerre. In fact, it does not mention St Patrick at all.

When J. H. Todd published his book *St Patrick, Apostle of Ireland* in 1864 it sparked great controversy because Todd suggested this lack of historical record raises serious doubts as to whether St Patrick's mission to Ireland was ever commissioned or sponsored by the Papacy. Similar concerns apply to the notion that St Patrick had any close or positive relationship with Roman ecclesiastical authorities in Britain or Gaul.[11] Whatever was happening in the church of the fifth century, St Patrick's place within that church remains a mystery.

In the most reliable Chronicle for this period, Prosper of Aquitaine tells us that in 431 CE, Palladius was ordained by Pope Celestine and sent as the first bishop 'to the Irish believing in Christ'.[12]

Prosper appears not to have heard of Patrick, who according to Irish ecclesiastical traditions is supposed to have been appointed by Rome the following year, in 432 CE, after Palladius's sudden and unexpected death.

We know that Palladius was a confident of St Germanus and had close relations with the Church in Auxerre, where he worked before being appointed to a senior position in Rome. This makes Prosper's silence about St Patrick even more remarkable and suspicious.

The one place we would expect to find some record of St Patrick's life and mission is within the ancient annals of Ireland. Conspiracy theorists will be disappointed to discover that at last we can find some references to St Patrick in entries for the fifth century but these are still very unclear and contradictory. For example, in the entry given for the year 4357 (335 CE) the *Annals of Ulster* record, 'According to some, Patrick was born here ... but this is incorrect.' Then, for the year 4395 (352 CE): 'Patrick was brought as a captive to Ireland, but this is incorrect.'[13] Again for the year 4416 (358 CE): 'Patrick was released from captivity, but this is incorrect.'[14] These dates contradict other entries recorded for St Patrick in the Irish annals. The fact that another scribe felt it necessary to comment 'this is incorrect' on all three occasions, shows how uncertain the information was.[15]

The annals of Ireland are rightly venerated as a priceless national archive but within them even the identity of the person we know as St Patrick is very unclear. They contain references to various ecclesiastical figures called Patrick whose lives cannot easily be distinguished. The *Annals of Ulster*, for example, were compiled in the north of Ireland where St Patrick is said to have founded many churches. The Irish annals include the following entries which make very interesting reading:

431: St Patrick was ordained bishop by the Holy Pope, Celestine the First, who ordered him to go to Ireland to preach and teach faith and piety to the Gaeidhil (Irish) and baptise them. (A4M)[16]

432: Patrick came to Ireland this year, and proceeded to baptise and bless the Irish. (A4M)[17]

432: Bishop Patrick holds Ireland and begins to baptise the Scotti (Irish). (AI)[18]

441: The testing of Holy Patrick in the Christian faith. (AI)

442: Bishop Patrick was approved in the Catholic faith. (AU)

443: Bishop Patrick flourishing in the fervor of the faith and in the doctrine of Christ in our Province. (AU)

457: Repose of Old Patrick, as some books state. (AU)[19]

461: Here some read the repose of Patrick.

492: The Irish state here that Patrick the Archbishop died.

493: Patrick, son of Calpurn, first primate and chief apostle of Ireland whom Pope Celestine the First had sent to preach the gospel and disseminate religion and piety among the Irish ... resigned his spirit to heaven.

In an entry for the year 441 CE, nine years after St Patrick arrived in Ireland and began his mission, the *Annals of Ulster* state that he was 'confirmed in the Catholic faith'. This is an intriguing entry, not easy to explain. It implies that for the nine years before 441 CE, St Patrick was not confirmed or 'approved' in the Catholic faith, or that for some reason he still needed to be confirmed in that faith.[20]

It completely contradicts the claim in the *Annals of the Four Masters* that he had been ordained in Rome by Pope Celestine in 431 CE before he was sent to Ireland.

For the same year, the *Annals of Inisfallen* record 'the testing of Holy Patrick in the Christian faith'. These are strange remarks, yet to be fully understood or satisfactorily explained. Perhaps St Patrick did something wrong to lose his credentials in the eyes of the authorities, and then did something right to retrieve them.

All that can be gleaned from what is recorded in the annals, is that if St Patrick was ordained by Pope Celestine in 431 CE and came to Ireland in 432 CE, was not confirmed in the Catholic faith until ten years later in 441 CE but was 'flourishing in the faith and doctrine of Christ' within a year in 442 CE, then everyone else in the Irish church, in Britain, on the continent and in

Rome was completely clueless about what was going on because no one else appears to have heard about him. Was St Patrick's presence not important enough to record? Considering all these uncertainties, the only reasonable inference is that any reliable information which existed was lost or greatly obscured in the centuries after St Patrick's death.

The uncertainties which surround St Patrick may have been compounded by the fact that there were several figures called Patrick whose lives may have been confused or woven together. Tirechán tells us that Palladius was also called 'Patrick'.[21]

One of Ireland's most rigorous historians, D. A. Binchy, said that when no trustworthy historical information is available it is legitimate even for historians to engage in speculation, since this is the only resource left. What follows is pure speculation. What was going on at that time which might help to explain the anomalies and the deafening silence? There has to be a rational explanation for Patrick's absence from records which survived from the fifth and sixth century.

St Patrick tells us in his own writings that attempts were made by unnamed Church leaders to remove him from office and his mission to Ireland. Patrick was already working in Ireland when a conflict arose with those he calls his 'seniors'. Had St Patrick become *persona non grata* as a result of these disputes, to the extent that his position was not recognised or sanctioned by emerging leaders in the Church who were becoming influential in Britain and Gaul? This Latin phrase *persona non grata* refers to 'an unwelcome person'. It was a legal term used in diplomacy that indicates a proscription against a person entering a country. In non-diplomatic usage, when someone was *persona non grata* it suggests that he or she had for some reason been ostracised, so as to be figuratively non-existent. This appears to have happened to Patrick.

Speculation centres on issues of concern raging within the western Church at that time and events which must have affected St Patrick's life and ministry, either directly or indirectly.

In his *Chronicle*, which is known to be reliable, Prosper of Aquitaine informs us that St Germanus had been sent to Britain by Pope Celestine in 429 CE as part of an official mission by Rome to combat the Pelagian heresy, said to be rampant in Britain and Ireland at that time. These visits were part of an initiative undertaken by diocesan Church authorities in Gaul on behalf of Pope Celestine to bring the British and Irish churches in line with the teachings of Rome.[22]

Pelagius had been condemned as a heretic, largely through the influence of Augustine and Jerome, whose stance against him was ill-tempered, vitriolic and racist.[23] Shortly afterwards, Pelagius disappeared and was never seen again. Whether he went to the desert, as some traditions claim, or was killed by the champions of orthodoxy, we will probably never know. Patrick must have been aware of these controversies, since he was probably just beginning some form of biblical study and spiritual formation in preparation for the mission to Ireland, at the time that St Augustine's *Confessions*, which had been completed in 397 CE, was beginning to circulate.

These issues dominated the Church's agenda on the continent and in Britain, throughout the time of St Patrick's mission in Ireland. St Augustine died in 430 CE, which is probably around the time Patrick returned to Ireland. From the evidence available it is difficult to know which side he may have leaned to in this dispute, if any. James Kenney says St Patrick's writings show 'the unconscious influence of the Anti-Pelagian controversy and his declaration of faith resembles that of Pelagius'.[24] Some scholars suggest that Patrick's way of thinking shows a strong leaning towards Pelagius, while others say his letters reflect the teachings of Augustine.[25] It is important at this stage simply to acknowledge the silence that surrounds St Patrick in all historical records from this period, which has yet to be explained.

In relation to the Pelagian controversy, we frequently find references to this as an 'arch heresy'. Writers speak of 'the evil poison of Pelagianism' and Pelagius is demonised as a heresiarch. In the midst of serious theological and ecclesiastical controversy, it might be helpful to ask, who exactly were these dastardly Pelagians? Where was the ecclesiastical stronghold from which their 'devilish poison' threatened the life of the western Church?

After being castigated in St Augustine's influential book *Contra Pelagius* (Against Pelagius), Pelagianism was condemned as a heresy, especially by influential bishops in Gaul who were in conflict with the type of monasticism pioneered by St Martin. They initially lobbied and then supported Augustine on this issue in efforts to combat the influence of early forms of monasticism that were unwelcome to many diocesan clergy.[26] In a letter written to the Irish church in 638 CE Pope John says, 'We have learned that the poison of the Pelagian heresy has revived among you and so we urge you to put out of your minds completely this poisonous crime of superstition … this detestable heresy.'[27]

Pelagianism never existed as an organised, separatist religious movement. It became a convenient and powerful stereotype, used by the authorities in Rome and North Africa and their supporters in Gaul to counter what was essentially an alternative way of thinking within the Church. Augustine and Jerome, then Pope Celestine, Prosper of Aquitaine and St Germanus of Auxerre were all at the forefront of efforts to combat the teachings of Pelagius. When we meet references to the 'evil poison' of Pelagianism it can be helpful to read between the lines to 'Early Irish, Welsh and Breton Christianity'.

Prosper records that Pope Celestine freed Britain from 'the disease' of Pelagius by sending Germanus of Auxerre to Britain in 428 CE. He describes how Celestine had challenged 'the enemies of grace' also by 'ordaining a bishop (Palladius) for the Irish' (in 431 CE). Prosper remarks that by these actions 'he (Pope Celestine) made the Barbarian island (Ireland) Christian while taking care to keep to the Roman island (Britain) Catholic'.

Germanus, Pope Celestine, Prosper of Aquitaine and Augustine were of the same party. Prosper records, 'Augustine was always in communion with us … people in Gaul who rejected (his) writings were deprived of the liberty to speak evil.' This confirms that the Church in Britain, Ireland and parts of Gaul was seen to be 'Pelagian' by the papal authorities and diocesan bishops who supported the teachings of Augustine. In a challenging recent study, the Irish author Dara Molloy has argued strongly that the early Irish church (which had developed indigenously before the arrival of Roman influences towards the end of the sixth century) was strongly sympathetic to the teachings of Pelagius and that Rome sought to 'rectify' this.[28]

After the death of Pelagius, grave concerns had been expressed by some Church leaders that within Irish, British and Gallic churches, sympathies towards the teachings of Pelagius were still strong. Pope Celestine sent St Germanus to Britain in 429 CE to combat those who followed these teachings. As an essential part of this anti-Pelagian mission, Pope Celestine also sent Palladius to Ireland in 431 CE as its first accredited Catholic bishop.

This suggests that efforts made by Rome at this time to challenge and undermine the teachings of Pelagius formed part of a deliberate strategy to confront and control the British and Irish churches and the influence of indigenous Celtic spiritual traditions, wherever they existed. Papal letters that survive describe how Celestine launched a strong crusade against Pelagianism at this time. His appointment of Palladius to Ireland must have been designed to support this strategy, hoping to bring the Irish church into line with Rome's official teachings.[29]

The key question is, where did St Patrick stand in relation to all this? These events all took place at exactly the same time Patrick was being prepared for his mission to Ireland. Can the silence which greets us in usually reliable sources be explained because Patrick may have been associated with a religious group accused of being Pelagian, or some other marginal group classified as heretical? This would certainly help to explain St Patrick's absence from existing historical records.

At the beginning of the fifth century, such groups were in conflict with the diocesan bishops who had given their full support to St Augustine's teachings. Some of these bishops had recently been appointed to the Church in Gaul, where they quickly acquired positions of influence, wealth and responsibility, replacing 'Celtic' bishops who were sympathetic to Pelagius.

This was part of a deliberate strategy developed by the Church, directed by newly appointed bishops who once held positions of executive responsibility in the imperial administration. The Roman Empire may have collapsed early in the fifth century but its legacy survived and was rejuvenated in many ways by the Church. In a detailed study of the fall of Rome, Peter Heather says:

> At the top end of Roman Society, the adoption of Christianity made no difference to the age-old custom that the Empire was God's vehicle in the world.[30]

By 438 CE, the Senate in Rome was a Christian body. The Church was able to rejuvenate a sense of Roman 'imperialism' through an influential and growing ecclesiastical organisation.[31] It adapted many traditional customs and values of the Empire, including dioceses with a hierarchical structure based on the order of deacons, priests and bishops. The Pontiff, based in Rome, continued to dress in purple, the sacred colour of imperial rule. This was a potent, traditional symbol of secular and divine authority. These are only a few examples of the many customs, traditions and structures of administration adopted by the Church from its 'secular' forerunner.

After Rome had fallen to the Barbarians, rules and doctrines developed by the Church and administered by the Curia, offered new hope for the preservation of unity and order.

A strategy was being developed for the 'Romanisation' of western Christendom. It would take another five hundred years before this policy finally came to absolute fruition with the Norman Invasion of Ireland but this strategic goal, which formed an essential component of St Augustine's teachings, was eventually achieved.

This process began during Patrick's lifetime and, together with Pelagius, St Patrick may have been one of its first victims. As the fifth century progressed, the monastery of Lerins appears to have become a centre for the promotion of Catholic orthodoxy based on St Augustine's teachings, disseminated through supportive diocesan authorities. Churches in Britain, Ireland and parts of Gaul and Spain were caught in the midst of this influential political development.

The story of the struggle for pre-eminence between the sees of southern Gaul is a complicated one but before long, bishops were appointed from Rome and Lerins to replace Celtic bishops in Gaul.[32] These developments had a major impact in Brittany.

We catch glimpses of tensions that existed at this time between early forms of Christian monasticism influenced more by Celtic and Egyptian traditions and an emerging urban diocesan hierarchy strongly supportive of Rome. St Ambrose, a close friend and mentor of St Augustine, was afraid to visit Gaul in 392 CE because of the conflict that was raging there between monks and diocesan bishops.[33]

Could these tensions between monasticism and expanding diocesan structures help to shed light on those 'missing years' in the life of St Patrick?

Shortly after sending Palladius as a bishop to Ireland, Pope Celestine wrote to the bishops in Vienne and Narbonne condemning the practice of appointing 'wanderers and outsiders' over the heads of the appointed local clergy.[34] He makes no secret of his dislike of 'monastic bishops' and says:

> It is not surprising they who have not grown up in the Church act contrary to the Church's usages, and that, coming from other customs, they have brought their traditional ways with them *into our church*. Clad in cloak, and with a girdle round the loins, they consider they will be fulfilling the letter rather than the spirit of the scriptures ...
> Such a practice may be followed as a matter of course rather than reason by those who dwell in remote places and live their lives far from their fellow men. But why should they dress in this way in the churches of God, changing the usage of so many years, of such great prelates, for another habit?[35]

Pope Celestine's description of these 'wanderers and outsiders' who practiced an ascetic Christian lifestyle based on the need for 'purity of heart' through which they considered themselves to be fulfilling the biblical law is an appropriate description for the approach taken by St Martin and St Patrick.

According to an ancient tradition, St Patrick spent four years in spiritual formation with St Martin's community and was tonsured there. These groups had an uneasy relationship with diocesan authorities. Some may have been sympathetic to the Priscillians, as St Martin was.[36]

St Columbanus never mentions St Patrick or Pelagius by name but he does make an intriguing and surprisingly defensive remark which may help shed light on issues of concern at the time he was writing. In his letter to Pope Boniface IV, written in 613 CE, Columbanus seeks to assure Rome, that the early Irish church was and always had been part of the one true Catholic and Apostolic Church. What he actually says is: 'No Jews, schismatics or heretics can be found amongst us.'[37] Is it possible that St Patrick had been forgotten and erased from history because he had been associated with one or more of these three groups?

One of the most controversial claims found in many of the ancient sources is that St Patrick's ancestors were Jewish.[38] This has always been dismissed as a legend without historical foundation but if there is any truth in this claim then it would certainly help explain why the surviving records are so silent with regard to St Patrick. In the sixth century, when anti-Semitism was pervasive, this would have been a factor strong enough to guarantee a journey into historical oblivion.

Considering that St Patrick is such an anonymous figure in all the surviving records from the fifth and sixth centuries it is a miracle that his two letters survived. But survive they did, God bless them, through all the great dangers and difficulties of this turbulent period in history that followed the collapse of the Roman Empire, fuelled by the Barbarian invasions in Europe and the Anglo-Saxon invasion of Britain.

A cult of St Patrick must have existed somewhere, possibly in the north of Ireland where his writings were preserved by friends or followers. Suddenly, in the closing decades of the seventh century after more than two hundred years of historical and ecclesiastical silence, something happened to turn Patrick's 'biography' upside down. St Patrick was about to reappear from the historical oblivion with great fanfare and glory, in hagiographical documents published by the Church in Armagh. Whatever may have happened in the previous two hundred years, around 685 CE someone decided it was time to open the file and prepare Ireland's apostle for an official resurrection.[39] Bishop Aed of Sletty, who was active in efforts to reform the Church in Ireland and encourage wider acceptance of Rome, commissioned an Irish scribe called Muirchú to write an official 'biography' of St Patrick. This has shaped our image and understanding of Patrick to the present day. By the time Muirchú put pen to paper, the world was a very different place to that which St Patrick had known when he first came to Ireland.

On the margins of Western Europe where Celtic traditions were strong, Christianity was rapidly being Romanised and organised more effectively at an international level with diocesan structures capable of propagating official Church teachings and doctrines. As part of a well developed and deliberate strategy, ecclesiastical, political and military alliances had been formed between the Roman Church and the Franks in Gaul and with the Anglo-Saxons in Britain. Such alliances increased the Church's influence and authority and now gave it the secular muscle required to overcome opposition. A new world order was emerging. Christianity on the continent was becoming more homogenised and uniform. The Roman Church was now expanding westwards and growing stronger.

Roman ecclesiastical traditions were not only becoming more popular and in some parts of Ireland more desirable, they could now be effectively imposed. Those who refused to conform to Rome's teachings and accept reforms were becoming increasingly isolated and marginalised. It is within this historical context that Ireland's 'unknown apostle', St Patrick, was about to come out of the invisible closet into which history had so far confined him.

Muirchú was a genius. His *Life of St Patrick* would quickly find its way onto the front page of the Irish ecclesiastical record and gain great influence. To meet the changing circumstances of the times, whatever may have happened before,

Patrick's image and the ecclesiastical record now had to be acceptable. St Patrick was about to be presented to the Church and the world as a fully paid up, card carrying member of the Catholic Church, with a pristine behavioural record. Any talk of conflict with ecclesiastical authorities or the reason for his absence from historical records had to be discounted. Whatever uncertainties had existed in the past, whatever might have been the truth about St Patrick's place of origins or his obscure and controversial religious and ethnic background, St Patrick's story was about to go public and this time, therefore it had to be kosher.

This was not the time to mention any possible association there may have been with those now seriously out of favour, such as the three groups mentioned by St Columbanus. Greatly honoured and now to be remembered for all time, St Patrick was heralded as the sole founder of Irish Christianity, Ireland's patron saint and national apostle, founder and first archbishop of the Church in Armagh, blessed by Pope Celestine and in full communion with Rome. It wasn't exactly the truth, but for Ireland and the Irish Church at the end of the seventh century, it served far more than its purpose. That's how the 'Legend' of Saint Patrick was born.

---

*Notes*

1. From *Flash Forward*, a television series.

2. For a masterful and detailed study, see T. M. Charles-Edwards, *Early Christian Ireland* (Cambridge, 2000).

3. The Monastic City at Glendalough is a perfect example. A large monastery developed in 'Gleann dá loch', the 'valley of two lakes', where St Kevin lived as a hermit in the sixth century. See Michael Rodgers and Marcus Losack, *Glendalough: A Celtic Pilgrimage* (Dublin, 1996; Revised 2011).

4. For a radical and pioneering new study, see Dara Molloy, *The Globalisation of God* (Inismor, Aran Islands, 2009).

5. The Irish form of his name, Colm Cille, means 'dove of the church' or perhaps 'Messenger of the church' (*colum*: dove, or messenger (hence *columbarium*, a name given by the Romans to 'dovecots' for homing pigeons, used for carrying messages) *cill*: a church or monastic cell.

6. In the *Book of Armagh* St Patrick refers to his grandfather, Potitus, as a presbyter. C 1.

7. Adamnan helped convene the Synod of Birr in 697 CE, which introduced reforms in the Irish church. This reference to Patrick appears to have been added later to his *Life of Columba* in a second preface written after the Synod of Birr.

8. See Heinrich Zimmer, *The Celtic Church in Britain and Ireland* (London, 1902), p. 81. For an English translation of Cummian's letter, see Liam de Paor, *St Patrick's World*, Four Courts Press, Dublin, 1993, pp. 151–3.

9. For an English translation of Columbanus's letter, see Liam de Paor, *St Patrick's World* (Dublin, 1993), pp. 141–3.

10. For a detailed discussion, see Zimmer, *The Celtic Church in Britain and Ireland*, ch. 1.

11. J. H. Todd, *St Patrick, Apostle of Ireland* (Dublin, 1864).

12. For an English translation of Prosper's *Chronicle*, see Liam de Paor, *St Patrick's World*, pp. 70–87.

13. *Annals of Ulster (AU)*, trans. Sean Mac Airt and Gearoid Mac Niocaill, Dublin Institute for Advanced Studies (Dublin, 1983).

14. Dr Dan McCarthy, Fellow Emeritus at Trinity College, Dublin, kindly synchronised the *AU* dates given for St Patrick's birth, captivity and escape to 335 CE, 352 CE and 358 CE respectively. McCarthy's view is that the earlier Annalistic chronology for Patrick was: born c.416 CE, taken captive 432 CE, released or escaped 438 CE returned to Ireland c.458 CE, died 491 CE. See Dan McCarthy, *The Irish Annals: Their Genesis and History* (Dublin, 2008), pp. 142–6.

15. The Irish Annals cannot be trusted as a source of reliable historical information about St Patrick. The *Annals of Tigernach*, for example, which are thought to be the most reliable, say Patrick was born in 341 CE and taken captive to Ireland in 357 CE. AD 341: (*Patricius nunc natus est*); AD 357 (*Patricius captiuus in Hiberniam ductus est*). See *Annals of Tigernach*, trans. Whitley Stokes, i, *Revue Celtique* 16 (1895); facsimile edition published by Llanerch, 1993, p. 30 ff.

16. Statements about St Patrick's close relationship with Papal authorities must be viewed with extreme caution. This claim is impressive but is most likely the result of hagiographical interpolation.

17. *The Annals of the Kingdom of Ireland, Of the Four Masters* (A4M) i, De Burca (Dublin, 1990).

18. *Annals of Inisfallen*, trans. Sean Mac Airt (Dublin 1944 [1951]), Celt: The Corpus of Electronic Texts (UCC) [website] <http://www.ucc.ie/celt/published/T100004/index.html>

19. According to the *Féilire Aengus* this 'Sen Patrick' (Old Patrick or Patrick Senior) was St Patrick's tutor.

20. *Probatus est in fide Catolica*: *AU*, p. 40, 41.

21. See Thomas O'Rahilly, *The Two Patricks* (Dublin, 1942; repr. 1981).

22. Prosper states that Pope Celestine saw Britain as the stronghold of Pelagianism and ordered those who shared such views to be banished from Italy. Prosper says Celestine 'was at no less pains to free Britain from the same plague. For certain men who were the enemies of Grace had taken possession of the land of their birth'. *Contra Collatorem*, XXI; Nora Chadwick, *Age of the Saints in the Celtic Church* (Durham, 1960; facs. edn, Llanerch, 2006), p. 15. For the conflict between Augustine and Pelagius, see Gerald Bonner, *St Augustine of Hippo: Life and Controversies* (Norwich, 2002), ch. 8, pp. 313 ff.

23. Jerome calls him a 'fat dog weighed down with Irish porridge'. Jerome, *Comm. on Jeremiah*, Prologue 3.

24. James Kenney, *The Sources for the Early History of Ireland: Ecclesiastical* (Dublin, 1997), p. 167, see n. 44.

25. See Daniel Conneely, *The Letters of St Patrick*, ed. Patrick Bastible (Maynooth, 1993).

26. Pohle, Joseph. 'Pelagius and Pelagianism', *The Catholic Encyclopedia*, 11 (New York: 1911), *New Advent* [website] <http://www.newadvent.org/cathen/11604a.htm>

27. See Liam de Paor, *St Patrick's World*, p. 149.

28. See Prosper of Aquitaine on Pope Celestine and Pelagius in de Paor, *St Patrick's World*, p. 70 ff.; Dara Molloy, *The Globalisation of God*.

29. Chadwick, *Age of the Saints*, p. 31 ff.; See also Kenney, *The Sources for the Early History of Ireland: Ecclesiastical*, p. 161 ff. The mission of Palladius in 431 CE was not successful. Some

accounts say he was not welcomed in Ireland and may have been killed there. Others say he went to Britain and died among the Picts.

30. Peter Heather, *The Fall of the Roman Empire: A New History* (London, 2005).

31. Heather, *The Fall of the Roman Empire*, p. 125.

32. See Kenney, *Sources*, pp. 163–5. For an outspoken and still controversial overview of the 'Romanisation' of the Western Church, see Heinrich Zimmer, *The Celtic Church in Britain and Ireland*. Lupus of Troy, who accompanied St Germanus on the visit to Britain in 429 CE to combat the teachings of Pelagius, was a monk from Lerins.

33. Chadwick, *Age of the Saints*, p. 31.

34. *Peregrine et extranei*: 'wanderers (pilgrims) and outsiders'.

35. Epistle 4, Mansi, III, p. 264. *Emphasis added.

36. See ch. 16, 'Martin of Tours'.

37. This statement has been taken to confirm that the Irish church always saw itself as being part of the universal Catholic Church and not a separate 'Celtic' Church. For an English translation of Columbanus's letter, see Liam de Paor, *St Patrick's World*, pp 141–3.

38. *Quidam sanctum Patricium ex Iudeis dicunt originem duxisse*: 'Some say St Patrick's origins was of the Jews'. See 'Vita IV' in Ludwig Bieler, ed., *Four Latin Lives of St Patrick*, (Dublin, 2005), p. 50. See 'Was St Patrick Jewish?' in Marcus Losack, *St Patrick and the Bloodline of the Grail: The Untold Story of St Patrick's Royal Family* (Annamoe, Wicklow, 2012), p. 119 ff.

39. Zimmer described this as 'resuscitation'. See *The Celtic Church in Britain and Ireland* (London, 1902).

CHAPTER FIVE

# *Our Man in Armagh*

One of the easiest and most effective ways to promote a deception is by the misspelling of words. Names can be distorted and misspelled to such an extent it requires long and patient effort to trace their true and proper form.[1]

A file labelled 'Saint Patrick' must have been tucked away somewhere, perhaps in the basement at the monastery of Armagh. It had gathered a lot of dust by the time Muirchú opened it and he knew that his task would not be easy. More than two hundred years had passed since St Patrick's death and the information which had survived about him was obscure. Muirchú began his narrative with surprising frankness and honesty. He says St Patrick's life was uncertain and controversial. Scribes had found 'discrepancies' and 'so many had expressed doubts, they had never arrived at a coherent narrative of events'.[2] Muirchú complains of 'uncertain sources' and 'unreliable memories'. He also expresses genuine anxiety bordering on fear about the responsibility he had been given, concerned that he was entering what he describes as the 'deep and dangerous sea' of fifth-century church history.[3]

The information about St Patrick was obviously complex and uncertain but what could possibly make an investigation into this subject so dangerous? This is how Muirchú described what he found when he opened the file at the end of the seventh century:

My lord Aed: Many have tried to bring certainty to the order of this narrative according to what their fathers and those who were from the beginning servants of the Word have handed down to them, though because of this most difficult work of narration and the different opinions and very great suspicions of so very many persons, they have never managed to achieve consensus or certainty with regard to an agreed history.

For that reason, unless I am deceived, according to this proverb of ours 'as boys are led out into an amphitheater' [we have found ourselves] being led through this deep and dangerous sea of holy narration where there are waves and unpredictable currents swelling without restraint between very violent eddies and whirlpools, uncharted waters never tamed or brought to order by any previous craft except by my father Cogitosus.[4]

I have taken this initiative now with something tried and appropriated, the infant sailing boat of my own little intellect but just in case I am accused of fashioning something great from something small, know that I am working without sufficient literary sources, authors who cannot be identified, dependent on unreliable memories and the bad language that characterises this controversial subject ...

I do this with pious affection and holy charity, obedient to the command of your holiness and authority, even though I may be feeling weighed down with great uncertainty, I shall now take steps to unfold a few of the many deeds of holy Patrick.[5]

Muirchú had been commissioned by the Church in Armagh to write an official 'biography' of St Patrick. Regardless of any difficulties, this had to be detailed and specific. 'Time, place and person' were demanded. Failure and further controversy was not an option. Muirchú's warning about uncertainties is quickly left aside as he launches into the main body of his narrative. He makes explicit geographical statements, in which Muirchú claims to know 'without doubt' that Patrick came from Britain:

> Patrick, also named Sochet
> A Briton by race [*Brito natione*]
> Born in the Britains [*in Brittanniis natus*]
> His father Calpurnius [a deacon] the son
> [As Patrick says] of an elder, Potitus
> Who hailed from Bannauem Thaburniae –
> A place not far from our sea ...
> This place, as I am informed beyond
> Hesitation or doubt is Ventra.
> His mother's name was Conchessa.[6]

Muirchú had access to a copy of St Patrick's *Confession*. He follows it closely in the first part of his narrative. He tells us that Patrick's family came from 'Bannauem Thaburniae'.[7] This is an alternative spelling to the way it appears in the *Book of Armagh* version of Patrick's *Confession*, but it is still clearly recognisable.

According to author David Howlett, who has made a detailed study of his text, Muirchú used numerology or gematria when composing his narrative. Individual words, sentences and whole paragraphs were constructed using alpha numeric values, based on letters in the Hebrew alphabet. This might help explain a difference in spelling in this case.[8]

Muirchú is the first person we know to claim that he could identify the location of Bannavem Tiburniae. He said he knew without doubt it was called 'Ventra'. Unfortunately, Muirchú's 'Ventra' has never been identified. We don't know whether it was a town or village or even if it existed. He states clearly, that it was in Britain and his narrative is one of those later sources used to support the view that St Patrick came from Britain.[9] Muirchú identifies St Patrick's origins exclusively with Britain. He provides detailed geographical descriptions using names which appear to refer to Britain and have always been translated as Britain. Let's take a closer look at the words he used in Latin, to see whether his geography is clear enough to be trustworthy.

Muirchú tells us St Patrick was 'a Briton' by nationality (*Brito natione*) born 'in the Britains' (*in Brittanniis*). When Patrick escaped from Ireland the ship took him back to 'the Britains' (*ad Brittanias nauigauit*). When Patrick left his homeland 'in the Britains' (*in Brittanniis*), he went to study in Gaul with St Germanus. Muirchú describes how St Patrick crossed the sea 'to the south of Britain' to get there.[10]

While Patrick was in Gaul news reached the continent that Palladius had died 'in the Britains' (*in Brittanniis*). After Patrick had finished his religious training in Gaul and was ready to embark on his mission to Ireland he 'came through to the Britains'.[11]

Muirchú tells us that at that time 'the whole of Britain' (*tota Brittannia*) was frozen in the cold of unbelief.[12] Patrick crossed the Irish Sea[13] (presumably from somewhere on the west coast of Britain) before he landed at Wicklow Harbour, on the southeast coast of Ireland.[14]

Muirchú goes overboard in a geographical sense, by including so much detailed, descriptive geography in his narrative. He uses several names which as far as Muirchú is concerned, all clearly refer to the island of Britain and are applied exclusively to Britain.[15]

These geographical descriptions are designed to emphasise the 'fact' that St Patrick came from Britain and remove any lingering doubt about that. His narrative is impressively well constructed but is it trustworthy?

Hagiography is a particular genre of medieval literature, designed with one objective in mind, to publicise the life of a saint and emphasise their holy and miraculous deeds.

Hagiographers cannot be viewed as reliable historical witnesses. Medieval hagiographers were professional spin doctors. We cannot treat this information as trustworthy in the way we should be able to trust history, geography or biography, even though what Muirchú writes sounds very convincing. As Binchy once said, with Irish hagiography, nothing is impossible.

Let's try to step inside Muirchú's shoes for a moment and appreciate his genius. When Muirchú described St Patrick's place of origins and episodes that took place in his life, he did this by creating a geographical picture. In other words, Muirchú created a 'map'. Through the use of creative and pseudo-historical narrative, he uses this 'map' to explain and convince his readers as to where St Patrick came from, where he received his religious training and the various journeys St Patrick is alleged to have undertaken. Some of these journeys can be identified from St Patrick's writings but others cannot. Muirchú's 'map' was carefully designed and deliberately crafted to locate St Patrick's origins in Britain. To understand his work, we have to be able to 'read' his map.

Authors Ward Kaiser and Denis Wood have written a fascinating study of maps called *Seeing through Maps: the Power of Images to Shape our World View*. When asked if there is any such thing as a true and accurate map, they say, 'Maps are merely descriptions of the world or part of it, from a particular perspective or bias.'[16] To understand what this bias is, they suggest we look first at what stands at the centre of the map, because this reflects a certain world view. This is true of all maps, but especially those from the medieval period. A good example is a twelfth-century map of the world called the *Mappa Mundi*, preserved at Hereford Cathedral, England. In this map, Jerusalem stands at the centre of the world. This reflects a particular religious world view held by some at that time.[17]

Muirchú's 'map' was designed to explain key episodes in St Patrick's life and locate those events for the reader. His genius as a hagiographer is that he appears to speak with authority, to the extent that his narrative has shaped our image of St Patrick's biography for more than a thousand years. Most writers are still convinced that, in terms of his origins, Britain stood at the centre of St Patrick's world.

Kaiser and Wood invite us to reflect more deeply on what we can learn from maps, saying that every map reflects an agenda and we can detect that agenda by observing what has been included and what has been excluded from the map. This is a sign of any map maker's priorities and defines their 'mental geography'. A map of Ireland designed to advertise cathedrals or sites of historical and archaeological interest, for example, would be very different to one designed to show golf courses. Can we detect any form of bias or hidden agenda in the 'map' Muirchú created for us?

Muirchú was commissioned by the church in Armagh to write the Church's first official 'biography' of St Patrick and he was expected to provide clear and specific information. He admits in his prologue 'time, place and person' were demanded. Those who funded his work had a strong political and ecclesiastical agenda which may have influenced the choices he made about what to include or leave out.[18]

This is where maps become really interesting. What Muirchú left out or excluded from his map is just as significant as what he included. We know Muirchú had access to a copy of St Patrick's *Confession*, so we can compare both documents and see what he included and what he excluded from Patrick's own writings. For example, any reference to St Patrick's difficulties with 'seniors' in the Church, those who were seeking to discredit Patrick's reputation and remove him from office, are excluded. A conflict with (and estrangement from) certain figures who represented the ecclesiastical authorities stands at the centre of St Patrick's *Confession*, but Muirchú makes no reference to it.

Muirchú also excluded any reference to another tradition which said that Patrick was taken captive from a place on the continent, in Brittany.

We do not know what stories Muirchú had found in the files, or what sources he used, apart from St Patrick's *Confession*, but he was probably aware that Patrick's family had been associated with Armorica, the Roman name for Brittany. This is a reasonable assumption to make because Muirchú tells us that St Patrick's mother was called Conchessa, but he does not include the second part of that tradition, as it is passed down through most of the other sources, that she was 'of the Franks' and a close relative of St Martin of Tours. In all the other ancient Lives of St Patrick which mention Conchessa by name, these extra details are always included, even in Jocelyn.

If Muirchú knew St Patrick's family had a 'French' connection, he chose not to mention it. One possible explanation is that it did not suit his objective as a hagiographer, which was to emphasise the pureness of Patrick's pedigree as an apostle who came to Ireland from Britain.

Muirchú's real genius can be appreciated when we understand the context in which he was writing. This was a critical time in Irish, British and European history. Recent developments in Britain had serious implications for Ireland and for the church in Armagh. Muirchú's narrative cannot be understood in isolation from these events which influenced much of what Muirchú wrote about St Patrick and perhaps ultimately determined the whole design of his 'map'.

### The Synod of Whitby, 664 CE

At the end of the year in which St Columba had died, 597 CE, Pope Gregory sent St Augustine to Canterbury, England, as part of a Roman mission. This began as a fairly small undertaking, centred on the church in Kent. Things changed dramatically when a new alliance was forged between the Roman Church and senior members of the Anglo-Saxon royal family. This was brought into effect through decisions taken at the Synod of Whitby in 664 CE. At this Synod, the king of Northumbria, who was concerned about the practical implications of differences between the Roman Church and the Irish tradition with regard to the date for Easter, decided to accept the need for uniformity and submit the English Church to the authority of Rome.

After Whitby, the Irish Church also came under pressure to reform. The Catholic Church in Britain had begun to establish a very close alliance with the Anglo-Saxons and now benefited from English military expansion. By the time Muirchú started writing his *Life of St Patrick* the Anglo-Saxons had occupied coastal areas of northwest Britain and reached as far north as Carlisle and Dumbarton in Scotland.

The Irish Church was watching these developments with grave concern especially when news came through that the English had taken the Kingdom of Strathclyde, an ancient and symbolic stronghold for the Irish. From an Irish perspective, the threat of an English invasion was not only real, it was immanent. The invasion of Brega in 684 CE shows how the ambitions of the Northumbrians now extended to Ireland.[19] From Strathclyde or the Isle of Man, which had been occupied by the Northumbrians for fifty years, it was only a short distance across the sea to Armagh.

For the first time in her history, Ireland faced the military might of the English, allied to the ecclesiastical authority of Rome. Threats concerning the use of force had been made clear to the Britons, a Celtic speaking people who inhabited the island of Britain before the Anglo-Saxon invasions in the fifth century. It was implicit in 603 CE when Bede records that St Augustine of Canterbury 'urged the British bishops to cement Catholic unity' and backed this with a threat that 'if they refused to unite with their fellow Christians, they would be attacked by their enemies (the English) and if they refused to preach the faith of Christ to them, they would eventually be punished by meeting death at their hands'.[20] Bede said that St Augustine's threat proved itself to be a prophecy, soon to be fulfilled, when around one thousand two hundred British (Celtic) monks from the Monastery at Bangor in North Wales were killed by Anglo-Saxon forces at the Battle of Chester in 612 CE.

Anglo-Saxon military advances during the closing decades of the seventh century created a potentially serious situation for the Irish who were deeply divided. Some favoured Roman reform, while others wished to remain faithful to established traditions of Irish monasticism, in many ways autonomous and independent from Rome. Meanwhile, Ireland was also in the midst of a civil war. A secular power struggle was taking place between rival chieftains, most notably the northern and southern O'Neills. The church in Armagh had a pivotal role in this conflict. Catholic reform was top of the ecclesiastical, political and civil agenda. A religious component underscored the secular conflict. A violent struggle was taking place between two opposing religious factions. On one side, a group called the Romani had already adopted Roman customs for the celebration of Easter, and was seeking to bring the whole Irish Church under the authority of Rome. Standing against them, the Hibernensi held fast to Irish monastic traditions and resisted Roman reforms.[21] Carney writes:

> Armagh set out to claim jurisdiction over the whole island from about the mid-sixth century. The claim *legatus totus Hiberniae* implies a claim to jurisdiction over all Ireland and Papal authority for such jurisdiction.[22]

In the closing decades of the seventh century, Armagh became the head-quarters of the Romani movement. It was also the mother house for the *Paruchia Patricii* – 'Patrick's Fraternity' – a growing federation of monasteries and churches claiming jurisdiction over the whole of Ireland on the basis that St Patrick was their founder. There were important financial aspects to these arrangements. Membership of such monastic federations required loyalty to the founding saint with financial obligations. Armagh would receive gifts of land, rentals and tithes in return for the blessings and privileges of coming under the banner of St Patrick, the federation's patron saint.[23]

The church in Armagh was developing a strong federation in the name of St Patrick. It was in direct conflict with monasteries established by St Columba, which had suffered set backs as a direct result of decisions taken in Northumbria at the Synod of Whitby. The secular and religious landscape in Ireland was changing rapidly. It is no coincidence that Bishop Aed commissioned Muirchú to write an official 'biography' of St Patrick at this time, as a means of strengthening public support for Armagh's growing ecclesiastical ambitions. His *Life of St Patrick* would influence the outcome of this dispute in ways that St Patrick could never have imagined. Bishop Aed had recently allowed his own congregation at Sletty to be incorporated into the *Paruchia Patricii* after visiting Bishop Segene, who was Abbot of Armagh from 662–688 CE.[24]

Muirchú was a member of this new federation and had a vested interest in the outcome of these events. In fact, the church in Armagh was politically involved at the highest level in its desire to reform the Irish Church and bring it more closely under the authority of Rome. Cummian, a leading activist, had recently written a threatening letter to Segene, Abbot of Iona, about the Easter controversy. In this letter he strongly advised Iona to accept Roman reform, so there could be uniformity within the Irish Church.

Aed, Muirchú and Cummian were all members of the Romanising party. They were well educated and highly motivated political and ecclesiastical activists whose objective was to introduce reforms whilst at the same time enhancing the claims of Armagh. Events taking place in Ireland were beginning to mirror those in Northumbria.

We sense how divisive the situation was from Bishop Tirechán, another key member of the federation, whose notes are preserved alongside Muirchú's narrative in the *Book of Armagh*. Tirechán was an influential figure in Connacht and the west of Ireland. He appears to speak with genuine concern and compassion, when he says:

> My heart is troubled within me for love of Patrick, since I see renegades and robbers and warriors of Ireland who hate Patrick's *Paruchia*; they have stolen from him what was his. And now they are afraid since, if the heirs of Patrick were to reclaim their territory, they could recover the

whole island. God gave the whole island (to Patrick) with its people. All the primitive churches of Ireland are his.[25]

The 'renegades and robbers' were the so called 'dissidents' that Tirechán despised, members of the Columban Church or those who still supported the older, Irish monastic foundations and refused to accept either the legitimacy of the claims of Armagh or the customs and reforms now being required of the Irish Church, by Rome.[26]

### The Synod of Birr, 697 CE

Aed and Muirchú are listed among clergy who attended the Synod of Birr in 697 CE, where the famous 'Law of Adamnán' was agreed.[27] This was the Irish Church's response to developments which had taken place at Whitby, in Britain. The Synod of Birr had been convened in Ireland to secure an agreement between the southern and northern Irish churches, to introduce certain reforms and accept the authority of Rome.[28]

Author David Howlett has argued strongly that as part of this agreement, the new Roman cycle for calculating the date of Easter and other Roman ecclesiastical customs were accepted in the north of Ireland while St Patrick was recognised as Ireland's national apostle in the south. Howlett is convinced that claims about St Patrick being the founder of Irish Christianity and patron saint of all Ireland were formulated in a more precise fashion at this time.[29]

The conflict taking place within the Irish Church and between the chieftains cannot be viewed in isolation from the ecclesiastical and military pressures being applied externally from Rome and Britain. Changes which took place in the aftermath of the Synod of Whitby were having a huge impact on the independence and safety of the Irish tradition. That is why it is incorrect to describe the Synod of Whitby as an insignificant event in the context of the wider affairs of the Church and for the British and Irish churches in particular.

St Wilfrid was a young and ambitious cleric who had acted as spokesperson for the Roman party at Whitby. The Irish were greatly concerned about his role in Church affairs and tried on several occasions to have him removed. They were especially concerned about Wilfrid's ambitions towards Ireland. Having tasted the fruits of success at Whitby, Wilfrid appears to have set his sights on becoming Metropolitan Archbishop not only of the whole of northern Britain but also Ireland. This is confirmed by ecclesiastical records.[30]

In 669 CE, five years after the Synod of Whitby, Theodore of Tarsus had been sent to Britain by Pope Gregory, as head of the Roman mission.[31] Theodore's attempt to divide dioceses led to a conflict with Wilfrid, who travelled to Rome from November 679 CE to March 680 CE to protest the diminution of his authority.[32]

The Papal authorities approved his petition but when he returned to Britain, their opinion was rejected and Wilfrid was imprisoned for a short time by the secular and religious authorities in Northumbria, who appear to have briefly returned to their traditional loyalties.

After his release, Wilfrid moved to the south of England where he lived from 681–686 CE. Wilfrid's ambitions may have posed a threat to the church in Ireland. In 704 CE he returned to Rome to continue his personal 'crusade'. Speaking as if he was the Archbishop of York (which at that time he was not) Wilfrid vouched for the Catholic orthodoxy not only of the Anglo-Saxons in Northumbria but also 'all the inhabitants of northern Britain and Ireland and adjacent lands'.[33]

> For all the northern part of Britain and Ireland and the islands which are inhabited by the people of the English and the Britons, also the Scots [Irish] and the Picts he [Wilfrid] confessed the true and Catholic faith.[34]

Wilfrid's restoration in 687 CE probably sparked concerns in Armagh about who was going to be the future Metropolitan Archbishop in Ireland. During at least two visits to Rome, Wilfrid appears to have tried to persuade the Papal authorities that he was the right person for the job. If Wilfrid (who was English) had been granted authority in Ireland, this would have presented difficulties for the Irish and may have resulted in a greater loss of 'independence' for the Irish tradition.

Despite their serious differences, the Romani and Hibernensi shared nationalist sympathies. Both groups must have been anxious to find a compromise and resolve domestic difficulties. Wilfrid's reputation would have suggested they guard themselves against him. This would have been even more the case if the Irish Church was aware of events taking place in Gaul, where Ebroin, one of the Dukes of Theodoric, king of the Franks, offered 'a full bushel of gold solidi' if the king of Friesland would 'send Wilfrid to him alive, or slay him and send his head'.[35] Wilfrid's political and ecclesiastical ambitions were not restricted to Britain and Ireland. For some reason, a price had been put on his head on the continent. Some of Wilfrid's clerical friends in Gaul appear to have been involved with activities which had already led to several deaths.[36] Eddius Stephanos, his close friend and biographer, describes how Wilfrid gave support to the exiled Merovingian king, Dagobert II, who was being protected at the Monastery of Slane in Ireland where he had been educated since he was a young child.

Immediately following the Synod of Whitby in 664 CE, Wilfrid became deeply involved with arrangements for Dagobert to return to Gaul to reclaim his right to the throne.[37] Before leaving Ireland, Dagobert had married an Irish princess called Mathilde. They travelled to England in 668 CE to meet Wilfrid in York. Two years later, Mathilde died in childbirth before the royal couple left England. Dagobert was only twenty years old at the time.

Author Martin Lunn says, 'Wilfrid lost no time in finding a suitable replacement and was swift to ensure Dagobert's next wife was chosen with care.'[38] Wilfrid now arranged for Dagobert to marry Gizelle de Razés, daughter of the Count of Razés, who was niece of the king of the Visigoths. Returning to France, Gizelle and Dagobert II were married in the Church of St Mary Magdalene at Rennes-le-Château, in 670 CE. It was through the agency of Wilfrid who was now appointed Archbishop of York, that Dagobert was restored to his kingdom, after the death and disposition of Childeric II. These events place Wilfrid at the centre of what has been called 'The Merovingian Conspiracy'.[39] According to a controversial genealogical table compiled by Henri Lobineau, Gizelle de Razés was Wilfrid's God-daughter.[40]

Dagobert was crowned around 674 CE but his reign was to be short lived. After returning to France, he appears to have reneged on promises made to Wilfrid by not cooperating with the authorities of the Roman Church, much to the dismay of local diocesan clergy.

Dagobert was assassinated shortly afterwards, an event linked to Wilfrid and efforts to influence the Merovingian succession. The circumstances that surround Wilfrid's contact with clergy in Gaul, which led to the murder of Dagobert II, are very suspicious.[41]

Whatever political and ecclesiastical intrigues may have been taking place, great pressures appear to have been placed on the Irish Church during the last thirteen or fourteen years of the seventh century from the restoration of Wilfrid in 686 or 687 CE to the death of Bishop Aed in 700 CE. Muirchú's *Life of St Patrick* can only be fully understood in the context of these complex political and ecclesiastical realities. According to David Howlett, this was a period in Ireland when Cogitosus and Muirchú both used hagiography as a medium to support ideas as to which saint would be accepted as the national apostle of Ireland and which church should become the Metropolitan See.

Cogitosus had argued for St Brigid and Kildare. Armagh argued for Patrick. In simple terms, Armagh won and St Patrick instead of St Brigid became the national apostle and patron saint of Ireland.[42]

The church in Armagh benefited greatly from Reforms but an ability to compromise and avoid further internal division, which opened the doors to 'Romanisation', also allowed the Irish Church to retain a degree of freedom and independence. Muirchú's 'biography' of St Patrick ensured an ecclesiastical triumph for Armagh, presenting St Patrick as the apostle and patron saint of Irish Christianity and as the founder of the Church in Armagh, which he may not have been. This probably helped keep Wilfrid out of Ireland, reducing tensions and threats of an English invasion.

Muirchú may have invented stories to include senior figures from Anglo-Saxon royal families who were related to strategic places such as the Isle of Man,

Wales and Strathclyde, perhaps to create the impression that St Patrick's religious authority was already well established with these people and, therefore, within the regions over which they had influence in Britain.[43] Howlett says, Muirchú's *Life of Patrick* is a sophisticated work of hagiography which implements a national, political and ecclesiastical agenda. This shaped and determined what Muirchú said about St Patrick, much of which is fictitious.

This relates also to St Patrick's place of origins. Howlett argues that Muirchú's objective was to bring Patrick into relationship with powerful figures in Ireland and Britain, to establish an ecclesiastical pedigree for St Patrick and a line of protection for the Irish Church.

This line extended through the western coast of Britain southwards from Strathclyde to Anglesey, northwards to the Picts and east towards the Saxons, the region in which Wilfrid was claiming authority:

> Muirchú is with an implicit geographical argument turning the tables, not only denying that Wilfrid is or can be Metropolitan of Ireland but suggesting that *the Briton Patrick* is the rightful metropolitan not only of Ireland but the entire archipelago on the western and north western side of the British Isles, the same islands and peoples mentioned by Wilfrid in Rome'.[44]

Muirchú's *Life of St Patrick* was created as part of a strategic effort to secure the claims of Armagh and perhaps even safeguard Ireland's national interest through the medium of hagiography. This required an impressive but essentially fictional reinvention of St Patrick's 'biography'.[45] Professor Binchy speaks with authority on this subject when he describes how the secular claims and ascendency of the Northern Uí Neill which was one of the most powerful clans in Ireland at this time, went hand in hand with the religious claims and ascendency of Armagh:

> The Armagh canon is merely one of the numerous forgeries by means of which, in the course of the seventh century, the community of Armagh sought to buttress its claim to supremacy over the other monastic federations.[46]

Muirchú may have expressed doubts and misgivings about having to 'create big things out of something small' but thanks to his efforts, St Patrick provided the church in Armagh and perhaps even the nation of Ireland herself with what was needed to resolve current difficulties and avoid more serious conflicts. The information about St Patrick that had been available to Muirchú may have been uncertain and controversial but that kind of image was not helpful for the Irish Church at the end of the seventh century. If Muirchú was aware of uncertainty as to where St Patrick came from, he tries to correct that.

His task was to remove any doubt or confusion, which he did by creating a 'map' deliberately designed and crafted to emphasise St Patrick's close connections with Britain. We should not underestimate his ability to shape the map the way he and the church in Armagh wanted it to be shaped.[47]

Muirchú's description of various journeys allegedly undertaken by St Patrick appears at first sight to be very convincing, but the template he uses is essentially hagiographical.[48] The result was an outstanding success from Armagh's point of view. Muirchú had convinced most readers he was speaking with authority – he had dealt with any remaining doubts or potential conflicts and revealed everything of substance that could be found in the file.

His narrative was so influential that it has defined our image and understanding of St Patrick for more than a thousand years. But can we trust Muirchú's statement that St Patrick was British? Muirchú claimed to know the location of Bannavem Tiburniae and said it could be identified 'without doubt' with a place he called 'Ventra'. Writers may be sceptical about the claims of hagiography but most have accepted Muirchú's statement that St Patrick came from Britain, as if this is historically reliable and no longer in dispute. If so, the local tradition preserved at Château Bonaban claiming St Patrick was taken captive from Brittany, cannot be trusted. Who is telling the truth?

As our friend in Washington DC advises intelligence agents when he is teaching them how to write better reports – just because someone says something is true does not mean it necessarily is true, unless some real evidence is provided in support.

Muirchú provides no historical evidence to support his claim that St Patrick came from Britain. What he does provide is an impressive 'map' which dominated the front page of the ecclesiastical press in Ireland at the end of the seventh century.[49] Muirchú had rescued St Patrick's story from historical oblivion and created a new ecclesiastical authority for Ireland's national apostle.

To make this transition possible, he presented Ireland's new patron saint with all the required qualifications. This included a personal portfolio of his holy and miraculous deeds, a list of powerful and aristocratic English associates, an original 'British' passport and some pristine ecclesiastical credentials that were well documented and now clearly and officially stamped 'Roman, British, orthodox and Catholic'.

Muirchú was faithful to his sources in one very important respect. If he had found the name 'Britanniis' as a description of St Patrick's homeland in the copy of Patrick's *Confession* available to him, he retained this name with exactly the same spelling. He used this name to good effect in his narrative. When he designed his 'map' to locate St Patrick's place of origins, Muirchú made sure this name applied to Britain. If the claims recorded by local Breton historians and preserved at Château Bonaban are authentic, for St Patrick this phrase may not have referred to the island of Britain but a region on the continent we now call Brittany. If it can be shown that St Patrick was taken captive from Brittany and not Britain, then Muirchú had applied this name to the wrong country. This may have been an innocent error due to a continuing confusion in surviving records. Muirchú may not have known the true location of Patrick's *Britanniis* but was determined to resolve contradictory claims he found in the existing sources. He admits the information that had survived was uncertain and he was expected to bring certainty to St Patrick's biography.

On the other hand, could Muirchú have been responsible for some kind of deliberate 'fraud' or deception, falsifying the evidence to suit a particular domestic or political purpose? Fraud and deception were not issues of concern to medieval hagiographers. Their primary objective was to bring glory to the saint whose life was being documented and the church with which he or she was associated. The more miraculous, extravagant tales that could be told the better! Fabrication was the lifeblood of hagiography and the ends always justified the means.

From a historical point of view, however, it would be helpful to know if Muirchú 'tampered with the truth', especially in relation to St Patrick's place of origins. In the quotation chosen to head this chapter, Conor MacDari remarks on how names can be misspelled or distorted to such an extent that great effort is sometimes required to establish their original and true meaning.

One thing is certain: Muirchú cannot be accused of bad spelling. In fact, he used the same basic form of spelling for St Patrick's homeland *in Britanniis* as it appears in the earliest surviving copy of St Patrick's *Confession* and in so doing, may have remained faithful to his source.[50] The question is, did Muirchú introduce anything to distort the original meaning of this name as St Patrick would have understood it?

Muirchú was a master of words and as Dan Brown has said, 'Language can sometimes be very adept at hiding the truth.'[51] It is possible that Muirchú may have made a confession of his own related to this issue towards the close of his narrative.

Every good writer knows that beginnings and endings are important. At the very beginning, Muirchú was honest about the uncertainties which surrounded St Patrick, saying there was no clear record of events. Minds were confused; sources which had survived were unreliable and contradictory. Muirchú hints at more sinister controversy when he describes 'this deep and dangerous sea of church history'. Then, at the very end of his narrative, he makes another intriguing statement which is potentially the most controversial of all. Muirchú brings closure to his narrative with a reflection on illusions or 'delusions'. First he mentions stories related to 'illusions' that can be found in the bible, then concludes by saying, '*so also this delusion was arranged to secure concord between the people.*'

The Latin word he uses is *seductio*, which can mean 'leading astray', 'delusion' or 'deception'.[52] Was Muirchú trying to tell us something? Could this be a subtle reference to some of the claims about St Patrick which had been made in his narrative? Did he decide to end with one final flourish – the good old scribe that he was – with an intellectual honesty that has never been fully understood or appreciated?

Was Muirchú admitting 'between the lines', so to speak, that his presentation of St Patrick was 'a delusion arranged to secure concord between the people'?[53] If so, we have good reason to distrust everything Muirchú said about St Patrick, including his claim that St Patrick's homeland and the place where he was taken captive could both be identified in Britain. If Muirchú was being intellectually forthright about the 'illusion' or 'delusion' he had created, then he deserves to be remembered as one of the most honest hagiographers ever to have emerged from the murky waters of the medieval world.[54]

Muirchú's influence cannot be underestimated because his narrative gave birth to the 'Legend' of St Patrick. If he created a deliberate illusion, however, Muirchú is admitting something far more serious. He may have been trying to tell us that he 'cast a spell' over St Patrick's story. This 'spell' was so powerful that it has shaped our image and understanding of St Patrick's biography for more than a thousand years. It appears to have convinced almost everyone that St Patrick came from Britain. Most scholars who have written about St Patrick and those who have read and accepted their works, have more or less been 'bound' by the spell that Muirchú cast around St Patrick's place of origins and have continued to be bound and blinded by the 'spell' of Britain, to the present day.

Was the truth about St Patrick's origins and therefore his real identity, suppressed when his file was tidied up by Muirchú at the end of the seventh century? Muirchú may have been the first, but fortunately he was not the last to write a 'Life of St Patrick'.

Information about St Patrick must have survived elsewhere, perhaps in Irish monasteries on the continent. Other documents survived which included accounts not found in Muirchú. Some of these present a very different record of St Patrick's origins and where he was trained and ordained for the mission to Ireland.

A unique sequence of events was about to unfold that would allow uncertainties to come back to the surface. A thousand years passed by before certain developments took place through which a very different account of St Patrick's story came to light. In 1640 CE, on the brink of Oliver Cromwell's invasion of Ireland, an Irish Franciscan called John Colgan and some close friends were determined to collect and preserve as many ancient documents as they could, related to the origins of Christianity in Ireland and the lives of the early Irish saints. As a direct result of these efforts, several important old manuscripts written in Latin and Old Irish were about to enter the public domain for the first time. Colgan published seven of these manuscripts in 1647, together with extensive notes and a commentary.

These were priceless ancient manuscripts dated from the eighth to the twelfth century. Some had built on Muirchú's account and repeated his claim that St Patrick came from Britain. Others included stories and traditions which cannot be found in Muirchú and completely contradict what Muirchú had said. Many of these documents record that St Patrick was taken captive from Brittany.

The survival of these ancient Lives of St Patrick was a miracle. If they had fallen into the hands of Cromwell's army, they might have been lost forever. Instead, they were smuggled out of Ireland and taken to Louvain in Belgium saved from destruction just in the nick of time. These documents hold a number of clues that can help us to identify the truth about St Patrick's place of origins.

Protected by providence for almost a thousand years, they had been waiting for someone, somewhere in the unforeseen future to get down on their knees and dig deep into the ashes of the hearth fire of history to see what treasure can be found there.

*Notes*

1. Conor MacDari, *The Bible: an Irish Book* (London, 2005).

2. For Muirchú's original Latin text and an English translation see David Howlett, *Muirchú Moccu Mactheni's 'Vita Sancti Patricii'* (Dublin, 2006), p. 46. Also Ludwig Bieler, *The Patrician Texts in the Book of Armagh* (Dublin, 2004), p. 62 ff.

3. For another translation of Muirchú's narrative, see James Kenney, *The Sources for the Early History of Ireland: Ecclesiastical* (Dublin, 1997), p. 332.

4. Cogitosus's *Life of St Brigid* is one of the earliest Irish hagiographies dated c.650 CE. For an English translation see Liam de Paor, *St Patrick's World* (Dublin, 1993), p. 207 ff.

5. Ludwig Bieler, *PTBA*, p. 62 ff.

6. *Patricius qui et Sochet uocabator, Brito natione in Brittannis natus, (patre) Cualfarni (o) diacono ortus filio, ut ipse ait, Potiti presbiteri, qui fuit uico Bannauem Thaburniae, chaut procul a mari nostro, quem uicum constanter indubitanterque conperimus esse Ventre, matre etiam conceptus Concessa nomine;* Muirchú, *Vita* 1:1–5, Bieler, *PTBA*, p. 66. Note that Muirchú describes Calpurnius as a deacon (*diacono*) and Potitus as a presbyter (*presbiteri*). Howlett translates presbyter as 'priest'.

7. In the Book of Armagh version of St Patrick's *Confession* the name is spelled 'Bannauem Taburniae'. Bieler, *Clavis Patricii II: Libri Epistolarum Sancti Patricii Episcopi* (Dublin, 1993), p. 56 ff. Howlett gives 'Banna Venta Burniae' and suggests this place can be identified as the 'market town of the promontory of Bernia', perhaps Sabrinae – 'Severn' or Berneich – 'land of the

Bernicians'. Howlett also suggests Ventra can be identified with Carleaon in Gwent. A question mark admits the uncertainties. No evidence is provided to support these locations. See Howlett, 'Vita Sancti Patricii', p. 46 ff.

8. Gematria is based on numeric values given to Hebrew Letters. Muirchú must have had access to a manual of the Hebrew alphabet designating these values although such a manual has never been discovered in Europe. See Howlett, 'Vita Sancti Patricii', pp. 180–6.

9. It is possible that 'Ventra' could be Muirchú's rendering of 'Nemthor' a name mentioned as the birthplace of St Patrick in St Fiacc's Hymn and other, later sources. The names are linguistically similar.

10. Mari dextero Brittannico (16.8) lit: following the right hand – (sun-wise) in Irish deisal. Muirchú's description of St Patrick's journey to Gaul in which he sails 'southwards from Britain' is suspiciously similar to other accounts which describe a journey the family are said to have taken from Strathclyde to Armorica, to visit relatives there.

11. Peruenit Brittannias is a plural form meaning 'arrived in the Britains' or 'came through the Britains' or perhaps 'came to the Britains'. See Bieler, PTBA, pp 74 ff. Howlett, 'Vita Sancti Patricii', p. 58.

12. Bieler, PTBA, p. 98; Howlett, 'Vita Sancti Patricii', p. 106.

13. Mari nostro means 'our sea', which presumably means the Irish Sea. See Muirchú, 'Vita Sancti Patricii', I:5.

14. In Howlett's translation, Muirchú says St Patrick was 'born into the famous port amongst us which is called Mouth of the Dee'. See Muirchú, XI:44, Howlett 'Vita Sancti Patricii', p. 61. This may have been a port at the mouth of the Vartry River, once called the Dee, now Wicklow Harbour.

15. For example, Muirchú includes the name for St Patrick's homeland in Brittanniis (I:2) which is recognisably the same as that found in the Book of Armagh version of St Patrick's Confession. He includes another spelling, 'Britannias', but for Muirchú this appears to refer to the same region. Muirchú's use of different names for 'Britain' is suspicious and appears contrived. He may have included some of the names found in his sources, assuming these all referred to Britain and/or presenting them as referring to Britain.

16. Ward Kaiser and Denis Wood, Seeing through Maps: the Power of Images to Shape our World View (Massachusetts, 2001).

17. The Mappa Mundi was drawn from a Jewish-Christian perspective. An Islamic or Buddhist cartographer would have seen the world from a different perspective and created a different map.

18. Muirchú was under serious pressure from the church in Armagh to write a definitive 'biography' of St Patrick. Political and ecclesiastical demands influenced his narrative and the nature of the 'map' he created.

19. See T. M. Charles-Edwards, Early Christian Ireland (Cambridge, 2000), p. 438. The army eventually arrived in force, five hundred years later, with the Norman invasion of Ireland in the twelfth century.

20. See Bede, Ecclesiastical History, ii: 2, 3.

21. In his Letter to Coroticus St Patrick strongly identified himself with the Irish when he said 'they despise us because we are Irish' – indignum est illis Hiberionaci sums – LC 16. This allows for the possibility that St Patrick may have been identified with the forerunners of those who were known later as Hibernensi, not the Romanising party, who were called the Romani.

22. James Carney, Studies in Irish Literature and History (Dublin, 1979), p. 399. Hibernia was the Roman name for Ireland.

23. D. A. Binchy, 'Patrick and his Biographers', Studia Hibernica, 2 (1962) pp. 60–4.

24. Bishop Aed died c.700 CE. The original foundation of his church is attributed to St Fiacc, said to have been a poet and disciple of St Patrick. *Fiacc's Hymn* is one of the oldest hymns written in Ireland. See Kenney, *The Sources for the Early History of Ireland: Ecclesiastical* (Dublin, 1997), p. 340.

25. See Liam de Paor, *St Patrick's World,* p. 160; also 'Armagh and the Patrick of Legend', in Kenney, *Sources,* p. 319.

26. 'To Patrick belongs the church although the community of Columcille has encroached upon it.' Whitley Stokes, *Tripartite Life of St Patrick* (London, 1887), p. 97.

27. Adamnán's 'Law' introduced important social changes, such as the right of women and clergy to be accepted as non-combatants in battle.

28. With regard to the 'Romanisation' of the church in Ireland, see J. B. Bury, *The Life of St Patrick, His Place in History* (London, 1905), p. 261 ff.

29. Howlett, *'Vita Sancti Patricii',* p. 180 ff.

30. Much of what follows is drawn from David Howlett's study, in which he identifies key issues surrounding the compilation of Muirchú's narrative. See David Howlett, *Muirchú Moccu Mactheni's 'Vita Sancti Patricii'* (Dublin, 2006), but also T. M. Charles-Edwards, *Early Christian Ireland* (Cambridge, 2000) p. 429 ff.

31. At the Synod of Hertford in 672 CE, Theodore was designated 'Archbishop of Canterbury' but at the Synod of Hatfield a few years later (679 CE) he was entitled 'Archbishop of All Britain'. See Bede, *HE,* iv, v. Howlett, *'Vita Sancti Patricii',* p. 181.

32. Theodore of Tarsus was Greek and may have appreciated the 'orthodoxy' of the Celtic Tradition.

33. See Howlett, *'Vita Sancti Patricii',* p. 181–2 and B. Cosgrave, ed., *The Life of Bishop Wilfrid by Eddius Stephanus* (Cambridge, 1985).

34. *Pro omni aquilonali parte Brittanniae ac Hiberniae insulisque quae ab Anglorum et Britonnum, necnon Scottorum et Pictorum gentibus colebantur ueram et catholicam confessus fidem.* Howlett, *'Vita Sancti Patricii',* p. 182. See also 'Life of Wilfrid', trans. J. F. Webb, *Lives of Saints* (London, 1986), p. 188.

35. Eddius Stephanus, *Life of Wilfrid,* trans. J. F. Webb (London, 1986).

36. Stephanus informs us that a party travelling to Rome with another Bishop called Winfred had been attacked by Wilfrid's enemies when they passed through the territory of the Franks, in what appears to have been a case of mistaken identity. Webb, *Life of Wilfrid,* chs 24 and 27.

37. This is a controversial subject with intriguing implications for the study of St Patrick, which we will explore more fully elsewhere. The timing of these events suggests that Dagobert's arrival in York may have been related to changes which took place at Whitby, through which Wilfrid's influence (and Rome's) had been greatly enhanced. See Marcus Losack, *St Patrick and the Bloodline of the Grail* (Annamoe, Wicklow, 2012).

38. Martin Lunn, *Da Vinci Code Decoded* (New York, 2004), p. 56 ff.

39. Some accounts say that it was after the assassination of Dagobert II that Wilfrid presented his own 'God daughter' as claimant to the throne. Others record that Giselle de Razes was an English princess. For various accounts of these events see Michael Baigent, Henry Lincoln and Richard Leigh, *Holy Blood and Holy Grail* (London, 1996), pp. 257–81; also Lionel and Patricia Fanthorpe, *Mysteries and Secrets of the Masons* (Dundurn, 2006); Nicholas de Vere and Tracy Twyman, *The Dragon Legacy: A Secret History of an Ancient Bloodline* (San Diego, 2004); see also *Portail Histoire Bourgogne Franche-Comté* [website] <gilles.maillet.free.fr.> and Ron Schuler, 'The Dagobert Code', *Ron Schuler's Parlour Tricks* [website] <http://rsparlourtricks.blogspot.ie/2005/12/dagobert-code.html> published online 23 December 2005.

40. Baigent, Lincoln and Leigh, *Holy Blood and Holy Grail*, p. 276.

41. Stephanus, *Life of Wilfrid*, chs 28, 33.

42. Howlett, *'Vita Sancti Patricii'*, p. 182 ff.

43. One example is Moneissan. Muirchú describes how she came from Britannia (Britain) to visit St Patrick in Ireland. She was the daughter of a Saxon king. Muirchú also includes a reference to Coroticus, the king who ruled Strathclyde at the time of St Patrick.

44. See Howlett, *'Vita Sancti Patricii'*, p. 183 ff. The Isle of Man was half way between Armagh and Wilfrid's stronghold at Hexham. *Emphasis added.

45. The longest story in Muirchú's narrative relates to the Easter Controversy. The second longest is that of Daire, who is said to have given St Patrick land at Armagh for a church. Armagh wanted to secure its position as the Metropolitan See of Ireland. It was not in that position before the end of the seventh century. See Howlett, *'Vita Sancti Patricii'*, p. 180 ff.

46. Binchy, 'Patrick and his Biographers', p. 52. Armagh is still the Primatial See for the Roman Catholic Church and the Church of Ireland (Reformed).

47. Muirchú uses several different names for Britain including 'Britanniis', 'Britannias' and 'Britannia', which all refer to the island of Britain in the context of his narrative. Howlett never questions the established view that St Patrick came from Britain and agrees that when Muirchú used the name 'Britanniis' or 'Britannias' (both plural forms) this referred to the regional divisions of Britain under the Romans. Howlett, *'Vita Sancti Patricii'*, p. 141.

48. Bury trusted Muirchú's narrative with regard to St Patrick's origins in Britain. See 'The Home of St Patrick', Bury, *The Life of St Patrick*, p. 322 ff.

49. The situation can be compared to recent events in the United States. After the election of President Obama, the *Washington Post* dealt with the interesting case of Charles Freeman Jr, who stepped down from an appointment to chair the National Intelligence Council. Freeman had raised issues of concern about the power and influence of the Israeli Lobby on Capitol Hill. If he had been allowed to take up the appointment offered by newly elected President Obama, Freeman said he would have challenged analysts to remember that 'it is not how highly classified information is, but how reliable it is, even if it is on the front page of a newspaper', *Washington Post*, 12 March 2009. Muirchú's 'Life of St Patrick' was not just on the front page of the newspaper on the Hill of Armagh at the end of the seventh century, that newspaper was also the only one in town.

50. In the *Book of Armagh* the spelling is 'Britanniis'. Muirchú's text has 'Brittanniis'. The difference is small enough and may reflect changes by copyists.

51. Dan Brown, *The Lost Symbol* (New York, 2009), p. 196.

52. *Haec etiam seductio ad concordiam populorum facta est.* See Howlett, *'Vita Sancti Patricii'*, p. 125; de Paor, *St Patrick's World*, p. 197.

53. If Howlett's theory is correct, this is exactly what Muirchú sought to achieve, on behalf of the church in Armagh.

54. Howlett says Muirchú's *Life of St Patrick* is 'a work of narrative and architectronic genius that emerged from a culture more deeply learned than any modern critic has yet imagined'. See Howlett, *'Vita Sancti Patricii'*, pp 180–6.

# CHAPTER SIX

# Illuminating Manuscripts

> When seen, these pages moved. They moved and were
> Replaced in storytelling sequence each time the page
> Was turned and every time the vellum caught the light, its
> Passages of polished gold sent gleams into the room.[1]

The suppression of all things Irish by the British in Ulster following the Nine Years War in 1603 and the Flight of the Earls in 1607 was a disaster for Ireland and the Catholic Church. The violent nature of English oppression created huge sympathy towards Ireland especially within Catholic nations on the continent. St Anthony's College, Louvain was founded in Belgium in 1607 to provide support. It quickly became a centre for Irish intellectual, spiritual and missionary activities. This college was established specifically for the propagation and preservation of Catholic faith in Ireland and Scotland, driven by concern to preserve information about Ireland's ecclesiastical and historical past.

Following the Reformation, there had been a Scots-British interpretation of Irish history which was offensive to the scholars at Louvain.[2] This led to the preservation of several old manuscripts that contained ancient traditions about St Patrick, St Brigid and St Columba.

Fr John Colgan was born in Ireland and joined the Franciscans in 1620 before moving to Louvain. He visited libraries on the continent, searching for information about the early Irish saints. At the same time, Michael O'Clery, one of an intrepid band of native Irish antiquarians who compiled the famous *Annals of the Four Masters*, was sent to Ireland in 1626. He combed the countryside in efforts to discover and preserve as many ancient documents as possible.[3]

Several old manuscripts collected by these scholars were published by Colgan in 1647. His book *Trias Thaumaturga* is one of the great treasures of the seventeenth century and an essential resource for the study of St Patrick. It contains seven, ancient Lives of St Patrick written in Latin and Old Irish together with a commentary by Colgan himself, concerning the homeland and family of St Patrick.[4]

Without these documents, the clues required to locate Patrick's place of origins may have been lost forever. These manuscripts are classified as 'secondary sources' which means that, unlike St Patrick's own writings, they cannot be treated as reliable historical evidence. Nevertheless, they contain threads of truth passed down from earlier generations and copied from ancient records, woven into the complex fabric of hagiographical legends.[5] The challenge is to disentangle those threads and see if they point in a particular direction.

These documents will now be examined, focusing first on those manuscripts which identify St Patrick's birthplace and homeland in Britain, since this is currently the accepted and established tradition. Where St Patrick was born appears to have been more important to seventeenth-century writers than where he was taken captive. It is important to recognize these as two separate issues. In his own writings, St Patrick does not tell us where he was born. He only gives the name of the place where he was taken captive.

*St Fiacc's Hymn on the Life of St Patrick* is the first 'Life' in Colgan's collection and is regarded as one of the most ancient documents. Fiacc or Fiecc is said to have been one of Patrick's first converts who became Bishop of Sletty, or Slebte in County Leix; a church incorporated into the *Paruchia* of Patrick in the seventh century.[6] This ancient hymn is written as a poem in Old Irish with a Latin version transcribed by Colgan.[7]

The earliest surviving copy was probably not compiled in its present form before about 800 CE but it contains information copied from a much earlier date. *Fiacc's Hymn* states that St Patrick was born in a place called 'Nemthor'. This is the earliest recording of 'Nemthor' or 'Nemthur' as Patrick's birthplace:[8]

> In Nemthor, as our minstrels own,
> Heaven's radiance first on Patrick smiled,
> But fifteen summers scarce had thrown
> A halo round the holy child[9]

This name was not given by St Patrick in his own writings but its value soon becomes apparent. Colgan published notes attached to *St Fiacc's Hymn*, compiled by a person called the Scholiast or 'the Scholar'. These notes cannot be dated earlier than the ninth century in their present form and could even be as late as the eleventh or twelfth century but they contain specific claims about St Patrick which are very significant and have always been taken seriously.[10]

The Scholiast identifies Nemthor with 'Alcluid', which according to Bede was the ancient name of the fortress of the Britons at Dumbarton, near Strathclyde.[11] This is the earliest record we have, claiming that St Patrick was born in Scotland.

The true location of Nemthor must have been uncertain at the time these notes were written. The Scholiast had to clarify its location and did so by identifying it with Alcluid. Whether these notes were added in the ninth or twelfth century, it shows there was still uncertainty about where St Patrick came from.

That St Patrick's family was connected with this part of Scotland forms part of an ancient, established tradition that still forms part of the Scottish historical record.

'Nemthor' is an old and mysterious name. A clue to its meaning and possible location comes through etymology. It has Gaelic or Celtic and Latin roots. The prefix *Nem* possibly derives from the Gaelic *noem* meaning 'holy' or *neam*, a name for heaven. According to Colgan and other ancient writers, the suffix *thor* or *tor* cames from the Latin word *turris*, which denotes a tower or lighthouse.[12]

The Romans used lighthouses in most of the fortified coastal ports of the Empire, to assist the navy. Wood fires kindled at the top of these towers provided a beacon for ships entering a harbour at night. Colgan used this argument to support the view that Patrick was born in Strathclyde although there is no archaeological or historical evidence to confirm a lighthouse existed there at the time of St Patrick. From an etymological point of view other interpretations are possible. The suffix *thor* could be the Gaelic *tor*, which designates a sacred high place or pointed hill as with Glastonbury Tor in England or Tor Abb (Hill of the Abbot) on the Island of Iona.

In the early days of Christianity in Europe during the fourth and fifth century, within monastic communities, to claim a person was 'born' in a particular place could mean two very different things. It might not refer to the place of actual physical birth but to the place where they were spiritually 'born' to a life of discipleship.

The claim that St Patrick was born in Nemthor could have preserved a memory of the place he received spiritual formation and was spiritually nurtured as a Christian. It could have been the place where St Patrick accepted the religious life, perhaps where he was tonsured.[13] Some scholars have identified Nemthor with the city of Tours on the River Loire, where St Martin's monastery was established towards the end of the fourth century. The argument in favour again stems from etymology. *Nem* is a Celtic word meaning 'holy' and *Thor* or *Tor* may be related to the city of Tours, hence Nemthor or *Nem-Thor* could be a reference to 'Holy Tours'.[14]

A possibility that St Fiacc's 'Nemthor' could perhaps be identified on the continent at Tours rather than Strathclyde, seems to be confirmed from accounts that describe St Patrick's mother, Conchessa, as being 'of the Franks' which is recorded in Old Irish as *di Frangeaib di* (of the Franks was she) with the additional comment 'through a sister of St Martin of Tours' (*ocus suir do Martin hi Hin Nemthur*).[15] This description appears to support the view that 'Nemthor' could be a name associated with Tours. The significance of this interpretation will become more apparent later, when we consider evidence that suggests St Patrick was trained and tonsured with St Martin of Tours or within Martin's community.

At this stage in our inquiry, the meaning and precise location of Nemthur must be viewed as uncertain, despite claims made by the Scholiast. The identification with Strathclyde is too late to be completely trustworthy.[16]

Etymology suggests this name is open to interpretation and therefore cannot be identified exclusively with one particular place whether in Britain or Brittany, until more reliable evidence becomes available.

Many of the ancient documents accept the identification of Nemthor with Strathclyde and, as a result, locate St Patrick's parental home near Bannavem Tiburniae in the same place.

The *Second Life*, *Third Life* and *Fourth Life* of St Patrick published by Colgan repeat the claim that Patrick was born or 'nurtured' in Nemthor, adding extra details in saying this was a town in the district or region of 'Taburne' where there was a military base in which the Romans pitched their tents for shelter during the winter months.[17] Describing Nemthor in the 'Plain of Taburniae' clearly links its location to St Patrick's parental home at Bannavem Taburniae.[18] Just because this claim is repeated in several of the ancient documents does not guarantee its reliability. Authors copied from existing manuscripts, so the argument from greater numbers is not sustainable.[19]

When St Patrick describes how he was taken captive from his parental home near Bannavem Tiburniae this provides a significant clue to help identify its geographical location. A *tiburnia* was the name given to a Roman military base in Gaul. In Britain it was called a *taburne*.[20] Some of the ancient writers may have passed on reliable information when they interpreted these names by making specific associations. If so, 'Bannavem Tiburniae' possibly refers to a place located near the 'foot' or perhaps 'mouth' of a river where there was a military camp, perhaps where Roman Legions pitched their tents for protection during the winter months. The problem is, Roman military bases existed in many different locations, often situated at the mouths of rivers! This description could also apply to the Roman port at Aleth at the mouth of the River Rance in Brittany, which was the location for a military base for the Legion of Mars.[21]

Like Muirchú's narrative, written at the end of the seventh century, the notes attached to *St Fiacc's Hymn* by the Scholiast in the ninth century greatly influenced other writers. They added fuel to the fire of a growing tradition that identified St Patrick's birthplace in Scotland. This is reflected in Colgan's *Sixth Life*, written in the twelfth century by a monk called Jocelyn.[22] Jocelyn follows others in claiming that St Patrick was born and brought up in village called 'Taburnia' near the town of 'Emptor', which is recognizable as 'Nemthor'.[23] He goes a step further, however, when he says that both 'Nemthor' and 'Tiburnia' were near the Irish Sea. Muirchú said St Patrick was born 'not far from our sea' by which we have assumed he meant the Irish Sea, but Jocelyn is the first and only writer to explicitly name the Irish Sea.[24] Jocelyn identifies Nemthor as the place where St Patrick was born and raised as a child, adjacent to a fortress located on the Rock of Dumbarton, near Strathclyde.[25] He locates Nemthor and Bannavem Tiburniae in Britain, following Muirchú.[26]

So far, we have considered those texts that locate St Patrick's birthplace and parental home, in northern Britain. The manuscripts published by Colgan in 1647 include other claims which present us with a very different understanding of the location of these places. When considering these accounts, St Patrick's association with Strathclyde becomes less certain.

The *Seventh Life* of St Patrick published by Colgan is known as the 'Tripartite Life' because it is divided into three parts. The original manuscript probably dates in part to the tenth century but includes several intriguing stories some of which must have been passed down from a much earlier date. It repeats the claim that St Patrick was from the Britons of Strathclyde and born in Nemthor. What it does not say quite so clearly is that Patrick was born in Strathclyde.[27]

St Patrick originated from the Britons of Strathclyde. Nemthor, denoting a heavenly tower, was where his family lived and the place of his birth.[28]

This is the first of several claims about St Patrick's origins which are uncertain or contradictory. The statement above can be interpreted in at least two different ways. Taken as a whole, it seems to claim St Patrick was born in Nemthor which was also the place where his family came from, identified with Strathclyde in Scotland. Another possible interpretation is that St Patrick's family origins were associated with the Britons of Strathclyde (perhaps through his father's side of the family) but the family was living in another place called 'Nemthor' when St Patrick was born. If this is the intended or original meaning, then Nemthor and Strathclyde may have represented two different places, perhaps located in different countries. The problem with the Strathclyde tradition is that the earliest surviving reference is given in notes attached to *St Fiacc's Hymn* by the Scholiast and dated perhaps to the ninth but possibly as late as the twelfth century. This is several hundred years after St Patrick's death and, therefore, must be considered unreliable.

Some modern writers accept the Strathclyde tradition, but many do not. The historical evidence strongly suggests that the Romans had no significant settlement that far north in Britain at the time of St Patrick. The established view taken by most scholars is that St Patrick was taken captive from somewhere in Britain but opinions differ widely as to which part of Britain. If the Strathclyde tradition is authentic, it is surprising that Muirchú failed to record it. Muirchú was aware of St Patrick's conflict with Coroticus, the king of Strathclyde, but does not attempt to identify Bannavem Tiburniae or Ventra with Strathclyde.[29]

Several of the ancient documents published by Colgan in the seventeenth century preserve other accounts that challenge and sometimes completely contradict the notion that St Patrick was taken captive from Britain. Some claim that St Patrick was born in Strathclyde but was taken captive from Brittany (Armorica) when he was visiting with his family on the continent. One of the ancient authors goes further, claiming to know 'without doubt' that St Patrick was born in Brittany and that he grew up there as a child.

Colgan's *Fifth Life* of St Patrick is an intriguing document written by a monk called Probus.[30] The text has been dated to the ninth century and is probably one of the most reliable of all the ancient Lives of St Patrick, specifically in relation to material included in Book I which appears to be the most archaic and original. Other parts of the document may have been written by a later author and show signs of interpolation.

The name 'Probus' is intriguing. It comes from the Latin word 'probo' which means, to probe. Someone had obviously probed into the uncertainties which surrounded St Patrick. This author presents an account radically different to all others. Probus claims that St Patrick was a 'Briton' by nationality but that he came from the village or town called 'Bannaue' in the province of Neustria.[31] The reference to Neustria is very significant. Unlike Britanniis, Bannavem Tiburniae or Nemthor, the geographical location of Neustria is historically well documented and can be clearly identified. Neustria was the name applied by the Franks to a region in northwest Gaul between the Meuse and the Loire. The Province of Neustria formed part of the Merovingian kingdom in Gaul which included coastal regions of north-west Brittany. Neustria was the 'new' land of the Franks (*neu* = new) as Austria was the 'south land' (*aust* = south).[32] Neustria means the newly conquered land, a name which dated from the time of Clovis who was born in 465 CE about the time of St Patrick's death. He was of Merovingian descent and reigned as king of the Franks from 481– 511 CE. Clovis invaded Brittany and, as a result, the north-west coast of Armorica between Aleth and Mont St Michel became part of the province of Neustria. In the tenth century, Normandy replaced Neustria as the name for this region but in Latin, the province of Neustria always referred to that part of ancient Gaul which is now divided between Normandy and Brittany.

The significance of the account given by Probus cannot be underestimated. It correctly refers to Neustria a province.[33] For the first time in the ancient documents we have discovered an alternative record in which St Patrick's birthplace is not located in Britain but on the continent.[34] This is how Probus writes about St Patrick's place of origins:

> St Patrick, who was also called Sochet, was a Briton by nationality [*Brito fuit natione*] in which nation also having suffered many misfortunes in his youth he was fashioned for the salvation of his whole tribe and fatherland …[35]

This man was born in Brittany[36] [*in Britanniis*] from his father Calpurnius who was the son of Potitus the Elder; his mother's name was Conchessa; from the village of Bannaue in the region of Tiburniae, not far from the Western Sea [Mare Occidentale]. We have established beyond doubt this village belonged to the province of Neustria in which giants are said to have lived.

The phrase *in Britanniis natus est* could mean St Patrick was born 'amongst the Britons' or more specifically, 'he was born in Brittany' accepting that a region called 'Britanniis' existed on the continent at the time of St Patrick. Brittany is, therefore, a more accurate and authentic translation, since Probus locates St Patrick's homeland on the continent, in Neustria and not on the island of Britain.

Probus claimed to know without doubt that Bannavem Tiburniae was a village 'not far from the Western Sea' which belonged to the province of Neustria. The Latin name he gives for this sea (Mare Occidentale) applied to the whole ocean to the west of the Roman Empire. For Probus, it clearly refers to the ocean off the north-west coast of Brittany. Muirchú and Jocelyn both claimed that St Patrick's birthplace was in Britain and they located St Patrick's 'Bannavem Tiburniae' close to the Irish Sea. Probus may have been trying to correct this by saying it was 'not far from the Western Sea' in the Province of Neustria, which clearly refers to the northern coast of Brittany. This document is unique because it describes St Patrick's home from a continental perspective.

It is also very significant that Probus uses the same phrase to describe Bannavem Tiburniae as St Patrick did for the Wood of Foclut. Both are described as 'close beside the Western Sea'. If this is deliberate and authentic, it allows for the possibility that both places existed in the same geographical location.[37] The significance of this document has probably never been fully appreciated. Probus is telling us very clearly that Patrick's parental home, the place from which he was taken captive, was in a region called 'Britanniis' that was definitely not located in Britain but on the continent.

He says St Patrick was from the nation (or stock) of the Britons (*Brito fuit natione*) but this may not necessarily have been a reference to the island of Britain, exclusively. The ancient Britons were associated with both Britain and Gaul, especially the coastal region of Armorica. If Patrick's origins were identified by Probus with these ethnic Britons on the continent, this would explain his claim St Patrick was British or from 'the nation of the Britons'. Alternatively, if Calpurnius came from Strathclyde and Probus was accounting for St Patrick's nationality on his father's side of the family, this could also explain how St Patrick was of the same 'nation' as the Britons.

Probus adds more detail when he says St Patrick was of the nation of the Britons 'in which nation he suffered the misfortunes of his youth'. If this is a reference to St Patrick being taken into captivity when he was sixteen years of age, which seems likely, then it confirms that as far as Probus was concerned, the place where St Patrick was taken captive was located in this 'nation of the Britons', which is described as being on the continent, close beside the Western Sea, in Brittany (*in Britanniis*) in the Province of Neustria.

Probus coins another phrase from Muirchú when he says he knew this location to be true 'without doubt'. This again suggests that he may have been writing with the specific intention of correcting errors he found in Muirchú's account.[38] The information given by Probus has geographical integrity and reveals a genuine consistency.

He provides the most direct and impressive reference so far in all the ancient Lives, which identifies St Patrick's homeland as a specific region on the continent. Compared with Muirchú's account, which seems geographically contrived, the information given by Probus is much more concise and has profound implications for our traditional understanding of St Patrick.[39] Probus is not simply claiming that Patrick was taken captive from this region; he is claiming emphatically that St Patrick was born and grew up there, until the time he was taken captive.[40] This is radically different to any other account in the ancient Lives but it is not incompatible with what St Patrick says in his own writings, if Patrick's homeland was located on the continent. If St Patrick's 'Britanniis' refers to Brittany rather than Britain, it is remarkable how some of the contradictions in the ancient sources and uncertainties in Patrick's own writings, begin to disappear.[41]

The association with giants at the end of the passage quoted above is intriguing. This could be a reference to the huge standing stones characteristic of Brittany.

In another passage, Probus speaks of the circumstances in which St Patrick was taken into captivity. In case anyone still has misgivings, there can be no doubt about what is being said. Probus states clearly that Bannavem Tiburniae was located in Armorica, the Roman name for the coastal province in northwest Gaul. He also states emphatically that this was St Patrick's homeland:

> While he was still in his homeland [*patria*] with his father Calpurnius and his mother Conchessa, also with his brother Ructhi and sister Mila, in their city Armuric [Armorica] great strife broke out in those parts …
> In a devastating attack on Armuric [Armorica] and other places round about it, the sons of Rethmitus, king of Britannia [Britain or Brittany?] slaughtered Calpurnius and his wife Conchessa; they led away captive their sons Patrick and his brother Ructi, together with their sister, Mila.[42]

Several versions of this story survived in various ancient manuscripts but the account given by Probus again differs significantly from others. In most accounts, St Patrick's family travelled by sea from Strathclyde to Brittany to visit relatives, when St Patrick was taken captive. Probus is saying something very different. There is no mention of Strathclyde. Patrick was already resident in his homeland in Armorica, when the attack took place.[43]

Probus is credited by some scholars as being one of the most reliable of the ancient authors. Others have dismissed his work as inconsistent and contradictory, claiming that Probus begins by saying Patrick was British (*Brito fuit natione*) and born in Britain (*in Britanniis*) then immediately contradicts this when he locates Patrick's birth in the Province of Neustria, on the continent. This reflects a misunderstanding and misrepresentation of his geographical descriptions. Probus is clearly referring to Brittany and not the island of Britain, so any apparent contradictions cease to exist. In fact, contradiction only exists in the minds of those who are convinced that St Patrick came from Britain and who take the view that these names refer exclusively to Britain. By interpreting his work in this way, we are misrepresenting what Probus says. If by saying St Patrick was born as a Briton (*Brito fuit natione*) Probus meant St Patrick came from the nation or ethnic stock of the Britons and that he was born in Brittany (*in Britanniis*) in a village called 'Bannau' in the region of 'Tiburnia' (Bannavem Tiburniae) which was close beside the Western Sea (Mare Occidentale) in the province of Neustria (ancient Normandy including parts of Armorica) Probus was being exceptionally consistent from a geographical point of view.

In fact, he is the first ancient author to be so clear and consistent using terms we can understand and clearly identify. Probus provides reliable geographical information to support his claims, more than any of the other ancient authors. He locates St Patrick's homeland in Brittany and he claims that St Patrick was taken captive from this region.

What is of greatest significance in relation to local traditions about St Patrick which have been preserved in Brittany today is that what Probus says matches perfectly the information provided for guests at Château Bonaban.

One of the most controversial statements made about St Patrick in some of the ancient sources is that his ancestors were Jewish and had settled in Brittany. This claim has usually been dismissed as a legend. It is one of those stories passed down through the centuries which is impossible to verify but may have greater significance for understanding St Patrick than has so far been imagined. This claim can also be found in several of the ancient documents.

For example, the *Fourth Life* of St Patrick, published as part of Colgan's collection in 1647, opens with a bold statement that Patrick's ancestors were Jewish, having been driven from the Holy Land following the destruction of the Temple in Jerusalem by the Roman Legions under Titus, in 70 CE. The author of this ancient document begins his account of St Patrick as follows:

> Some say that St Patrick was of Jewish origin. After our Lord had died on the cross for the sins of the human race, the Roman army, avenging His Passion, laid waste Judea, and Jews taken captive were dispersed amongst all the nations of the earth. Some of them settled among the Armoric Britons, and it is stated that it was from them that St Patrick traced his origin.[44]

The author describes how Jewish families were dispersed from the Holy Land to Armoric Letha, where they settled and he says this land was beside the Tyrrhene Sea.[45] These places can be identified on the north west coast of Brittany, adjacent to the Bay of Mont St Michel in the same region where Château Bonaban is now located.[46]

O'Hanlon thought Colgan's *Fourth Life* was one of the most ancient documents and suggested it retained an archaic tradition that St Patrick was born on the continent, in Brittany. Bury also said this document contained some very old source material (he called it 'W') which could be dated from internal evidence to before the seventh century. The *Fourth Life* is the original document on which the second and third Lives depended, but they drew from it in different ways. The reference to St Patrick's Jewish origins appears in a prominent position at the very beginning of the earliest document, but appears to have been removed by later copyists.

Beginnings and endings are always important for a writer, which suggests that the introduction to the *Fourth Life* was placed there for a reason. Why was this passage not included in the *Second Life* or the *Third Life*? When the manuscripts are compared, it suggests that this section may have been suppressed when the two later documents were compiled. This can clearly be seen because the *Second Life* and the *Third Life* begin in a very disjointed way, as if the statement which appears at the very beginning of the *Fourth Life* was deliberately excluded by the clumsy hands of an unsympathetic editor.[47]

If Bury was right, the record of St Patrick's ancestors being Jewish must have formed part of the earliest material, which predated the Armagh Movement that took place in the seventh century. The reference to St Patrick's Jewish origins is probably the more original, archaic tradition, erased by later copyists. If it was erased intentionally, perhaps this was because of the reference to St Patrick's ancestors migrating from the Holy Land to Brittany, which contradicted other claims that he came from Britain. Another possible explanation is that it was erased because of the reference to St Patrick's ancestors being Jews, which would not have been looked on with favour in some quarters of the Church at the time these later documents were written.[48]

In relation to the truth as to where St Patrick was taken captive, it is important to note that the *Fourth Life* directly associates St Patrick's family with Armorica, saying that Patrick's ancestors migrated there after their expulsion or dispersion from Jerusalem in 70 CE.

If Bury is right, then this name belongs to archaic material that predates Muirchú. It must, therefore, be considered significant and perhaps more trustworthy than Muirchú's narrative or the other ancient documents that depended on Muirchú.

The name 'Letha' or 'Armoric Letha' is not mentioned by St Patrick in his own writings but it appears in many of the ancient sources in a variety of different and unusual contexts. It provides one of the best clues available to help identify St Patrick's place of origins more precisely because it has a historical and geographical integrity not easily invented. Fortunately, it can be identified. This time there is reliable historical and geographical evidence to support a specific location. Letha or Armoric Letha must have been on the continent within the coastal region of Armorica.

*Summary*

Most of the ancient Lives of St Patrick were compiled over a five-hundred-year period from the end of the seventh to the twelfth century before they were rescued from oblivion and published by Colgan in 1647. These documents cannot be taken as first-hand historical evidence because they were written long after St Patrick's death. Scholars have sometimes underestimated the value of these 'secondary sources' and have dismissed them as if they can never be trusted. Hagiographies are not reliable as historical records. Without doubt they contain much that is false or imaginary. Gibbon was probably not far from the truth when he said the sixty-six Lives of St Patrick that were extant in the ninth century 'must have contained as many thousand lies'.[49]

In relation to the quest for knowledge as to where St Patrick came from, however, we cannot reject these documents out of hand because they contain geographical references which provide clues to help resolve uncertainties about the key places mentioned in Patrick's *Confession*. The ancient Lives of St Patrick have preserved some of the missing pieces in the geographical jigsaw puzzle. They are the only records we have apart from St Patrick's writings and the truth remained hidden within these legends for centuries.

Some of the manuscripts published by Colgan in 1647 claim that St Patrick was born in Britain but they contain other traditions which associate St Patrick and his family directly with Armorica. Colgan was aware of this when he examined these manuscripts. As they arrived on his study desk in 1645, he found himself in the privileged position of being the first person able to compare them.

There were uncertainties and contradictions in the various stories and traditions recorded over the centuries. Some said St Patrick came from Britain, others from Brittany. Probus claimed to know without doubt that St Patrick's homeland was located in a specific coastal region of northwest Brittany and that he was not only taken captive from there, but born on the continent.

In relation to the local traditions about St Patrick recorded in Brittany, what has become clearly apparent is that the early Breton historians are not alone in their claim that St Patrick was taken captive from there. This claim appears directly or indirectly in several of the ancient manuscripts published by Colgan, including Colgan's *Fourth Life*, the notes of the Scholiast, and especially the *Life of St Patrick* by Probus. All these documents have, in their own unique way, recorded that St Patrick was taken captive from a place called 'Armoric Letha' which was known to the ancient Irish writers as 'Lethania Britannia'. This belonged to a coastal region of Brittany, known to the Romans as 'Armorica'.[50] This is the same region in which Château Bonaban is located, suggesting again that the local tradition recorded there about Patrick, may be authentic. If these accounts are trustworthy, it means that St Patrick's homeland and the place from which he was taken captive were not located anywhere in Britain but on the continent. The existence of these accounts strongly challenges the established tradition that St Patrick was taken captive from Britain. The region that was known to the ancient Irish writers as 'Armoric Letha' provides the key to resolve some of the uncertainties that surround St Patrick's place of origins. In our quest to rediscover the truth about St Patrick it is essential that we establish its precise geographical location.

---

*Notes*

1. Paul Richard, 'Page of Enlightenment', *Washington Post* <http://articles.washingtonpost.com/2009-04-04/news/36898995_1_rosenwald-choir-books-monastery> published online 4 April 2009.

2. Padraig O'Riain, 'Introduction', John Colgan, *Trias Thaumaturga*, ed. Eamonn De Burca (Dublin, 1977).

3. *Annals of Ireland by the Four Masters*, 7 vols, de Burca (Dublin, 1990).

4. John Colgan, *Trias Thaumaturga* (*Trias Thau.*), first published in Louvain, 1647. Facsimile edition published by Edmund Burke, Dublin, 1993 for De Burca Rare Books. See Appendix V, 'Concerning the Homeland and Family of St Patrick', p. 219 ff. Four of Colgan's Lives of St Patrick were published by Ludwig Bieler with a commentary in *Four Latin Lives of St Patrick* (Dublin, 1971).

5. See also James Kenney, *The Sources for the Early History of Ireland: Ecclesiastical* (Dublin, 1997), pp. 165–82 and 319–56.

6. The second line, *ut refertur in historiis* (as we read in the histories), argues against it being written by a contemporary of Patrick, but it contains old traditions related to Patrick's origins. Kenney, *Sources*, p. 340.

7. *St Fiacc's Hymn* in Colgan, *Trias Thau.*, p. 4.

8. Old Irish: *Genair Patraic inNemthur.* The Latin version says: *Natus est Patricius Nemthurri* – 'Patrick was born in Nemthor'. Prof. Luce suggested a literal translation could be 'Patrick was born a Nemturrite'. When Colgan examined this manuscript he said St Fiacc introduces him as 'the Nemturrinate'. (Colgan, *Trias Thau.*, p. 4.) This name appears in various forms, including 'Emptor', 'Nemthor' and 'Nemthur'. We do not know if it is the same place Muirchú called 'Ventra'. This could be possible. as when ancient texts were copied the letters 'n' and 'v' were interchangeable.

9. 'St Fiacc's Hymn', *Ecclesiastical Record* (1868), O'Curry MS, Catholic University. The earliest manuscript is in Old Irish, probably eighth century. See Kenney, *Sources*, p. 340.

10. For *St Fiacc's Hymn* see Whitley Stokes, *Tripartite Life of St Patrick* (London, 1887), ii, pp. 402–26. For the notes added by the Scholiast see pp. 413–26.

11. 'Nemthur is a city in northern Britain, called Al Cluid': *Nemthor est civitas in septemtrionali Brittannia nempe Alcluida.* Scolion 1, Colgan, *Trias Thau.*, p. 4; Stokes, *Tripartite Life*, p. 413.

12. Colgan interpreted 'Nem-thur' as the Latin *Nem-thurris*, meaning a 'heavenly tower' or 'holy tower'. Villemarque suggested a lighthouse. See Villemarque, *La Legende Celtique* (Paris, 1864).

13. Another way of interpreting the words of *Fiacc's Hymn*, is that Patrick was born a 'Nemthorite'. This suggests a different meaning. If St Patrick was a 'Nemthorite' perhaps his family was part of an ethnic or religious group identified with 'Nemthor'.

14. 'St Patrick was born at Holy Tours. This, according to Fr Colgan, who embraces the opinion of all the Irish and British writers in the present question, is handed down as an established tradition among the natives of Armoric Gaul and those who live contiguous to that venerable city (Tours).' *Life of St Patrick*, (Paris, 1870), p. 13, 14. Those who support the theory of Tours, say this became 'Nemthor' or 'Nempthur' in various translations, being an error for *Naem Tour*, or 'Holy Tours', in Gaelic. Colgan disagreed with this interpretation, but he accepted there was an ancient tradition that St Patrick was born in Gaul when he said, 'Dom Philip O'Sullivan Beare, in his life of our saint (Patrick) makes him a native of Bretagne in France. This is the account of Probus too, whose words are plain. In his life of our saint (Patrick) Probus says, 'St Patrick was a Briton, of the village of Banave, in the district of Tyburnia, adjacent to the Western Ocean, which village we undoubtedly find to be in the province of Neustria.' See *Life of St Patrick*, (Paris 1870), p. 13 ff.

15. Stokes suggests 'Hidemthur'. Stokes, *Tripartite Life*, n. 2, p. 8.

16. The Rock of Clyde is a prominent feature of the landscape with an ancient history, but there is no historical or archaeological evidence for the existence of a lighthouse or Roman military base.

17. 'So he [Patrick] was born in that city, Nemthor by name ... Patrick in the Plain of Tiburnia. Now the Plain of Tents is so called because in it at a certain time the Romans had pitched their tents there in the cold of winter ... for this reason it was named *Campus Taberne*, that is, the Plain of Tents.' Colgan, *Trias Thau.*, p. 11. It would seem doubtful even the Romans would have pitched their tents anywhere near Strathclyde for protection during the winter, unless the climate in Scotland was milder in those days.

18. The name 'Taburnia' or 'Taberne' is given in these manuscripts without the word 'Bannavem' placed before it, unlike the name given in Patrick's *Confession*. This is a sign of a later secondary development.

19. 'Alcluth' or 'Alclud' was also an ancient name for the city of Aleth (St Malo) in Brittany.

20. Most surviving copies of St Patrick's *Confession* include the name 'taburnia' which reflects the usage common in Britain. In the fifth life published by Colgan, written by Probus, the name 'tyburnia' or 'tiburniae' is recorded. Probus identifies St Patrick's homeland in Brittany and he appears to have been one of the few ancient writers who knew where St Patrick came from and where St Patrick's 'Bannavem Tiburniae' was located. For original texts of the manuscripts of Patrick's *Confession* see *Saint Patrick's Confessio* [website] <http://www.confessio.ie>, a superb website and resource on St Patrick developed by the Royal Irish Academy.

21. John O'Hanlon, *Lives of the Irish Saints* (Dublin, 1875), iii, p. 509, n. 68. If the pre-fix 'bon' or 'ban' refers to the 'foot' of the river this would be an accurate geographical description of the site where Château Bonaban is now located. At the time of St Patrick, the river Rance flowed inland from its 'mouth' at Aleth, to its 'foot' at Bonaban.

22. Jocelyn was a monk of the Augustinian Canons which John de Courcy brought from England and established at Downpatrick after the Norman Invasion of Ireland in the twelfth century. O'Hanlon considered it the most unreliable of all the ancient 'Lives'. See O'Hanlon, *Lives*, iii, p. 461, n. 317.

23. Colgan, *Trias Thau.*, p. 64.

24. Jocelyn follows Muirchú saying that Patrick fled to Britain after his escape from slavery in Ireland.

25. 'On a certain promontory overhanging the town of Empthor was erected a fort, the ruins of whose walls may yet be traced... and the place, being in the Valley of Clud [Clyde], is called in the language of that people Dun Breatan [Dunbarton] that is, the Mountain of the Britons.' Jocelyn, *The Life and Acts of St Patrick* in *Ancient Lives of Saint Patrick*, ed. James O'Leary (New York, 1880) *Project Gutenberg* [ebook] <http://www.gutenberg.org/files/18482/18482-h/18482-h.htm> published online 1 June 2006, ch. XI.

26. Jocelyn, *The Life and Acts of St Patrick*, ch. XVII.

27. Colgan, *Trias Thau.*, p. 117 ff. See Stokes, *Tripartite Life*, i, p. 3 ff.

28. *De Britanniis Alcluidensibus origenem duxit Sanctus Patricius... Nemthur, quod ex vocis etymo coelestem turrem denotat, patria et nativitatis locus fuit.* Colgan, 'Septima Vita', *Trias Thau.*, p. 117 ff.

29. See David Howlett, *Muirchú Moccu Mactheni's 'Vita Sancti Patricii'* (Dublin, 2006), p. 111 ff.

30. Lanigan identified Probus with Coneachair, senior lecturer at the monastery of Slane in Ireland not far from Newgrange and the Hill of Tara, all sacred sites associated with St Patrick. Coneachair died at Slane in 950 CE when Vikings attacked and burned the monastery. Others suggest Probus may have been an Irish monk who died at Mayenne in 859 CE. If so, he may have been familiar with traditions unknown to Muirchú or perhaps for some reason excluded by him.

31. *Brito fuit natione:* 'of the nation or stock of the Britons'. This phrase refers to St Patrick's ethnic origins or nationality, possibly Scots/Welsh through Calpurnius and Gallic through Conchessa.

32. An association with Muirchú's 'Ventra' is possible because of the similar spelling. Neustria should not be confused with Nemthor which was always presented either as a town, sacred hill, lighthouse or religious monument.

33. Neustria appears as 'Nentria' in some Latin manuscripts, where the 'u' and 'v' are interchangeable. This sounds suspiciously similar to Muirchú's 'Ventra'. It has been suggested that Probus is simply copying Muirchú's narrative but the reference to Armorica shows clearly

that Probus was referring to a place on the continent. An anonymous Life of St Patrick, published in Paris in 1870, understands Probus to be referring to Neustria. 'This is the account of Probus too, whose words are plain. In his life of our saint [Patrick] Probus says, "St Patrick was a Briton, of the village of Banave, in the district of Tyburnia, adjacent to the Western Ocean, which village we undoubtedly find to be in the province of Neustria."' *Life of St Patrick*, (Paris, 1870), p. 13. Hoey thought the reference to Neustria rather than 'Nempthur' was part of an original, authentic tradition linking St Patrick's origins to France.

34. In his *Confession*, St Patrick's homeland is identified as *in Britanniis*. Probus claims St Patrick was also born there.

35. This appears to be a reference to St Patrick being taken into captivity. If so, it confirms that Probus identified St Patrick's homeland and place of birth with the location of 'Bannavem Tiburniae'.

36. Probus, 'Vita Auctore Probo' in Bieler, ed., *Four Latin Lives of St Patrick* (Dublin, 1971), p. 192.

37. C 23: *haut procul a mari occidentali*; in Ludwig Bieler, *Clavis Patricii II: Libri Epistolarum Sancti Patricii Episcopi* (Dublin, 1993), p. 71; See Probus 1:5 in Bieler, *Four Latin Lives*, p. 192.

38. It has been suggested that Probus was copying from Muirchú's account. Compare Probus's *quem uicum indubitanter comperimus esse Nentriae provinciae* (Probus 1:6, Bieler, p. 192) and Muirchú's *quem uicum constanter indubitanturque conperimus esse Venta* (Muirchú 1.6, Howlett, 'Vita Sancti Patricii', p. 46 f.) The inclusion of the reference to Armorica in a later passage clearly shows that Probus meant the coastal region Brittany, and that it is more reasonable to understand that he is referring to the province of Neustria.

39. The theory that 'Britanniis' refers to a 'Britain' on the continent is controversial and will be examined in greater detail in due course.

40. *Hic in Britanniis natus est* can therefore only mean 'he [St Patrick] was born in Brittany'. Unlike some of the other documents, Probus makes no mention of Nemthor or Strathclyde.

41. One of the largest 'menhirs' or megalithic stones can be found just outside the medieval town of Dol-de-Bretagne, which is not far from Château Bonaban. There is a spectacular group of stones, still known as 'the Giants of Kerzerho', at Erdeven, near Carnac. For a map of the alignments see *The Megaliths of Carnac* [website] <http://menhirs.tripod.com/intro.html>; also Julian Cope, *The Megalithic European* (London, 2004).

42. *In ciuitate eorum Arimuric*. See Bieler, *Four Latin Lives*, p. 195. Canon Flemming translates this as 'in their own sea-side city' on the basis that Caesar said all the towns on the sea coast of Armorica were called 'Armoricae'. He quotes Camden, *Britannica* (Abridged, London, 1701), i, p. 13. See William Flemming, *Boulogne-sur-Mer* (London, 1907), p. 68 ff.

43. We will explore the significance of these stories in more detail later, in relation to the question as to where St Patrick was born.

44. *Quidam sanctum Patricium ex Iudeis dicunt origenem duxisse: Nam postquam Dominus noster pro salute humani generis passus est Romanus exercitus in ultoniem passionis Iudeam reastauit, et Iudei in capitiutatem deducti per omnes terranum partes disperse sunt et eorum pars apud Brittones Armoricos locum tenuit ex qua sanctus Patricius nationem duxisse fertur.* 'Vita Quarta', Bieler, *Four Latin Lives*, p. 51.

45. *Terram quae Aemorica dicitur iuxta mare Tyrrenum possideret.* 'Vita Quarta', 1:14, Bieler, *Four Latin Lives*, p. 51.

46. The location of the mysterious Tyrrhene Sea will be established in ch. 17, 'Barefoot Hermits'.

47. See Bieler, *Four Latin Lives*, pp. 50–1 (Vita II: i, IV: i) and p. 118 (Vita III: i).

48. For a more detailed enquiry into the question of St Patrick's Jewish origins, see Marcus Losack, *St Patrick and the Bloodline of the Grail: The Untold Story of St Patrick's Royal Family* (Annamoe, Wicklow, 2012).

49. Edward Gibbon, *Decline and Fall of the Roman Empire*, 8 vols (London, 1862), iv, p. 53.

50. See Richard Woods, 'Brittany and Beyond' in *The Spirituality of the Celtic Saints* (New York, 2000).

# CHAPTER SEVEN

# *Armoric Letha*

Sometimes a legend that endures
For centuries, endures for a reason.[1]

The *Life of St Patrick* recorded by Probus was not the only manuscript published by Colgan to claim that Patrick was taken captive from Brittany. Several other references can be found in the ancient sources which associate St Patrick and his family with the same coastal region in which Château Bonaban is now located. As we consider these, a more complex and intriguing picture of the life of St Patrick begins to emerge.

*St Fiacc's Hymn* is thought to be one of the oldest documents for information about St Patrick, apart from Patrick's own writings.[2] It also links St Patrick to a place called 'Letha', a name which appears prominently in four different verses. The author describes in a poetic way how Patrick travelled 'far away beyond the seas, to the southern part of Letha'. However, there is apparent confusion as to the precise geographical location of this place. In two verses it clearly refers to a region on the continent; in two others it appears to refer to Ireland:

> He sent him [Patrick] across the Alps
> Over the sea marvellous was his course
> Until he stayed with Germanus in the south
> In the southern part of Letha (v. 5)[3]

> They prayed that the saint would come
> That he would return from Letha
> To covert the people of Erin (Ireland)
> From error to life (v. 9)

> [Patrick] preached the Gospel to all
> He wrought great miracles in Letha
> He healed the lame and the lepers
> The dead he restored to life (v. 17)

> Patrick preached to the Scotti [Irish]
> He endured great toil in Letha
> With him will come to Judgement
> Everyone whom he brought
> To the life of faith (v.19)[4]

Fortunately, other references to Letha or Armoric Letha have survived in the ancient sources which help to identify its true location, removing further doubt or confusion.

In notes attached to *St Fiacc's Hymn* that were written by the Scholiast, we find another version of the story given by Probus. This describes the circumstances in which St Patrick was taken into captivity. Probus said St Patrick was taken captive when he was resident in his 'homeland' in Armorica.[5]

The Scholiast also records that Patrick was taken captive from Brittany but he gives a slightly different version of these events. He says the family were simply visiting Armorica at the time, having travelled by ship from Strathclyde to see relatives who lived on the continent. Consistent with Probus is the fact that Armorica is again identified as the place where Patrick was taken captive.

The region in question is named as 'Letha' or 'Letavia'. Here is the account as it appears in the notes of the Scholiast, which were originally written in Old Irish. Patrick's family are said to have travelled to the 'Britons of Armorica, that is, to the Letavian Britons' (Britons of Letha):

> This is the cause of his enslavement. Patrick and his father Calpurn, Concessa his mother, a daughter of Ocmus, and his five sisters, Lupait and Tigris and Liamain and Darerca and the name of the fifth Cinnenum, [and] his brother the deacon Sannan, all travelled from the Britons of Ail-Cluade [Strathclyde] over the Ictian Sea southwards on a journey to the Britons of Armorica[6] that is, to the Letavian Britons,[7] for there were relatives of theirs there at that time, and, besides, the mother of the children, namely Concessa, was of the Franks and she was a close female relation of [Saint] Martin ...[8]
>
> That was the time at which seven sons of Sectmaide, king of Britain, were in exile from Britain. So they made a fierce attack on the Britons of Armorica where Patrick was with his family, and they slew Calpurn there, and they brought Patrick and Lupait with them to Ireland, and they sold Lupait in Conaille Muirthemne [County Meath] and Patrick in the north of Dalriada [County Antrim].[9]

This passage is significant. If the geographical description is reliable then Letha must have formed a local or regional subdivision within Armorica itself. Several versions of this story can be found in the manuscripts published by Colgan and other documents. All of them include an account of a journey allegedly made by Patrick's family, travelling from Strathclyde to Armoric Letha, where St Patrick was taken captive. These accounts differ only in details given about the family, the list of travellers and the names of the attackers.[10]

Some say St Patrick had five sisters called Lupait, Tigris, Liamain, Darerca and Cinnemon, and one brother called Senan. Others mention only two sisters, Lupait and Tigris and no brothers. A similar list of names is recorded in Breton historical sources.[11]

At an early stage in this enquiry, having returned home to Ireland from Brittany and begun more extensive reading and research, I stumbled across a reference to Letha in one of my favourite old books, *Lives of the Saints from the Book of Lismore*, edited by Whitley Stokes, which helped to clarify its meaning and possible location.

In some of the best books, the real treasures are found in the footnotes. This reference would have been meaningless to me, if I had not learned from a guidebook that Aleth was the ancient name for St Malo in Brittany, which is close to the site where we discovered a local tradition about St Patrick at Château Bonaban.[12] Stokes mentioned that St Patrick was known by various names, including 'Patricius il Letha Luind'. He suggested that 'Letha' meant 'on the continent' without giving a specific geographical location.[13]

'Aleth' is the old name for the Roman port at the mouth of the River Rance, now St Malo. If the references to Letha or Armoric Letha are linked to Aleth, then perhaps St Patrick's connection with the St Malo region could be confirmed? In the late Roman period, Aleth was a place of considerable note: 'that point, where the sun rises, considered as the leading one formerly, in fixing geographical, astronomical positions'. At the time of St Patrick it was an important military base for the Legion of Mars. The history and strategic significance of this port for the Roman navy is well documented.[14] A prefect of the Legion of Mars had a residence there and ships based at Aleth guarded both sides of the English Channel in efforts to combat piracy in the Iccian Sea.[15]

From an etymological point of view, 'Letha' is connected to the Greek *lethe* meaning forgetfulness or oblivion, cognate with the Latin *latere* which means, 'to be hidden'. It can refer to something which has been hidden or escaped our attention.[16]

In classical mythology, it was the name for a river in Hades whose water, if drunk, caused forgetfulness of the past. Heideggar understood 'lethe' to mean 'concealment of being' or 'forgetfulness of being and true identity', which is strangely appropriate in relation to our quest for the truth about Patrick![17]

The name 'Letha' may also be derived from *Laeti*, a Latin word used by the Romans for communities of barbarians (literally, babblers, those from outside the Empire who spoke in foreign tongues) who were given lands on which to settle within the Empire. This was granted on condition they provide recruits for the army. The son of the veteran was usually compelled to follow the profession of his father. Military service was an obligation because the *Laeti* considered themselves to be part of a military race.[18] The soldiers not only held an estate distinct from the rest of the people, they formed an influential ruling caste from within which sovereign power was derived. Historical records mention the *Laeti* from the fourth century onwards, but these military alliances had been taking place for a long time.[19] Breton historians writing from an early period have claimed that a colony of the *Laeti* was established in Brittany at the time of the rebellion of Magnus Maximus in 383 CE and that St Patrick's family were part of this migration, having belonged to the Britons of Strathclyde.

Scholars have been aware for some time of the link between Letha and Armorica. Camden identified Letha as a coastal region in Brittany.[20] O'Hanlon understood that 'Armoric Britain' was called 'Letha' or 'Leatha' by the Irish and he refers to it as a 'maritime district of British Armorica'. It appears as 'Letha' or 'Lethania' in ancient Irish sources.[21] Some writers called it 'Letavia'.[22]

In the ancient Lives of St Gildas, 'Letha' is clearly identified with Brittany. This document states that in Gaul there was another region called 'Britain' on the continent, known as 'Letavia', which must be another reference to Armoric Letha:

> Armorica, formerly a territory in Gaul, but was at that time called Letavia by the Bretons, in whose possession it was.[23]

This suggests that 'Letha' or 'Lethania' had replaced 'Armorica' as the name for at least part of this region which we know as Brittany.[24] The identification of 'Armoric Letha' as a region which surrounded Aleth or St Malo, is self evident, although the importance of Aleth in relation to Patrick's place of origins appears to have been overlooked and neglected by many writers.[25]

Geoffrey of Monmouth gives an account of close contact between the ancient Britons in Britain and Brittany, in which the reference to the city of Aleth is so precise it must have come from a reliable source. Geoffrey records how a delegation of Britons sailed from Britain to Armorica to appeal for help from King Salomon of Brittany. The ship docked at the port of Kidaleta. Breton historians date King Salomon's rule to 405 CE, around the time that St Patrick escaped from slavery in Ireland.

> Then the wind standing fair, he got ready his ship and hoisting sails they pursued their voyage, arriving at the city Kidaleta.[26]

'Kidaleta' or 'Quidalet' was another name for the city of Aleth.[27] Locals still refer to it by its ancient designation as *la cité*.[28] This suggests that Aleth may have been the capital of Armoric Letha. According to Geoffrey, the king of Brittany was resident there and it was a centre for local government, where foreign delegations were welcomed. The location of Armoric Letha is crucial to the study of St Patrick. Although this place is not named directly in St Patrick's own writings, there are several references in the ancient Lives of St Patrick that are very significant and they all point firmly in the direction of Brittany. It applies to a specific local region on the coast of north-west Brittany between Aleth, Dol and Mont St Michel.

This becomes apparent when we consider a number of significant references to Letha in the ancient sources. One of the earliest can be found in Cogitosus's *Life of St Brigid*, dated to c.650 CE. In this account a bishop called 'Conleath' had been invited to Kildare (the place where Brigid's monastery was located in Ireland) by St Brigid to share her ministry. Cogitosus writes:

> How many miracles she [St Brigid] wrought no man can fully tell. She blessed the vestments of Conleath which he had brought from Letha.[29]

Bishop Conleath may have come from Letha or was sent there to get vestments for St Brigid, having contact with the Church in that region.[30] The identification of Letha with lands adjacent to the Bay of Mont St Michel can be confirmed from a reference in the *Life of St Ailbe*. The following story appears in the context of Ailbe's visit to Brittany. The association with Dol-de-Bretagne is so direct it points to a specific geographical location.

> St Ailbe arrived at the city called Dolo Moir [literally 'Dol by the Sea' – Dol-de-Bretagne] at *the farthest limits of Letha* where he and his people stayed in a hospice.[31]

Dol-de-Bretagne is one of the most ancient ecclesiastical sites in Brittany and is still close to the sea. This reference confirms that 'Letha' was the name of a specific local region within Armorica, close to Aleth and Dol. When St Ailbe arrived in Letha he is said to have met St Samson and helped repair Samson's chalice. St Samson was from a noble family, the son of Amon of Dyfed and Anna of Gwent. He was born about 486 CE. In Brittany, he founded a monastery at Dol. He is recorded as being present at a church council in Paris between 556 and 573 CE. St Samson was buried at Dol and his stone sarcophagus (now empty) is preserved in the beautiful chapel in front of the high altar in the local cathedral named after him.[32]

The reference to St Samson, Letha and Dol confirms without doubt, that Dol-de-Bretagne existed within the region of Armoric Letha.[33] There has been uncertainty and confusion as to the precise geographical location of this region, which has greatly influenced our traditional understanding of St Patrick's place of origins.[34]

In his *Confession*, Patrick tells us that he was taken captive from his father's estate at Bannavem Tiburniae. If there is any truth in the Armorican tradition, this home must have been located in a coastal area of northwest Brittany, close to the Roman port at Aleth.

One of the earliest historical references is recorded by Nennius (c.675 CE) in his History of the Britons.[35] This is how Nennius described events taking place in Brittany in 385 CE:[36]

The seventh Emperor was Maximus. He withdrew from Britain with all his military force, slew Gratian, the king of the Romans, and obtained the sovereignty of all Europe. Unwilling to send back his warlike companions to their wives, children and possessions in Britain, he conferred upon them numerous districts from the Lake on the summit of Mons Jovis, to the city called Cant Guic and to the western Tumulus, that is, to Cruc Occident. These are the Armoric Britons and they remain there to the present day.[37]

Nennius's 'Mons Jovis' has sometimes been mistakenly identified with St Bernard's Pass in the Alps, but the evidence points rather to the Brittany peninsular. The description of Mons Jovis as a very steep rock and *super verticum* suits Mont St Michel perfectly, as Dr Lanigan suggested.[38] French historian, Bizeul, identifies Nennius's 'Mons Jovis' as Mont St Michel, 'Cant Guic' as Nantes and 'Cruc Occident' or 'tumulus occidentale' (the western tomb or burial mound) as Le Cap St Mahe, at the furthest extremity of Brittany.[39]

Taking a minimalist approach, the region which Nennius describes as 'Armoric Letha' probably refers to the coastal area of north west Brittany, between the coastal town of Perros Giuirec and Mont St Michel and inland as far as the highest point of Les Monts D'Arée, at La Reservoir du St Michel. Historians who take a maximalist approach suggest the settlement may have extended south-east as far as the Loire and south-west as far west as Quiberon.

The location of Armoric Letha is one of the key missing pieces in the geographical jigsaw puzzle of St Patrick. Although it may be difficult to determine its precise boundaries, this region must have included a specific local area along the coast of northwest Brittany between St Malo (Aleth) and Mont St Michel, adjacent to what is now the Bay of St Malo. This is precisely the place where Château Bonaban is located, supporting the integrity of the local tradition about St Patrick that is recorded in Brittany.

The establishment of a British settlement in Brittany at the time of the rebellion of Maximus in 385 CE is an historically controversial subject but of critical importance to locating the homeland of St Patrick. Disagreement centres on when the name 'Britain' or 'Bretagne' was first applied to Armorica. If a major settlement took place under Maximus, when he took control of the western Empire from 383–389 CE, this would support the case that a name change may have occurred at this time, at which point a coastal region in Armorica would have been known as 'Britanniis' or 'Britannia'.

This presents us with a number of intriguing possibilities. If St Patrick was born around 385 CE, as Bury suggested, this is precisely when the new political regime was established by Maximus. If St Patrick's family moved to Brittany at this time as the majority of Breton historians claim, then St Patrick would have grown up being familiar with 'Britanniis' as the name for his homeland.

This would be the case especially if he was born in Brittany, or moved there with his family as a baby or at a very young age.

*Summary*

The ancient Lives of St Patrick published by John Colgan in 1647 have presented us with a number of different accounts about St Patrick's origins which show inherent contradictions and cannot easily be reconciled. If there is any truth in several of the accounts found in these old manuscripts which associate St Patrick's origins with Armoric Letha, it allows for the possibility that an authentic local tradition may also have been preserved in Brittany.

From the evidence gathered so far, it would appear to be the case that a local tradition in Brittany claiming that St Patrick's home at Bannavem Tiburniae was located in this region, close to the present site of Château Bonaban, is historically possible.

For those who take the view that St Patrick came from Scotland or Wales, the number of references to Brittany which can be found in the ancient sources, has to be accounted for. They cannot simply be dismissed as the fruit of hagiographical fantasy or the imaginative genius of the early Breton historians.

If St Patrick and his family came from Britain and he was taken captive from Britain, why have so many conflicting stories been preserved which associate St Patrick's origins so directly with such a specific local region in Brittany? This becomes even more significant when we consider more detailed claims about various members of St Patrick's family and their close relationship to the early Breton aristocracy, as recorded by many of the early Breton historians.

Against this, we must come to terms with the fact that almost the full weight of academic opinion is strongly against the view that St Patrick came from Brittany.

Most Patrician scholars are entirely convinced at present that St Patrick came from Britain. In fact, it is said to be the only thing we can know about St Patrick with absolute certainty. Breton historians writing in the eighteenth and nineteenth centuries obviously thought otherwise, as did the authors of some ancient Lives of St Patrick.

Why have scholars not taken up the gauntlet dropped into the path of Patrician Studies by these alternative accounts? The bulk of the evidence considered so far points firmly in the direction of Brittany as the most likely location of Bannavem Tiburniae, the parental home from which St Patrick was taken captive.

Before presenting any further evidence, however, we must face up to the opinions of respected scholars who continue to reject this possibility. It is of paramount importance to consider their views and take their expertise fully into account. M. de Gerville was convinced that the established tradition claiming that St Patrick was taken captive from Britain, was a 'gross' historical error. If he is right, then we have all been misled about St Patrick and the origins of Christianity in Ireland. The quest for the truth about St Patrick is too important to remain neglected.

Let's find out what happened after the ancient manuscripts were published by Colgan in 1647. How would all these different stories and traditions associated with St Patrick be viewed by Colgan himself and then by the scholars who came after him?

---

*Notes*

1. Dan Brown, *The Lost Symbol* (New York, 2009), p. 23.

2. *Fiacc's Hymn* is an ancient hymn written in Old Irish. The earliest surviving copy dates from the seventh or eighth century. It says Patrick was born in 'Nemthor' but does not identify this place.

3. *Profectus est trans Alpes omnes, Trans Maria, fuit faelix expedition, Et remansit apud Germanum, In aistrali parte australis Lethanie: St Fiacc's Hymn*, v. 5.

4. 'St Fiacc's Hymn', *Ecclesiastical Record* (1868), O'Curry MS, Catholic University. Albion is an ancient name for Britain and Scotland (Alba).

5. *Cumque adhuc esset in patria...in ciuitate eorum Arimuric.* See Probus 1:12: Bieler, ed., *Four Latin Lives of St Patrick* (Dublin, 1971). p. 195.

6. *Co Bretnaib Armuirc Letha.*

7. *CoBretnaib Ledach.* The name appears elsewhere as Letha, Letavia or Lethania.

8. The Scholiast records that pirates plundered 'Letha' in 'Armoric Britain'. They killed Calpurnius and brought Patrick to Ireland. *Facerunt praedas in Britanniae Armoricae regione Letha, ubi Patricius cum familia fuit.* Scholion 5, n. 82. This supports Probus's claim that Patrick and his family had connections with a region on the continent known as 'Britannia' or 'Britain', in Armorica. See Notes on *Fiacc's Hymn*, p. 36, trans. Whitley Stokes, *Tripartite Life of St Patrick* (London, 1887), ii, pp. 414–5.

9. In the Franciscan Liber Hymnorum (FLH) the journey is 'from the Alclyde Britons to the Armoric Britons of Letha', or 'Lethic Britons': 'a Bretnaib Ailcluade' 'coBretnaib Armuirc Letha... coBretnalb Ledach'. Notes to *St Fiacc's Hymn* in Stokes, *Tripartite Life*, p. 412 ff. *Emphasis added.

10. See Stokes, *Tripartite Life*, ii, p. 461, n. 318, also p. 439; M. F. Cusack, *Life of St Patrick, Apostle of Ireland* (London, 1877), p. 376 and 'The Scholiast' in Stokes, *Tripartite Life*, p. 413, p. 433.

11. In Latin, 'Tigris' means 'little tiger', but these names will be explored in a future enquiry when we examine genealogies which suggest St Patrick's family may have been related to Scots-British royal families and the early Merovingian Dynasty in Gaul. See Marcus Losack, *St Patrick and the Bloodline of the Grail: The Untold Story of St Patrick's Royal Family* (Annamoe, Wicklow, 2012).

12. Philippe Barbour, *Cadogan Guide to Brittany* (London, 2008).

13. *Anecdota Oxoniensia* (Oxford, 1890), facs. edn trans. Whitley Stokes, as *Lives of the Saints from the Book of Lismore* (Llanerch, 1990). See notes on p. 294 (p. 153).

14. See Jacques Doremet, *De Antiquité de la Ville et cité d'Aleth, ou Quidalet*, ed. Thomas de Querci (St Malo, 1894; Slatkine Reprints, 1971), p. 17; Jacques Doremet, *L'Antiquité d'Aleth* (La Cane de Montfort, 1628).

15. Iccian Sea: the stretch of water between south-west Britain, Ireland and the north-west coast of Gaul.

16. Online Etymological Dictionary <http://www.etymonline.com/>

17. *Mythweb* [website] <www.mythweb.com>

18. See Francis Palgrave, *History of Normandy and Britain* (London, 1861), ch. 1.

19. The *Notitia Dignitorum* is an official document compiled in the fourth and fifth centuries, which lists Roman civil and military posts. Title XLII contains a list from Gaul, *per tractum Rodunensem et Alanorum*. See M. Poslan, *Cambridge Economic History of Europe* (Cambridge, 1966), p. 187.

20. Camden, *Britannica* (Abridged, London, 1701), col. cxxxii.

21. Sharon Turner (who rejects the idea that this region was known as 'Britannia' or 'Brittanniis' at the time of St Patrick) equates 'Letha' with the Welsh or Celtic 'Llydaw', meaning 'sea coast', and accepts it was a synonym to Armorica. See Sharon Turner, *The History of the Anglo-Saxons* (London, 1852).

22. 'Letauia appears to be an ancient name for at least a portion of Gaul. Latin inscriptions also indicate a goddess named 'Litauis' (consort of Mars Cicollus) was invoked in Gaul. She may have been a mother goddess and symbol of the sacred land and its national sovereignty, like Eriu in Ireland.' Source: <kmatthews.org.uk/arthuriana/brittany.html>

23. 'In the Armorican region of Gaul there is another Britain called Letavia': *In Armorica quondam Galliae regionem tunc autem Britannis a quibus possidebator Letavia dicebatur*. See Hugh Williams, trans., *Two Lives of Gildas by a monk of Ruys and Caradoc of Llancarfan* (Cymmrodorion Series, 1899; facs. edn Llanerch, 1990), ch. 16. Also Bouquet, 3, p. 449: The MS Vita Caoci says, *Provincia quodam Armorica deinde Littau, nunc Britannia Minor vocator*. 'The province of Armorica known as Littau (Letavia) also called *Britannia Minor* (Little Britain or 'Lesser' Britain)'. Cotton Library, Vesp. A. 14, p. 32.

24. 'Brittany which, as we have said, was formerly called Letavia, was at that time ravaged in a cruel manner as much by its own inhabitants as by foreigners.' *Two Lives of Gildas* 32.

25. Canon John O'Hanlon is one of only a few scholars who have recognised the significance of Aleth. See O'Hanlon, *Lives of the Irish Saints* (Dublin, 1875), iii, p. 509, n. 67.

26. See Geoffrey of Monmouth, 'History of the Kings of Britain', in *Six Old English Chronicles*, trans. J. A. Giles and Aaron Thompson, (1848), p. 243.

27. Jacques Doremet, *De Antiquité de la Ville et cité d'Aleth, ou Quidalet*, ed. Thomas de Querci (St Malo, 1894; Slatkine Reprints, 1971).

28. This might explain why Probus says, 'while they were in their city, Armuric' but we should think of Armoric Letha as a region, existing within Armorica, centred around Aleth and Dol and the coastal hinterland.

29. Cogitosus, 'Life of St Brigit the Virgin', in *Celtic Spirituality*, trans. Oliver Davies (New York, 1999), p. 122 ff. In his prologue Muirchú tells us that 'his father' Cogitosus was the first to write an Irish hagiography: Howlett, *Muirchú Moccu Mactheni's 'Vita Sancti Patricii'* (Dublin, 2006), p. 41. Cogitosus says Brigid and Conleath were buried together in separate tombs located on either side of the high altar inside the Church at Kildare.

30. The name 'Conleath' suggests a link with Letha (*Con leath*: Con of Letha) and that he was a Gallic bishop. There appears to have been a certain rivalry between St Brigid and Rome. Todd refers to the 'curious tale' told by Cogitosus, that Conleath was eaten by wild dogs because he

had set out for Rome in opposition to St Brigid's command. Todd was aware 'Letha' signified Armorica but in this case he suggested it referred to Italy. See J. H. Todd, *St Patrick, Apostle of Ireland* (Dublin, 1864), p. 23, n. 2.

31. St Ailbe had just built a monastery 'in that region, in which he left the holy sons of Goll'. Liam de Paor suggests this may refer to 'sons of Gaul' and that the region being referred to was Gaul. *Emphasis added.

32. St Samson is remembered as the founder of the ancient ecclesiastical settlement at Dol, c.530 CE. St Samson's Cathedral is a very historic and prayerful place to visit, greatly loved and cared for by its local Breton, Catholic congregation. Samson is venerated as one of the seven founding saints of Brittany. A 'Life of St Samson', *Vita Sancti Samsonis*, was written between 610 and 820 CE. It includes important information about Celtic Christianity and early contacts between the Churches in Ireland, Britain and Brittany.

33. In the 'Life of St Ailbe', Dol is described as being at 'the farthest limits of Letha'. If the description given by Nennius of the British settlement under Maximius is accurate, this could mean Dol was the northern limit, especially if Nennius's 'Cruc Occident' is a reference to Mont St Michel, as seems most likely.

34. Stokes was prone to errors of interpretation with regard to the location of certain key sites related to St Patrick's origins. For example, he mistakenly identified Armorica with Scotland when he said, 'the place where Patrick was captured, *Bannavem Tiburniae*, has not been identified but it was probably somewhere on the sea coast (ar-mor-ica) of north Britain': *Tripartite Life*, i: p. cxxxvii.

35. Gildas also mentions the rebellion of Maximus and the fact that many of the British soldiers who crossed into Gaul and Spain with Maximus never returned home. See 'The Works of Gildas' in *Six Old English Chronicles*, ed. J. A. Giles (London, 1868), p. 304.

36. Nennius records that Mellobaudes was Maximus's 'master of the horse' or military chief of staff. He talks about the 'war' between the Britons and the Romans and the 'victory' of Maximus. Nennius was writing in north Wales at about the same time Muirchú was compiling his *Life of St Patrick* for the Church in Armagh.

37. Nennius, 'History of the Britons: Historia Brittonum' in *Six Old English Chronicles*, ed. J. A. Giles (London, 1858), p. 394 ff. Kenney dismisses this account as 'pure fantasy' but the detailed geographical references are grounds to question this view.

38. *Quod est super verticem montis Jovis:* See John Lanigan, *Ecclesiastical History of Ireland*, 4 vols (Dublin, 1822; 2nd edn, Dublin, 1829), p. 109, n. 129. See Louis Blondel, *Notice Historique du Mont-St-Michel, de Tombelaine et d'Avrenches* (Avrenches, 1823). L'Abbé Desroches identifies Nennius's Mons Jovis with Mont St Michel, noting that the Forest of Cokelunde was in the environs of Mont St Michel, *cette forêt était dans l'environs de Tomba* [Mont St Michel] *qui se nommait encore Mont de Jupiter, Mons Jovis de Nennius:* Jean-Jacques Desroches, *Histoire du Mont St Michel*, i (Caen, 1838), p. 59, n. 1.

39. Dr Lanigan notes that in Gale's version, Nennius's 'Cantguic' is given as *Tantguit* and 'Cruc-Occident' is given as *cumulum occidentalem*. See Lanigan, *Ecclesiastical History of Ireland*, 4 vols (Dublin, 1822; 2nd edn, Dublin, 1829) i, p. 107. If 'tumulum' is a preferred reading for 'cumulum' this points towards Mont St Michel, which may have been known as the 'tumulus of the west', 'western mount' or 'western tomb'. Of all the places Nennius mentions, 'Cant Ctuic' is perhaps the most difficult to identify. Canturk (Carantec) or Perros Guiros (Perroz Gireg) on the coast near Roscoff, are both possibilities. See Lanigan, *Ecclesiastical History of Ireland*, i, p. 107, and p. 109, n. 129.

# CHAPTER EIGHT

# A Survey of Scholars

Numerous are the *Lives of St Patrick* which have been written yet the evidence that has been gleaned and preserved is bewildering and conflicting. The authentic facts of his life are few compared with the cloud of fable which has served to obscure them.[1]

Several of the old manuscripts collected by John Colgan in 1647 preserved stories and traditions about St Patrick which had been passed on faithfully for more than a thousand years. When Colgan examined the documents he knew there were conflicting accounts about St Patrick's origins. Two different places had been mentioned. Colgan said they were 'far removed' from each other. There was disagreement and confusion about the location of Bannavem Tiburniae which some said was in Britain and others in Brittany. This created a problem which had to be accounted for. St Patrick's birthplace was too important to be left unresolved and there appears to have been a reluctance to distinguish between where St Patrick was taken captive and where he was born.

In Colgan's opinion the associations with Brittany were false and the Strathclyde tradition was more reliable. Having read, studied and compared all the ancient documents, Colgan was aware that some writers identified Brittany as St Patrick's homeland and the place where he was taken captive but he concluded they were mistaken. He decided that St Patrick must have been taken captive from Strathclyde and that Nemthor, the alleged place of St Patrick's birth, was also located there. Colgan failed to explore the possibility that where Patrick was taken captive and where he was born were two separate places. Colgan opted to locate both of these places in Scotland:

> Not in the stated place [i.e. Brittany or Armoric Letha] but in another [place] far removed, in the region of Alcluda in the Plain of Taburnia, and in the town of Nemh-thor or Nemthurris, that is to say, 'heavenly tower'; many other older writers record [this which is] a more reliable tradition.[2]

Colgan discredited Probus saying the author was 'not sufficiently skilled in Patrician matters and the location of places'.[3] An aversion to this manuscript was shared by the Bollandists who refused to publish it at first, claiming it was full of lies. There is no rational explanation as to why Probus was singled out for censorship. Political and/or ecclesiastical factors may have intruded into the publication process.

In her recent study of the Irish annals, Bernadette Cunningham concluded that the Louvain manuscripts (which were edited by Colgan and others) show clear evidence of 'something more than a manuscript being tidied up for publication'.[4] Cunningham provides evidence to show how this affected material directly related to St Patrick and she makes a remarkable statement concerning this material when she says:

> The more extensive revision of Patrician material [in the annals] is not typical of the manuscripts [AFM] as a whole and must be regarded as exceptional. Its importance is that the attempt to alter the traditional chronology to accord with that contained in the printed ecclesiastical annals of Baronius [published in 12 vols between 1588 and 1607] provides evidence of changing attitudes to historical evidence'.

Cunningham suggests that

> It marks a point where the native Irish historical record was modified in the light of the international standards dictated by Counter-Reformation historiography.

If material relating to chronology was affected in this way, could material relating to geography and social or ecclesiastical background have also been affected? Colgan's views may have been influenced by his loyalty to the Church. He ended his commentary by referring to official Church teaching as the ultimate authority:

> Truer, however, and received is the opinion of our native and foreign writers *that St Patrick was born in Great Britain.* Thus [it is written] in the official records of the Lateran Canons, printed at Montes in Hanover in the year 1635, Reading 4, of the Office of St Patrick: Patrick, the apostle of the Irish, *was born of Christian and Catholic parents from the island of Great Britain.*[5]

If it can be shown that St Patrick came from Brittany and not Britain, it is perhaps ironic that John Colgan and his colleagues may have been misled.

Having opened St Antony's College as a resource to challenge an established Scots-British interpretation of Irish history, which was offensive to the scholars at Louvain, the decision to reject the claims of France and locate St Patrick's place of origins exclusively in Britain served to sustain rather than reverse the historical momentum of that tradition. Having said that, it must be admitted that in relation to the quest for truth about St Patrick conspiracy theorists cannot afford to be denominational. A belief that St Patrick came from Britain was endorsed by many others including the influential Protestant antiquarian and Archbishop of Armagh, James Ussher and his views were accepted by many other scholars on the continent, except for some of the Breton historians who refused to accept his authority.[6]

Ussher strongly supported the theory of Britain and stubbornly resisted attempts to question it.[7] Camden, one of the most respected Scottish historians of his time, also claimed that St Patrick came from Britain and that he was born in Scotland on the banks of the River Clyde.[8] The ancient claims of Brittany had been silenced at least for a time. Minds became closed to the possibility of any alternative to Britain. The documents suggesting that St Patrick was taken captive from Brittany were rejected. A conservative approach dominated the study of St Patrick for the next two hundred years. Then suddenly, in the second half of the nineteenth century, an Irish scholar decided it was time to let the genie out of the bottle. The established view that St Patrick was born in Britain was seriously challenged for the first time since Probus by Irish scholar Dr John Lanigan, in his magnificent *Ecclesiastical History of Ireland* published in 1823.[9]

Lanigan was convinced that St Patrick came from north-west Gaul. He presented as much evidence as he could to support the view that a region on the continent was known as 'Britain' even before the time of St Patrick. Lanigan argued that it was named after a local Celtic tribe, the Brittanni. According to Lanigan, most of the ancient writers had misunderstood and misrepresented the meaning of this name when they assumed that St Patrick had come from the island of Britain.

O'Hanlon publically acknowledged the significance of Dr Lanigan's research.[10] He agreed that some of the evidence clearly suggested that St Patrick had been a native of Gaul but this did not prevent him holding fast to the traditional theory of Britain.

Lanigan claimed to have identified Bannavem Tiburniae with 'Bononia Tarvannae' or 'Tarabannae', now Boulogne-sur-Mer, in France. This stretched etymological evidence beyond acceptable limits.

He failed to provide the conclusive evidence required to convince sceptics. But his theory attracted some very interesting converts. Thomas Moore (1779–1852) a well-known Irish entertainer, poet and singer-songwriter, best known for his lyrics of 'The Minstrel Boy' and 'The Last Rose of Summer', became one of his first disciples. Moore was a man of many talents. Extensive literary achievements included a *The History of Ireland* in which he said that Dr Lanigan had shown clearly that Bannavem Tiburniae was in Armoric Gaul, being the same town as Boulogne-sur-Mer, in Piccardy.[11] Moore's comments are worth recalling. Having given the claims of Scotland thoughtful consideration, he strongly disputed them.

Respecting [St Patrick's] birthplace, there has been much difference of opinion – the prevailing notion being that he was born in Al Cluit, now Dumbarton, in North Britain. It is only, however, by a very forced and false construction of some of the evidence on the subject that any part of Great Britain can be assigned as the birthplace of St Patrick.

His [St Patrick's] own *Confession* proves him to be a native of old Gallican, or rather Armoric Britain. The country anciently known by this name comprised the whole of the northwest coasts of Gaul.[12]

As far as John Colgan was concerned, the ghosts of France had been laid to rest in 1647. Dr Lanigan's research had brought them back to life for a while but there was not much discussion of St Patrick's origins during the next forty years.[13] This was not surprising as the Land of Saints and Scholars found herself being dragged by the devil to the doorsteps of hell. In 1845 Ireland was plunged into Famine, also referred to as The Great Hunger. One and a half million Irish died during the country's worst period of illness and starvation from 1842–1846.[14]

The number who died was matched by those forced to emigrate either to save lives or find work. Many of those who secured a passage to America and Canada on the so-called 'coffin ships' never reached their intended destination, dying from infection due to the crowded and unhealthy conditions on board or from the fatal sickness which emerged after they landed. As if things weren't bad enough, the old demons of sectarianism were growing fatter on both sides of the Irish Sea in the continuing conflict between British imperialism and Ireland's struggle for independence. Some of these began prowling around Patrician Studies, waiting to pounce.

In 1864, less than twenty years after the greatest sufferings of the Famine, J. H. Todd published a major study of St Patrick. This quickly turned into a catalyst for controversy which exploded into accusations of heresy and sectarianism with verbal attacks that became public and personal. Todd (1805–1869) was a member of faculty at Trinity College, Dublin and President of the Royal Irish Academy. His book *St Patrick, Apostle of Ireland* is credited with being one of the first real biographies of St Patrick.[15] Todd became a lightning rod for controversy when he claimed there was no historical evidence to support the traditional view that St Patrick was sent to Ireland by the Pope as part of any official mission of the Catholic Church.

This view aroused anger and resentment in many quarters. Todd was accused of holding historical bias as a Protestant and being anti-Catholic as a writer but his book was influential, causing others to respond. He must have known the sensitive nature of his subject. Having warned his readers that he was going to reject the established tradition that St Patrick was commissioned by Pope Celestine, he said that he hoped none would 'suppose him to have been influenced by any controversial prejudice in coming to that conclusion'.[16] We are too far from the action to know whether Todd was being truly humble, sensitive and sincere or had part of his tongue in his cheek when stating these things. Perhaps there is an element of truth in both. Binchy reflects the atmosphere of the times when he said:

> There is a nationalism in religious matters which can be as strong an emotional force as political nationalism and which reacts just as vehemently against any attempt by historians to query its foundations.[17]

Todd was a disciplined, structural thinker and an excellent scholar. In relation to uncertainties surrounding Patrick's place of origins he was aware of conflicting claims in the earliest sources and refused to commit to any particular theory. As a historian, he tried to remain faithful to the maxim that all we can know for certain about Patrick is the information given in St Patrick's own writings and he acknowledged the difficulties which exist because of those writings. Most scholars accepted Muirchú's account that St Patrick came from Britain but Todd had studied the manuscripts thoroughly enough to know that some of the ancient authors recorded that St Patrick had been taken captive in Brittany. He allowed for this possibility when he said, 'If this story be true, "Bonavem Taburniae" where St Patrick was taken captive, must have been in Armoric Britain'.[18] Todd was familiar with Lanigan's idea that St Patrick was born in France but thought it was 'contrary to all ancient traditions on the subject'.

Like others, Todd became disenchanted with the quest to identify geographical locations. He decided the subject was not worth pursuing further saying, 'The question does not seem of sufficient importance to the object of this work to be allowed to occupy much space.' Dr Lanigan was not alone in supporting the case for France but this was a sensitive and controversial subject and it was only a matter of time before Scottish historians would decide enough was enough.[19] In 1872, when J. H. Tukner began a presentation to the Royal Society of Scottish Antiquaries in Edinburgh the case for Britain was so firmly established he exclaimed with great confidence:

> The unanimous tradition of Christendom represents the apostle of Ireland [Patrick] as having been born amongst the Britons of Strathclyde or Clydesdale, southwest Scotland.[20]

Even though fifty years had passed since Dr Lanigan's theory was first published, it was clearly still a cause of concern for the Scots, who had always claimed St Patrick as one of their own. Tukner had been invited by the Royal Society to put matters right and exorcise the Scottish historical record of Dr

Lanigan's ghost. They chose their knight well. Tukner was also a structural thinker, trying to move towards a scientific method of scholarly inquiry. He began his presentation to the Royal Society of Scottish Antiquarians by saying:

> The question of St Patrick's origins should only be approached with the calm and unbiased temper appropriate to the investigation of scientific problems. It is only by such a method, by casting aside all spirit of partisanship that we can hope to arrive at the determination of the truth and to see the results of enquiries acknowledged and embraced by others.[21]

Lanigan's theory had clearly upset some British historians who held strongly to the established tradition. Tukner was determined to bring the full weight of his intelligence and expertise to refute the claims of Brittany in the strongest possible terms. After delivering what appeared to be a masterful analysis of the evidence and assuming the Royal Society would endorse his conclusions, Tukner almost gloated in the possibility that he had solved 'the problem' of St Patrick's birthplace, which he certainly had not. Having begun the evening by saying a spirit of goodwill and genuine historical inquiry should never be lost in the face of nationalist sympathies and sectarian bias, he launched into a bitter personal attack, accusing Lanigan of 'one of the most deliberate attempts ever made to set aside the voice of tradition'.

Then Tukner attempted to destroy Dr Lanigan's academic reputation with remarks that were both condescending and racist when he referred to him as that 'mere Irish scholar'. This remark was deplorable from a personal and academic point of view, especially in the aftermath of the Irish Famine.

From an ecumenical perspective the evening went from bad to worse. Tukner said Lanigan had attempted 'to deprive north Britain of the glorious St Patrick, of whose apostolic labours and the success which crowned them she has long been proud'.

Then he drove his warhorse deeper into the mire when he accused Dr Lanigan of 'hagiocleptsy' (saint stealing) and said Lanigan's theory was an attempt to 'undermine the true position of north Britain and Scotland in the history of the Christian Church'. The French hypothesis was obviously still causing quite a stir forty years after John Lanigan's book had been published. Nationalism was running high in Scotland in 1872.

Dr Lanigan was an excellent scholar who had done more than enough to win his own spurs. His thesis had not been built on thin air. His research was magnificent in its originality and detail. Much of what he said can be more fully appreciated now, having stood the test of time. Lanigan was unable to supply the final piece of really conclusive local evidence which is still required to copper-fasten the case for France. If he had been aware of claims and local traditions recorded by the early Breton historians perhaps things would have been different. But Lanigan held fast to his own theory of Boulogne-sur-Mer, which is about three hundred and fifty kilometers to the north of St Malo.[22]

Switching to more conciliatory remarks, Tukner identified two key issues which had to be resolved if the continental hypothesis could be taken seriously. Firstly, he said it had to be shown that Bonavem or Bannavem Tiburniae could be identified at a specific location on the continent with evidence that could not be applied equally to Strathclyde or Wales or any other place in Britain. Secondly, he suggested that more evidence was required before it could be accepted that 'Britanniis' or 'Britannia' applied to a region in north-west Gaul at the time of St Patrick, with sufficient historical evidence to support the view that Patrick may have been referring to a place on the continent when he used this name in his writings.

Tukner's sharp and brilliant mind had cut through to the heart of the Patrician problem. These two issues still form the essential historical criteria by which any theory concerning St Patrick's place of origins will be judged. In Tukner's view, Dr Lanigan had failed on both accounts.[23]

After presenting what he considered to be enough evidence to confirm St Patrick's birth in Scotland, Tukner loosened his grip on Dr Lanigan's throat and admitted, 'That St Patrick's family was connected with Armorica, that it may even have been Armorican in its origin, is not impossible.' Tukner was satisfied with his own defence of Strathclyde as the place where St Patrick was born but he expressed grave doubts about the geographical location of Bannavem Tiburniae. He was not the first and would not be the last to admit feelings of frustration bordering on despondency when he said:

> I despair of being able to localise with certainty either Bannau [the Bonnavem Tiburniae of St Patrick's *Confession* or Tiburnia, the Taburnia or Taburne of the other lives.[24]

Having summoned the courage to accept this, he speaks as a true Scotsman in claiming that wherever it was it must have been somewhere in Scotland. And he concluded his 'Inquiry into the Birthplace of St Patrick' by agreeing with Dr Wylie and others whose view now forms part of the Scottish historical record.[25]

> The most probable site for Bonaven of St Patrick is the confluence of the River Aven or Avon with the main stream of the Clyde, near where the present town of Hamilton stands. A more exact correspondence of locality with the name as it has been transmitted to us could not be desired.

As far as Tukner and the Royal Society of Scottish Antiquaries were concerned, the matter was now closed. St Patrick had been born in Scotland and the family estate at Bannavem Tiburniae, from which St Patrick was taken captive, was also located there. It was more a case of slamming the stable door after the horse had bolted.

If only the jigsaw puzzle was that simple! One of the greatest errors in Tukner's presentation was his misunderstanding and misrepresentation of the evidence with regard to Probus. Basing his case on false etymology, Tukner argued that Probus was being geographically consistent because the Province of Neustria was simply another name for the region of Strathclyde. This gives an example of the extent to which Tukner was prepared to tailor the evidence to support his own theory. This is a temptation we all have to resist in any study of St Patrick. At the same time, Tukner was right when he said that Dr Lanigan had not provided sufficient evidence to prove a case. However, both Tucker and Dr Lanigan contributed greatly and we must honour them for that.

Todd's controversial statement about the Pope inspired a religious Sister Frances Clare (Mary Cusack) to undertake her own private investigations. In 1877, she published a very attractive *Life of St Patrick*. Cusack's study can best be admired for its detailed analysis of the original sources. Unlike some writers she was determined not to accept the established view without investigating the evidence herself.

Sr Mary said the quest to resolve St Patrick's place of origins depended on three things. Firstly, the meaning of the name 'Britanniis' since Patrick had said this was his homeland. Secondly, the location of Bannavem Tiburniae and thirdly the meaning and location of Nemthur, a name which is not found in St Patrick's writings but forms part of an ancient tradition where it is recorded as his birthplace. Unlike Todd, she stubbornly refused to shrink from the demands of further inquiry, saying the questions which surround Patrick's origins were of 'considerable interest'. She agreed with Lanigan that names which appear in the ancient sources for Britain and Brittany are very similar and could easily have been confused. In her opinion, Lanigan had provided enough evidence to show that when Patrick used the name 'Britanniis' he must have been referring to a region on the continent. In her desire to restrict this to Boulogne, by following Dr Lanigan's theory enthusiastically, she went too far in dissociating this region from the place we now call Brittany.[26]

A magnificent contribution to the study of St Patrick was made in the closing decades of the nineteenth century by another Irish Scholar. Dr Whitley Stokes supported the traditional view that St Patrick came from Britain but he knew the subject was fraught with historical uncertainties and remained cautious. Stokes had detached himself from sectarian controversies and focused his energies more positively elsewhere, by translating the early manuscripts collected by Colgan. In 1887, he published a Rolls Edition of the *Tripartite Life of Saint Patrick* for Her Majesty's Stationary Office in Dublin. This book is an essential resource for the study of St Patrick. Stokes is the perfect example of a brilliant scholar who wrestled deeply with the conflicting sources and tried to form a sensible opinion about St Patrick, based on the evidence.

The complexity of this subject has left many writers bewildered and often deeply torn between the conflicting demands of historical analysis and the claims of established tradition. Stokes accepted that St Patrick was probably born at Nemthor, which in his opinion may have been the old name for Strathclyde. He knew that Bannavem Tiburniae, the place from which St Patrick had been taken captive, had never been securely identified. He decided that it was '*probably somewhere on the Western Sea coast (Armorica) of North Britain*'.[27]

Stokes was aware of several references to Armorica in the ancient sources, all clearly referring to a coastal region in northwest Gaul which had been given that name by the Romans. Instead, he drew on a dubious and misguided etymological interpretation of 'Ar-mor-ica' (by-the-sea) to support the view that Bannavem Tiburniae must have been located near Strathclyde. To have suggested in this case that Armorica referred to a coastal region of northern Britain was inexcusable.[28] Despite his geographical errors, Stokes was clear about how little we can know for certain about St Patrick. He laid the historical foundations for St Patrick's biography when he said:

> All the facts that can be stated with certainty about St Patrick are these: He was born in the latter half of the fourth century and was reared a Christian. He had relations (*parentes*) 'in the Britains' and he calls these 'Britains' his *patria* (fatherland or homeland). Patrick's father lived at a place called *Bannavem Tiburniae* near which he had a small farm, and there in his sixteenth year Patrick was taken captive.[29]

*Summary*

The ancient Lives of St Patrick were compiled over a period of a thousand years from the seventh to the seventeenth century. They contain many stories and traditions about St Patrick some of which may be authentic, having been based on earlier written sources or passed down faithfully through several generations in an oral tradition until eventually written down by the scribes.

In the nineteenth century, John Lanigan looked at the evidence in these secondary sources and realised St Patrick's origins were closely associated with a place on the continent in north-west Gaul. His thesis was supported by some writers but he was unable to convince the majority because he had failed to supply conclusive local evidence. The key issue is that most historians refused to accept that Armorica had been called 'Britain' at the time of St Patrick. As a result of these uncertainties, Dr Lanigan's theory would soon be forgotten and the accepted theory that St Patrick came from Britain became even more firmly established.

As we entered the twentieth century and the era of modern scholarship, a hope remained that experts would apply their wisdom and academic expertise to this complex subject and resolve some of the uncertainties. Ireland deserved to know the truth about St Patrick and why the origins of Irish Christianity have been shrouded in so much legend and controversy. Any such hopes would quickly be dashed. Scholars of the nineteenth century have been criticised for not having the same standards of scholarship as more recent authors but in relation to discussions about St Patrick's origins things went down hill rapidly after Whitley Stokes. Despite a huge renaissance in Patrician scholarship, the consensus of academic opinion would cling firmly to the established tradition. Patrick's 'French Connection' would continue to be discounted by the vast majority of writers.

Throughout the twentieth century and especially today there is a strong consensus among scholars that St Patrick came from Britain. Before we can progress further we must consider their positions and examine the strength of the evidence on which the established theory of Britain is based.

---

*Notes*

1. John O'Hanlon, *Lives of the Irish Saints* (Dublin, 1875), p. 399.

2. John Colgan, *Trias Thaumaturga*, ed. Eamonn De Burca (Dublin, 1977), ch. 2, p. 221. It is clear from this passage that Colgan located Nemthor and Bannavem Tiburniae in Scotland. Translation by John Luce.

3. *Probus vero non satis peritus rerum Patricianarum & locorum probatur.* See Appendix V, 'On the Homeland and Family of St Patrick', in John Colgan, *Trias Thau.*, p. 220.

4. See Bernadette Cunningham, *The Annals of the Four Masters: Irish history, kingship and society in the early seventeenth century* (Dublin, 2010), p. 167.

5. Even the statement from the Lateran Canons is unclear and open to interpretation. Does it mean that St Patrick was born in Great Britain or just that he was born to parents who were in Great Britain or who had come from Great Britain? *Emphasis added.

6. See Ussher, *Britannicarum Ecclesiarum Antiquitates*, Cap XV11, pp 426, 427.

7. Thomas Moore, *History of Ireland* (New York, 1835), i, pp 203 ff. See also Ussher, James, *A Discourse on the Religion Anciently Professed by the Irish and the British* (London, 1631).

8. Camden, *Britannica* (Abridged, London, 1701), p. 43.

9. John Lanigan, *Ecclesiastical History of Ireland*, 4 vols (Dublin, 1822; 2nd edn, Dublin, 1829), i.

10. O'Hanlon said, 'We are obliged to acknowledge that St Patrick was living with his family in Armorica, at the time of his captivity.' See O'Hanlon, *Lives of the Irish Saints*, iii, p. 486. O'Hanlon died before completing his magnificent study. Twelve volumes were intended, one

for each month of the year, but only the first ten volumes were published, the last posthumously. Thankfully, O'Hanlon's detailed and masterful study of St Patrick had already been completed.

11. Moore, *History of Ireland*, i, p. 203 ff. Moore followed Lanigan when he assigned Boulogne, fourteen miles south of Calais, France, as St Patrick's birth place (in AD 387 CE).

12. This is an example of how some writers tend to follow a particular theory even though conclusive evidence is lacking. Moore's analysis shows there were some historians who felt the Strathclyde tradition was unsafe. Moore, *History of Ireland*, i, p. 210 ff. See also William Sullivan, *Historical Causes and Effects from the Fall of the Roman Empire 476 to the Reformation 1517* (Boston, 1838).

13. Kenney regarded it as a fact that St Patrick was born in Britain but also recognised that the location of Bannavem Tiburniae was uncertain. 'He was born in Britain at a place which has not been identified.' Kenney, *The Sources for the Early History of Ireland: Ecclesiastical* (Dublin, 1997).

14. The 1841 census recorded a population over 8m. The figure for 1851 was 6.5m. *Census Finder* [website] <www.censusfinder.com>

15. J. H. Todd, *St Patrick, Apostle of Ireland* (Dublin, 1864).

16. 'Preface', *St Patrick, Apostle of Ireland*, Todd, p. vi.

17. D. A. Binchy, 'Patrick and his Biographers', *Studia Hibernica*, 2 (1962), p. 17.

18. Todd, *St Patrick, Apostle of Ireland*, p. 356.

19. O'Sullivan Beare suggested that St Patrick was a native of Bretagne or Brittany. See Ludwig Bieler, 'O'Sullevan Bear's Patriciana Decas: a Modern Irish Adaptation', *Journal of the Galway Archaeological and Historical Society*, 22 (1946–1947), pp. 19–33. Hoey accepted Boulogne and suggested Nemthur was 'Holy Tours', H. E. Manning, ed., *Essays on Religion and Literature* (London, 1865), pp. 106–37.

20. J. H. Tukner, 'An Inquiry as to the Birthplace of St Patrick', *Archaeologica Scottica*, v (1890), pp. 261–84.

21. *Ibid.*

22. Lanigan's identification of Nemthur with the tower at Boulogne and the claim that St Patrick's home at Bannavem Tiburniae must have existed on the site of some ancient ruins nearby was not supported by conclusive local evidence. The same applies to Canon Flemming's impressive efforts to support Dr Lanigan's theory. See William Flemming, *Boulogne-sur-Mer* (London, 1907).

23. Lanigan's claim that 'Britanniis' denoted a region on the continent was supported by some impressive historical evidence but not enough to be deemed conclusive by the experts, who remained sceptical.

24. Tukner almost capitulated to Lanigan's hypothesis when he said, 'It could be admitted that Bannavem Tiburniae or Bonavem is Boulogne,' and admitted that St Patrick resided there for some years of his life. Tukner allows for this possibility, but not for the possibility that Patrick was born there.

25. 'Succat or St Patrick was born on the banks of the Clyde ... the present towns of Hamilton and Dumbarton compete for his birthplace – near one of the two he must have seen the light.' Wylie did not concern himself with the French connections. Like others, his choice of material is selective. See J.A. Wylie, *History of the Scottish Nation* (London, 1887), ii, p. 108 ff.

26. Colgan appears to have accepted that the name 'Britain' was applied to part of Belgium and the north-west of Gaul, not only in the time of St Patrick but at a later age. Following Lanigan, Cusack differentiated between this 'Britain' and the region we now call Brittany in France.

27. Whitley Stokes, *Tripartite Life of St Patrick* (London, 1887), i, p. cxxxvii. *Emphasis added.

28. Stokes, *Tripartite Life*, i, p. 29 ff. As noted, it was a prelude to other geographical errors made in relation to the identity of places associated with St Patrick in the secondary sources. This includes 'Armoric Letha', 'Nemthor', the 'Isles of the Tyrrhene Sea' and 'Mount Hernon' or 'Arnon'. The true location of these places will be considered later.

29. Stokes, *Tripartite Life*, i, p. cxxxiii.

# CHAPTER NINE

# Historians and Hagiographers

The 'problem' of St Patrick can still be seen
To bar the very portals of early Irish history.[1]

The meaning of 'Britanniis' holds the key to unlock the truth about the location of St Patrick's homeland. This name is given in the earliest surviving copy of St Patrick's *Confession*, preserved in the *Book of Armagh*. If this is an accurate copy from the autographed original, St Patrick said this is where he came from and it is probably the place to which he returned after escaping from slavery in Ireland, to be reunited with surviving members of his family.

The reason for saying 'if' is because we simply do not know whether the *Book of Armagh* version was copied accurately from the original *Letter* written by Patrick. Words may have been changed by the scribes and perhaps even by those who published the manuscripts. The inclusion of the word 'deacon' as a description of Calpurnius suggests later interpolation, reflecting ecclesiastical influences.

In his *Letter to Coroticus*, Patrick describes his father as a Decurion (*decurione*) which is probably more authentic. Other names may have been changed. The name for St Patrick's homeland is given as 'Britanniis' in the *Book of Armagh* but appears as 'Brittannias' in other copies of St Patrick's *Confession* that have survived. Whichever form may have been used originally, what did this name mean for Patrick? Did it apply to Britain or Brittany or perhaps to both?

If there is any truth in the claim that Patrick came from Brittany, then it has to be shown that the name 'Britanniis' or 'Britannia' applied there around the time St Patrick was born. This is a controversial subject which has never been resolved.

When J. B. Bury's *Life of St Patrick and His Place in History*, was published in 1905 it was also acclaimed by scholars as a genuine biography of St Patrick, reflecting the more stringent discipline of historical inquiry associated with the so-called 'era of modern scholarship'.[2] Bury's expertise was the late Roman period and he was convinced that St Patrick had come from Britain. He claimed that passages from the *Confession* 'prove that St Patrick regarded Britain as his native land and that his family lived there continuously from the time of his captivity till his old age'.[3]

Bury placed far too much trust in Muirchú's authority when he said, 'His biographer in the seventh century writes unhesitatingly that he was of the British nation or native of Britain and born in Britain.' We hear strong echoes from Muirchú when Bury exclaims, 'That Patrick's family were British provincials and lived in Britain there can be no question.'[4] He discounted the evidence for Strathclyde on the basis that it was very unlikely the Romans had settlements that far north at the time of St Patrick. Instead, he suggested that Bannavem Tiburniae was in south-west Britain, in the region of the lower Severn.[5]

Bury was not alone in helping the theory of Britain to become more firmly established in the first decades of the twentieth century. Heinrich Zimmer had published a challenging study of St Patrick in 1902 which held fast to this view, making a statement that cannot be justified from the evidence of St Patrick's own writings:

> According to his [Patrick's] own statement he was born in the British borough of Bannaventa, which must have been somewhere near the modern town of Daventry.[6]

Bury's reputation as a historian had encouraged others to accept it as 'fact' that Patrick came from Britain. In 1905, when N. J. White produced the first critical edition of St Patrick's *Confession*, the established tradition became enshrined in a respected academic translation. Although White remained faithful to the plural form 'Britanniis' as it appears in the *Book of Armagh*, translating this as 'in the Britains', he assumed that it referred exclusively to the island of Britain.[7] Then an academic bombshell dropped through the roof of Trinity College, Dublin.

In March 1942, Thomas O'Rahilly presented a study of St Patrick which shook conservatives and liberals alike.[8] He was convinced that our traditional understanding of Patrick's biography had been created by the fusion or perhaps confusion between the records of two or three different saints, all called Patrick. O'Rahilly suggested that details from the life of Palladius (who had been sent to Ireland by Pope Celestine as part of an official Roman mission in 431 CE)[9] and Patrick (author of the *Confession* and *Letter to Coroticus*) had been woven together to make a composite figure, our traditional St Patrick.[10] Conflicting references in the Irish annals mention several figures called Patrick whose records or legends may have become confused.

According to O'Rahilly, the Patrick we know from Muirchú and the *Book of Armagh* is a contrived figure who exists only in the ecclesiastical 'cyberspace' of seventh-century Irish hagiography. This composite figure is a 'virtual' St Patrick, without historical foundation. If there is any truth in this, then we have good reason to distrust anything Muirchú said about St Patrick, including the statement that he came from Britain.

In relation to St Patrick's origins (the Patrick who wrote the *Confession*, that is) O'Rahilly favoured Britain but like Bury he rejected the evidence for Strathclyde. Instead, he came up with yet another suggestion and conjectured that Bannavem Tiburniae was in south-west England.[11] In so doing, it is ironic that O'Rahilly himself may have confused the real St Patrick with a later namesake, who is closely associated with Glastonbury.

Once the claims of Strathclyde had been rejected, the uncertainties which surround Patrick's biography became more complex. If Scotland had to be discounted, which part of Britain did St Patrick come from? How would scholars react to this latest challenge to the established tradition? R. P. C. Hanson (1916–1988) was Professor of Historical and Contemporary Theology at the University of Manchester, regarded as one of the foremost authorities on St Patrick. He began by warning us that from a historian's perspective there are few things we can know about St Patrick. Hanson then insists that the one thing we can know for certain is that Patrick was born in Britain.[12] He suggests Patrick was probably taken captive somewhere along the west or south-west coast of Britain, from a place accessible to Irish pirates but despaired the precise location could ever be discovered:

> The fact is that we do not know where Bannavem Tiburniae was [located] and short of an archaeological miracle, we probably never shall. But the probability is strongly in favour of locating it in the Lowland Zone of Roman Britain and in the south western part of that zone, in Somerset, or Dorset or Devon.[13]

Hanson's contribution to the study of Patrick was immense. In his final chapter, he provides a moving tribute to St Patrick. In relation to St Patrick's origins, however, following Bury, he may have relied too much on Muirchú. Hanson rejected the possibility that St Patrick's family came from Strathclyde, claiming there was no significant Roman presence north of Hadrian's Wall during St Patrick's lifetime.

The strength of the established tradition shaped the opinions of many writers. When D. A. Binchy joined the fray in 1962 he began his study by saying the quest for reliable historical information about St Patrick was 'like an effort to solve a jigsaw puzzle from which most of the important pieces are missing'.[14] It was the perfect analogy but Binchy appears to have resigned himself to failure even before he began when he decided that 'most of the essential pieces of the Patrick puzzle have been lost and are unlikely to be recovered'.[15]

Binchy was not the first and would not be the last to quit the table in dismay. He thought the ancient Lives of St Patrick were completely untrustworthy and regarded them as worthless for authentic historical information. Historical caution was then thrown to the wind when he exclaimed, 'St Patrick must have been born in Britain.'[16]

According to Binchy, Patrick's birth, family, homeland, ecclesiastical training and spiritual formation were all located in Britain. He claimed that the traditions which linked him to France were all spurious:

> So much is certain [St Patrick] was consecrated bishop in Britain. His mission was financed by members of the British hierarchy.[17]

Binchy believed that when Patrick escaped from Ireland he travelled back to Britain and was supported in his mission to Ireland by the British Church. He says, 'Patrick may never have been in Gaul ... he was consecrated bishop in Britain and his mission to the Irish was organised and financed by certain members of the British hierarchy.'

Unfortunately, like so many others who have wrestled with this subject, Binchy does not provide any real or indisputable historical evidence to support these claims. Nevertheless, this view is now reflected in some of the most respected and authoritative, current academic writings.

T. M. Charles-Edwards, Professor of Celtic at the University of Oxford, who recently published a major study of Early Christian Ireland, also states emphatically that St Patrick's family came from Britain. He says St Patrick belonged to the local nobility of a Romano-British *civitas* and that when Patrick escaped from Ireland he returned to Britain and was trained within the British Church, like his grandfather.[18]

Nora Chadwick, Liam de Paor and Máire de Paor excelled in their studies of St Patrick and like so many others they were convinced that Patrick came from Britain. Chadwick was more sympathetic towards the traditional theory and took the view that Patrick's home at Bannavem Tiburniae was probably Strathclyde or the Solway Firth area.[19] Liam de Paor suggested Birdoswald, which is a short distance west of Carlisle, close to the northern frontier of Roman Britain.

Continued uncertainties and disagreement about the location of Bannavem Tiburniae are, therefore, reflected in the diverse opinions of scholars, while the notion that St Patrick came from Britain is still taken for granted almost unanimously. Máire de Paor said, 'We can be sure of only one thing – Patrick was a native of Britain.'[20]

In fact, the claim that St Patrick's origins can be associated exclusively with the island of Britain became so firmly established during the twentieth century it is not unreasonable to say that it is now taken for granted as a historical 'fact', even though no conclusive evidence has ever been given in support.

Dr Thomas O'Loughlin helped pioneer an innovative graduate programme in Celtic Studies for the University of Wales in Lampeter. He is widely respected as a contemporary authority on Patrick, having published his own detailed and in many ways excellent study.[21]

After giving the statutory warning that we must be extremely wary of claims made in the secondary sources, O'Loughlin says this view can be taken too far and that we must not dismiss the uniqueness of these documents, to assess their true value. At last we have found a modern writer who is willing to keep the door open and admit the ancient Lives of St Patrick might contain some information of value.

O'Loughlin is aware of the difficulties which surround St Patrick's biography but he does not try to examine the evidence for Brittany. When dealing with the geographical place names in St Patrick's *Confession* he warns us to be very sceptical of claims made by Muirchú in the *Book of Armagh*. Muirchú no longer knew where these places were and engaged in 'guesswork'.[22] He repeats the mantra expected from all Patrician scholars, 'The only reliable historical information about St Patrick is that which is contained in St Patrick's own writings,' and he allows for the fact that St Patrick's family home at Bannavem Tiburniae has never been positively identified.

Unfortunately, he then makes certain statements which cannot be justified from the evidence of St Patrick's *Confession*: 'Patrick tells us that he was born in Britain.' 'Patrick tells us that his parents' home was in Britain.'[23] These statements are further compounded by somewhat hasty and unjustified conclusions when the author states categorically that 'all we can say with certainty is that Bannavem Tiburniae was in Britain and that the Wood of Foclut was located in Ireland'.

St Patrick said absolutely no such thing.

The extent to which scholars support the established tradition and have made categorical statements about Patrick's British origins as if this overcomes or short-circuits uncertainties in both the primary and secondary sources is very surprising. Most twentieth century writers have taken this position.[24] This is not a criticism of their otherwise outstanding scholarship, which greatly enhances our understanding of St Patrick and the origins of the early Irish Church. It is simply to make the point that it is not appropriate for academic theologians and historians to claim on the one hand that the only reliable information we have concerning St Patrick is contained in his own writings (where most of the key geographical references have not been identified and are still uncertain) and then on the other to make categorical statements insisting that the one thing we can know for certain is that St Patrick came from Britain. Yet this is exactly how some of the most reputable scholars repeat the traditional view, without providing a shred of reliable historical or geographical evidence to support this view.[25]

Throughout the twentieth century a belief that St Patrick came from Britain appears to have been accepted as an established historical fact. This has shaped the image of St Patrick that is found today in most popular writings, religious publications, heritage magazines, educational resources provided for schools and colleges, and even guidebooks and tourist information services.[26] One of the most accredited text books recommended to Irish students, *A Course in Irish History*, edited by T. W. Moody and F. X. Martin, states that 'He [St Patrick] was a native of Roman Britain' and that some time after his escape from slavery in Ireland, Patrick was 'back in Britain' where 'he was welcomed by relatives as a long lost son'. What we appear to be dealing with here is a conservatism in Patrician scholarship that has crept into the highest eschelons of media and academic publications and which is totally spellbound by the established tradition that St Patrick's homeland and the parental home from which he was taken captive were both located in Britain. This view has been widely promulgated despite the fact that there is no real evidence to support it. This raises the possibility that we have all been misled by the experts and that our traditional image of St Patrick may have been shaped by what the Breton antiquarian M. Charles de Gerville called 'a gross historical error'.

Trying to gather sufficient evidence to present a coherent and convincing argument in the hope of being able to verify the local traditions discovered at Château Bonaban seemed much more daunting in light of the established academic consensus even though the evidence for Brittany appeared to me to be more impressive than anything Britain had to offer. The quest for answers continued, trusting that various clues present in the secondary sources are significant and that there was a real possibility that a local tradition preserved in Brittany could perhaps be vindicated with greater perseverance.

---

*Notes*

1. Dáibhí Ó Cróinín, ed., *A New History of Ireland* (Oxford, 2005), ch. 4.

2. J. B. Bury, *The Life of St Patrick, His Place in History* (London, 1905).

3. Bury, *Life of St Patrick*, p. 290.

4. Bury, *Life of St Patrick*, p. 290, note for p. 16.

5. Bury, *Life of St Patrick*, p. 17.

6. Heinrich Zimmer, *The Celtic Church in Britain and Ireland* (London, 1902), p. 43.

7. See C 23, C 32, C 43 in N. J. White, *Translation of the Latin Writings of St Patrick* (London, 1918); and *The Writings of St Patrick* (London, 1932).

8. Thomas O'Rahilly, *The Two Patricks* (Dublin, 1942; repr. 1981).

9. 'Chronicle of Prosper of Aquitaine', trans. Liam de Paor in *St Patrick's World* (Dublin, 1993), p. 72 ff.

10. O'Rahilly, *Two Patricks*, p. 33. Fragments attached to Tirechán's narrative in the Book of Armagh record that Palladius was also called Patrick. See de Paor, *St Patrick's World*, p. 203.

11. For Patrick's alleged connection with Glastonbury, see William of Malmesbury, *The Antiquities of Glastonbury*, trans. Frank Lomax (Llanerch, 1992).

12. 'It is certain that Patrick was born in Britain.' R. P. C. Hanson, *St Patrick His Origins and Career* (Oxford, 1997), p. 1.

13. Hanson, *St Patrick His Origins and Career*, p. 116.

14. D. A. Binchy, 'Patrick and His Biographers', *Studia Hibernica* No 2, 1962.

15. See Binchy, 'Patrick and His Biographers', p. 27, p. 167.

16. 'We can only be certain of the very few unequivocal facts he tells us about himself in his own writings: that he was born in Britain.' Binchy, 'Patrick and His Biographers', p. 164

17. See Binchy, 'Patrick and His Biographers', pp. 27, 167.

18. St Patrick 'followed his father and his grandfather into a clerical career in Britain'. T. M. Charles-Edwards, *Early Christian Ireland* (Cambridge, 2000), p. 217.

19. Nora Chadwick, *Age of the Saints in the Celtic Church* (Durham, 1960; facs. edn, Llanerch, 2006), p. 18.

20. Máire de Paor, *Patrick: The Pilgrim Apostle of Ireland* (Dublin, 1998), p. 22 ff. Also see Liam de Paor, *St Patrick's World*, p. 88.

21. Thomas O'Loughlin, *Discovering St Patrick* (London, 2005).

22. Thomas O'Loughlin, *St Patrick: the Man and His Works* (London, 1999), p. 20.

23. O'Loughlin, *Discovering St Patrick*, p. 47, n. 12. See also p. 78.

24. This includes most of the well-known Patrician Scholars, including N. J. White, J. B. Bury, R. P. C. Hanson, D. A. Binchy, T. M. Charles-Edwards, David Howlett, Tom O'Loughlin, Dáibhí Ó Cróinín and Ludwig Bieler, alongside many others, who represent a formidable army of converts.

25. Newport White's publication of St Patrick's Writings in 1905, together with Bieler's critical edition have become the standard references to date. In 1911, Dr John Gwynn produced his edition of the *Book of Armagh*, prefaced by a penetrating study of Patrician documents. Gwynn favoured Wales rather than Scotland as Patrick's place of birth and suggested Gwent. John Ryan also supported the view that Patrick was from Britain in his influential book *Irish Monasticism*.

26. See *A Course in Irish History*, ed. T. W. Moody and F. X. Martin (Dublin, 1994).

# CHAPTER TEN

# Britain or Brittany?

Truth has its own gravity
And eventually draws people back.[1]

One single Latin word holds the key to identifying the truth as to where Patrick came from. In the earliest surviving copy of St Patrick's *Confession* in the *Book of Armagh*, Patrick uses 'Britanniis' three times and in two of these references it is given as the name for his homeland. This is still rendered as 'Britain' in the most respected academic translations of St Patrick's writings. Before presenting specific local evidence which supports the case for Brittany, it is important to understand the historical foundations on which the theory of Britain is based.

*The Evidence for Britain*
The evidence put forward in support of the established view can be summarized as follows. Firstly, it is argued that the name given for St Patrick's homeland is the name for Roman Britain. The ancient name for Britain was 'Alba' or 'Albion' but after the invasion by Julius Caesar in 67 BCE, the Romans called it 'Britannia'. Those who are convinced that St Patrick came from Britain, claim that when he used the phrase *in Britanniis* or *in Britannias*, he must have been referring to Britain.

At first sight, this seems very reasonable. The island of Britain was called 'Britannia' by the Romans. However, a complication has to be accounted for. The Latin name given in the *Book of Armagh* appears as 'Britanniis', which is a plural form. Those who hold to the traditional view say there is a simple explanation for this. Britain was divided into several provinces by the Romans, hence St Patrick was describing his homeland as being within these provincial regions.

Britain was subdivided by the Romans, a process which took place over a considerable period of time. It was divided at first by Caracalla in 212–296 CE into two regions, called Britannia Superior (in the south) and Britannia Inferior (in the north). In 296 CE during the reforms of Diocletian, these two provinces were restructured and each was again divided in two. Britannia Superior became Britannia Prima, governed in the west from Cirencester, and Maxima Caesariensis, governed in the east from London. Britannia Inferior became Britannia Secunda governed from York and Flavia Caesariensis governed from Lincoln.

Another Province called Valencia in the far north beyond Hadrian's Wall was added in 369 CE by the Emperor Valentinian, probably including

Dumfries, Galloway and the Scottish borders. The boundaries of Valencia are difficult to determine. Security deteriorated rapidly, almost as soon as this region was established. There may have been a brief period of stability when Maximus led a successful campaign against the Picts and Scotti (Irish) in the years before his rebellion in 383 CE but the existence of a well-established Roman settlement that far north at the time of St Patrick is unlikely.[2]

Secondly, those who support the view that Patrick came from Britain claim that no alternative meaning or translation is possible because the region we now call Brittany in France was not known by the name 'Britanniis' or any similar name in the late fourth century, at the time of St Patrick's birth and teenage years. In other words, if St Patrick used this word for his homeland, he could only have been referring to the island of Britain and not to any region on the continent.

These are the two essential pillars of evidence on which the theory of Britain is based and with which it continues to be justified. They provide support for the established view, which is taken by scholars who accept these arguments as trustworthy. This 'evidence' forms the basis for the most accepted English translations of St Patrick's writings.

On closer examination, both pillars appear to rest on uncertain and potentially unsafe foundations. Let's consider first the Roman name for Britain.

It cannot be doubted that the Romans applied the name 'Britannia' (in a singular form) to the island of Britain but there is less evidence to show that the various regions or sub-divisions were commonly referred to using a plural form. Only two of the five regions incorporated the name 'Britannia' (Britannia Prima and Britannia Secunda). If St Patrick was born in Strathclyde, this was located in Valencia. Roman Britain was part of a very large island. It seems strange that St Patrick would describe his homeland using such a broad and uncertain geographical reference.

St Patrick wrote his *Confession* in Ireland at a time when the Irish were familiar with British geography, especially Wales and the north-west. If St Patrick came from Strathclyde, it is strange that he does not mention this in his *Letter to Coroticus*, who was king of Strathclyde. Patrick obviously knew exactly where to send this letter so that it could be delivered securely.

If St Patrick came from a specific region within Britain and wanted us to know its location, why did he not simply give us the name for that region in which his family lived? The existence of historical uncertainties, especially with regard to the plural form, advises against being hasty in drawing any conclusions.

To regard St Patrick's use of 'Britanniis' as a reference to the island of Britain exclusively would only be appropriate if it can be shown with absolute certainty that no other meaning could possibly be given to this name. Following more detailed research it became clear that the evidence for the established tradition is far from conclusive and there are enough uncertainties to raise questions as to whether it could be in error. When the late John Luce, retired Professor of Classics and former Provost at Trinity College, Dublin, kindly agreed to translate these passages for me he drew attention to the fact that the Latin name 'Britanniis' is in a plural form. He suggested this may not have referred exclusively to the island of Britain.

In Luce's opinion, an alternative translation might be 'amongst the Britons', if St Patrick was describing his homeland in terms of two different geographical regions both associated with the culture and settlements of the ancient Britons. If one of these regions included the place we now call Brittany and this was St Patrick's homeland, then 'in the Britains' could still be an acceptable literal translation, but not if this is taken to refer to the island of Britain, exclusively.

Likewise, if the region we now call Brittany was known to St Patrick as 'Britanniis' or 'Britannia' then an alternative and more authentic modern translation of these names as they appear in St Patrick's *Confession*, would be 'in Brittany'.

It could be argued that this is not being faithful to the original plural form but if it can be shown that St Patrick's homeland was located in this region on the continent, then using the single form Brittany is justified because it gives geographical clarity and an authentic translation for the modern reader.

If there is any truth in the claim that St Patrick came from Brittany, it has to be shown that 'Britanniis' or 'Britannia' were names that may have applied to this region around the time of Patrick's birth, in the closing decades of the fourth century.

### The Evidence for Brittany

A coastal region of north-west Gaul was known to the Romans as 'Armorica'. Scholars are agreed that at some stage, the name 'Britain' was also applied to this region, giving rise to today's Brittany, or Bretagne in French. There is disagreement among historians as to when exactly this name change came into effect.

This is a matter of critical importance for knowing the truth about St Patrick's place of origins. If the name 'Britanniis' was applied to this region at the time of the rebellion of Maximus in 385 CE, then Patrick may have grown up knowing this to be his homeland.

In 1823, when Dr John Lanigan first put forward his thesis that Patrick came from France, he presented evidence to support the view that a region called 'Britain' or 'Britannia' existed on the continent from an early period, even before the time of St Patrick. Lanigan identified various ancient sources which suggested that a tribe called the Brittanni or Pretanni (from which the ancient Britons could trace their ancestry) was located in north-west Gaul. This tribe may have applied their name to the land in local ethnic geography, a situation common amongst the Celts as it is with all indigenous peoples.[3]

Bede says the ancient Britons originated as colonists, having arrived in Britain from Armorica. He also claims that the island of Britain took its name from these Britons. If true, then the existence of a region called 'Britain' in Armorica is not impossible.[4]

One of the earliest and most reliable accounts which appears to refer directly to a region called 'Britain' on the continent can be found in the writings of Sulpitius Severus (363–425 CE). Severus was a native of Aquitania and is best known for his *Chronicle of Sacred History* (published in 403 CE) and a biography of St Martin of Tours, a copy of which is preserved in the *Book of Armagh*. What he writes must be taken seriously because he is a reliable historical witness, contemporary with St Patrick, one of the few sources we have from a person who lived during the closing decades of the fourth century.

Severus describes a church synod at Ariminum which took place in Italy in 359 CE, shortly before the time of Patrick. He provides some fascinating information about local 'ethnic' geography in the following passage, in which the Latin names given for the 'Britons' and/or 'Britain' are open to interpretation:

> More than four hundred western bishops were summoned. For all of these the Emperor had ordered provisions and lodgings to be provided. But that appeared unseemly to the men of our part of the world that is, to the Aquitanians, the Gauls and Britons [*Britanniis*] so that refusing the public supplies they preferred to live at their own expense.
> Three only of those from Britain [Britannia] through want of means of their own, made use of the public bounty, after having refused contributions offered by the rest for they thought it more dutiful to burden the public treasury than individuals.[5]

Severus appears to be referring to two different places both of which were called 'Britain' or associated with the Britons. In the first part of the passage he tells us that men from 'his own part of the world' – namely Aquitanians, Gauls and Britons (*Britanniis*) – refused financial support because they preferred to live at their own expense. On the other hand, three delegates who appear to have represented the Church in Britain (Britannia) having no means of their own, made use of the public funds they had been offered. Severus could be describing two different regions by his use of the names 'Britanniis' and 'Britannia'. The 'Britons' that Severus identified as being from 'his own part of the world', probably came from a region on the continent most likely to have been Armorica. The three who accepted financial support may have been from the island of Britain.

Severus appears to refer to the Armorican Britons in Latin as 'Britanniis'. This is precisely the same name which is used to describe St Patrick's homeland in the earliest surviving copy of St Patrick's *Confession*, preserved in the *Book of Armagh*. Did this name refer to a place, a people or to both? For Severus the name 'Britanniis' reflects a cultural as well as a geographical identity. Just as the Aquitanians are from Aquitania, the Galls are from Gallis so he says the Britons from his part of the world (which is on the continent) are from Britanniis. He uses different words to make this clarification. If this is a correct interpretation then Severus distinguished these Armorican Britons from the Aquitanians and Gauls and perhaps also from those Britons from the island of Britain who availed of the public purse. The geographical distinctions recorded by this author who was writing at the end of the fourth century are very significant as this is the time when St Patrick was born.

Severus gives reliable testimony that in his part of the world various ethnic groups existed in three separate regions. Severus was from Aquitania. The person with whom he converses in his *Dialogues* is a Gaul. It is also significant that he does not refer the coastal peninsular as Armorica, suggesting that this region had been renamed or was known as 'Britanniis' at the time he was writing. If this is correct, then our understanding of local ethnic geography on the continent at the time of St Patrick, in relation to regional divisions of Gaul, will need to be revised.[6]

Severus includes another significant reference to Britain, in relation to the rebellion of Maximus in 385 CE. He speaks as a contemporary witness to these events when he says:

> A faint rumour had spread that Maximus had assumed imperial power in the Britains [*intra Britannias*] and he would in a short time make an incursion into Gaul.[7]

The Latin name given (Britannias) is again in a plural form which leaves open a possibility that it could be a reference to Brittany as well as Britain. This would be the case, for example, if Severus was saying the usurpation of Maximus began and was centred in or launched not only from Britain but also from within Brittany. In other words, Maximus had assumed imperial power in or 'within the Britains' (*intra Britannias*). If so, this allows for the possibility that a coastal region in Armorica was known as 'Britannia' at the time of St Patrick.

Several Breton historians, prolific in their writings between the seventeenth and nineteenth centuries, record that Maximus landed considerable forces at the mouth of the River Rance at the port of Aleth and subdued Gaul and Spain from Brittany whilst his other forces landed near the Rhine before going north to take over the imperial palace at Trier. They are convinced that the name 'Brittany' or 'Bretagne' was introduced at this time.

Severus published his book in 403 CE. He was probably writing it when Patrick was still a teenager, around the time St Patrick was taken captive. The geographical references given by Severus are ethnically and geographically specific and appear to reveal local geographical distinctions within Gaul which are more complex at a regional level than we usually see from maps of the western Empire in the final years before the fall of Rome.

However we may interpret the descriptions given by Severus, what is not disputed by anyone is that by the time of Gregory of Tours, writing in 575 CE, a coastal region of Armorica was called 'Britain' and probably had been for a considerable period of time.[8] Gregory frequently and consistently refers to Brittany using both Latin names 'Brittaniis' and 'Britannia'.[9]

As far as Gregory is concerned, these names are synonymous and it is important to note they are both applied exclusively to Brittany, not to the island of Britain.[10] Those who specialise in local ethnic geography estimate that it takes between one hundred, and one hundred and fifty years at least for new geographical names to become more widely known and established in historical records. This allows for the possibility that the names familiar to Gregory may have been introduced much earlier, perhaps at the time of St Patrick.

When Gregory writes about Brittany he uses the two names given for St Patrick's homeland, which can be found in all surviving copies of St Patrick's *Confession*. He includes specific local geographical references that clearly identify 'Brittaniis' or 'Britannia' as a local region on the north-west coast of Brittany, close to Aleth, Dol and Mont St Michel.

From the description he gives, this 'Britain' existed as an independent region with its own Breton culture and some unusual religious and political customs.[11]

Gregory describes the great slaughter which took place at this time among the Bretons and Saxons. The troops marched out of Brittany (*exercitu a Brittaniis*).[12] The stronger men crossed the River Villaine but those less strong and the camp followers beside them were not able to wade through. They had to stay on the far side of this river.[13]

Gregory applies the name 'Brittaniis' in this case to a very specific local area in the vicinity of the River Villaine, which is close to the region where Château Bonaban is located today. The local French municipality is still called Isles et Villaine.

Gregory also distinguishes Brittany (which he refers to as 'Brittaniis' and 'Britannia') from the Gauls (*Galliis*). Gregory was based in Tours which for him is clearly part of Gaul but for him, 'Britanniis' is a separate, independent region near the coast around St Malo and Dol.

If St Patrick came from Brittany, this passage may help to shed light on a geographical description given by St Patrick, which may also be distinguishing Brittany (Britanniis) from Gaul. In his *Confession*, St Patrick describes how he would love to have the opportunity to make a journey from Ireland to 'Britanniis' to visit his homeland and family, and then to proceed further into 'the Gauls' (*Gallias*) and see his religious friends. He says:

> As a result, even if I would wish to leave them and make a journey *in Britanniis* and I would most dearly love to make that journey so as to see my homeland and family – not only that but also to proceed into the Gauls [*in Gallias*] to visit the brethren and see the face of the saints of my Lord.[14]

The journey Patrick describes would make perfect geographical sense if his homeland was in Brittany. If St Patrick's family were resident in Brittany, the religious friends or 'saints' he longed to see again may have been based at Tours, which was in Gaul.[15]

Severus's description of regional or local ethnic geography allows for this possibility. The same local geographical distinction is evident in the *Life of St Maclovius* or St Malo, an early Irish or Welsh saint who travelled to Brittany and placed himself under a hermit named Aaron, who had established the first monastery on the island adjacent to Aleth where the old walled city of St Malo is now located. A disorder on the island had compelled Malo to leave. After being driven away from his monastery, he is said to have cursed Brittany or the Bretons (Britanniis) and travelled into the Gauls (*Gallias*).[16] This suggests that 'Britanniis' and 'Gallias' were considered as separate but adjacent regions within the area we have traditionally thought of in more general terms, simply as Gaul.

Severus is our most reliable witness, writing at the time of St Patrick's birth, towards the end of the fourth century. In his writings, he uses plural forms when referring to 'the Britains' (*Britanniis*) the Gauls (*Galliis*) and the 'two Spains'. This may be a reflection of divisions that existed within the western Diocese of the Empire at the time of St Patrick, caused by civil wars and local rebellions. Considering these references, it is surprising that so many writers have discounted the possibility that St Patrick may have been referring to Brittany rather than Britain when he used the Latin name 'Britanniis'.

Part of the reason for this is a strong disagreement among scholars as to when the name 'Brittany' or 'Bretagne' was first applied. The transition from the name 'Armorica' to 'Brittany' is a controversial subject riddled with uncertainty, linked to a serious political controversy that relates to the turbulent relationship and historical rivalry between Britain and France.

Dr Christopher Snyder, Head of the Department of History and Politics at Marymount University, says the Breton succession crisis became a permanent part of the continuing struggle between these two great powers and the transition from 'Armorica' to 'Brittany', that is the establishment of the Britons in this region, is a little understood process.[17]

The big political hot potato is whether the British occupied this region as refugees or conquerors. This is a very sensitive political issue, as we shall see, that relates to another matter of crucial importance to the study of St Patrick. Was a settlement of the ancient Britons in Brittany established with its own monarchy, which was therefore independent of the French kings?[18] According to many of the early Breton historians this took place at the time of the rebellion of Maximus in 385 CE.

Gibbon recognised what he calls 'the obscure state of Britain' during the late Roman period and accepted that Brittany's history is riddled with uncertainty and political controversy.[19] He accepts that a coastal region of Armorica eventually acquired the name 'Little Britain'. Gibbon says these lands were filled 'by a strange people who under the authority of their counts and bishops preserved the laws and languages of their ancestors'. What he would not allow for is the possibility that it was called 'Britanniis' at the time of St Patrick.[20]

Gibbon's attitude towards events taking place in Brittany has always been influential but is it trustworthy? Hadrian Valesius, in his *Notia Galliarum*, argued that a region on the continent called 'Britain' had existed from a much earlier date. It was known to Valesius (writing from a continental perspective) as 'Britannia Cismarina', which means a Britain 'on this side of the ocean'.[21]

Gibbon was aware that many Breton historians claimed the government of Armorica was established as a monarchy before declaring its independence from the Roman Empire in 409 CE. He examined the evidence given by various French historians concerning an earlier foundation for this 'Britain' and thought they were wrong. Gibbon refused to accept that any significant migration and settlement of Britons took place in Brittany before the middle of the fifth century, saying 'beyond that era the Britons of Armorica can be found only in romance'.[22]

Gibbon's authority as a historian of the Empire was strong enough to shape prevailing opinion. Naturally, his view was embraced by those who held to the established tradition that St Patrick came from Britain. Unfortunately, Gibbon had no interest in St Patrick. He mentions St Patrick and Ireland only briefly in dismissive racist remarks.[23] He also had a very negative attitude towards the ancient Lives of St Patrick and although he must have been familiar with their writings, his stance towards most of the early Breton historians is equally dismissive.[24]

Gibbon's approach to these matters has influenced our understanding of St Patrick's origins for many years and may be the reason why the intriguing accounts about St Patrick's family which can be found in Breton sources have been neglected. Sharon Turner takes the most conservative view, claiming the coastal region of Armorica was not called Brittany until 513 CE. However, she admits 'the first British colonists of Armorica have been excluded from

European history and wherever they did appear, their history has been wrapped in legend and fable'. As a result, the authentic history of Brittany is unknown.[25]

If Gibbon is right, then local traditions preserved at Château Bonaban and many of the claims recorded about St Patrick by local Breton historians, have to be wrong. Fortunately, Gibbon's attitude towards events taking place in Britain and Brittany in the fourth and fifth centuries did not go unchallenged.

Others took a different view, providing impressive historical evidence to support their claims. Dr Lappenberg (1759–1819) placed the first British settlement in Armorica much earlier, during the rebellion of Maximus in 383 CE. He describes this as a *milites laeti* consisting of British warriors in Armorica, which gave the region a distinct character and new name, Bretagne.[26]

Other scholars from both sides of the Channel and in Ireland also take the view that Brittany became an independent region during the settlement that took place under Maximus and was called 'Britanniis' or 'Britannia' at that time.[27]

Breton historians have addressed this question in great detail, since it concerns their own country, its history and origins. Pierre Toussaint de Saint-Luc's study is meticulous and there is no doubt in his mind that the name for this region changed from 'Armorica' to 'Brittany' or 'Bretagne' at the time of the rebellion of Maximus in 383 CE.

This is a detailed and fascinating historical study, by an author whose essential concern is not St Patrick's place of origins. This makes it all the more remarkable that several Breton historians understand the origins of the name 'Bretagne' as being confirmed from the ancient Lives of St Patrick, published by Colgan, and others which they had read.[28] In a detailed and masterful study of St Patrick published in Dublin in 1875, John O'Hanlon recognised the significance of the settlement under Maximus when he said:

> Several ancient and modern writers have derived the Armoric Britons from the followers of Maximus, who appear to have spread along and ravaged the northern coasts of France, to their remote extremity of Brittany. The Bretons of this province, however, have an obscure history; *but after the time of Maximus, the westernmost corner of Gaul began to be styled Britannia.*[29]

Gildas (516–570 CE) and Nennius (630–688 CE) are two of the earliest sources we have for the history of Britain during this period. They both record that a British colony was established in a coastal region of Brittany at the time of Maximus. Gildas identified the first settlement of Britons in Armorica with Maximus and says this region began to be called 'Britannia' at this time. He claims that when Maximus entered Gaul with the British legions, launching a bid for imperial power in 383 CE, he broke his vows to the Emperor and discarded Roman laws 'whilst keeping the Roman name for Britain'.[30]

When Nennius wrote his *History of the Ancient Britons* in the seventh century, he records that when Maximus withdrew Roman forces from Britain in 383 CE a large number of British troops were settled in Armorica. It is possible that the name 'Britain' may have been applied to this region as part of an official policy introduced by Maximus at this time. Nennius refers to these colonists as 'Armoric Britons' and the region in which these troops and their families were settled is identified in several of the ancient Lives of St Patrick as 'Armoric Letha'.[31]

In 1777, M. Deric published a fascinating *Ecclesiastical History of Brittany*. This includes more detailed local information about this region, especially valuable for our study because it comes from a Breton perspective. He says:

> The lands that Maximus gave to these foreigners were said to be uncultivated. These migrants were called 'Létes' or 'contes' – 'Laeti' in Latin [from Laetus], which described their status and condition [as serfs or half-free colonists] and which was given to 'those Barbarians who were in the service of the [Roman] Empire and who had been granted special military benefits [or favours]'.
>
> They were required to cultivate their new lands, called 'Létiques', and to provide a certain number of recruits for the Roman army. During this period Armorica was also called 'Letavi' or 'regio læta' – land of the Contens' as well as 'Ledaw' or 'Leidaw'.[32]

M. Daru writes in detail about the army of Britons in Armorica at the time of Maximus in 383 CE. He says this changed the whole existence of this region, which he calls 'La Bretagne continentale' (a Britain on the continent) and claims the name 'Little Britain' (La Petite Bretagne) was applied to this region at this time to distinguish it from the island of Britain, which is still called 'Grande Bretagne' in French.[33]

Unlike more recent English-speaking writers who hold fast to the notion that Patrick came from Britain, M. Daru quotes various sources to support his claims and also documents more ancient texts which support the view that Brittany was called 'Britanniis' at the time of Maximus.[34] Dom Morice claims the soldiers of Maximus landed at the mouth of the River Rance at the Roman port of Aleth.[35] From there, they occupied the coastal territories of the Diablintes in a place 'close to the sea' between Aleth, Dol and St Brieucc.[36] These accounts provide significant details which help to clarify the location of the settlement which took place under Maximus, and provide an historical context for the local traditions that have been preserved about St Patrick.

The information given by the early Breton historians is geographically very explicit and points directly to the local area where Château Bonaban is located.

M. Deric provides etymological and local geographical evidence to support his view that a settlement in Brittany under Maximus was based in the coastal region between St Malo, Dol and Mont St Michel, linked to the names of certain local villages, which still exist today.[37]

On the outskirts of Dol-de-Bretagne, we find the local parishes of Baguer Pican, Baguer Morvan and Miniac-Morvan. According to M. Deric, 'Bagner' is a Celtic word which refers to 'a troop' of soldiers, 'Morvan' comes from the Celtic word for great (mor in Gaelic) or sea (mer in French) and 'wan' or 'gan' which derives from a Celtic word for birth. He suggests that the names of these villages refer to 'a troop of soldiers born from (or close to) the great sea'.[38] M. Deric is convinced that these names are unequivocal signs of the existence of the British colony established by Maximus. He quotes the fifth-century Prefect of Gaul, Sidonius Appolinaris when he suggests that the territory covered by the British settlement in Armorica under Maximus was even larger, stretching from the west coast of Brittany to the Loire Valley.[39]

References to this settlement in Brittany also appear in the writings of the twelfth-century British historians, William of Malmesbury and Geoffrey of Monmouth. These accounts are often maligned by those who say both writers were influenced by spurious legends and a form of ethnic British 'imperialism' that created a fictional account of British history in the final century before the fall of Rome. From what we learn through other sources, however, the account they give of the settlement in Brittany, in essence, is historically plausible.[40]

The origins of Brittany or 'proto-Bretagne' are cloaked in uncertainty and political and historical controversy, but from the evidence available from a variety of sources that have been considered so far, it would seem reasonable to take the view that the name 'Britanniis' or 'Britannia' may have applied to Brittany at the time of the rebellion of Maximus in 385 CE. If so, this is most likely to have been St Patrick's homeland and the place from which he was taken captive. If St Patrick's parental home at Bannavem Tiburniae was located in Brittany, then St Patrick's own writings would provide the strongest and most reliable historical evidence of all to confirm that 'Britanniis' is a reference to Brittany and not the island of Britain exclusively.

*Summary*

Detailed consideration has now been given to the controversial historical question as to whether the Latin names 'Britanniis' or 'Britannias' could refer to Britain or Brittany in the context of St Patrick's writings. Although to some extent uncertain because of the lack of historical records, the evidence suggests that either or both of these names could have applied to a region on the continent in the closing decades of the fourth century.

The establishment of a colony in Brittany may have been one of the most significant events in European history at the time of St Patrick, shortly before the fall of the Rome. It can be identified within a coastal area in north-west Brittany, including the Bay area between Aleth, Dol and Mont St Michel.

This region was known to early Irish writers as 'Armoric Letha' or 'Lethania Britannia'. On the basis that the evidence seems to weigh in favour of the existence of a British settlement in Brittany at the time of Magnus Maximus in 385 CE the map below has been designed to show the regional divisions of Britain and the location of this settlement.

Caledonia

Strathclyde

Valencia

Hadrian's Wall

Hibernia

IRELAND

Maxima Cæsarensis

Flavia Cæsarensis

Britannia Secunda

Londinium

ROMAN BRITAIN
Showing the Rebellion
of Magnus Maximus
383 - 388 CE

Britannia Prima

Iccian Sea

British forces land at the Roman port of Aleth at the mouth of the River Rance, establishing a settlement in Brittany known to ancient Irish writers as Armoric Letha

Aleth

Gaul

BRITTANY
(Britanniis)

Tours

If we accept that St Patrick was taken captive from Brittany, this has enormous implications for understanding the original meaning of the name 'Britanniis' in St Patrick's *Confession*. Despite the abundance of evidence that tends to support the case for Brittany, the fact remains that most scholars still hold firmly to the traditional view that St Patrick came from Britain. Could the experts have got it wrong and if so could the misinterpretation or misunderstanding of one single Latin word have completely distorted our image and understanding of the truth about St Patrick for more than a thousand years?

Enough doubt and uncertainty exists to question the integrity of the established tradition. This raises the interesting and controversial question of translation which must be addressed before proceeding further. The Latin phrase *in Britanniis*, which appears in the *Book of Armagh* version of St Patrick's *Confession*, has, until now, always been rendered in English as 'Britain' in most accredited academic translations. This continues to be the case, even in the most recently published versions.[41]

N. J. White and Ludwig Bieler were two of the most influential scholars, acknowledged as experts in this field. Their translations of St Patrick's writings from Latin to English have helped to shape established opinions about St Patrick's origins.

Bieler dedicated most of his life to the study of St Patrick; he was an expert Latinist and one of the foremost authorities on the subject. Bieler's translation of St Patrick's *Confession* has rightly been praised and currently forms the accepted standard for academic research. It is based on a comparative study of the original manuscripts and a meticulous consideration of the process of textual transmission.

After studying and comparing the most ancient manuscripts, White and Bieler were both convinced that St Patrick came from Britain and they were also convinced the Latin name 'Britanniis' refers exclusively to the island of Britain in the context of St Patrick's writings. If they are right, then everything discovered so far in relation to Brittany must be false. This presents the greatest challenge of all to surmount.

Ludwig Bieler is one of the most respected scholars in the field of Patrician Studies. Without reference to his works this inquiry might never have been completed. If the local tradition discovered at Château Bonaban is to have any lasting credibility, before further progress can be made it is essential to come to terms with Bieler's expertise and analysis.

Having come so far in this quest and despite the size of this scholarly giant, there is no alternative but to try and climb onto his shoulders if we are going be able to see the truth about St Patrick's story from a different perspective.

---

*Notes*

1. Dan Brown, *The Lost Symbol* (New York, 2009), p. 61.

2. Charles Thomas, *Christianity in Roman Britain to AD 500* (Berkeley and Los Angeles,1981), p. 197.

3. Lanigan suggested this 'continental' Britain was centred around Boulogne but he admitted that it was impossible to ascertain how far this region may have extended either to the north or south. See John Lanigan, *Ecclesiastical History of Ireland*, 4 vols (Dublin, 1822; 2nd edn, Dublin, 1829) pp. 103–7.

4. Bede said, 'The original inhabitants of the island were the Britons, from whom it takes its name, and who, according to tradition, crossed into Britain from Armorica'. Bede, *History of the English Church and People*, trans. Leo Sherley-Price, Penguin (USA, 1980).

5. *Sed id nostris, id est Aquitanis, Gallis ac Britannis, indecens visum; repudiatis fiscalibus propriis cum sumptibus vivere maluerunt. Tres tantum ex Britannia inopia proprii publico usi sunt, cum oblatam a ceteris collationem respuissent, sanctius putantes fiscum gravare quam singulos:* Sulpitius Severus, 'Sacred History' in *The Nicene and Post Nicene Fathers*, xi, eds Philip Schaff and Henry Wace (New York, 1894), p. 116, xli.

6. See William Flemming, *Boulogne-sur-Mer* (London, 1907), p. 20.

7. *Iam tum rumor incesserat clemens, Maximum intra Britannias sumpsisse imperium ac brevi in Gallias erupturum.* Sulpitius Severus, 'Sacred History', xlix.

8. Gregory of Tours (539–594 CE) is one of our earliest witnesses for events in Gaul, although he was more closely associated with the diocesan church in Tours than with rural, religious groups in Brittany. See Gregory of Tours, *History of the Franks*, trans. Lewis Thorpe (London, 1974).

9. Gregory says, 'the following events occurred in Brittany' (*in Brittaniis haec acta sunt*). Again, 'At this time a Breton called Winnoch, who practised extreme abstinence, made his way from Brittany to Tours (*tunc Winnocus Britto in summa abstinentia a Brittaniis venit Toronus*) … he wore no clothes except sheep skins from which the wool had been removed.' Gregory of Tours, *History of the Franks*, p. 287.

10. Gregory describes how Macliavus, a count of Brittany (*Comte Britannorum*) gathered a band of Britons (*a Britannia viris*). *Macliavus quondam et Bodicus Brittanorum comites sacramentum … Cui tandem misertus Deus, collectis secum a Brittania viris.* Gregory of Tours, *History of the Franks*, v. 16.

11. Gregory describes how the Bretons (*Britanniis*) made incursions towards Rennes, which is south of St Malo. The local Breton queen had influence over Bayeux, which is to the north of Mont St Michel. This region was clearly struggling to retain its independence. The Bretons had their own unique dress and hair style, called the 'Breton rite'… 'When [Queen] Fredegund learned this expedition was being led by Beppolen, whom she had hated for many a long year, she ordered the Saxons settled in Bayeux to cut their hair according to the Breton rite and to dress in the Breton fashion (*ritum Brittanorum tonsos atque cultu vestimenti conpositos*) and then to march in support of Warroch.' Gregory, *History of the Franks*, p. 556.

12. Gregory, *History of the Franks*, p. 558.

13. 'They came to the River Villaine, crossed it and reached the River Oust.' (*Interea venerunt ad Vicinoniam amnem, quo transmissi, ad Uldam fluvium pervenerunt*) Gregory, *History of the Franks*, p. 556.

14. *Pergens in Britannias et libentissime paratus eram, quasi ad patriam et parentes; non id solum, sed eram usque Gallias vistare fraters, et ut viderum faciem sanctorum Domini mei.* (C 43) Note: *patriam* means homeland or fatherland and *parentes* in Latin refers not to parents but members of St Patrick's extended family.

15. Lanigan understood that at the time of St Patrick, Brittany was distinct from Gaul and not part of it. Lanigan, *Ecc. History*, p. 118.

16. *Maledictis Britannis in Gallias abut.* St Maclovius, Maclaw or Malo (490-565 CE) is remembered as one of the founders of the monastery at Aleth. St Malo is named after him.

17. Dr C. Snyder, 'The Medieval Celtic Fringe', *The ORB: Online Encyclopedia Book for Medieval Studies* [website] <http://www.the-orb.net/encyclop/early/origins/rom_celt/celtic.html> pubd online 2 June 2003.

18. See Richard Woods, *The Spirituality of the Celtic Saints* (New York, 2000), ch. 6.

19. 'The youth of the island (of Britain) crowded to (Maximus's) standard; he invaded Gaul with a fleet and an army, long afterwards remembered as the emigration of a considerable part of the British nation'. Gibbon, *Decline and Fall of the Roman Empire*, 8 vols (London, 1862, iii, p. 360.

20. Gibbon held strongly to a particular view, following the well-known French historian, Lobineau, who claimed 'Brittany' or 'Bretagne' was not introduced until about 458 CE. Gibbon was even more cautious, insisting this name was not established until after the arrival of Britons who fled to the continent, following defeat by the Anglo Saxons in 550 CE. Gibbon, *DFRE*, iv, p. 130 ff. See G. A. Lobineau, *Histoire de Bretagne*, 2 vols (Paris, 1707), i.

21. Hadrian Valesius, *Notia Galliarum*, pp 98–100.

22. See Gibbon, *DFRE*, iv, p. 391, n. 136.

23. 'The meanest subjects of the Roman Empire assumed the illustrious name of Patricius, which by the conversion of Ireland has been communicated to a whole nation.' Gibbon, *DFRE*, iv, p. 300, n. 26.

24. Dean Milner appreciated this when he noted that according to the opinions of French authors Daru and Deric, the government of Armorica was established as a monarchy from the period of its independence from Rome, which Gibbon dates to 409 CE. Milner appears to be one of the few authors to mention alternative accounts recorded by Breton historians, that the monarchy and name change came into effect at the time of the usurpation of Maximus. See Gibbon, *DFRE*, iv, p. 131, n. (a) added by Milner.

25. Sharon Turner, *The History of the Anglo-Saxons* (London, 1852), p. 179.

26. Johann Martin Lappenberg, *A History of England under the Anglo-Saxon Kings*, i, trans. Benjamin Thorpe (London, 1865), p. 59 ff. These soldiers are described as *milites limitanei*, *laeti*, hence the designation 'Letha'. See *Geschichte von England*, i, p. 56. Lappenberg expressed surprise that in relation to this controversial question, Gibbon rejected the authority of French authors he had followed and trusted elsewhere. See editorial notes by W. Smith in Gibbon, *DFRE*, iv, p. 391–2.

27. Commenting on C 43 in which St Patrick says he would have longed to visit his native country 'Britanniis' and afterwards proceed into the Gauls, Tukner says, 'It is most important to observe that he [Patrick] speaks of the Britains *Britannise* not *Britannia*. Had he used the singular, it might be supposed that he meant Brittany in Gaul; but those who wish to make out that he was born in the latter country must show that *Britannise* can here mean anything else than the island of Britain, or that the plural appellative was commonly applied to Brittany of Gaul.' Tukner's argument implies acceptance of the fact that Brittany could have been known as *Britannia* (at least in the singular form) at the time of St Patrick.

28. *Les plus ancient auteurs, qui ont écrit la vie de S. Patrice, prouvent qu'il y avoit des Bretons dans l'Armorique depuis l'an 383 jusqu'a après 389. On ne doit pas neanmoins conclude de la, que se pays eut alors absolutement perdu sont ancient nom d'Armorique pour prendre commencement celui de Bretagne.* See Pierre Toussaint de Saint-Luc, 'Histoire de Conan' in *Dissertation Historique sur L'Origins des Bretons*, i (Paris, 1739), p. xxxiv, p. 6.

29. John O'Hanlon, *Lives of the Irish Saints* (Dublin, 1875), ii, p. 447. See notes 164–8. *Emphasis added.

30. See 'The Works of Gildas' in *Six Old English Chronicles*, ed. J. A. Giles (London, 1868), p. 307.

31. Breton historians identify the region of 'Armoirc Letha' described by Nennius as between Mont St Michel, Nantes and le Cap Finistere, lands which stretched from the coast to the Loire River. Daru identifies Nennius's 'Mon Jovis' or 'Mon Jupiter' with Mont St Michel, Cantguic with Nantes (Cantiguine) and 'Cruc Occident' with Le Cap Finistere. See P. A. Daru, *Histoire de Bretagne* (Paris, 1826), i, p. 51. Deric quotes Sidonius Appolinaris (Lib 1 Ep 7) to confirm it stretched from the coast to the Loire River. Gilles Deric, *Histoire Ecclésiastique de Bretagne*, (Paris, 1778), ii, p. 135.

32. Deric, *Histoire Ecclésiastique de Bretagne*, p. 136 ff. Deric claims L'Abbe Gallet had provided proof that many Britons passed into Gaul under Maximus and never returned to the island of Britain.

33. Daru, *Histoire de Bretagne*, i, p. 18.

34. (i)*Armorica in Gallia ad oceanum provincial, incoepit Britannia appelari, nomine accepto a Britannis quorum Legiones duce ex insula Britannica, rebellante Maximo, in irrpterunt, ducc Conano Britanno insulari.* Laccary, *De Colonis in Gallias ab Exterior Ductis*, ch. 24, for the year 382 CE; (ii) *Maximus Armoricanum regum, quod postea minor Britannia dicebator, petivit...vocavit igitur Maximus Conanum et dedit ili Armoircanum regum, et minorem britanniam jussit appelari.* Matthew of Westminister (entry for the years 390, 391, 392); (iii) *Maximus in Gallias transit, partem Galliae sibib subolitam Brotonibus tradidit, unde usque ad hancdiem minor Britannia appelatur.* In Sigebert's Chronicle, for the year 385. Daru, *Histoire de Bretagne*, p. 54.

35. *L'embouchure de la riviere de Rence*, see P. H. Morice, *Histoire de Bretagne*, 2 vols (Paris, 1742–6), p. 6. *Maxime et son allie passerent la mer et virent debarquer a l'emboucher de la Rance.* See Daru, *Histoire de Bretagne*, p. 44. Lobineau rejected the notion of a settlement in Brittany at the time of Maximus. See G. A. Lobineau, *Histoire de Bretagne*, 2 vols (Paris, 1707), i, p. 6.

36. See Deric, *Histoire Ecclésiastique de Bretagne*, p. 123, 124 and P. H. Morice, *Memoires Pour Server de Preuves a l'Histoire de Bretagne*, 3 vols (Paris, 1742–6), p. 8.

37. Deric gives a very specific location for this region of the *Letes* or soldiers who formed part of the settlement under Maximus: *cependant les Troupes Bretons, en penplant une partie du Pagus Dol, and quelques portions de celui Aleth.* See Deric, *Histoire Ecclésiastique de Bretagne*, p. 147. He records that the centre of administration was at Dol: *Le chef Lieu de cette Colonie étoit Dol.* Deric, *Histoire Ecclésiastique de Bretagne*, p. 133.

38. Bagner: *troupe*; Morvan: *morl merl sea*; *wanl ganl ne* (birth or beginning): *Troupe que est nee dans un lieu environment de la mer:* 'a colony of soldiers born (or established) near the sea'. Deric, *Histoire Ecclésiastique de Bretagne*, p. 132, notes (a) and (b).

39. See Deric, *Histoire Ecclésiastique de Bretagne*, p. 135 n. (a).

40. Breton historians describe various stages of migration of the ancient Britons to Armorica. The first was in 284 CE under the Emperor Constantine Chlorus. Deric suggests this is when the *Letes* were first established in Armorica. The next was in 364 CE, a date which he thinks marked the beginning of an independent Brittany.

41. See Pádraig McCarthy, trans., *My Name is Patrick: St Patrick's Confessio*, (Dublin, 2011).

# CHAPTER ELEVEN

# *Misquoting Saint Patrick*

A single word, misunderstood, can rewrite history.[1]

Ludwig Bieler came to Dublin in December 1939 at the outbreak of the Second World War. He remained in Ireland and dedicated the rest of his life to the study of St Patrick. Bieler's critical analysis of the ancient manuscripts and translations of St Patrick's writings into English, building on those presented by N. J. White in 1905, are viewed as the most reliable scholarly editions available.[2] Bieler once said, perhaps prophetically, 'In Patrician Studies no question is ever finally settled or at rest.'

Like most twentieth-century scholars, however, he was convinced that St Patrick came from Britain as if this particular matter was no longer in dispute. Bieler states categorically that St Patrick 'was a fifth-century Latin writer, born in Roman Britain, trained for ecclesiastical office in Gaul'.[3] Having advised his readers that 'the search for St Patrick's birthplace is quite hopeless,' he suggests:

> Patrick must have been born in that part of Britain which was Romanised – probably in the south-west, which lay open to Irish raids. Among the numerous identifications that have been attempted, Ravenglass in Cumberland would be most acceptable from a geographical and historical point of view.[4]

Bieler was convinced that Bannavem Tiburniae was not the place St Patrick was born, nor the primary home from which his father worked. Instead, he thought it was a second home which, from the description given, sounds like the Roman equivalent of a holiday home or country residence, close to the sea. This is stretching the evidence beyond acceptable limits. St Patrick tells us that there were several male and female servants in his father's house who were killed when it was attacked by pirates. If so, it must have been quite a substantial residence.

> The city where Calpurnius was a magistrate must have been situated in that part of Britain in which Roman civilisation had got a firm foothold. It is probably there Patrick was born but the name of that place is unknown. *When Patrick was captured by Irish pirates he was apparently spending a holiday at the family's country seat … the place must have been near the Irish Sea.*[5]

I had turned towards Ludwig Bieler hoping to gain insight from his knowledge of the original texts, to see if there was any linguistic evidence to support the case for Brittany. Bieler was more familiar with these documents and the process by which manuscripts were transmitted than any other scholar. His expertise would hopefully shed light on the original meaning of the Latin names given for St Patrick's homeland.

In the various manuscripts which survived, place names are often spelled differently. Scholars refer to these as 'variant readings'. In the earliest surviving copy of St Patrick's *Confession* in the *Book of Armagh*, for example, the name given for St Patrick's homeland is 'Britanniis'. This name is mentioned three times and the spelling is always the same.[6] In six other extant copies of St Patrick's *Confession* other spellings include 'Brittanniis', 'Brictanniis' and 'Brittannia'.[7] Presumably, when he wrote his original letter, St Patrick used only one form of spelling.

The key question is, which country or region was he referring to? To find different spellings for a place name is not unusual or surprising, although the variations are surprisingly low.

Scribes sometimes made mistakes in copying and may have introduced alternative forms as geography and place names changed in society. Texts were edited at times with deliberate changes or additions, called interpolations. It is a miracle that certain place names associated with St Patrick's origins were preserved through the centuries in a clearly recognisable form.

Without the expertise and discipline of the scribes who faithfully copied these names, we would have been left completely in the dark.

Through a critical examination and comparison of all the existing manuscripts, Bieler attempted to identify what he calls *Theta*, the original text or archetype of St Patrick's *Confession*, from which all later copies developed. In terms of Patrician Studies this can loosely be compared to the scientific discovery of a genetic code or DNA on which all human development is based and the quest to identify the place from which the human species originated. Scientists claim DNA contains 'indisputable memory', which is a reliable record of human genetic inheritance and development. Could any such 'indisputable memory' about St Patrick's place of origins have found its way into the genesis of manuscripts?

Bieler never claims absolute precision when trying to identify the archetype of St Patrick's *Confession* from which later copies were 'cloned' but he was prepared to offer some tentative conclusions. He was confident that the text of the *Confession* could be identified, as this would have existed around 630 CE. This is two hundred years before the earliest surviving text in the *Book of Armagh*, which was copied by the scribe Ferdomnach in 807 CE.[8]

Bieler speculates that a file containing copies of Patrick's writings (and perhaps the autographed original of St Patrick's *Confession*) may have been kept in the library at Armagh or perhaps in Saul, County Down in 'the Barn' where St Patrick built his first church in Ireland. He suggests that the archetype *Theta* is 'nothing more or less than a publication of these files'.[9]

In relation to the name given for St Patrick's homeland, there are two predominant alternative spellings in the earliest manuscripts, including 'Britanniis' and 'Brittannia'. Bieler regarded 'Britanniis' as the original or preferred reading in the *Book of Armagh*, where it always appears in a plural form but he was convinced that 'Brittannia' (singular) was the archetype from which other forms of spelling originated.[10] This means that in Bieler's opinion the name 'Brittannia' is most likely to have been the word used by St Patrick in his original letter (as this existed in 630 CE) and 'Brittanniis' or 'Britanniis' was presumably a secondary or later development.[11] Bieler does not provide any historical or geographical evidence to support his opinion.

In his study, Bieler does provide a commentary. This was the most obvious place to discuss (however briefly) any controversial matters, but he does not address the issue. For example, there is only one place in the commentary where he mentions *in Britanniis*, in the context of C32. The translation he gives is: 'I was not present, nor was I in Britain, nor did I take the initiative (that is, to come to his own defence).'[12] This inevitably raises the controversial question of translation. We expect academic translations to be based on reliable historical and geographical evidence, especially in relation to place names and geographical references.[13]

When N. J. White published the first critical edition of St Patrick's *Confession*, together with an English translation in 1905, there was a strong consensus of opinion that St Patrick came from Britain. White translated *in Britanniis* as 'in Britain'. Some scholars remained cautious in translation, rendering this phrase as 'in the Britains'. This is a more accurate literal translation because it keeps the plural form. It retains and maintains at least some degree of uncertainty which characterises the original phrase and therefore allows for the possibility that the 'Britain' referred to by Patrick may not have been the island of Britain exclusively.

Retaining the plural form keeps open a possibility that the name may have referred to Brittany. Translating this phrase as 'in Britain' in a singular form immediately restricts and potentially changes the original meaning. White's text formed the basis for Bieler's translation of St Patrick's *Confession*, in which 'Britanniis' is again translated as 'in Britain' eradicating the plural form of the original. As a result, this name is taken to refer to the island of Britain exclusively.

Such decisions have had serious historical and geographical implications in relation to our understanding of the location of St Patrick's homeland. In fact, the translation (or possible mistranslation) of this one single Latin word has probably shaped our image and understanding of St Patrick's origins, more than any other name in the whole corpus of Patrician literature. The examination of factors that may have led to the creation of the established translation end in a chicken-and-egg situation: Which came first? The historians who argued that the names 'Britanniis' and 'Brittannia' could only have referred to Britain or the decision of pre-eminent Latin scholars that there could be no other form of translation? It is impossible to separate the two.

This shows how influential translations (and translators) can be, especially the accredited ones. As soon as the claim that St Patrick came from Britain was accepted by most reputable scholars, it became enshrined in translation and was thereby given greater credibility. Inevitably, it created the impression for readers that St Patrick's place of origins in Britain was a fact when the complex and uncertain nature of the available historical evidence suggests it was not. Bieler does not provide supporting evidence or reasoning – either for his suggestion that 'Brittannia' is the archetype or for his decision that *in Britanniis* should be translated as 'in Britain'. This inevitably leaves his position open to criticism and raises serious questions.

Could Bieler's analysis and translation of these names have been influenced in any way by his conviction that St Patrick had come from Britain and that all the places connected to his homeland were located in Britain? Did Bieler opt for 'Brittannia' as the original archetype because it was closest to the accepted name for Roman Britain and therefore seemed to him to be most authentic and appropriate? If so, is it possible that he failed to appreciate the deeper significance of the plural form 'Britanniis' which appears so consistently in the earliest surviving copy of Patrick's *Confession* in the *Book of Armagh*?

Bieler's suggestion that 'Brittannia' rather than 'Britanniis' is the archetype (the original word used in St Patrick's *Confession*) implies that the scribes in Armagh were not so well informed as other copyists. This implication is improbable. The name 'Britanniis' (in a plural form) is unusual; the scribes in Armagh were probably being faithful to the text they had received and the Armagh scriptorium reveals its fidelity in this instance by retaining this name despite the opportunities they had to change the spelling. Even Muirchú chose to retain it as one of the names he used to create his 'map'. Perhaps a change from 'Britanniis' to 'Brittannia' reflected a later secondary development?

David Parris, a specialist in Old French at Trinity College, Dublin, has shown that the name 'Bretagne' in French is derived from the singular Latin name 'Britannia' according to recognised laws of language change when Latin names become established in French. However, the plural form 'Britanniis' may have been used by St Patrick in his *Confession* as the name for his homeland in Brittany, designating a place that was established during the time of the rebellion of Maximus in 383 CE. This region is perhaps being described by St Patrick as 'in the Britains', or 'amongst the Britains' and it carried the Roman name for Britain although it was on the continent and had to be distinguished from the island of Britain. At the same time, David Parris's comments might point to the truth that Brittany was originally called 'Britannia' at the time of the settlement under Maximus, as the writings of Sulpitius Severus and Gregory of Tours and the Chronicle of Fredegar all seem to suggest.

Serious historical uncertainty characterises the late fourth and fifth century. Taking into account the information gathered from various sources and the evidence of St Patrick's own writings, this tends to suggest that Patrick may have come from a particular coastal region in Brittany, which was known as 'Britanniis' or 'Britannia' to continental writers such as Sulpitius Severus and Gregory of Tours.

These are the same names which are given for St Patrick's homeland in surviving manuscripts of St Patrick's *Confession*, which is surely more than a coincidence.[14] The uncertain nature of the conflicting but intriguing accounts in the secondary sources should not have allowed such definitive decisions to have been taken with regard to translation. Those who were convinced that St Patrick came from Britain should have remained open to the possibility of error and focused their attention to the existing uncertainties, until such time as sufficient evidence was found to resolve matters. An abundance of references that can be found in the later secondary sources, together with claims widely recorded in the nineteenth century by Breton historians that link St Patrick and his family very closely to Brittany deserved to be taken more seriously. Greater respect and consideration should also have been given to the challenging hypothesis presented by Dr Lanigan, the claims made by Probus in his *Life of St Patrick*, and the references to Armoric Letha as the place where St Patrick was taken captive found in the Colgan's *Fourth Life* and the notes of the Scholiast to *St Fiacc's Hymn*, all of which have been neglected in more recent Patrician scholarship as if 'the problem' of St Patrick had ceased to exist.

Despite uncertainties, Bieler held fast to the traditional view which located St Patrick's homeland in Britain. Armorica is not even considered as a possibility.[15]

In his recent study of biblical manuscripts called *Misquoting Jesus*, Bart Ehrman wrestled with the question of preferred readings when old manuscripts have to be translated and he concluded that 'the reading that best explains all the others is more likely to be the original'.[16] When we apply this to St Patrick's place of origins, it does not really matter whether 'Britanniis' or 'Brittannia' is the preferred reading or even the archetype, if it is accepted that both names could have referred to Brittany at the time of St Patrick.

We may never know for certain which of these two names St Patrick may have used. Only the discovery of an autographed original of St Patrick's *Confession* would clarify that. The plural form suggests a reference to two separate regions that were linked not only by name, but through a shared political, geographical and ethnic identity.

In the writings of Sulpitius Severus and Gregory of Tours it appears that both were applied to Brittany, although in relation to a specific coastal region of north-west Armorica these two authors emphasise the name 'Britanniis'. This suggests that perhaps the *Book of Armagh* copy of St Patrick's *Confession* may have preserved the original name that was used by St Patrick. This leaves no alternative but to ask whether there has been a fundamental error with regard to the established tradition concerning St Patrick's origins. Have scholars been misquoting St Patrick by misunderstanding the meaning of these original words, in the same way Errman suggests we have misquoted Jesus? If there has been a fundamental misunderstanding of the meaning of these Latin names for St Patrick, could there have also been an equally serious error in accepted translations?

If St Patrick's homeland was in a coastal region of Brittany, or even if this is a reasonable historical possibility, there can no longer be any justifiable reason for translating the phrase *in Britanniis* as if it refers to the island of Britain exclusively.

Before considering further detailed local evidence to support a radical new proposal that St Patrick's homeland was in Brittany and that Bannavem Tiburniae, the place where he was taken captive, was also located there, we must show that this view is not incompatible with anything St Patrick said in his own writings.

The easiest and most obvious way to do this is by experimenting with a revised translation of the three passages in St Patrick's *Confession* where this name appears. If a revised translation still makes sense in the context of Patrick's own writings, this will provide a strong foundation from which to consider more detailed evidence from Brittany. St Patrick tells us that after escaping from slavery in Ireland he was eventually reunited with his family *in Britanniis*.

In the following revised translation we will render this phrase as Brittany to see if this still makes sense. Although Brittany is a name in singular form, unlike the plural of the original, it has been included for greater simplicity and clarification. An authentic literal translation in English would be 'in the Britains' only if it is made clear this name included a reference to the coastal region of north-west Brittany.

The first occasion when the name 'Britanniis' appears is when it is given as a description for St Patrick's homeland in *Confession* 23. A revised translation would read as follows:

> After many years (of captivity?), I was in Brittany again with my family who received me like a son and sincerely begged of me that at least now, after all the many troubles I had endured I should not leave them to go anywhere else.[17]

This makes perfect geographical sense, if Brittany was St Patrick's homeland. The second time it appears is when Patrick describes how sad he felt after some personal confidence he had shared with a close friend had been betrayed. A meeting had been held to discuss this matter and Patrick explains that he was not present at the meeting (which probably took place in neighbouring Gaul) nor was he *in Britanniis* and he disclaims any responsibility for asking his friend to stand up for him in his absence. A revised translation could be:

> I feel very sad to talk about one of my closest friends, with whom I had trusted the secrets of my soul … I found out from some of the brethren at the gathering that was held about me – I was not present at it nor was I in Brittany nor did it originate from me, that he would stand up for me in my absence.[18]

This also makes sense, if St Patrick was familiar with Brittany as his homeland and the tribunal or 'gathering' that was held about him had taken place in Brittany or a nearby region.

The third and final occasion this name appears is when St Patrick describes how he might have wished to leave Ireland for a time because he longed to visit his family and return to his homeland *in Britanniis* and then proceed to visit his religious friends and associates in Gaul (*Gallias*). He felt he could not do this because it would detract from his mission. A revised translation would be:

> As a result, even if I would wish to leave them and make a journey to Brittany – and I would most dearly love to make that journey so as to see my homeland and family – not only that but also to proceed further into the Gauls to visit the brethren and see the faces of the saints of my Lord.[19]

This also makes perfect sense if St Patrick's homeland and remaining family were in Brittany and the religious colleagues he longed to see were based at the community of St Martin of Tours, located nearby in Gaul.

If a region called 'Britanniis' existed on the continent at the time of St Patrick on the north-west coast of Armorica and it was distinguished in local ethnic geography from neighbouring Gaul, then nothing St Patrick has described or said in his writings would be incompatible with what has been suggested above as a revised authentic translation of these three passages. If this is accepted, then for the sake of historical integrity, established translations will need to be revised.

After St Patrick's death, the precise geographical location of most of the key place names in St Patrick's *Confession* became confused or lost to historical memory. Uncertainties about St Patrick haunted the scribes and hagiographers for more than a thousand years. Muirchú, the Scholiast, Probus and even Jocelyn were all concerned about these uncertainties. So were the early Breton historians, and several other eminent scholars on all sides of the Irish Sea. Each of them tried in their own way to clarify matters. The uncertainties have continued to haunt us, even today.

Nothing Bieler said gave reason to abandon the quest or discount a possibility that St Patrick was taken captive from Brittany and that St Patrick may have understood this place to be his homeland. The more the scales continue to tilt towards Brittany, the more obvious it seems that a local tradition preserved by Breton historians and made available to guests at Château Bonaban could be authentic and reflect the most trustworthy record concerning St Patrick.

---

*Notes*

1. Dan Brown, *The Lost Symbol* (New York, 2009), p. 195.

2. Ludwig Bieler, *Clavis Patricii II: Libri Epistolarum Sancti Patricii Episcopi* (Dublin, 1993).

3. Bieler, 'Preface', *Libri*, p. 1.

4. Bieler clearly recognised that the place where St Patrick was born and the place from which he was taken captive were not necessarily the same. He followed Bury by taking the view that when St Patrick escaped from Ireland the ship took him to Gaul.

5. Ludwig Bieler, *The Life and Legend of St Patrick* (Dublin, 1949), p. 52. *Emphasis added.

6. Bieler identified *in Britanniis* as the preferred reading in all three passages where this name occurs. In other words, in his opinion, 'Britanniis' is the original name given for Patrick's homeland in this manuscript. C 23, C 32, C 43.

7. Bieler documents all the different spellings which can be found for these words in the various copies of St Patrick's *Confession* which have survived, including 'Britannis', 'Brictanniis', 'Brittanniis' and 'Brittania', etc. See Bieler, *Libri*, p. 70, 71. He uses 'Brittanniis' in his Latin text.

8. Bieler says, 'In reconstructing [*Theta*] we have regained two hundred years or more of textual history and gone back from the time of Ferdomnach to a period that precedes the great Armagh movement of the seventh century, or, at the latest, coincides with its beginnings.' Bieler, *Libri*, p. 29.

9. Bieler, *Libri*, p. 28.

10. Bieler classifies 'Brittannia' as part of what he identifies as the 'indirect tradition', which is preserved in Muirchú, Vita II, III and IV, the *Tripartite Life* and Colgan's Vita V, written by Probus. See C 23, 'Brittannia' in Bieler, *Libri*, p. 70, n. 4; also p. 23: 'The Indirect Tradition' and p. 27: 'the archetype' (*Theta*).

11. Bieler notes that 'Britanniis' occurs in the *Book of Armagh*, which was written in Ireland. He gives a slightly different form, 'Brittanniis', as his preferred reading. The difference in spelling in this case is minimal. See Bieler, *Libri*, p. 70, C 23. Other forms of spelling are found in copies of St Patrick's *Confession* which are continental or English. See Bieler, *Libri*, p. 11.

12. See Bieler, *Libri*, p. 159. David Parris, a specialist in Old French at Trinity College, Dublin, regards 'Bretagne' as being derived from the singular Latin name 'Britannia' according to recognised laws of language change when Latin names become established in French.

13. This is true of most academic as well as more popular translations of Patrick's *Confession* and other related documents. White retained the plural form for *in Britanniis* in his Latin text but was also convinced St Patrick came from Britain and this may have influenced his translation. Daniel Conneely and the Maynooth scholars who edited and published Conneely's work posthumously, remained faithful to the original plural form both in the original and in their translation, 'in the Britains'. See Daniel Conneely, *The Letters of St Patrick* (Maynooth, 1993).

14. The copy of St Patrick's *Confession* which has survived in the *Book of Armagh*, despite political, ecclesiastical and hagiographical influences, might therefore be one of the earliest authentic records with regard to geographical location of St Patrick's homeland and the original name used by St Patrick.

15. Binchy suggests Bieler was being too respectful of established traditions when he said, 'a tradition may be accepted as true if there is no reason to the contrary'. See Bieler, *Life and Legend*, p. 26; D. A. Binchy, 'Patrick and his Biographers', *Studia Hibernica*, 2 (1962), p. 18.

16. Bart D. Errman, *Misquoting Jesus: The Story Behind Who Changed the Bible and Why* (New York, 2005).

17. *Et iterum post paucos annos in Britanniis eram cum parentibus meis.* See Bieler, *Libri*, p. 70, C 23.

18. *Et comperi ab aliquantis fratribus ante defensionem illam (quod ego non interfui nec in Britanniis eram nec a me oriebatur ut et ille in mea absentia pulsaret pro me.* See Bieler, *Libri*, p. 75, C 32.

19. *Pergens in Brittanniis et libentissime paratus eram quasi ad patriam et parentes; non id solum, sed etiam usque ad Gallias uisitare frates, et ut uiderem faciem sanctorum Domini mei.* Bieler, *Libri*, p. 82, C 43. *Patriam* means homeland or fatherland and *parentes* in Latin refers not to parents but rather members of St Patrick's extended family.

# CHAPTER TWELVE

# The Forgotten City

History is an amazing presence.
It's the place where vanished time gathers.[1]

At the time of St Patrick's birth, Aleth was the most important defensive port on the north-west coast of Brittany, between Brest and Cotentin.[2] It was used by the Romans to patrol the Iccian Sea, an old name for the wide, open stretch of water south of what is now the English Channel between Ireland, Land's End in Cornwall and Brittany.[3] Following the rebellion of Maximus, it became an important regional centre for political and military administration. St Patrick's father, Calpurnius, could easily have been employed here as a Decurion, providing a cavalry of ten men and horses for the Roman army.

The *Notitia Dignitatum* (an official record of Roman military bases) mentions that there was a Roman Prefect (*Praefectus Militum Martensium*), at Aleth, under the command of the Duke of the Armorican Tract (*Dux Tractus Armoricani et Nervicani*). Aleth, therefore, provided the location for a Roman *taburnia* or military camp for the Legion of Mars. Historians are agreed that this reflects the position at the end of the fourth century, which is about the time St Patrick was born. In fact, there were very substantial Roman naval military facilities at Aleth.[4]

Unlike the various locations in Britain that have been suggested as the place where St Patrick may have lived and been taken captive, the historical and archaeological evidence to support the case for Aleth is substantial. Significant remains from the late Roman period have been discovered. A network of ancient local Gallo-Roman roads has been identified and mapped by local archaeologists.[5] The name 'Aleth' itself provides an obvious connection with the region called 'Armoric Letha', which is frequently associated with St Patrick in many of the ancient sources as being the place from which St Patrick was taken captive. If Patrick was taken captive from Armoric Letha (also known as 'Lethania Britannia') then St Patrick's parental home at Bannavem Tiburniae must have existed somewhere in the region of the ancient city of Aleth. According to local Breton historians, it was a very strategic site at the time of the settlement under Magnus Maximus in 383 CE and they record that St Patrick's father, Calpurnius, inherited lands there at the time of the rebellion.

The site of the ancient city can be visited in St Servan, a suburb of St Malo.[6] The Roman port at Aleth was eight hundred metres south of the island on which the old walled city of St Malo is now located. It is still called l*a cité d'Alet* and *le fort de la cité* or 'fortress of the city'. The original Gallo-Roman settlement is located on an impressive rocky promontory within an area of about fourteen hectares. In its prime, it dominated the mouth of the River Rance and formed a peninsula which until about ten years ago was joined to the mainland by a narrow sandy isthmus which once carried a Roman road.[7] Archaeological excavations undertaken in 1973 found extensive remains from the late Roman period, dated to 385–400 CE.[8] This includes the foundations of a tower or lighthouse dated to 390 CE, at the base of the existing Solidor Tower, which was built at the end of the fourteenth century.[9] A Roman lighthouse supervised maritime traffic and access to the military base at Aleth.[10] It was a prominent feature in the local landscape at the time of St Patrick.

Archaeologists have also documented the remains of a military fort, the perimeter of which is estimated to be about one hundred and eighty metres. There were ramparts girding the ancient city, controlled by eight turns or entries. The remains of other port installations include two or possibly three basins for the safe harbouring and repair of ships next to a naval fortress or *castellum*. These facilities were adjacent to the Roman tower. French author René Henry has published an excellent recent study which includes several maps, detailing the facilities which existed during the late Roman period, shortly before the fall of the Empire and barbarian invasions of Gaul.

The significance of these local studies in relation to uncertainties which have surrounded Patrick's biography cannot be underestimated. No such archaeological evidence has ever been provided to support the case for locating Bannavem Tiburniae in Britain.

René Henry's research is not intentionally focused on the origins of St Patrick but it provides all the documentary evidence needed to strongly support the claims of the region surrounding Aleth to be identified as the place where St Patrick was taken captive. This includes maps relating to the ancient local roads in the late Roman period, geographical and geological analysis of the area, including coastlines and the ancient river courses as these existed at the time of St Patrick and also remains of the ancient forests, which will be considered in greater detail shortly, as these have considerable potential significance in relation to the possible location of the Wood of Foclut.[11]

Aleth was an important centre for political administration as well as a military base for the Roman navy. The fact that there was a Roman military fortress or *tiburnia* at Aleth is important. It probably helps to explain why Patrick links the words *Bannavem* and *Tiburniae*. At the time of St Patrick, a tributary of the River Rance flowed directly from its 'mouth' at Aleth to its 'foot' at Bonaban. This supports the integrity of local traditions which claim that the estate owned by St Patrick's family was located on or close to the present site of Château Bonaban. This would not have been far from the Roman port and military base. The château is located on an escarpment which is a very ancient site. Substantial remains from the prehistoric and Roman periods have been discovered in the local area.[12]

A network of modern roads has led to the disappearance of some former navigation channels and it is no longer possible to travel directly from Château Bonaban to Aleth by boat but the old main road towards St Malo is still called *La Rue d'Aleth*.

The significance of Aleth and Letha for understanding many of the geographical references preserved in the ancient documents related to St Patrick should not be underestimated. These are important pieces in the geographical and historical jigsaw puzzle which can help identify the location of not only those places which are mentioned in St Patrick's *Confession* but others associated with St Patrick in the secondary sources which have never been clearly identified.

The region in which Aleth was located was known to early Irish writers as 'Armoric Letha' or 'Lethania Britannia'. In the ancient sources, it is identified as the place where Patrick was taken captive. If so, then St Patrick's parental home at Bannavem Tiburniae must have existed somewhere in the region of the ancient fortified city of Aleth, which provided a military base for the legion of Mars.

According to local Breton historians, it was a very strategic site at the time of the settlement under Magnus Maximus in 383 CE. They record that after Maximus launched a rebellion against the incumbent Emperors Gratian and Valentinian, a settlement of the ancient Britons was established in Brittany. According to Breton historians, Conan was placed in charge of this settlement and appointed as Duke of the Armorican Frontier as well as being crowned as the first king of the Bretons in 383 CE. Writing in 1864, L'Abbé Lecarlatte records that as part of this new settlement in Brittany, Maximus settled a large military force in this coastal region between the city of Aleth as far north as Mons Jou (Mont Dol or perhaps Mont St Michel). The troops were placed under Conan's command. These military posts are remembered in the names of certain local villages including Bagar Pican, Bagur-le-Petit, Bagor Morvan and Miniac Morvan (near Dol), all names that derive from the troops of 'Bagaude' who were stationed there at the time of Maximus.

What is especially intriguing about various accounts recorded by the early Breton historians is that St Patrick's father, Calpurnius, and other members of the family are named as being directly involved with the establishment of this settlement as founding members of the Breton aristocracy. Breton historians record that Conan and St Patrick's father, Calpurnius, were cousins and that both were related to an important royal lineage that originated from Albanie

(Scotland). According to these accounts, following the death of his first wife Ursula in tragic circumstances, Conan married St Patrick's sister, Darerca, as his second wife. Dom Morice records that it was as a direct result of this marriage that St Patrick's father, Calpurnius, inherited lands in the territory of the Diablintes, close to the sea, adjacent to the ancient city of Aleth.

The Diablintes were a Celtic tribe that once occupied the coastal region between Aleth (St Malo), Dol and Mont St Michel. This is precisely the region in which Château Bonaban is located, providing yet one more of the missing pieces of the jig saw puzzle that must be gathered so that more of the truth about St Patrick's place of origins can be revealed.

In a *Historical Essay concerning the Monuments of Dol,* L'Abbé Lecarlatte includes more detailed information about the new colony that was established in Brittany, recording that Conan gave Calpurnius (his new father-in-law) direct responsibility for the government of Aleth.[13] He records that a large troop of Roman soldiers under the direct command of Calpurnius was stationed on a tract of land or plain in the vicinity of Cancale (Cancaven) that was called *Bonnaban* or *Bonnaven Taburnie,* 'the plain of tents'. He identifies this as 'Bonnaban' which is clearly a reference to Bonaban.[14]

L'Abbé Lacarlatte was writing in 1864, twenty years after M. Charles de Gerville had published his own research, which identified the ancient site where Château Bonaban is now located, in the cantons of Letha, near Aleth, as being the place from which St Patrick was taken captive. M. de Gerville's work was published by the *Journal of British Archaeological Association in London* in 1849.[15] He claims that St Patrick was born in the ancient diocese of Dol (in Brittany) and he says this can be identified with a small parish in the bishopric of Dol, between Cancale and St Malo, in the Canton of Châtauneuf. His purpose in writing was to correct the established view (that Bannavem Tiburniae existed in Scotland) which he considered to be 'a gross historical error'.

Other references can be found in the *Lives of the Saints of Brittany* that identify Aleth and the coastal region between St Malo, Cancale and Dol as the place where Calpurnius owned lands and served as a Decurion or governor after being appointed by Conan to this position.

M. Charles de Gerville provides specific local geographical information when he describes how Irish pirates made an attack on Cancale and 'Bonnaban', near the Roman port at Aleth. During this attack Calpurnius was killed and St Patrick was taken captive, together with many of the servants who worked at the Calpurnius estate. This is clearly a reference to the site where Château Bonaban is now located. M. de Garaby insists that St Patrick was born in Brittany and he includes some intriguing information about St Patrick as one of the saints of Brittany, together with St Patrick's sisters, Darerca, Lupite and D'Agris or Tigris.[16]

In some of the manuscripts published by Colgan at Louvain in 1647, it is stated that St Patrick was born at Nemthor. This place has never been securely identified, although it is often associated with Dumbarton and the Rock of Clyde. Ancient writers understood 'Nemthor' to mean a lofty rock or perhaps a lighthouse or 'heavenly tower'. There is no evidence to suggest the existence of a Roman lighthouse or tower at Strathclyde, but excavations at Aleth confirm the existence of a tower during the late Roman period. On that basis, 'Nemthor' could have some association with this tower as plausibly as any other. If so, it would add further weight to the evidence that links St Patrick to this particular local coastal area in Brittany.[17]

A strong case can also be made that 'Nemthor' may be a reference to 'Holy Tours'. If St Patrick was initiated into the religious life at St Martin's monastery, this might explain the origin of the tradition that he was 'born' there. Similarly, if St Patrick's mother, Conchessa, was closely related to St Martin of Tours, as many of the ancient sources claim, then it is reasonable to consider the possibility that Patrick may have been born at Tours. Conchessa may have gone there to be close to her relatives on her uncle's side of the family, especially if the political and military situation in Brittany was insecure or unsafe around the time she was expecting to give birth.

It is very difficult, if not impossible, to know the true meaning and geographical location of Nemthor, but the evidence available suggests that it is more likely to have been a reference to a place in Brittany or at Tours, rather than somewhere in Britain. The location of St Patrick's birthplace will be explored more fully in due course.

If the established tradition which locates St Patrick's place of origins in Britain is in error with regard to the meaning of the Latin name 'Britanniis' and the true location of Bannavem Tiburniae, could it also be mistaken with regard to other geographical references given by St Patrick in his writings?

At the end of the fourth century, the elevated ground on which Château Bonaban is now located was close to the coastline as it existed at that time and would have been vulnerable to any attack from the sea.

A local tradition preserved in Brittany claims that St Patrick was taken captive from his father's estate at Bonaban (Bonabes de Tiberio) which existed on or close to the present site of Château Bonaban. It describes in detail how Irish pirates landed on the coast at nearby Cancale and proceeded to make their way up through a local forest before attacking the estate owned by Calpurnius. The forest through which the pirates launched their attack is named locally as the Forest of Quokelunde, 'La Forêt de Quokelunde', also spelled 'Coquelunde' or 'Cokelunde'.

The description given of this attack is very place-specific and concurs with local geography. This raises another intriguing possibility. Could this Forest of

Quokelunde perhaps be identified with the Wood of Foclut mentioned by St Patrick in his *Confession*? The names 'Quokelunde' and 'Foclud' appear to be similar. St Patrick remembered this wood in the context of a dream, when he heard the 'Voice of the Irish' calling him to return to Ireland as an apostle. If the local traditions have proved trustworthy in relation to the location of Bannavem Tiburniae, could it also be possible that the Wood of Foclut was also located in Brittany?

---

*Notes*

1. John O'Donohue, *Anam Cara: Spiritual Wisdom from the Celtic World* (Great Britain, 1997).

2. John O'Hanlon, *Lives of the Irish Saints* (Dublin, 1875), p. 509; and O'Brien's Irish Dictionary, at *DEAS*.

3. The Iccian Sea is mentioned in several ancient records, including the Irish Annals, where it appears in Gaelic as *Muir N'Icht*. This name comes from the Roman port of Iccius, known as *Portus Itius*, now Boulogne-sur-Mer in France. See Extracts from Cormac's Glossary in Whitley Stokes, *Tripartite Life of St Patrick* (London, 1887), p. 571. The Iccian Sea formed part of the Western Sea or 'Mare Occidentale'. Today, the French call it La Manche.

4. For an excellent record of the Roman fortifications and the strategic significance of this military port see 'Alet et Les Curiosolites' in *Bulletin Archaeologique*, Ass. Bretonne, S. Brieuc, 1849, p. 39 ff.

5. Gilles Manet, *De L'etat Ancien et De L'etat Actuel dans La Baie de Mont Saint Michel* (St Malo, 1829); For maps of the local, Gallo-Roman roads, ancient river courses, forests and remains of the Roman port at Aleth, see René Henry, *Au Péril de la Mer* (Paris, 2006). This was an area of significant Roman defensive positions, military roads and ports. See: Chart of Roman Roads, *Statistique Monumentale du Department du pas De Calais* (Commission des Antiquities, 1840).

6. The ancient episcopal see of Aleth was transferred to St Malo in the twelfth century.

7. See Henry, *Au Péril de la Mer*. 'La Cité' is the site of the ancient city of Aleth, which at the close of the Roman Empire replaced Corseul as the capital of the Coriosolites.

8. For documentation relating to the 1973 archaeological excavations see: 'Origine Gallo-Romaine de l'Éveche d'Alet', *Annals de la Societé d'Histoire et Archaéologie de Saint Malo* 95, 1974; L. Langouet, *Alet Ville Ancienne* (Rennes, 1973), and 'L'Histoire d'Alet', *Dossiers du Centre Régional d'Archéologie d'Alet*, 2 (1974); C. Brenot, 'Monnaies d'Alet', *Annales de Bretagne*, 76/1 (1969), p. 247–61, and 'Les monnaies romaines des fouille d'Alet', *Les Dossiers du centre regional d'archeologie d'Alet*, 2 (1974).

9. A tower on this site was known as Oreigle Tower in the ninth century.

10. The Cathedral at St Malo is dedicated to St Vincent. The tower in the transept was constructed with Gothic style in 1422, but is built on the foundations of another tower which also existed at the time of St Patrick; remains can still be seen in the wall which separates the chancel and the transept crossing.

11. The maps included which are of special importance in relation to Brittany, the Bay of Mont St Michel (Gulf of St Malo) and the settlement at Aleth during the late Roman period include: 'L'Armorique Celte et Gallo Romaine', p. 21, which shows the ancient Roman roads and tribal settlement of the Diablintes; 'Le Golfe de St Malo', p. 23, showing local geography and

coastlines as these existed at the time of St Patrick; Aleth and its environs with ancient Roman roads marked, 'La Cité d'Aleth et ses environs', p. 26; The Roman port installations including the fortress, Solidor tower, naval facilities and dockyard, 'Istallations Romaines dans 'l'anse Solidor', p. 29; and an artist's impression of Aleth during the Roman period, p. 31. Henry, *Au Péril de la Mer* (Paris, 2006).

12. In his detailed study of this region, French author Louis Blondel mentions the existence of an ancient settlement called 'Bonaban' on the coast between St Malo and Mont St Michel. He calls it the ancient commune of Bonaban.

13. *Calpurnius vint dans L'Armorique avec son epouse et ses enfants. Le Marriage s'accomplit, Conan donna a sa nouvelle famille un etablissement considerable pres d'Aleth, don't son beau-père eut le commandement.* See L'Abbe Lecarlotte, *Essai Historique sur les Monumnets de Dol* (1864), p. 370 ff. See also p. 377 ff. and p. 499 ff.

14. L'Abbé Lecarlotte, *Essai Historique sur les Monumnets de Dol*, p. 56.

15. *Journal of British Archaeological Association* (London, 1849), pp. 229–46.

16. Joseph de Garaby, *Vies des Bienheureux et des saints de Bretagne* (Saint-Brieuc, 1839), p. 90.

17. Nemthor's identity is uncertain. It could also be a reference to Tours (*Naem-Tour*) or 'Holy Tours'. The argument in favour of it being a reference to Tours, Mont St Michel or perhaps even the Roman lighthouse at Aleth outweighs the evidence presented for any alternative site in Britain or Lanigan's theory of Boulogne-sur-Mer.

CHAPTER THIRTEEN

# *The Wood of Foclut*

A help to Ireland was Patrick's coming.
The cry of the Children of the Wood
Of Foclut was heard far away.[1]

The Wood of Foclut is one of the few geographical references that are recorded in St Patrick's *Confession*. Patrick remembered this wood in the context of a dream. His account of what happened is deeply moving and has strongly influenced our popular understanding of some of the events that shaped his life.

In this 'vision of the night' St Patrick tells us that he saw a man who had come *as if* from Ireland. This person was carrying many letters and began reading them to Patrick. As he was opening the first letter, St Patrick describes how he heard the 'Voice of the Irish' and says in that same moment he could hear the voice of 'those who live beside the Wood of Foclut' calling him to 'come and walk once more among them'. He woke up suddenly, feeling 'heartbroken'. This was no ordinary dream, it was a nightmare. However traumatic it was, St Patrick understood this dream as a call from God to return to Ireland as an apostle. Here are St Patrick's words, as they are recorded in the earliest copy of his *Confession*, preserved in the *Book of Armagh*.

> And there, in a vision of the night I saw a man coming as it were from Ireland, whose name was Victor, carrying many letters. He gave me one of them to read and as I did so, I heard the *Voice of the Irish*. In that moment, as I was reading from the beginning of the letter, I thought I could hear the voice of those around the Wood of Foclut which is close beside the Western Sea.[2]
> It was as if they spoke with one voice, saying 'We beg you, holy youth, to come and walk once more among us' … I woke up suddenly feeling my heart was broken and had to stop reading. Thank God that after all these years the Lord has granted them according to their cries.[3]

Something in this dream had disturbed St Patrick greatly. It seems to have brought back traumatic memories. His account of the dream has traditionally been interpreted as being a recollection of his experience as a slave in Ireland. The 'Voice of the Irish' must have come from those in Ireland who Patrick knew during captivity. He says he heard this 'voice' from those who lived near the Wood of Foclut, calling him to return to them. Part of the difficulty with this particular interpretation is that we will never know the true meaning of St Patrick's dream.

It would be foolish to take what St Patrick says in the context of a dream to support an argument in favour of one particular geographical location over another. Nevertheless, most writers have interpreted Patrick's dream as confirmation of the fact that the Wood of Foclut must have existed in Ireland. It is widely assumed that in this dream St Patrick experienced a calling to return to those he knew or met during the seven years when he was held as a slave there. There is nothing in St Patrick's account to justify making such an assumption. As we have noted, Jeremy Taylor, who is a qualified Jungian therapist and expert in dream analysis, warns about the dangers of trying to interpret dreams and he strongly advises that we guard against what he calls 'mistaken literalism'. In his opinion, 'only the dreamer knows the meaning of a dream'. We can benefit from Taylor's experience by approaching this subject with caution.

At the same time, because St Patrick has left us with so few geographical references in his writings, the account of this dream is significant. The location of the Wood of Foclut is potentially very important for our enquiry. We will, therefore, assume, as most writers have always done, that when St Patrick wrote about this dream he was remembering a real wood or forest called 'Foclut' which was known to him from personal experience and had a definite geographical location. In other words, this wood existed somewhere and had a historical and geographical reality. It did not exist simply as part of St Patrick's experience of the 'dream world' arising from the depths of his unconscious mind. There is nothing in St Patrick's dream which should lead us to assume that the wood must have existed in Ireland, even though this has been the traditional interpretation.

St Patrick recalled the Wood of Foclut in the context of a dream he experienced many years before. In his *Confession*, Patrick does not say the Wood of Foclut was located in Ireland. The only geographical reference given is when he describes this wood as being 'close beside the Western Sea'. Again, some writers have pushed a speculative form of dream interpretation even further by not only assuming the Wood of Foclut was in Ireland but also that when St Patrick describes this wood as being 'close beside the Western Sea', he must have been referring to the Atlantic Ocean off the west coast of Ireland.

The temptation to draw such conclusions has been irresistible, especially since there has been an established tradition within the early Irish church claiming that the Wood of Foclut existed near Killala, in County Mayo, on the west coast of Ireland.[4] Lanigan and Flemming located Bannavem Tiburniae in France, but accepted the established tradition about Foclut. 'The Woods of Foclut were situated within five miles of Killala, and St Patrick in his *Confession* speaks in familiar ways of the inhabitants who dwell in the neighbourhood of the woods, whose voices sounded familiar in his ears when he was far away in Gaul.'

The earliest source claiming to know the true location of the Wood of Foclut is the work of an Irish Bishop called Tírechán, who published a narrative on St Patrick towards the end of the seventh century. This is more than two hundred years after St Patrick's death. Tírechán said the Wood of Foclut existed in his own diocese near Killala, County Mayo. His claim was embraced by the Irish church in the seventh century, enshrined in Ireland's ecclesiastical records when Tírechán's narrative was included in the *Book of Armagh*.[5]

Bishop Tírechán identifies this wood as the location for an important ecclesiastical centre in the west of Ireland, which he claims St Patrick founded. He calls it 'the Great Church of St Patrick'. Tírechán must have read or had access to a copy of St Patrick's *Confession* because he is aware of the significance of St Patrick's dream, which he builds upon in a very creative and skillful way to serve the purpose of his narrative. According to Tírechán, after Patrick returned to Ireland as an apostle he began to consecrate many priests and bishops, he baptised countless people and taught them how to write the alphabet.

Tírechán gives a very impressive and detailed account of various journeys St Patrick is said to have undertaken around Ireland. In doing this he creates a hagiographical 'map' just like Muirchú. He describes how St Patrick founded churches all over the country from Leinster, Munster and Connacht to Ulster. When describing these journeys, Tírechán lists a number of these churches and names the local chieftains who gave land to St Patrick for this purpose.[6]

In the midst of these accounts we find several references to the Wood of Foclut. As we listen to these stories, we must bear in mind that they are designed to bolster the ecclesiastical claims of the church of Armagh to jurisdiction over these churches and the lands associated with them. In other words, however much these stories might convince us that Bishop Tírechán must have been telling the truth, it now appears more than likely that he may have made the whole thing up.

Binchy always reminded his readers to appreciate that with Irish hagiography nothing is impossible. Nothing Tírechán says should be taken as true, simply because Tírechán has said it. Just as Muirchú may have created the legend or 'illusion' that St Patrick came from Britain, so Tírechán's narrative may have created another misleading claim that the Wood of Foclut was located in his own diocese, near Killala in the west of Ireland. What follows is a description of the main references to the Wood of Foclut found in Tírechán's narrative.

The family or tribe of the Amolngids, were the traditional landowners and chieftains in a particular region of Connacht where Tírechán's diocese was located. They appear in reliable genealogies of the ancient Irish kings.[7] Tírechán describes in detail how, after Easter, St Patrick went to Tara where he overheard a conversation between two nobles. One of them is introduced to us as Ende, son of Amolngid:

> I am Ende, son of Amolngid, son of Fiachae son of Echu, from the west-ern district, Mag Domnon and the Wood of Foclut.[8]

According to Tirechán, when St Patrick heard the name 'Foclut', he felt great joy and said to Ende, 'I shall go out with you, if I am alive, because the Lord told me to go there.'[9] St Patrick is said to have baptised Conall, Ende's son, and after blessing him, gave him to a bishop called Cathiacus for educ-ation and fostering. He was helped by Mucneus, the brother of Bishop Cathiacus, 'whose relics are in Patrick's great church in the Wood of Foclut'.[10]

Tirechán describes how six of the sons of Amolngid came before the high king in Tara, asking for judgement in a property dispute. Standing against them were St Patrick, Ende and Ende's young son (the seventh son) as the king pro-ceeded to examine their case of inheritance. Patrick and King Loiguire passed judgement that they should divide their inheritance into seven parts and Tirechán says that 'Ende offered his part to Patrick's God and to Patrick'. This implies that it was given to the church in Armagh and the Patrician *Paruchia*. Tirechán explains, 'It is for this reason, some say, we are servants of Patrick to the present day.'[11]

St Patrick and the sons of Amolngid are said to have concluded a treaty with King Loiguire of Tara acting as guarantor. They pledged to travel together to Mons Aigli (Croagh Patrick) and

> Patrick agreed to pay the price of fifteen men [as he states in his writings] in silver and gold, so that no wicked person should obstruct them, for by necessity they had to arrive at the Wood of Foclut before the end of a year's time, at the second Easter, because of the children crying with a loud voice, whose voices he had heard from their mothers' wombs say-ing, 'Come Holy Patrick, to save us.'[12]

This is the first clear sign that Tirechán had reworked Patrick's account of the dream and was using this to bolster the claims of the church in Armagh and the *Patricii Paruchia* by locating the Wood of Foclut in his own diocese. Tirechán's St Patrick is soon back, across the River Moy in the west of Ireland with the Amolngids, where he met two maidens and 'he blessed for them a place in the Wood of Foclut'.[13] Tirechán arranged all these journeys to bring St Patrick into Connacht by the 'second Easter'. This suggests some degree of complicity or familiarity with Muirchú, who brings St Patrick to Tara for the 'first' Easter. Connacht may have been claiming the second place of honour, after Armagh, in the *Paruchia Patricii*.

Tirechán was writing towards the end of the seventh century, two hundred years after St Patrick's death. Like Muirchú, his narrative was created with a specific hagiographical agenda which was to safeguard the claims of his own diocese to inheritance rights and support a reform movement for greater Romanisation which was being sponsored at that time by the church in Armagh.

Nothing Tirechán said about the Wood of Foclut should be viewed as historically reliable. To closely associate the 'sons of Amolngid' with St Patrick must have served Tirechán's political and ecclesiastical purposes but what he says about St Patrick and the Wood of Foclut is not to be trusted unconditionally. There are probably snippets of truth tucked away in the crevices and folds of his narrative but the vast majority of what he writes could be entirely fabricated. These stories are so graphic they sound very plausible and even authentic; such was the genius of Irish hagiography in the seventh century. The influence of these stories on our image and understanding of St Patrick in general and the location of the Wood of Foclut in particular, should not be underestimated. Tirechán's influence on the development of an ecclesiastical tradition concerning the location of the Wood of Foclut has been enormous.

In *St Fiacc's Hymn*, which is viewed as one of the earliest documents, no specific geographical location is given. The author simply says:

A help to Ireland was Patrick's coming. Afar was heard the cry of the Children of Fochlud's wood.[14]

In notes attached to *Fiacc's Hymn* by the Scholiast, however, which were written much later (at least five hundred years after St Patrick's death) we find a more detailed statement which promulgates the claims made by Bishop Tirechán. These notes show how the Irish church had embraced and been entranced by the Tirechán tradition:

The Wood of Fochlut *[Caill Foclaid]* is the name of the district which is in Tirawley in the north-east of Connacht, and there is a church there to this day.[15]

The Scholiast follows Tirechán's narrative closely, claiming that the Wood of Foclut was in Hy-Amalgaidh (tribal lands associated with the Amolngids) around Tirawley, near Killala in County Mayo. A similar claim appears in the *Tripartite Life of St Patrick* and many of the other ancient manuscripts that adopted the Tirechán tradition.

As we examine these stories more closely, we can see how the ancient writers developed their material, guided not by any information that could be considered historically reliable, but by the imagination and creativity of pure hagiographical genius.

In the *Lebar Brecc* Homily on St Patrick, for example, the original account given in St Patrick's *Confession* is alluded to but extra descriptive detail is added. The author refers initially to St Patrick's dream, which took place after he had escaped from Ireland and was reunited with his family. The voices now come, not simply from those associated in St Patrick's mind with the Wood of Foclut, but from their mothers' wombs. Foclut is again geographically located in the west of Ireland.

> His (St Patrick's) parents begged him now to stay with them. Nevertheless the angel came to him in his sleep having many letters in Gaelic. And when he was reading them out he heard a great cry from the infants in their mothers' wombs in the region of Connacht. Those children were of *Caille Fochlad* (Wood of Foclut) and this is what they were saying: 'Come, Holy Patrick, to make us whole.'[16]

In the notes attached to *St Fiacc's Hymn* by the Scholiast, we can detect a further development of the story, which is now completely embellished by hagiography to support a particular agenda and emerging tradition. The children are given names. Pope Celestine heard the voices too, when he was conferring orders on St Patrick. Patrick heard the voices 'coming from their mothers'' wombs and the voices could be heard all over Ireland and as far away as Rome.

> Now when orders were conferred on Patrick (Pope) Celestine heard the voice of the children calling him. These are the children here mentioned, namely Crebiu and Lesru are their names … And this is what they said out of their mother's womb: 'All the Irish are crying unto thee.' And they are often heard repeating that throughout all Ireland even as far as Rome.[17]

This elevates the children of Foclut to a very high place of esteem and creates a link with the Papacy and the Roman Church. It also serves to confirm an established tradition that the Wood of Foclut was in Ireland. As the story develops further, St Patrick is said to have baptised the children in the Wood of Foclut, at Cell Forcland to the west of the Moy, where their remains can still be found.[18]

From a comparison of these stories we can see how Patrick's original account of the dream was used by some of the ancient writers to link St Patrick not only to Rome but also to St Germanus of Auxerre. Patrick is alleged to have told St Germanus about many visions he had about the voices of the children who came from the Wood of Foclut. Germanus instructed St Patrick to go to Pope Celestine so that holy orders could be conferred:

After Patrick had read the canon with Germanus and the ecclesiastical order, he told Germanus that he had often been invited (to Ireland) in heavenly visions and that he had heard the voice of the children (from the Wood of Foclut).

Germanus said, 'Go to (Pope) Celestine so he may confer orders on you, for he is proper to confer them.' So St Patrick went to him, but he did not give him that honour, for he had previously sent Palladius to Ireland to teach.[19]

None of these extra details can be found in St Patrick's own writings. They are a clear reflection of the Romanising influence.

By the ninth century, the meaning and significance of the original dream had become embellished by ecclesiastical fables and, as a result, the true location of the Wood of Foclut may have been lost to historical memory. Many of the accounts about this wood found in the later secondary sources are entirely fictional and the only purpose they serve is to support the claims of the church in Armagh and strengthen the Romani movement in the Diocese of Connacht and elsewhere, locating the Wood of Foclut in Ireland and associating St Patrick and his mission more closely with the authority of St Germanus and Rome.

The development of these hagiographical accounts can be viewed as part of the 'Romanising' process which deeply affected St Patrick's biography, especially towards the end of the seventh century, more than two hundred years after St Patrick's death. This was promoted by the church in Armagh to provide St Patrick in particular, and the Irish church in general, with the credentials necessary to safeguard its image and future. An essential requirement was that St Patrick's mission to Ireland was supported by the papacy and that St Patrick himself was always in communion with Rome.

This process of later hagiographical development is clear to follow. An original historical reference (as it was given by St Patrick in his *Confession*) is shaped to suit a political and ecclesiastical agenda. This creates false 'information' which is essentially fraudulent. Muirchú and Tirechán were highly skilled, political and ecclesiastical spin doctors who applied their genius to completely reinvent St Patrick's 'biography'. Tirechán was followed by others, whose religiously creative imagination reshaped St Patrick's original account of his dream. In the hagiographical process the first stage of development takes place when the Wood of Foclut is identified with a specific geographical location: Bishop Tirechán's own diocese in the west of Ireland. In his own writings, St Patrick does not give enough information to identify any one particular location.

In the next stage, the 'Voice of the Irish' that St Patrick heard in his dream calling to him from the Wood of Foclut is said to have been the voice of children who lived beside the wood. Then the voice is said to have come from the children while they were still in their mothers' wombs. As the hagiographical process develops, the children are given names and then baptised by Patrick, as are their mothers.

Finally, the original account of the dream is woven into an elaborate story of St Patrick's meeting with Germanus of Auxerre and later with Pope Celestine.[20] While he is conferring holy orders on St Patrick, Pope Celestine starts to hear the voices himself. The children of Foclut are now recognised as saints and their voices could be heard all across Ireland and even as far as Rome.[21]

The final 'spin' takes place when all the choirs of heaven join in, to celebrate St Patrick's ordination in Rome and sing the praises of Ireland's apostle. The mysterious 'Voice of the Irish' which Patrick heard calling to him from the Wood of Foclut in a dream, now becomes a fully fledged church choir. It is the last masterful stroke from the brush of hagiography through which St Patrick's story becomes entirely embellished and Romanised. In these accounts, it is St Peter's successor who sends St Patrick to preach the gospel in Ireland:

> When they were conferring the rank of bishop upon him [Patrick], the three choirs answered, namely, the choir of heaven's household, the choir of the Romans and the choir of the children of the Wood of Foclut. This is what they sang, '*Hibernensis omnes clamant ad puer*' [All the Irish are calling for you]. So Peter's successor sent Patrick to preach to the Gael.[22]

These references have been included not only because they reveal the growing influence of the Romani movement but also because they helped to perpetuate Tirechán's claim that the Wood of Foclut existed in Ireland. Just as most writers accepted Muirchú's claim that St Patrick came from Britain so there has been widespread acceptance of Tirechán's claim, which locates the Wood of Foclut in the west of Ireland. This now forms part of an established tradition which has never been seriously questioned.[23]

In his landmark 'biography' of St Patrick, Bury appreciated that St Patrick was describing a dream and said 'This is the dreamer's description of the dream.' He recognised that the story was embellished by later accounts: 'As the story was told in later days, the cry that pierced his heart was uttered by the young children of Foclut, even by the children yet unborn.' But Bury was not alone in giving Tirechán's claim far too much historical credibility when he remarked, 'There is nothing of this in St Patrick's words ... yet the tradition betrays the true instinct of the significance of the dream.'[24]

The only reliable historical source for information about the Wood of Foclut is the account given in St Patrick's *Confession* and even this must be viewed with caution, because St Patrick remembered this place in the context of a dream. His description of that wood is part of his memory of that dream, which he had experienced many years before.

Some scholars have recognised the historical and geographical difficulties. The Tirechán tradition, when it is supported by the established interpretation given to Patrick's dream, implies that Patrick was held captive in the west of Ireland, where he must have known people who were now calling him to return to them. Tirechán's account, therefore, has implications for the location of St Patrick's place of captivity. Dr Lanigan was one of the first to recognise the difficulty when he suggested that if Patrick was held as a slave in Antrim or Down in the north-east of Ireland as many of the ancient sources suggest, then why would he hear voices coming from a Wood in Connacht, in the far west of Ireland?[25]

From what he says in the *Confession,* St Patrick appears to have been held captive more or less in complete isolation on a remote hillside where he tended animals for his slave master. He does not give the impression that he got to know many other people. Bieler tried to explain the dilemma by saying Patrick may have travelled to Connacht, an unlikely privilege for a slave. Bury also accepted Tirechán's claim, saying the Wood of Foclut must have been in the west of Ireland and that St Patrick (because of what he said when describing his dream) must, therefore, have been held captive in that region.[26] Bury may have misrepresented St Patrick's words and the meaning of his dream when he wrote, 'It is certain, from his own words, he (St Patrick) served near the Forest of Fochlad.'[27]

The following statement shows just how widely the Tirechán tradition has been accepted even by reputable historians:

> When the boats of his captors reached their haven, Patrick was led – so we should conclude from his own story – across the island into the kingdom of Connacht, to serve a master in the very furthest parts of the 'ultimate land'. His master dwelled near the Wood of Foclut, 'nigh to the Western Sea' in north-western Connacht, to this day a wild and desolate land, through the forest has long since been cleared away ...
>
> A part of this land belonged to Amolngaid, who afterwards became king of Connacht and it is still called by this name, Tir-awley, 'the land of Amolngaid'. But the Wood of Foclut was probably of larger extent than the district of Tirawley.[28]

Bury appears to have swallowed some of the claims of hagiography, hook, line and sinker when he writes, 'the cry that pierced his heart was uttered by the young children of Fochlad' and 'even by children that were still unborn.'[29]

Established traditions concerning St Patrick's origins have had a powerful influence on our understanding of his biography and this has influenced the views of many writers, despite the lack of evidence to support them. Even J. H. Todd accepted Tirechán's narrative as trustworthy.[30] Having crossed the

River Moy and entered the district of the Amolgmids (*Tír Amalgaidh*) Todd describes how Patrick 'made his way to the Wood of Fochlut, of which he had dreamt many years before, and which had clung ever since to his imagination'.[31]

Hanson suggested that if both Muirchú and Tirechán had not described Patrick's captivity as taking place in County Antrim, rather than Connacht, no one would have questioned Tirechán's claim, which located Foclut in the west of Ireland. Yet still, Hanson says, 'there is no reason to doubt Tirechán's statement that it was in Tirawley, on the borders of Sligo and Mayo.'[32]

T. M. Charles-Edwards of the University of Oxford, who recently helped to republish Bury's *Life of St Patrick*, affirms the historical integrity of the Tirechán tradition and attempts to solve the dilemma as to where Patrick was held captive by following Bury and locating this in the west of Ireland.

After six years of slavery, when Patrick was about twenty-two years old, a dream directed him to escape. Discussing Patrick's escape, Professor Charles-Edwards states that

> This was not an easy feat, for the district in which he was living as a slave was beside the Wood of Voclut, near Killala in the north of the modern County Mayo, close to the Atlantic coast.[33]

Professor Charles-Edwards is recognised as one of the leading authorities in Celtic Studies and the history of Ireland in the early medieval period. Tirechán's statements about the location of the Wood of Foclut are accepted by him to such an extent, however, he is willing to discard another tradition (which was supported even by Tirechán) that St Patrick was held in captivity in County Antrim.

This gives an indication of the powerful influence of hagiography, leading to potential errors in historical analysis. Once Tirechán's claim about the location of the Wood of Foclut is accepted, St Patrick's place of captivity is also identified with that region. This traditional view is constructed on what is essentially a risky and misguided form of dream interpretation.

Tirechán wrote his narrative about two hundred years after St Patrick's death. He claimed that the Wood of Foclut was in his own diocese in the west of Ireland. Understandably for a bishop of his time, he does not provide reliable evidence to support this. Medieval hagiographers were not constrained by the same standards which apply to modern historical analysis. The linguistic evidence which has been given in support of the Tirechán tradition is not convincing. In Tirechán's narrative the Wood of Foclut is identified with Fochloth (Fochlad) in Connacht, a place name which is said to have survived in modern Eoghill (Fochoill) near Killala, Tirawley, County Mayo.[34]

One or two astute scholars remained sensibly cautious and sceptical about Tirechán's claim. Macneill suggested the existence of such a forest in Connacht was 'a gratuitous assumption'.[35] He recognised that 'Fochlud' was not a clear or easy name to identify because so many different forms of spelling are preserved in the ancient manuscripts and decided it was best simply to call it the Forest of 'U'.[36]

O'Rahilly examined the origins of the name 'Foclud' and thought it came from an archetype, spelled 'Voclitu'.[37] He lists all the various forms in which this name appears in the *Book of Armagh* and other sources. The extent of these variations alone suggests the meaning of the original name was uncertain.[38] O'Rahilly doubted the connection between the name 'Fochloth' and modern Foghill in Connacht which he suggested could only be due to the 'deceptive resemblance' between these names. Despite these uncertainties, he held firmly to the established tradition. O'Rahilly said the context of St Patrick's dream makes it clear, 'the Wood of Voclut was close to the place of Patrick's captivity, the one place in Ireland that was quite familiar to him after he had spent six years there as a slave'. He continues, 'There is not the slightest reason to suppose that the Irish tradition was wrong in locating the Wood of "Voclut" near Killala'.[39]

Ludwig Bieler regarded any attempt to locate the Wood of Foclut outside Connacht as 'guesswork' and criticised those who were pushing aside 'traditions of considerable antiquity'.[40] The weight of scholarly opinion has always favoured locating it in Ireland. Such opinions are based on the assumption that 'Foclut' is the only Irish place name mentioned by St Patrick in his own writings and that Bishop Tirechán was telling the truth and could be trusted when he claimed that it existed within his own diocese.

In the context of the local traditions preserved in Brittany, another possibility had to be considered. Perhaps the name 'Foclut' or 'Foclud' was not originally Irish but rather the Irish form of a Breton or Brythonic name which may have been familiar to St Patrick from his experiences on the continent.[41]

If 'Foclut' could be identified with the Forest of 'Quokelunde' close to the present site of Château Bonaban, this would have significant implications for our traditional understanding of St Patrick's biography. The names look very similar, despite the differences in spelling. If they are connected and refer to the same wood how could these differences in spelling be accounted for?

The transmission of ancient texts is a very specialist field of study. Ludwig Bieler is a recognised expert, having dedicated most of his life to an analysis of the manuscripts. Bieler examined and compared all the ancient documents in which the 'Wood of Foclut' appears. This name was passed on with a variety of spellings, including 'Siluae Foclitae', 'Siluam Vocluti' or 'Silua Uocluti' in Latin and 'Fochloth' or 'Fochlad' in Old Irish.

Most translations render the name as 'Foclud' or 'Foclut' in English. Despite differences in spelling, all the forms listed agree as to the initial 'f', 'u' or 'v', then a 'c' or 'ch' in the body of the word and a 'd' or 't' towards the end. According to Bieler, the original word must have begun with a 'u' and this 'u' was changed to an 'f' as the manuscripts were copied in Ireland. As the change from 'u' to 'f' was taking place, scribes would modernise the spelling of the name independently.

Bieler decided *siluam Uocluti* was probably the original reading which he also considers the archetype, the earliest form of the name as this appears in surviving copies of St Patrick's *Confession*.[42] He accepted the traditional view that the Wood of Foclut was located in the west of Ireland although he was open to the possibility this might change if new evidence became available. Bieler recognised that difficulties arise from the assumption that Patrick heard people from a certain part of Ireland calling him to return to them, which would imply he had been there before. He may have misjudged Tírechán's motives, the context in which he was writing and the creative powers of Irish hagiography, when he says, 'Tírechán would appear to be a trustworthy reporter; asserting as he does that the See of Armagh might claim the whole country as his *paruchia*, he could not risk being proved wrong.'[43] This would not have applied if Tírechán had been in collusion with Armagh, not in competition.

Although Tírechán's narrative is hagiographical, most writers have trusted the Tírechán tradition concerning the location of the Wood of Foclut as though it was historically and geographically reliable. The key question is, was Tírechán telling the truth? If not, then could it be possible that when St Patrick dreamt about this wood, he was remembering the Forest of Quokelunde, which according to the Breton historians was the name of a local forest which surrounded the place where St Patrick was taken captive, not where he was held captive? If so, then the Tírechán tradition not only created an illusion based on what is essentially a false claim, it misunderstood and completely misinterpreted the meaning and significance of St Patrick's dream and, as a result, propagated false information about St Patrick and his true identity.

If there is any truth in local traditions about St Patrick recorded in Brittany, could 'Quokelunde' be the Breton name for a forest that was recalled by St Patrick in his dream and recorded in Ireland as the 'Wood of Foclut'? If this can be established as a definite historical and linguistic possibility, it would present a radical alternative to challenge our traditional understanding of St Patrick's story.

The next challenge in the quest to establishing whether the historical information provided for guests staying at Château Bonaban is reliable was to find out whether a forest called 'Quokelunde' existed there at the time of St Patrick and therefore was not simply the figment of someone's wild Celtic imagination.

*Notes*

1. *Fiacc's Hymn*. The name for the Wood of Foclut as given in Old Irish is *Caille Fochlad*, See Whitley Stokes, *Tripartite Life of St Patrick* (London, 1887), ii, p. 407.

2. *Siluam Vocluti quae est prope mare occidentale*. Bieler, *Clavis Patricii II: Libri Epistolarum Sancti Patricii Episcopi* (Dublin, 1993), p. 71, C 23.

3. C 23.

4. Todd accepted that Fochlut was a district of Hy Fiachrach in Co. Mayo. J. H. Todd, *St Patrick, Apostle of Ireland* (Dublin, 1864), p. 313. Bury said 'The Wood of Fochlud was probably of larger extent than the district of Tirawley,' and added that 'it may have stretched over Mayo to the western promontory of Murrisk'. J. B. Bury, *The Life of St Patrick, His Place in History* (London, 1905), p. 28. See William Flemming, *Boulogne-sur-Mer* (London, 1907), p. 13.

5. Tirechán was writing about the same time as Muirchú (670 CE). For the original text and translation, see Ludwig Bieler, *The Patrician Texts in the Book of Armagh* (Dublin, 2004), p. 123 ff.

6. Tirechán helped expand the *Paruchia Patricii* in the west of Ireland as Muirchú did in Armagh.

7. See King Lists in T. M. Charles-Edwards, *Early Christian Ireland* (Cambridge, 2000), p. 615, 627.

8. Siluae Fochlothi, Tirechán 14:2, Bieler, *PTBA*, p. 135.

9. Tirechán 14:3, Bieler, *PTBA*, p.135.

10. Tirechán 14:6, Bieler, *PTBA*, p. 135.

11. Tirechán 14:7, Bieler, *PTBA*, p. 135.

12. See Tirechán 15. Bieler, *PTBA*, p. 136.

13. Tirechán 43:3, Bieler, *PTBA*, p. 159.

14. Stokes, *Tripartite Life*, p. 407.

15. Notes on *Fiacc's Hymn* in Stokes, *Tripartite Life*, p. 421.

16. Stokes accepted that the Wood of Focult was located near Killala. See *Tripartite Life*, p. 445, n. 1.

17. Notes on *Fiacc's Hymn* in Stokes, *Tripartite Life*, p. 420 ff.

18. 'There is a church there to the east of the Wood of Foclud': *Cross Patraic ainm fri caille Fochlad unair*. Stokes, *Tripartite Life*, p. 131. '12,000 believed in Patrick in his Amalgada, and from the Wood of Fochlad.' Stokes, *Tripartite Life*, pp 135, 137.

19. Notes on *Fiacc's Hymn* in Stokes, *Tripartite Life*, p. 419.

20. Stokes, *Tripartite Life*, ii, p. 419 See also p. 445.

21. Stokes, *Tripartite Life*, ii, p. 421.

22. Stokes, *Tripartite Life*, p. 33.

23. See Patrick MacNeill, 'The Identification of Foclut', *Journal of the Galway Archaeological and Historical Society*, 22, (1947).

24. Bury, *The Life of St Patrick*, p. 42.

25. Dr Lanigan still assumed the Wood of Foclut was in Ireland. John Lanigan, *Ecclesiastical History of Ireland*, 4 vols (Dublin, 1822; 2nd edn, Dublin, 1829), i, pp 160–2, n. 67.

26. See Ludwig Bieler, 'The Problem of Silva Focluti', *Irish Historical Studies*, 3/12 (1943), pp. 351–64.

27. 'Fochlut is in the district of Hy Fiachrach, Co. Mayo'. Bury, *The Life of St Patrick*, p. 313, n. 4.

28. Bury, *The Life of St Patrick*, p. 29.

29. Bury, *The Life of St Patrick*, p. 27 ff. See also C 4, Bury, *The Life of St Patrick*, p. 334 ff.

30. 'Fochlut – in the district of Hy Fiachrach, county of Mayo', J. H. Todd, *St Patrick, Apostle of Ireland*, p. 313, n. 4.

31. See Todd, *St Patrick, Apostle of Ireland*, p. 447.

32. R. P. C. Hanson, *St Patrick His Origins and Career* (Oxford, 1997), p. 91; and Stokes, *Tripartite Life*, ii, p. 326.

33. T. M. Charles-Edwards, *Early Christian Ireland*, p. 217.

34. Colgan accepted this identification when he collected the ancient Lives of St Patrick. *Ad Fochladios: populos de Caille Fochlaidh in Tir-Amalgaid, Regione Connaciae* (Wood of Foclud: Tir-Amalgaid in the region of Connaught). John Colgan, *Trias Thaumaturga*, ed. Eamonn De Burca (Dublin, 1977), p. 6, n. 10.

35. Eoin MacNeill, *Celtic Ireland* (Dublin, 1921), p. 10.

36. Eoin MacNeill, 'Silua Focluti', *Proceedings of the Royal Irish Academy, Section C: Archaeology, Celtic Studies, History, Linguistics, Literature*, 36 (1923), p. 249–55.

37. Thomas O'Rahilly, *The Two Patricks* (Dublin, 1942; repr. 1981), n. 34, p. 60.

38. Various spellings in the *Book of Armagh* include 'Focluti' in the *Confession*; 'Foclitae' in Muirchú; 'Fochlithi' (three times), 'Fochlothi' and 'Focluth' in Tírechán. In Latin manuscripts the name appears as 'Uirgulti', 'uirgulti', 'uolutique', 'uirgulti', 'ueluti' etc. Thurneysen suggested these were all expansions of an original, 'Voluti'. O'Rahilly suggests the Irish forms given for this word, provide the archetype and that Latin forms are secondary. St Patrick, writing in Latin, was the first to mention this name and if the Latin form comes from a Breton name for a wood familiar to St Patrick, this might account for such diversity in spelling. See O'Rahilly, *The Two Patricks*, p. 60 ff.

39. O'Rahilly, *The Two Patricks*, p. 35.

40. Bieler, 'The Problem of Silva Focluti', p. 352.

41. Unlike St Patrick's homeland *in Britanniis* and the family estate at Bannavem Tiburniae, as far as I am aware, at the time of writing, no ancient or modern author has ever suggested that the Wood of Foclut may have existed on the continent, in Brittany.

42. Bieler concluded his study of the Wood of Foclut by saying in terms of location, nothing can be proved scientifically. Bieler, 'The Problem of Silva Focluti'.

43. See Bieler, 'The Problem of Silva Focluti', p. 363.

# CHAPTER FOURTEEN

# *Quokelunde*

A dream that has not been interpreted
Is like a letter that has not been opened.[1]

In Brittany a local tradition has been preserved that describes how St Patrick's family were resident from the time of the usurpation of Magnus Maximus in 383 CE. These accounts are significant because they provide a historical context for some of the key events that shaped St Patrick's life and destiny. Breton historians writing before the nineteenth century claim that Bannavem Tiburniae was located on or close to the present site of Château Bonaban. Irish pirates are said to have crept up through a local forest called Quokelunde before they attacked the estate, killed St Patrick's mother and father and dragged Patrick away to be sold into slavery in Ireland.[2] This is the information provided for guests staying at Château Bonaban, which is worth reading again:

> The first castle or rather fortress that was built here dates from the Roman period, during the fourth century. At that time, this place was called *Bonavenna* [or *Bonabes*] *de Tiberio*. It belonged to a Scottish prince, Calpurnius [St Patrick's father] who had come here to avoid Saxon forces who were invading Britain.
>
> One night, Irish pirates arrived in nearby Cancale. They spread through the Wood of Quokelunde, which stretched under Gouesnière-Bonaban as far as Plerguèr. Armed with pikes and axes, they slaughtered the prince and all his family.
>
> His property was looted and the castle burned to the ground; only his youngest son, Patrice, survived from this slaughter. He was taken captive to Ireland. There he looked after sheep and learned the language of the country of which he became the oracle and disciple.[3]

This raised an intriguing question that has never been considered before as historically possible. Could the Forest of Quokelunde be the Wood of Foclut, that Patrick remembered in a dream he experienced a few years later, after escaping from Ireland? Following more detailed research the geographical details given appeared to be significant and worth further consideration. The first task was to establish whether a forest called 'Quokelunde' existed in this region at the time of St Patrick. Considering the uncertainties which exist in records from the fifth century, the Forest of Quokelunde is well documented.[4]

It was part of a much larger forest called the Forest of Scissy or 'Chaussey'.[5] In the late Roman period, a huge oak forest covered much of Brittany. The forest of Scissy or Chaussey stretched along the coast from the Isle de Chaussey to Mont St Michel. Near the edge of this forest there were seven military roads which consolidated Roman power throughout northern and western Europe.[6]

This forest was held sacred by the Druids in the pre-Christian period. In early Christian times it was known 'the Desert of Scissy', because of the large number of hermits who lived there. One French writer described it as a *Thébaid Celtique* or 'Celtic Desert' referring to a place in Upper Egypt where desert monasticism originated in the fourth century. In his seventeenth-century *Histoire de Bretagne*, M. Deric describes it as the largest forest in Brittany.[7] Part of this vast forest covered the coastal region of north-west Brittany at the time of St Patrick, stretching from Alderney, Chaussey and Les Mintiers, as far as Dol. It surrounded 'Dolomhoir' now Dol-de-Bretagne.[8]

The forests of Brittany have long been associated with legend, but they are also remembered as a place of seclusion, religious worship and sanctuary. Valerosi describes the Forest of Scissy or 'Chaussey' as an 'Oak Millenarian' or 'Forest of a Thousand Oaks'. This description may refer to the forest itself or perhaps a monument or sacred grove of trees where monks or solitaries worshipped.

> It is the largest forest in the western region [of Brittany] stretching from the coast to the interior. *Monaci* [solitary ones, monks] have penetrated this forest to find peace and tranquility. Inside we find the sanctuary of a thousand oak trees which is adored by the *monaci* of the goddess Moira.[9]

It is unclear whether this reference is speaking about some form of pre-Christian monastic asceticism, related to a Goddess called Moira or early Christian monasticism related to Mary. The forest appears to have contained a religious sanctuary. Many hermits are said to have lived in this forest during the late Roman period. The Forest of Quokelunde formed part of this larger, more widely documented Forest of Scissy or Chaussey.[10]

A monastery existed at St Pair, called the Monastery of Scissy. This was associated with a holy man called St Senior, identified as a disciple of St Paterne, who is recorded as one of the earliest founders of local Christian monastic settlements. Breton historians claim that after St Patrick escaped from slavery in Ireland he returned to his homeland in Brittany and that eventually he was ordained as a priest by Saint Senior, the founding bishop of Dol.[11]

Probus records that Patrick was ordained as a bishop by St Senior. St Patrick refers to those who had made accusations against him and were seeking to have him removed from the mission in Ireland, as his 'seniors'.[12] 'Séigneur' is a title traditionally applied to holy men in France, clergy as well as nobles.

L'Abbé Desroches identifies the Forest of Quokelunde or 'Cokelunde' as a local forest, on the coast between Aleth and Mont St Michel.[13] Several other Breton historians clearly identify it within this same, small coastal region. The local geographical references are very detailed and specific.

The earliest reference to the Forest of Quokelunde that we can find is mentioned by Guillaume de Saint-Pair, a twelfth-century monk at Mont St Michel who wrote *Le Roman de Mont St Michel* around 1160 CE.[14] Here are the verses in Old French, with an English translation kindly provided by David Parris, specialist in Old French at Trinity College, Dublin:

*Desouz Averenches vers Bretaigne*
Below Avranches towards Brittany

*Eirt la forest de Quokelunde,*
Was the forest of Quokelunde.

*Don grant parole eirt par le munde.*
Much talked about in the world.

*Cen qui or est meir et areine,*
Where there is now sea and sand,

*En icel tens eirt forest pleine*
In that time [it] was all forest

*De meinte riche venaison;*
With much good game;

*Mers ore il noet li poisson:*
Now fish swim there:

*Dunc peust en tres bien aler,*
So you can easily travel,

*N'I esteust ja crendre meir,*
There was no need to fear the sea,

*D'Avrenches, dreit a Poulet,*
Going straight from Avranche to Poulet,

*A la cité de Ridalet.*
To the city of Ridalet [Aleth].

*En la Forêt aveit un mont*
In the forest there was a mount (vv. 49–61)

Guillaume de Saint Pair was describing part of an established medieval pilgrimage route to Mont St Michel. In this poem 'Avrenches' can easily be identified with Avranches, an ancient ecclesiastical centre which is located on the other side of the Bay of Mont St Michel from Dol-de-Bretagne. In the final verse of the passage quoted above (v. 60) the poem mentions the city of Ridalet (*la cité Ridalet*) known also as 'Quidalet', which refers to the city of Aleth (still known as *la cité*) on the opposite side of the bay from Mont St Michel.[15]

The description given by Guillaume de Saint-Pair can be trusted. Guillaume was a twelfth-century monk who was familiar with the pilgrimage route and the ancient traditions associated with it. He was resident at the Abbey as a member of the monastic community based at Mont St Michel and, therefore, had local knowledge. He describes how the forest was renowned for its venison, and the rivers and sea nearby for the fish.

When David Parris kindly sent me a translation of these verses I asked him whether they perhaps contained any *double entendres* or hidden meanings, that perhaps would suggest the influence of romance or Grail legends. His view was that Guillaume was writing 'pretty straight-down-the-middle Old French' which is a language that is simple in tone. In his opinion, hidden meanings and subtle twists came later with a group called *les grands rhétoriqueurs*. If this is correct, then we have good reason to accept what Guillaume is saying about the local landscape and trust his knowledge and understanding of local geography.

From the specific geographical references included in this poem, it is clear that the Forest of Quokelunde once stretched across the coastal region of north-west Brittany between Mont St Michel and St Malo. This is the place where Château Bonaban is located. According to Guillaume de Saint-Pair, the Forest of Quokelunde existed in the Bay area around Mont St Michel, between Aleth and Avranches, well known to pilgrims en route to Mont St Michel. It would be helpful to know whether Guillaume's knowledge about Quokelunde formed part of an oral tradition preserved at Mont St Michel or if he was drawing on earlier, written records which have since been lost, or perhaps are preserved in private archives.[16]

Although disputed by some writers in the past, the existence of this ancient forest is now acknowledged by historians.[17] Archaeologists have found evidence for a cataclysm, which may have taken the form of devastating flood caused by an encroaching of the sea. As a result the ancient Forests of Quokelunde and Scissy were submerged in water.[18] This affected the low-lying coastal region between St Malo and Mont St Michel. Breton fishermen, who farm mussels in the shallow waters of the Bay, frequently encounter old tree trunks preserved only a few inches under water in the Bay.

Some of these trees have been carbon dated and found to be very ancient (2700–250 BCE). French historians no longer doubt the existence of Quokelunde, although there is disagreement as to when exactly this forest was submerged. M. Manet and René Henry, amongst others, have dated the rise in sea level to 709 CE. This is also said to be the date when St Aubert built a new church on Mont St Michel. Châteaubriand dated the inundation of the sea during the reign of Childebert (511–558 CE) according to *Morery's Dictionary*.[19]

Local archaeological excavations have documented the remains of these ancient forests and the Gallic-Roman roads made of wattle and stone that once passed through them.[20] Remains of other Roman roads can be traced from Dol to St Pair and Corseul (Dinan), and Corseul to Aleth. In his excellent and more recent study called *Au Péril de la Mer*, French author René Henry has explored all the historical and archaeological evidence concerning the Forest of Quokelunde and provided a number of very informative maps and illustrations drawn by hand.[21] Archaeologists have identified the ancient course of the River Couesnon, which now flows into the sea at Pontorson. At the time of St Patrick, it flowed between the Forests of Scissy and Quokelunde. Local historical, geographical and archaeological evidence, therefore, allows for the possibility that Bonaban is the location of Bannavem Tiburniae, the place from which St Patrick was taken captive, since pirates travelling by ship from Ireland would have had direct access to the site.

The short walk from Château Bonaban to Bois-Renou allows for a clear view of the local landscape and especially the low-lying area of agricultural lands along the coast, called Le Marais. This is where the ancient Forest of Quokelunde once existed.

All these local geographical and topographical details are very significant in relation to the location of the villa owned by St Patrick's father, because they appear to confirm that many aspects of the local tradition preserved at Château Bonaban could be true.

The Forest of Quokelunde once stood in very close proximity to the ancient site where Château Bonaban is now located, along the stretch of coastline between Cancale, St Meloir and St Suliac. Cancale was situated on the coast at the time of St Patrick, as it still is today.

Geological surveys of this region confirm that the ancient site of Bonaban is on a raised granite escarpment, once accessible by sea and a river. These studies document the coastline at the time of St Patrick, before an inundation of the sea which is said to have taken place in 709 CE. Local research has identified a tributary of the River Rance which once flowed from its mouth at Aleth to where Château Bonaban is now located. The course of another old river has been detected between Cancale and the present site of Château Bonaban. This allows for the possibility that if pirates had arrived near Cancale before they attacked the estate where St Patrick's family was resident, they may have been able to reach this site by sailing up this river. These ancient river courses have been affected by recent local land-drainage schemes, but they can be seen very clearly on M. Henry's original maps.

The following map is based on the work of M. Manet and René Henry.[22] The site of Château Bonaban has been marked, showing its proximity to the Forest of Quokelunde together with coastlines and local river courses at the time of Patrick.

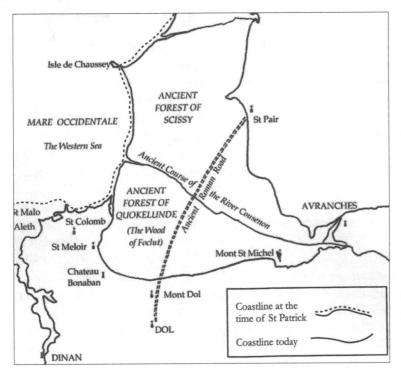

If this was the location of Bannavem Tiburniae and if St Patrick grew up there, then he would have been very familiar with this forest.

Local history and geography is, therefore, consistent with the local tradition which describes how Patrick was taken captive, as pirates from Ireland crept up through the Forest of Quokelunde before they attacked the Calpurnius estate.

Could this forest have been known to St Patrick and recorded in Ireland as the 'Wood of Foclut'? The names 'Quokelunde' and 'Foclut' show an intriguing similarity. When a Brythonic (Breton) name was transcribed in Latin and Old Irish certain letters would have been changed.[23] Old Welsh and Breton spellings reflect the fact that while the sounds of Latin had changed the spelling of Latin was retained, so that written words often required new pronunciation. A good example would be when a 'c', 'p' and 't' occurring after a vowel was pronounced 'g', 'b', 'd' respectively. This helps to explain the variety of spellings for 'Foclut' which can be found in the ancient manuscripts, sometimes written 'Foclud' or 'Foclut'. A Breton word beginning with a 'q' could be changed to begin with a 'u' or 'v' when written in Latin but appear with an 'f' in Old Irish. Perhaps the names 'Quokelunde' and 'Foclut' are connected and refer to the same forest? The difference in spelling might be accounted for by the transposition of letters or syllables that occurred when the name spoken by Patrick was recorded in Latin or transferred into Old Irish.

Dr Parris advised that Latin did not distinguish between 'v' and 'u' (nor between 'i' and 'j') and that these two vowels could also, on occasions, be consonants. Eventually, the distinction between the vowels 'u' and 'i' and the consonants 'v' and 'j' was reflected in writing, but we still call a 'w' a 'double u' when it is obviously a double 'v'. He said there was a known difficulty in representing 'w' sounds at the beginning of a word. Thus, what we call a 'wasp' and the Italians a *vespa*, in French is a *guepe*, originally pronounced something like 'gwesp'. Similar correlations are at work between the English 'warder' and French *gardien*, which was originally pronounced something like 'gwardien'.

Dr Parris recommended that the 'unde' or last part of the name Quokelunde should be removed and seen as a later Frankish addition. He suggested that the original name of the forest was probably pronounced something like 'Kwokel' to represent an initial 'w', as in the Latin 'Uoclut', which would have been recorded in Irish as 'Foclut'. Dr Parris's analysis strengthens the case for locating the Wood of Foclut in Brittany and the integrity of the local tradition about St Patrick which is preserved at Château Bonaban.[24]

Dr Christine Mohrman, an expert in fifth-century Latin, was one of the world's leading authorities in philology in 1961 when she was invited to speak at the Royal Irish Academy in Dublin.[25] Significantly, in relation to documents and traditions which survived about St Patrick, she said, 'Linguistic evidence does not tell lies, as hagiographical documents sometimes do.'[26] Mohrman felt that St Patrick's Latin was the most difficult to understand and criticise that she had ever encountered. The following are some of the conclusions Dr Mohrman offered following her intensive study of St Patrick's writings. She could find no trace of any quotations or borrowings from any book other than the bible.[27] In her opinion, 'For St Patrick, there existed only one book – Holy Scripture – and this book he almost knew by heart.'[28]

Mohrman agreed with Bieler that the biblical texts used by St Patrick must have been of Gaulish origin, but there was no evidence of any connection with southern Gaul or with the monastery of Lerins, as some later traditions claim.[29] Perhaps most significant of all, Mohrman said there is a blending of biblical elements with 'very normal, often colloquial elements which go back to his earlier days and to his contacts with Gaul'. She concluded, 'In his [St Patrick's] rather clumsy language there are certain elements which belong to living, colloquial Latin. These cannot possibly belong to early British Latin as they bear all the marks of living, fifth-century continental Latin.' Mohrman said St Patrick's Latin is very different to the tradition of early British Latin found in Gildas 'as if they belonged to a different world'. Her analysis suggests that St Patrick's religious formation probably took place without any formal or classical training in Latin.

This again might point towards Brittany and the coastal region of northwest Gaul, close to Armoric Letha as well as St Martin's community on the Loire. This monastery was a training ground for ascetic or 'monastic' spirituality and there was no significant emphasis on the classical Latin syllabus, including rhetoric, grammar and syntax, as would have been the case at the schools of Arles, Lerins or Auxerre.

During her presentations in Dublin, Mohrman did not attempt to address the specific question of St Patrick's place of origins. She was convinced from her study of St Patrick's Latin that his earliest connections were with rural Gaul and the structure of his language can only be understood in the context of rural Gaul.[30] If it had been possible to attend her lecture in 1961, an interesting question to ask would have been whether she thought St Patrick might have grown up on the continent during those early years when his language was formed. Mohrman appears to have accepted the established tradition that Patrick came from Britain, but concluded that Patrick's Latin could not have been influenced by the tradition of British Latin, such as we find in Gildas and even Columbanus, whose education was influenced by that tradition. In her view, St Patrick's Latin comes from 'another world' outside Britain, Auxerre, Rome or Lerins and probably derives from somewhere in rural Gaul. This could have been Brittany.

In relation to the Wood of Foclut, Christine Mohrman made an interesting remark during her lectures. She said there was a deeply human element in the way St Patrick described his dream in which some memories associated with this wood were recalled. She suggested that Patrick dreams 'the Irish' call him and that this call is realised and individualised by the voice of a people he had once known, from his youth: 'When he [St Patrick] reads from the letters that the Irish call him, *an image of his youth comes back to him and he hears the voices of the people he has known.*'[31] Could the 'image from his youth' that came back to haunt St Patrick in this dream perhaps have been a memory of traumatic events that took place in the forest that surrounded his father's estate on the day it was attacked and Patrick was taken captive? If so, the evidence, therefore, suggests that M. Charles de Gerville was correct when he identified St Patrick's 'Bannavem Tiburniae' with the ancient site on which Château Bonaban is now located.

What implications might this have for understanding St Patrick's dream and the meaning of his *Confession*? St Patrick tells us when this dream occurred. He had just returned to his homeland and been reunited with his extended family after many years of separation. Reading his account of the dream, there is immediately a sense that whatever memory Patrick had of the Wood of Foclut it was disturbing and traumatic for him. He tells us that he woke from the dream feeling 'heartbroken'.

This was no ordinary dream; judging by St Patrick's description of his feelings when he woke it sounds more like a nightmare. Despite this trauma, in the midst of this 'night vision', as he describes it, he received what he experienced to be a calling from God to return to Ireland and carry the gospel to those in need who were there. 'Thank God,' St Patrick said, 'after many years their cry was heard.'

Like other places mentioned by St Patrick, and despite the claims of Muirchú and Tírechán, the location of the Wood of Foclut is one of the great unsolved mysteries of St Patrick's life. As we have already suggested, there is nothing in this dream which should lead us to assume that the Wood of Foclut must have existed in Ireland, and we must also be wary of drawing any historical or geographical conclusions about what was remembered in the context of a dream that took place several years before. Having said that, could it be possible that St Patrick was remembering events which had taken place in the woods around his father's estate on the day he was taken captive? The trauma of being abducted by pirates and dragged from his home and family as a teenager would certainly have created difficult memories and affected him for the rest of his life.

St Patrick would never have been able to forget this experience of hearing voices, the shouts and screams of those who cried out in the face of outrageous violence being dragged away through the woods by barbarians from a foreign country. In his *Letter to Coroticus*, St Patrick tells us that on the day the raid took place, those who took him captive 'devastated the male and female servants' of his father's house. Those cries alone may have continued to haunt St Patrick even when he was an older man, especially if, as some of the ancient writers record, he witnessed his own parents being killed during the attack. Patrick's suffering would account for the traumatic nature of his memory and waking up suddenly, feeling 'heartbroken'.

Could the voices that haunted him in this dream have been the cries of those who were taken captive with him? If so, they could be identified in Patrick's heart with those who were still being held captive in Ireland, the voice of 'the Irish' slaves. It had not been too long since Patrick's escape from captivity; perhaps it troubled him in the depths of his conscience that he was free while they still suffered in captivity. Of the thousands of others he said were taken captive with him, most were presumably still being held in slavery in Ireland. Could the 'Voice of the Irish' have been the voices of those taken captive with him in the turmoil and violence of that fateful day, his own country men and women who were still held captive in Ireland? Is this how God called him, through the pain of a broken heart, to return to the land of his own captivity for the sake of others and for the gospel? For someone as courageous and faithful as Patrick, that would certainly have been one good reason to go back. Hanson said:

> Far be it from any historian to attempt the task of psycho-analysing St Patrick, but it is clear even to the most austere and dispassionate investigator of his writings that in his captivity, at the age of sixteen, Patrick suffered what we now call a severe psychological trauma from which, in a sense, he never recovered ...
>
> Even when as an old man he is writing the *Confession*, at least forty and perhaps fifty years after the event, he still cannot stop regarding himself as a helpless adolescent, cruelly torn from home and family ...

Hanson continues:

> Patrick does not pity himself because as he himself tells us, in his moment of helplessness and extreme need he found a helper and friend in God. He could never forget his terrible experience of being taken captive in his youth, but neither could he forget that through this experience he had met 'the one above all who is powerful, in all and through all, the one who drew him out of the deep mire and set him on top of the hill.[32]

This is one of the most remarkable qualities of St Patrick's personality, revealing his strength and depth of spiritual maturity. However much trauma there had been with all the danger and difficulties he experienced in his life, however much personal grief, loss and suffering, he never harbours a grudge against those who took him captive, or did him harm. St Patrick even ends his *Letter to Coroticus* offering the olive branch of forgiveness and reconciliation to those who had abused him. If there is reparation for wrongdoing, however evil it may have been, the message St Patrick wanted to proclaim is that God always forgives. Hanson said this is the real motive and keynote of St Patrick's *Confession*, not primarily written to hit back at his opponents or justify himself, but to declare gratitude to God.[33]

From the evidence gathered so far, we are now in a position to embrace the notion that three of the key geographical references mentioned by St Patrick in his *Confession*, Britanniis, Bannavem Tiburniae and the Wood of Foclut can all be identified within a very specific local region, on the coast of north-west Brittany, between Aleth (St Malo) and Mont St Michel. A final clue to support the possibility that all three of these places existed in the same local area is the meaning of the Latin name '*Mare Occcidentale*' or 'Western Sea'. It is the fourth coordinate which can help to explain all the others.

In his *Confession*, St Patrick describes the Wood of Foclut as being 'close beside the Western Sea'. This is a rare coupling of important geographical references. If the Wood of Foclut can be identified with the Forest of Quokelunde in Brittany, it allows for the possibility that when Patrick used the name 'Mare Occidentale' he may have been referring to the ocean extending westwards from the coast of Brittany.

At the time of St Patrick, the Forest of Quokelunde was 'close beside the Western Sea' which matches St Patrick's description perfectly. Is it possible that Irish raiders could have travelled so far to attack the estate of Calpurnius and carry St Patrick back with them to be sold as a slave in Ireland, towards end of the fourth century?

---

*Notes*

1. The Talmud

2. See Bertrand Robidue, *Histoire et Panorama d'un Beau Pays* (Rennes, 1953), pp. 14–19, 192.

3. Château de Bonaban, 35350 La Gouesnière, St Malo.

4. Quinault found many remains of a forest, 'La Forêt de Qokelunde' which after 1734 was called Scissy by L'Abbé Rouault. See L'Abbé Rouault, *Abrégé de l'Histoire des Solitaires de Scissy* (St Malo, 1734).

5. For detailed information on the ancient forests of Brittany, see Gilles Manet, *De L'etat Ancien et De L'etat Actuel dans La Baie de Mont Saint Michel* (St Malo, 1829), p. 6. See n. 26, also p. 52; n. 30, p. 55; n. 31, p. 56; n. 32, p. 60. Manet includes old maps of the Bay area on pp. 146 ff.

6. See John O'Hanlon, *Lives of the Irish Saints* (Dublin, 1875), iii, p. 455, n. 258.

7. 'Grande forêt, tres grande forêt la plus grande forêt de Bretagne,' Gilles Deric *Histoire Ecclésiastique de Bretagne*, ii (Paris, 1778). *Histoire de Bretagne*, p. 15–17. *L'éxistence de cette forêt est un fait sur lequel l'histoire ne perment pas d'élever le moins doubt*. p. 52. Édouard Le Héricher, 'Notes philologiques sur le Roman de Rou et le Roman du Mont-Saint-Michel', *Mémoires de la Société des antiquaires de Normandie*, 24/3 (1861).

8. *Dolomhoir au milieu d'une grand forêt; une vast forêt qui s'étendoit depuis Aldernay, Chosey, Chaussey et les Mintiérs jusqu'a Dol.* Deric, *Histoire Ecclésiastique de Bretagne*, p. 131–3, n. (c). See also Guillaume-Stanislas Trébutien, *Le Mont St Michel au Peril de la Mer* (Caen, 1841).

9. 'Forest of the Oak Millenarian' or perhaps 'The Forest of a Thousand Oaks': This reference surfaced on the internet but has been lost. If anyone can help identify the source, it would be appreciated. *ML*

10. For more detailed information on the Forest of Qokelunde, see Robidue, *Histoire et Panorama*, p. 17 ff. The location of the ancient Forest of Coquelunde is also mentioned in *Memoires des Antiquaries de France* for 1817–1869, vol. 17, p. 383. For other references to Quokelunde see Edouard le Hericher, *Histoire de L'Avranchin*, ii, p. 230. Also: *Les Annales du Mont St Michel*, i (1874), p. 109.

11. See Joseph de Garaby, 'St Patrick' in *Vies des Bienheureux et des saints de Bretagne* (Saint-Brieuc, 1839). L'Abbé Desroches also records the local significance of 'Saint Senier', the church of 'St Senier' de Beuvron and the ancient parish of 'St Senier', near Avranches. This is still an active local parish church about two miles from Avranches. See Jacques Desroches, *Histoire du Mont St Michel*, i (Caen, 1838), p. 80.

12. Latin: *senioribus*. C 26: Bieler, *The Works of St Patrick* (New York, 1952), p. 72.

13. *La Forêt de Coquelunde entre Ardevon et le Mont St Michel…la Forêt de Coquelunde envalie par la mer*. Desroches, *Histoire du Mont St Michel*, p. 72, p. 338. Louis Blondel identifies this forest: *cette forêt était dans les environs de Tumba (Mont St Michel) qui se nommait encore Mont St Jupiter*. See Louis Blondel, *Notice Historique du Mont-St-Michel, de Tombelaine et d'Avrenches* (Avrenches, 1823), pp 72, 79; see also Manet, *De L'etat Ancien et De L'etat Actuel dans La Baie de Mont Saint Michel*, who provides a detailed map on p. 26.

14. Guillaume de Saint-Pair, *Le Roman du Mont-Saint-Michel* (Caen, 1856).

15. Guillaume's poem is recognised as one of three Medieval Latin histories written at Mont St Michel.

16. Robert de Torigny was abbot of the Monastery at Mont St Michel from 1154–1186 CE, when Guillaume de Saint Pair was resident as a monk. Torigny is known to have been a prolific writer whose hobbies included the coats of arms of noble families throughout Christendom. He wrote a large number of books, many dedicated to the history of the Mont St Michel region including the Chronicle *Historiia Meriadoci* and other rare manuscripts compiled at Mont St Michel, now preserved in Avranches. Torigny also compiled certain genealogical tables, which appear to have been lost. One of Torigny's manuscripts is said to be preserved in private archives at Saint Sulpice Church in Paris. Could this shed light on uncertainties which surround the origins of St Patrick and the truth about his family in Brittany? See Michael Baigent, Henry Lincoln and Richard Leigh, *Holy Blood and Holy Grail* (London, 1996), p. 189 and p. 526 n. 21.

17. Desroches, *Histoire du Mont St Michel*. See also Loïc Langouet, 'La Forêt du Scissy et La marée de 709, Légende ou Réalité?' *Dossiers du Centre Régional d'Archéologie d'Alet*, 24 (1996), pp. 49–54.

18. Michel Rouze writes about the Forest of Quokelunde in his well-loved children's adventure and mystery stories. See Michel Rouze, *La Forêt de Quokelunde* (Paris, 1953).

19. See Boudent-Godelinière, *Mont St Michel* (1845), p. 14.

20. Langouet, 'La Forêt du Scissy'.

21. René Henry, *Au Péril de la Mer* (Paris, 2006).

22. Manet was the first to document local changes in sea level and map the former river courses, the ancient forests and Gallo-Roman roads that crossed the Bay area. Manet, *De L'etat Ancien et De L'etat Actuel dans La Baie de Mont Saint Michel*. See original map on p. 26.

23. Brythonic Gaelic (Welsh and Gaulish) has traditionally been classified is a 'P' Celtic language where as Irish and Scots Gaelic is a 'Q' Celtic language. The difference between them is the treatment of the proto-Celtic 'k' which became 'p' in the P-Celtic languages but 'k' in Irish. For example, in Welsh and Breton the word for head is 'pen' but it appears as 'ceann' in Irish and Scots Gaelic. The name for son is 'mab' (earlier 'map') in Brythonic but 'mac' in Goidelic. More

recently, Goidelic and Brythonic have been linked as insular Celtic languages and distinguished from continental Celtic. Quokelunde could reflect a Brythonic or continental (Gaulish) tradition. William Burley Lockwood, *A panorama of Indo-European languages* (Hutchinson, 1972), pp. 74–80.

24. L'Abbé Gervais de la Rue, writing in 1834, said that the name Quokelunde includes the common Scandinavian 'lundr' which means 'grove' or forest, attached to an older Celtic name. See Margaret Gelling, *Place-names in the landscape* (London, 1984).

25. Christine Mohrman, *The Latin of St Patrick* (Dublin, 1961).

26. Mohrman, *The Latin of St Patrick*, p. 54.

27. Mohrman, *The Latin of St Patrick*, p. 8, p. 26.

28. Mohrman, *The Latin of St Patrick*, p. 34.

29. 'The biblical elements (of St Patrick's Latin) seem to be of Gaulish origin but there is no evidence of a connection with southern Gaul.' This argues strongly against St Patrick being trained in Auxerre or Lerins. See Mohrman, *The Latin of St Patrick*, p. 32.

30. Mohrman, *The Latin of St Patrick*, p. 53.

31. Mohrman, *The Latin of St Patrick*, p. 20. *Emphasis added.

32. R. P. C. Hanson, *St Patrick His Origins and Career* (Oxford, 1997), p. 208.

33. Hanson, *St Patrick*, p. 202 ff.

# CHAPTER FIFTEEN

# Pirates of the Mare Occidentale

A wolf will not show itself –
Unless it's trying to tell you something.[1]

When trying to interpret a dream Jungian analyst Jeremy Taylor warns against the dangers of what he calls 'mistaken literalism'. The advice he gives is that we must be careful not to base any specific geographical or historical claims on whatever a person has described to us in the context of a dream.

Ever since the seventh century, when Bishop Tirechán claimed the Wood of Foclut existed in his own diocese in County Mayo, a particular form of dream interpretation has been applied to a passage in St Patrick's *Confession* which quickly became part of an established tradition continued to this day. This is based on an essentially speculative and misguided form of dream analysis. An initial error of interpretation that assumes the Wood of Foclut must have existed in Ireland because St Patrick describes in his dream how he heard the 'Voice of the Irish' calling to him from that wood, was compounded by further error when it was also assumed that when Patrick said the Wood of Foclut was close beside the Western Sea (Mare Occidentale) he must have been referring to the Atlantic Ocean off the west coast of Ireland.

In the context of his own writings, is it possible Patrick was referring to the ocean off the north-west coast of Brittany? In Roman geography, the 'Mare Occidentale' did not refer exclusively to the Atlantic Ocean off the west coast of Ireland. In Latin, *occident* means west, and *orient* is east. For Roman geographers, who approached the world from a continental perspective, the 'Mare Occidentale' meant, 'the sea of the setting sun'. It applied to the whole ocean west of the Empire, including that which existed off the west coast of France and Spain.[2]

Apart from ancient maps in which the name appears, there are few historical references to the Mare Occidentale. Those which do exist, suggest this refers not just to the ocean off the west coast of Europe, but to the seas adjacent to the coasts of France and Spain in particular.

The Mare Occidentale appears on a Piri Reis map dated to 1513, together with an interesting commentary. Piri Reis was a Turkish captain who later became the Chief Admiral of the Ottoman Navy. Notes in the margin attached to one of his maps include accounts of those who took part in the discovery of places shown on the map. The following passage is a translation of these notes as they apply to section XXII of the map, which deals specifically with the Mare Occidentale:

> This sea is called Western Sea [Mare Occidentale] but the Frankish sailors call it the *Mare d'Espagne* which means the Sea of Spain. Until now it was known by these names, but Columbus, who opened up this sea and made these islands known and the Portuguese ... have given it a new name, *Ovo Sano* [*Oceano* – Ocean], round like egg. Before this it was believed this sea did not have aim or limit, except that on the other side was dusk and darkness.[3]

Ireland was at the margins of the known world, beyond which there was only dusk and darkness. The ocean to the west of Ireland was basically an unknown and uncharted territory for classical geographers. It was always stretching the evidence beyond reasonable limits to assume that St Patrick must have been referring to such a remote part of the western ocean, when he described the Wood of Foclut as being 'close beside the Western Sea'. Valorosi described the Mare Occidentale as the ocean which 'bathes all the west of the Empire':

> Until now, nobody has pushed beyond the Island of Egamin [Erin/Ireland?] However there are a series of estuaries for the greater part unexplored that are used as bases for pirates who manage in this way to escape the boat vessels of the imperial military navy.[4]

Ludwig Bieler investigated the origins of the Latin 'Mare Occidentale' as part of his research into problems associated with the traditional location for the Wood of Foclut. He notes that in classical geographical records the word *mare* is often substituted by the word *oceanus*.[5] On various ancient maps the name 'Oceanus Occidentale' appears far more frequently than 'Mare Occidentale' but it still designates the sea which extends westwards from continental Europe, which we now call the Atlantic. The paucity of references, therefore, suggests that the 'Mare Occidentale' may have been a more familiar term within local or ethnic rather than classical geography, as would be the case, for example, for those who were resident in Brittany.

Is there any evidence which might provide clues to help clarify how St Patrick may have understood the meaning of this name? If there is any truth in the geographical descriptions given by Probus in his *Life of St Patrick*, the answer is yes. Probus includes a very significant remark when he describes Bannavem Tiburniae as being 'close beside the Western Sea' in the province of Neustria. He makes no claims regarding the geographical location of the Wood of Foclut but it is significant that Probus uses the same Latin phrase to describe the location of Bannavem Tiburniae that St Patrick used when describing the location of the Wood of Foclut. Both are described as being 'close beside the Western Sea' and the Latin phrase used by Probus – *haut procul a mare occidentali* – is exactly the same phrase as that given by St Patrick in his *Confession*.

If what Probus said is true, and if a local tradition recorded by the Breton historians is reliable, that pirates who attacked the Calpurnius estate crept up through a local forest called Quokelunde, which can be identified as the Wood called 'Foclut' in Patrick's *Confession*, then it is undoubtedly also true that when St Patrick tells us that the Wood of Foclut was 'close beside the Western Sea', he must have been referring to the ocean off the west coast of Brittany.

Could Irish pirates have travelled that far? A number of references can be found which help confirm the existence of piracy on the Mare Occidentale during the time of St Patrick. Stories recorded in the ancient Lives of St Patrick, link an important event in St Patrick's biography to a particular sea, which is called the Iccian Sea or 'Sea of Icht'. The event in question concerns the circumstances in which St Patrick was taken into captivity. The family are said to have crossed the Iccian Sea as part of a journey they made by ship from Strathclyde to Brittany, where St Patrick was taken captive. The Iccian Sea was a name given to the stretch of water between southern Ireland, south-west Britain and the northern coast of Brittany. For the Romans, this sea formed part of the Western Sea or 'Mare Occidentale'. Today, the French call it *La Manche*.

The location of the Iccian Sea is well documented and can be clearly identified. It was linked to the Roman port of Iccius (Boulogne-sur-Mer) from which Caesar embarked, during the invasions of the island of Britain in 55 and 54 BCE. The Iccian Sea is mentioned in the ancient annals of Ireland where it appears in Old Irish as 'Muir n-Icht', again connected with the Port of Iccius, located in northern Gaul. The annals record that towards the end of his reign (379–405 CE) one of the most famous of all Irish chieftains Niall of the Nine Hostages was engaged in seafaring expeditions on the Iccian Sea before he was killed during his second or third expedition in Gaul.[6]

> The Age of Christ 405: Niall of the Nine Hostages had been twenty-seven years in the sovereignty of Ireland. He was slain at Muir-n-Icht.[7]

In his book, *Oxygia*, Roderick O'Flaherty discusses the reign of Niall and says he was killed by a poisoned arrow when he was fighting on the River Loire. If this is true, it links Niall's excursions even more directly with Brittany.[8]

St Patrick tells us in his *Confession* that he was taken captive at sixteen years of age when pirates attacked his father's estate at Bannavem Tiburniae. If Patrick was born in 385 CE he would have been sixteen years old in 401 CE, which is the period the Irish chieftains were raiding in Brittany. It is therefore possible that St Patrick was taken captive during one of Niall's raids in Gaul. In his *History of Ireland*, Keating accepted this to be the case when he said:

He [Niall] sent a fleet to Brittany in France which is called Armorica, for the purpose of plundering that country; they brought 200 noble youths as captives to Ireland with them and it was in this captivity they brought Patrick who was sixteen years old.[9]

The Irish were not the only pirates operating in these waters. Piracy was rampant on the Western Sea or 'Mare Occidentale' during the late Roman period, especially in those final years which preceded the fall of Rome, when there were constant attacks along the north-western coasts of Gaul. Several groups were engaged in piracy and slave trading in the violent, unstable period during the late fourth and early fifth centuries. Slavery was a marked feature of native Irish (Celtic) and Caledonian-Pictish societies, as it was throughout the Roman Empire at the time of St Patrick.

Slave trading provided a lucrative income. With the breakdown of law and order in the Western Empire, the number of young men and women taken captive must have been enormous. In his writings, St Patrick tells us that he was taken captive along with thousands of others.[10] In his *Letter to Coroticus*, he mentions the policy of the Christians in Roman Gaul, which was to pay generous ransoms to the Franks for the release of Christians taken hostage.[11] This suggests that he was familiar with the situation on the continent. The busy Roman port at Aleth and its wealthy rural hinterland would have been a prime target for those seeking plunder especially after the legions had been recalled from Gaul around 405 CE. The soldiers of the Legion Martenensis, who had been stationed at Aleth, were recalled to defend Rome. Attacks were more common as the legions withdrew and lost whatever control they once had in Brittany.

In 407 CE the Vandals, Alans and Suevi and other barbarian tribes ravaged Gaul and the coastal region was constantly plundered until 417 CE. There were increasing attacks from pirates and Barbarian tribes arriving from the north. These attacks involved British, Irish and Frankish groups. In the political and military chaos, this region may have been denuded of people and resources. If St Patrick's family home was located near Aleth, at the 'mouth' of the River Rance, then from a historical point of view, Irish pirates could have been responsible for the attack.

Long before the Roman period there were established trading routes between Ireland and the coasts of Gaul and archaeological evidence confirms significant exchange between these two regions. With the prevailing westerly winds, the journey from southern Ireland to the coast of Brittany, in reasonable weather, would have taken no more than three days. Writing in the twelfth century, Gerald of Wales describes Ireland as three days sailing from Spain when he says, 'The farthest island of the west (Ireland) has Spain parallel to it in the south at a distance of three ordinary days sailing.'[12] If Spain could be reached in three days sailing, the same would obviously have applied to Brittany.

After his escape from slavery in Ireland, and intending to return to his homeland, St Patrick tells us he sailed for three days and nights before the ship on which he was travelling made land. The place where they landed seemed like a wasteland, almost devoid of people. Patrick and the crew had to walk for several days without food until they reached some kind of human habitation. It is possible the ship sailed to Brittany. If so, Patrick may have been an eye witness to devastations caused by Barbarian invasions of the Gallic peninsular, as Bury suggested.

Driving along the coast road from Château Bonaban to St Malo it is possible to enjoy views of the ocean which stretches out to the west. This could have been the sea St Patrick described as the Western Sea or 'Mare Occidentale'. The ancient site on which Château Bonaban is now located is still very close to the sea, which suggests that the local traditions that have been preserved in Brittany about St Patrick could be true.

The evidence, therefore, invites us to consider a radical new alternative to our traditional understanding of St Patrick's biography. Four of the key geographical references mentioned in the *Confession* can all be identified within a specific local coastal region of Brittany between the ancient Roman port of Aleth (St Malo) and Mont St Michel. This includes St Patrick's homeland *in Britanniis*, the family estate from which he was taken captive at Bannavem Tiburniae, the Wood of Foclut and the 'Mare Occidentale' or Western Sea. If these identifications are correct, then St Patrick's father and grandfather owned an estate on an elevated site close to the present site of Château Bonaban, only a few kilometres from the Roman port of Aleth.

René Henry's detailed maps have identified a large flat area of open ground close to Aleth and St Malo, at Cézembre, which would have been ideal for the Roman military. Soldiers could have pitched tents there during the winter months. Some of the ancient writers record that St Patrick's 'Bannavem Tiburniae' was identified with such a facility. Remains of Roman and Viking camps have been found on the prairies at Cézembre.[13] Much of the local area, covered by forest at the time of St Patrick, has been cleared for agriculture and new housing and road developments. A small part of the old Forest of Quokelunde may have survived in the grounds of Château Bonaban. It is possible that some of the oak trees growing around the lake are perhaps the descendants of trees which grew there at the time of St Patrick.

For those who may wish to visit, these oaks can be viewed as a natural remnant of the forest which once surrounded the family's estate at *Bannavem Tibur*niae where St Patrick may have been taken captive. Patrick may have played in this forest as a child and through his early teenage years, until that fateful day when he was abducted and sold into slavery in Ireland. Perhaps different memories of this forest, those which haunted St Patrick in his dreams and those which have shaped our understanding of its geographical location, can both now be freed from the shackles of historical uncertainty.

There is so much about St Patrick that we do not know. One of the most uncertain periods of St Patrick's biography includes the so-called 'missing years' between the time St Patrick returned to his homeland after escaping from slavery and the moment he set sail to return to Ireland as an apostle. This is the time when St Patrick undertook religious training and spiritual formation.

The question as to where St Patrick was trained and which church or religious group supported his mission to Ireland is an essential part of his biography which has always been controversial. The ancient Lives of St Patrick published by Colgan preserve several confused and contradictory accounts which mention different people in various contexts and a number of different geographical locations.

Many of these record that St Patrick's spiritual formation was associated with and guided by senior figures within the church of Rome, including St Germanus and Pope Celestine. These particular strands of tradition say Patrick was trained for many years under Germanus in Auxerre, that he may have spent time at the Monastery of Lerins or Arles, that he visited Rome on more than one occasion and was ordained by Pope Celestine before he went to Ireland as an apostle. This is not based on any reliable historical evidence, but appears to form part of the 'Legend' of St Patrick.[14]

Some of the ancient sources contradict these traditions and present an alternative version of events. According to these accounts, after Patrick escaped from Ireland he joined the community of St Martin, was tonsured and received his initial religious training there on the banks of the River Loire near Tours. After leaving Tours, Patrick joined a community of 'barefoot hermits' who lived on the 'isles of the Tyrrhene Sea'. It was here that St Patrick was ordained by St Senior and commissioned for the mission to Ireland and where he was given the *Baccaill Jesu* or 'Staff of Jesus', as a sign of his authority to preach the gospel there as an apostle. These mysterious islands are consistently mentioned in most of the ancient documents related to Patrick, although their location has never been securely identified. Evidence suggests they were also located in the Bay of Mont St Michel, off the north-west coast of Brittany, in the same local region as Château Bonaban. If so, St Patrick appears to have had a much closer relationship with this local coastal region in Brittany than has so far been acknowledged or understood.

Severus tells us that many young nobles were attracted to the monastery at Tours and if the claims recorded by the early Breton historians about St Patrick's family are true, St Patrick may have been one of them. Where did St

Patrick receive his religious training in preparation for the mission to Ireland? As we continue our quest to find our the truth about St Patrick it's time to visit those famous limestone caves where St Martin established an early Christian monastic community. Is there any evidence to support the possibility that St Patrick may have been there?

---

*Notes*

1. Gudhrun, a Danish Naturalist.

2. Bieler understood this when he said, 'Mare occidentale may denote any part of the sea to the north west of Europe': Perhaps a little recklessly, he then adds, 'Patrick probably thinks of the Atlantic coast of Ireland.' See Ludwig Bieler, *Clavis Patricii II: Libri Epistolarum Sancti Patricii Episcopi* (Dublin, 1993), p. 150; also *Irish Historical Studies*, iii (1943), pp. 351–64.

3. From notes concerning the Mare Occidentale, attached to Piri Reis Map, 1513, Legend xxii. See J. Hapgood, *Maps of the Ancient Sea Kings* (Illinois, 1966), p. 224.

4. The 'Island of Egamin' may be a reference to Ireland.

5. He concluded, 'The identification of Patrick's 'mare occidentale' with the Atlantic (off the west coast of Ireland) seems by no means untenable.' Bieler, 'The Problem of Silva Focluti', *Irish Historical Studies*, 3/12 (1943), pp. 351–64.

6. As well as attacking the north-west coast of Gaul, Niall had made incursions into Britain against Stilicho, whose success in repelling him and his Scots (Irish) was described by Claudian. 'By him', says the poet (speaking of Britannia), 'I was protected when the Scot [Irish] moved all Ierne [Ireland] against me, and the sea foamed with his hostile oars.'

7. Donovan, A4M, for the year 405 CE. See John O'Hanlon, *Lives of the Irish Saints* (Dublin, 1875), p. 488, n. 33 and William Flemming, *Boulogne-sur-Mer* (London, 1907), p. 8 ff.

8. Roderic O'Flaherty, *Oxygia* (Dublin, 1775), pp 393–412.

9. Geoffrey Keating, *History of Ireland*, ii, in Irish Texts Society, ed. and trans. P. S. Dineen (Dublin, 1908). Note that Keating describes Patrick as a 'noble' youth. Breton sources say St Patrick's family had a royal pedigree and that two of his sisters were founding members of the Breton aristocracy. For a study of St Patrick's royal pedigree see Marcus Losack, *St Patrick and the Bloodline of the Grail: The Untold Story of St Patrick's Royal Family*, (Annamoe, Wicklow, 2012).

10. C 1. *Hiberione in captiuitate adductus sum cum tot milia hominum*. See Bieler, *Libri*, p. 56.

11. LC 14.

12. Gerald of Wales, *The History and Topography of Ireland*, trans. John J. O'Meara (London, 1982), p. 33.

13. See René Henry, *Au Péril de la Mer* (Paris, 2006), p. 43 ff.

14. When J. H. Todd published his detailed study of St Patrick in 1864, controversy erupted because he suggested there was no historical evidence to associate St Patrick with Pope Celestine or the church in Rome. See J. H. Todd, *St Patrick, Apostle of Ireland* (Dublin, 1864), p. vi.

# CHAPTER SIXTEEN

# Martin of Tours

> Jesus did not predict that he would come clothed in purple with a glit-
> tering crown on his head. I will not believe Christ has appeared unless
> he comes in the form in which he suffered, naked and stripped of this
> world's glory, its power and possessions.[1]

Several of the ancient sources claim that St Patrick was trained and tonsured
in the community of St Martin. The credibility of this connection is strengthened by the claim that Patrick's mother, Conchessa, was 'of the Franks' and that
she was St Martin's niece.[2] If this is true, Martin and Patrick were closely
related.

The primary source for information about St Martin is Sulpitius Severus
(363–420 CE). His writings are a contemporary witness for the crucial period
from 385–400 CE when both the Emperor Maximus and St Martin were still
alive. This was the time of St Patrick's birth, childhood and teenage years. What
makes this author so intriguing is that Severus was a disciple and close friend,
familiar with Martin's approach to Christianity and how the teachings of the
gospel were being practised in St Martin's community. If Patrick received initial
ecclesiastical training and spiritual formation at Tours, this is where we may be
able to find more clues as to St Patrick's real identity.

The accounts given by Severus of the situation relating to church and state
during this period reveal there were diverse groups within the church and conflicts which had a direct impact on St Martin and perhaps, therefore, also on
St Patrick. Severus provides insight into these disputes and conflicting
approaches to the requirements of Christianity and the teachings of Jesus,
which may help explain why St Patrick was perhaps rejected by the church and
excluded from historical records for two hundred years after his death. The key
to the truth about St Patrick's biography is the link with St Martin of Tours.

Severus calls St Martin 'a truly blessed, holy person, in whom there was no
badness, judging no one, condemning no one, returning evil for evil to no one'.
He says, 'Never was there a feeling in his heart except for piety, peace and tender mercy.'[3] Martin was a very spiritual person, who understood Christianity
to be essentially an ascetic religion.

Christian discipleship required the renunciation of personal wealth and a
willingness to follow the essential teaching of Jesus, to avoid temptations associated with material grandeur. St Martin understood the command of Jesus to

'sell everything you have, give to the poor and come follow me' as an essential foundation for discipleship. To become a Christian, seek spiritual perfection and try to be worthy of eternal life, this command had to be put into practice.

Martin embraced the teachings of (Coptic) Egyptian Desert Spirituality, following the example of St Antony, to the extent that all members of his community wore simple garments made from camel hair which had been imported directly from Egypt.[4] Severus tells us that Martin continued to dress this way even after he became a bishop, which infuriated some clergy who thought ecclesiastical leaders should retain a sense of status which belonged to a more 'dignified' classical lifestyle.

He describes how Martin's approach to Christianity was influenced by Paulinus of Nola, who parted with his material possessions (which were substantial) and 'following Christ, showed himself the only one in these times to have fully obeyed the precepts of the gospel'.[5]

Severus also describes Martin's hermitage, two miles outside the city of Tours. This spot was so secret and retired that he enjoyed the chance for solitude, in the midst of other responsibilities. On one side it was surrounded by a precipitous rock; the river Loire had shut in the rest of the plain by a bay extending back for a little distance and the place could be approached only by one person at a time through a very narrow passage. Martin built a cell constructed of wood.

The other monks also built cells, although most were dug out of the rock in the overhanging mountain, which they hollowed out into caves. No one had anything called his own; all things were possessed in common.[6] It was forbidden to buy or sell anything, which Severus claims was the custom among most monks. No art was practised except by the scribes. Rarely did anyone go beyond the cell, except when they assembled at the place designated for prayer. They ate food together, after the hour of fasting was past. No one drank wine, except when illness compelled them. Severus informs us there were about eighty monks in St Martin's community, many from noble families. If St Patrick went there, we can imagine that he would not have felt out of place.

Severus also provides a reliable contemporary witness to the conflicts and difficulties which existed between St Martin and other church leaders. He tells us that some of the diocesan clergy despised Martin's appearance and Christian way of life, as a result of which there was controversy over Martin's election as Bishop of Tours. Some bishops accused Martin of being unworthy of the episcopate on the basis that his appearance was despicable, saying his clothes were poor and shabby, he was 'a contemptible person' and 'his hair was disgusting'. We can only try to imagine what was so despicable to them about St Martin's hair. For some reason it was offensive to other bishops.[7] Perhaps it was long, following the orthodox tradition, which required a monk never to cut his hair or shave the face again after monastic vows were taken. Martin's hair was obviously not compatible with what was expected or accepted by other clergy. This sheds some light on the kind of tonsure that was distinctive in his community.

If Patrick was trained in St Martin's community and tonsured there, as some of the ancient records claim, then Patrick would probably have worn his hair in the same style as St Martin. If so, this would have been equally offensive to those church leaders. Tonsure was to become one of the key issues of conflict between the Irish tradition and the Roman Church together with the calculations of a cycle related to the appropriate time for the celebration of Easter.

Severus tells us that some of the bishops attacked St Martin and 'sought to slander him'. Someone called The Avenger opposed Martin's election as bishop of Tours. The appointment was ratified by popular demand, in controversial circumstances. This did not go down well in some quarters. There was serious conflict within the church of Gaul at this time. Severus reveals something of the danger when he states openly that those who hated St Martin included many bishops, although he did not want to name names, saying, 'a good many of these people are still venting their spleen against my self'.[8] Severus was treading on a dangerous political and ecclesiastical tight rope. Whatever these conflicts and differences were they had created a dangerous situation for Martin and those associated with him.

Severus was a well-known writer, respected by the highest authorities in the church at the end of the fourth century but when approaching this subject he was clearly concerned to watch his words carefully. He tells us that he had originally intended to keep his record of St Martin private 'confined within the walls of my own house' but he thought it was disgraceful that the excellence of so great a man (St Martin) should remain concealed.[9] His *Life of Martin* was written when St Martin was still alive but Severus may have sensed danger and delayed publishing it until after his death. This shows how complex and potentially sinister the situation was. What was so dangerous about things happening in the church?

We don't have to read too far between the lines to find out what was going on and who Severus was talking about. Severus describes an emerging conflict between those who supported a simple form of monasticism of the kind sponsored by St Martin and those clergy who were linked more closely to a politically influential diocesan hierarchy. Monastic groups advocated the practice of asceticism and poverty, characteristic of Egyptian Desert Spirituality. Others, including some very influential wealthy and powerful bishops, were more attached to classical Roman social and economic values. This conflict appears to have been a very serious issue for senior members of the church.

St Ambrose of Milan refused to visit Gaul because of the conflict there between monks and diocesan clergy but this conflict was not restricted to Gaul.

It was characteristic of those areas where an expanding authority of the Roman diocesan hierarchy was interfacing with monastic expressions of Christianity in the 'Celtic' heartlands of Britain, Ireland and Gallic parts of Spain. St Patrick's life cannot be understood in isolation from these issues which were affecting the whole western church at this time.

Some of those associated with Martin were accused of being Pelagian. This included Severus himself. St Martin may have died before Pelagius visited St Augustine in North Africa, but views expressed by Pelagius were characteristic of the monastic movement at this time. Those who sympathised with him would soon be targeted by Pope Celestine, St Germanus, and Palladius, amongst others who strongly supported the teachings of St Augustine.[10]

Severus lets us know very clearly where he stood in relation to these disputes. As far as he was concerned, in their behaviour some bishops and a powerful clergy group within the church were betraying the essential teachings of the gospel and the original teachings of Jesus. He says, *'in Martin alone Apostolic authority continued to exert itself.'*[11] This is a remarkable statement, which shows his profound respect for Martin's way of being Christian.

Severus describes St Martin as a truly blessed and holy man 'in whom there was no falsehood – no lies or deception – judging no one – condemning no one – returning evil to no one'. He writes, 'never was there a feeling in his heart except piety, peace and tender mercy'. But there were those who 'as he led his retired and tranquil life, slandered him with poisoned tongue and viper's mouth.'[12]

In one of his books, Severus records a dialogue between himself and a 'man of Gaul'. He invites this person to speak the Celtic language or 'Gaulish'. This was Brythonic Gaelic, now preserved in Welsh and the Breton language.[13] This monk was a disciple of St Martin and a member of Martin's community. We know this because he speaks about fishing on the River Loire and catching a huge pike when he was responsible for finding food for the other monks who lived in the monastery.[14] The 'man from Gaul' also speaks about the serious conflict taking place in the western church at this time. St Martin's community had come under serious attack from Jerome, in a dispute related to issues of authority that manifested themselves shortly afterwards in the Pelagian controversy. When speaking about St Jerome the monk from Gaul says:

> He [Jerome] is in truth but too well known to us, for some five years ago I read a certain book of his in which the whole tribe of our monks is vehemently assaulted and reviled by him.[15]

Jerome and Augustine were influential and powerful figures in the church at this time. Anyone on the receiving end of Jerome's caustic criticisms would be vulnerable to condemnation and ridicule. Severus describes a church

Council at which 350 bishops were present and Jerome was in very high standing. At this council, heresies were condemned. Severus adds an intriguing comment that 'Jerome is said to stand in high favour with certain people who I am unwilling to name'. If this is a reference to St Augustine, which is possible, this reveals how precarious the situation was for St Martin's community and any other forms of 'Celtic' monasticism.[16] To have Jerome attacking you in his racist, vitriolic diatribes was one thing, but to have Augustine and Jerome teamed up against you, as Pelagius did, was sufficient to guarantee a theological death sentence, if not worse.

Telling of his conversion in 383 CE, St Augustine recalls a conversation in Milan with an imperial officer called Potitanus. This man told how, when he was stationed at Trier he and some companions walked together in the park outside the city walls. He entered one of the monastic huts, where he picked up a copy of the *Life of St Antony*, written by St Athanasius. When Augustine read this book it changed his life and led him and his wife to embrace celibacy. It brought about St Augustine's conversion to Christianity.

It is interesting to note that Potitanus was associated with members of the greatly feared Imperial Secret Police – known as *Agentes in Rebus*. Augustine was the first to develop a theological justification for the use of the secular powers and military agencies of the state to increase the church's influence and authority, including its ability to combat heresy. In relation to how these disputes were affecting monks in Gaul, the 'man from Gaul' is afraid to name names or speak in greater detail, noting somewhat despondently, 'Submission procures friends while truth gives rise to hatred.'[17]

Severus knew that by writing too openly about these matters he would be walking 'barefoot' into a political minefield, but he shows great courage by entering that field far enough for us to catch glimpses of how the western church was developing. Severus was an accomplished writer, well respected by established authorities. Jerome called him 'our friend Severus'[18] and St Augustine referred to him as 'a man excelling in learning and wisdom'.[19] Severus was a disciple of St Martin and had visited the monastery at Marmoutier on many occasions, so his writings are a priceless historical record of events taking place around him. The following passage describes the kind of approach to Christianity and spiritual formation that must have been typical of St Martin's community. It appears in a letter that may have formed part of extensive correspondence between Severus and St Paulinus of Nola. This letter provides an excellent summary of the essential teachings of St Martin and early Gallic monasticism, the kind of environment in which St Patrick probably received spiritual formation and training. If he was trained in St Martin's community, this is how St Patrick would have been taught to believe and practice the Christian faith:

If you wish to be with Christ, you must live according to the example of Christ, who was so far removed from all evil and wickedness, that he did not render a recompense, even to his enemies, but rather even prayed for them ... For I do not wish you to reckon those souls Christian, who [I do not say] hate either their brothers or sisters but who do not, before God as a witness, love their neighbours with their whole heart and conscience, since it is a bounden duty for Christians, after the example of Christ himself, even to love their enemies.

If you desire to possess fellowship with the saints, cleanse your heart from the thought of malice and sin. Let no one circumvent you – let no one delude you by beguiling speech. The court of heaven will admit none except the holy, the righteous and simple, the innocent and pure. Evil has no place in the presence of God. It is necessary that those who desire to reign with Christ should be free from all wickedness, hypocrisy and deceit. Nothing is so offensive and nothing so detestable to God, as to hate anyone. While nothing is so acceptable to him as to love everyone. The prophet knowing this bears witness when he teaches, 'Ye who love the Lord, hate only evil.'[20]

Everything is unrighteous which goes against the gospel of Christ and that is the case if you will quietly permit anything to be done to another which you would feel painful if done by anyone to yourself ...

Let grace grow in you with years. Let righteousness increase with age and let your faith appear the more perfect the older you become.[21]

A similar approach to Christianity can be found throughout the writings of St Patrick. Here too we find a strong emphasis on purity of heart.[22] Another intriguing similarity between the letters of St Patrick and the teaching of St Martin concerns the relationship between good and evil. Severus tells us an important aspect of Martin's preaching concerned the possibility of repentance and salvation, even for the Devil. In a saying with Pelagian overtones, St Martin told Severus a religious parable, centred on a dialogue between Martin and the Devil. St Martin told the Devil, 'Past sins could be cleansed by the leading of a better life.' The Devil replied, 'No mercy was shown by the Lord to those who had fallen away.' Martin said to the Devil, 'If you, O wretched being, would repent of your deeds with a true confidence, the Lord would promise you the mercy of Christ.'[23]

This is essentially the same kind of teaching we find in Pelagius and the Egyptian Desert Tradition, that good or evil comes through thoughts expressed in actions but through the agency of free will as human beings we have the opportunity to choose one path over another. We can be guided by the heart to act and think in a certain way or to refrain. According to this philosophy, even the Devil can be saved and redeemed through love, repentance (recompense made for evil actions) and forgiveness.

St Patrick takes a similar approach in his *Letter to Coroticus*. Even though the soldiers of Coroticus had attacked and killed some of Patrick's newly baptised converts, stolen goods and taken others as slaves to be sold into prostitution, the gospel standard of forgiveness for those who repent and make genuine redress for wrongdoing, is never lowered. St Patrick 'excommunicates' Coroticus for his evil actions while offering forgiveness and reconciliation if appropriate action was taken to restore what was stolen and redress the imbalance of the evil or wrongdoing committed. This is what makes St Patrick's understanding of Christianity so profound. It is very similar to the teaching of St Martin.

Severus includes another intriguing statement which might help shed light on St Patrick's decision to 'give up his nobility' for the sake of the gospel. He claims he got this saying from the lips of St Martin himself, and that it was not fabricated:

> The Lord Jesus did not predict that he would come, clothed in purple with a glittering crown on his head. I will not believe that Christ has come unless he appears in the form in which he suffered – naked and stripped of this world's glory, power and possessions.[24]

If this saying is a reflection of Martin's approach to Christian teaching, it may hold clues to the origins of early Irish monasticism. It reveals real differences between traditional Roman customs and values (purple as a sign of imperial power and ecclesiastical authority) and early forms of Christian monasticism such as that practised by St Martin, in which a different kind of nobility was expected – the nobility of a truly loving and compassionate heart, wearing only simple clothes, without the trappings of imperial power and wealth.

In relation to the origins of Irish monasticism, it is significant that the same story and very similar teachings appear in documents of the Céile Dé, an eighth-century monastic reform movement in Ireland. The following story appears in the Legend of St Moling from the *Book of Leinster*:

> On one occasion as he [St Moling] was praying in his church, he saw the youth coming towards him into the house. A purple garment was about him and he had a distinguished countenance. 'That is good, O Cleric,' the youth said. 'Amen,' said Moling. 'Why do you not salute me?' said the youth. 'Who are you?' said Moling. 'I,' said he, 'I am Christ, the Son of God.' 'That is not possible,' said Moling. 'When Christ approaches to converse with the Céile Dé, he never comes in purple, but in the form of the lowly, the sick and the poor.[25]

The same legend is recorded in the Book of Lismore, an ancient Irish manuscript dated to the fifteenth century which contains material from a much
earlier period. These stories may have developed directly from Severus's *Life of
St Martin*, which was preserved in the *Book of Armagh*.

### Martin and Maximus

St Martin was Bishop of Tours at the very time Magnus Maximus was being
dressed in purple and hoisted onto the shoulders of the Legions in Britain,
before making his bid for imperial power. Breton historians record that St
Patrick's family came to Brittany at this time – around 385 CE. Maximus led a
rebellion from Britain against the incumbent Emperors, Valentinian and Gratian. Gratian was killed by soldiers loyal to Maximus, who became Emperor of
the West, establishing his residence at the Royal palace in Trier. Gratian's
brother, Valentinian, fled for his life but eventually returned with the support
of Theodosius, Emperor in the East. Maximus was executed in 388 CE,
beheaded at the third milestone from Aquilaea.

Breton historians record that during his short reign as Emperor, Maximus
established a British colony in Brittany and that one of his relatives, Conan,
was crowned as the first king of Brittany and Duke of the Armorican Tract.
Conan is said to have been related to Maximus through the latter's marriage to
Ellen or Helen, daughter of a high king in Britain, who was called Eudes or
Eudav Hen. Several Breton historians who were writing before the end of the
nineteenth-century claim that St Patrick's father, Calpurnius, was a cousin of
Conan and that Conan married St Patrick's sister, Darerca. If there is any truth
in these claims, then St Patrick and Conan were brothers-in-law and both
Calpurnius and St Patrick were also not far removed as blood relatives of the
Emperor himself.

Sulpitius Severus does not mention St Patrick in his writings, but if any of
these accounts contain even half a grain of truth, anything Severus tells us
about St Martin, the Emperor Magnus Maximus and what was going on at this
time in the church in Gaul, is relevant to the study of Patrick. Severus records
in great detail the close relationship that St Martin had, first with the Emperor
Valentinian and then with his successor, Magnus Maximus. This is a priceless
record of events which took place at the Palace in Trier from 380–395 CE. In
his role as bishop, St Martin met on several occasions with both Emperors.
Severus describes them both as kings, which suggests that he recognised the
sovereign or royal lineage of the Emperor, Magnus Maximus. Severus tells us
that Martin had warned Maximus that Valentinian was plotting to kill him.
He pleaded with the new Emperor to show compassion towards two supporters
of the former Emperor, Gratian.

This was the time shortly before St Patrick may have been resident at St Martin's community at Tours. The following information sheds light on events and relationships which may have had a significant impact on St Patrick's life and destiny.

When Martin became a bishop, his new responsibilities brought him into contact with the Emperor Valentinian on the eve of the British rebellion, which took place in 383 CE. Martin had to visit the imperial court. Severus tells us that Valentinian was initially unhappy when he realised Martin was asking for things which he did not incline to grant, so 'he ordered him to be kept from entering the doors of the royal palace'. St Martin fasted for seven days then represented himself and managed to gain entry. The King did not rise to greet him but they were soon reconciled. Severus writes:

> Afterwards the King [Valentinian] often invited the Holy Man to the conferences and entertainments. The King offered him many presents which Martin totally refused, maintaining his poverty, as he did on all occasions.[26]

In 383 CE, after his brother Gratian had been killed by soldiers loyal to Maximus, Valentinian had to flee from the Palace at Trier, where Maximus now established his imperial headquarters. Martin's relationship with the new Emperor would be even more significant than it was with his predecessor. Severus had to be especially careful about what he wrote at this point. The rebellion of Maximus was viewed by the imperial families ruling on the continent not simply as 'usurpation' but a gross act of treason. As he begins this part of his narrative, Severus chooses his words very carefully to avoid causing offence and to minimise the damage and dangers to himself and others that publication would have caused. He gently invites us through what he writes, to approach this controversial subject and enter the political and ecclesiastical minefield with him by saying:

> And here to insert some smaller matters among things so great ... such is the nature of our times when all things have fallen into decay and corruption it is almost a pre-eminent virtue. Often invited [to the Palace at Trier] Martin kept away from the King's entertainments saying he could not take a place at the same table of someone who out of two Emperors had deprived one of his kingdom and the other his life.[27]

Trying to explain and justify the recent rebellion, the new King (Maximus) told St Martin that he 'had not of his own accord assumed the sovereignty', but was encouraged by his supporters in Britain. He claimed that he simply 'defended by arms the sovereign requirements of the Empire' and that a decision to bid for imperial power had been imposed on him by his own soldiers 'according to the divine appointment'.[28] Severus may be revealing his sympathy towards this rebellion when he says, 'it was as if he had the favour of God'.

He then presents us with an intriguing record of meetings which took place between St Martin and the new Emperor. A number of bishops from various parts had assembled at the request of Maximus who was 'a man of fierce character' and who was elated at that time in the victory he had won in the civil wars. Severus says:

> Maximus ruled the state – a man worthy of being extolled in his whole life, if only he had been permitted to reject a crown thrust upon him during an illegal rebellion by the soldiers, or had been able to keep out of the civil war. The fact is a great Empire cannot be refused without danger or preserved without war. And as we have, once for all, entered the Palace, I shall string together events that took place there, although they happened at different times. It does not seem right not to mention the Queen's admiration for Martin.[29]

Martin agreed to come to a royal banquet held at the Palace in Trier and what follows is probably as close as we can get to an eyewitness account of what happened. At the banquet, Martin's 'presbyter', a respected elder in the church, sat between Maximus's brother and uncle. St Martin sat near to the King. Maximus ordered the goblet to be given to Martin 'accepting and hoping that he should receive the cup from his right hand'. Martin gave it to his presbyter instead. This caused a great stir and news about the incident spread like wildfire. Severus describes this incident in greater detail:

> Martin was given a seat close to the King. About the middle of the banquet according to custom one of the servants presented a goblet to the King, who ordered it to be given to Martin, expecting that he should receive the cup back from Martin's right hand.
> When Martin had drunk from the goblet, however, he gave it to his own presbyter, because he said there was no one worthier to drink next to him, saying it would not be right for him to prefer either the King himself or those who were next to the King, before the presbyter. The Emperor, as well as those who were present, admired this conduct so much, this very thing, by which they had been undervalued, gave them pleasure.[30] A report then ran through the whole Palace what Martin had done at the King's dinner which no bishop would have dared do even at the banquet of the lower judges.[31]

Severus also tells about the close relationship which existed between Martin and the emperor's wife. Unfortunately, he does not name Maximus's wife, who now became Queen, but in Welsh tradition she is called Ellen or Helen. He says:

The new emperor frequently sent for Martin, received him into the palace and treated him with honour. His whole speech with him was concerning things present, things to come – the glory of the faithful and the immortality of the saints. In the meantime, the Queen hung upon the lips of Martin and no less than the woman mentioned in the gospel she washed the feet of the holy man with her tears and wiped them with her hair. She did not think of the wealth of the kingdom, the dignity of the Empire, the crown, or the purple. She could not be torn away from the feet of Martin.

At last she begged of her husband that all the other attendants should be removed from the holy man and that she alone should wait upon him at meals. Martin could not refuse. His modest entertainment was arranged for him by the Queen. She arranged his seat for him, set his table, gave him water to wash his hands, and served the food which she herself had cooked. While he ate, she fixed her eyes on the ground, stood quietly at a distance, like a servant, mixed his drink and gave it to him. When the meal was over she collected leftovers and crumbs of bread which became her banquet. A Blessed woman worthy by this display of piety to be compared to she who came from the ends of the earth to learn from Solomon.[32]

After this, the sequence of events recorded by Severus becomes more sinister, violent and dangerous, almost leading to Martin's execution. If St Patrick was a family relation to Martin and a member of his monastic community, the following account may provide clues not only to the kind of Christianity St Patrick may have been trained to observe but also the complex political and ecclesiastical factors which may have impacted on his life. St Martin's life was threatened because of his support for the Priscillians, a group that was strong in Spain and the first to be denounced by leaders in the western church as heretics.

The Priscillians were an ascetic sect, named after the leader, Priscillian, who was the Bishop of Avila.[33] A synod held at Bordeaux in 384 CE had condemned his doctrines, but he had appealed to the new Emperor. The Bishop of Ossanova, Ithacius, had attacked Priscillian and urged Maximus to put him to death.

This dispute caused great conflict within the church. Neither Ambrose of Milan, nor Martin of Tours would hold communion with Ithacius or his supporters, because they had appealed to the Emperor in a dispute over doctrine and were now trying to punish a heretic with death. Martin wrote a strongly-worded letter to reprove Ithacius for appealing to the state authorities in a matter that concerned the church. St Martin said it would be sufficient punishment if Priscillian was branded a heretic and excommunicated by the bishops, without punishing him with death.

Maximus yielded at first to Martin's lobbying on behalf of Priscillian by ordering the trial to be deferred and even promised there should be no bloodshed, but afterwards he was persuaded to turn the case over to his prefect Evodius. Priscillian and some others were found guilty on several charges and were beheaded in 385 CE. This was the first judicial death sentence for heresy and had the effect of spreading Priscillianism in Spain. At this news, Martin went to Trier to plead for the lives of the Spanish Priscillianists who were threatened with a bloody persecution, and also for two men under suspicion as adherents of the late Emperor Gratian. As a condition, before granting this request, Maximus stipulated that St Martin should resume communion with Ithacius and his friends. Since they were not excommunicated, the Emperor said this was no violation of any canon and Martin accordingly promised the Emperor he would do so, provided Maximus could pardon the two who were supporters of Gratian and recall the military tribunes he had sent to Spain. The next day Martin received communion with the Ithacians, an action which he thought was needed to save many people from death. Martin explained to Severus how deeply troubled he was by these events because he felt he had compromised too much and not followed his own conscience to stay away.

Priscillian was the leader of a controversial Christian group thought to be heretical by certain authorities within the church and it is intriguing to learn that St Martin was prepared to go to great lengths to support them. Severus tells us that the leader of this sect had been condemned to death along with two others 'who, when they were clerics, had recently adopted the cause of Priscillian *and revolted from the Catholics*'. Some were beheaded; others were transported to the Island of Sylina, 'beyond the Britains', a reference to the Scilly Isles.[34] For their part in the affair both the Emperor and Ithacius were censured by Pope Siricius. This passage is extremely significant; and the words of Severus speak for themselves:

> I will now come to an event which he always concealed, owing to the character of the times but which he could not conceal from us. The Emperor Maximus, while in other respects doubtless a good man, was led astray by the advice of some priests after Priscillian had been put to death. By his Royal power he protected Ithacius, a bishop, who had been Priscillian's accuser, together with other friends and confederates of his who it is not necessary to name. The Emperor prevented anyone from bringing it as a charge against Ithacius that by his actions a man had been condemned to death. Martin, who was constrained to go to the court wishing to act as an advocate for many situations which had

caused serious suffering, incurred the whole force of the storm which was raging.

The bishops retained in Trier were talking every day with Ithacius and had made a common cause with him. And it so happened that under their influence the Emperor had already resolved to send tribunes armed with absolute power into the 'two Spains' to search out heretics and deprive them of their life or goods.[35]

Some of the bishops were aware that such proceedings would not please St Martin. They were concerned that Martin would not commune with them and influence others to take the same approach. These clergy tried to persuade the Emperor not to let Martin into the city, unless he would declare first that he would make peace with the bishops who were living there. He frustrated their plans by saying that he would come with the peace of Christ.

St Martin met the Emperor (Maximus) and asked him first to act on behalf of some of Gratian's former colleagues, before making a further request that Roman tribunes with the power of life and death should not be sent to Spain. Martin not only wanted to safeguard from danger all the Christians in these regions who were to be persecuted in connection with that expedition, Severus tells us he was also concerned to *protect the heretics themselves.*[36]

The Emperor delayed seeing Martin. Some said he did not want to offend the other bishops. Rumours suggested the Emperor wanted properties belonging to the Priscillians. He needed resources as the Treasury was empty and civil wars were about to rage. Bishops in Trier who supported Ithacius then tried to have Martin killed. The Emperor was angry and 'not far from being compelled to assign to Martin the same fate of the heretics'. When this became known to St Martin he rushed to the palace, although it was night. He pledged to the King that he would agree to communicate (with the bishops) if the tribunes who had already been sent to Spain for the destruction of churches were recalled. Maximus granted his requests.

There was an ordination the next day of Felix as a bishop. Martin took part and received communion, judging it better to yield for the moment rather than disregard the safety of those over whose heads a sword was hanging. The bishops tried to get St Martin to put in writing that he had shared communion with them, but Martin refused. The next day Martin left the palace as soon as he could, filled with sorrow and feeling greatly disturbed that he had allowed himself to have been mixed up with such an 'evil' communion. He felt that his own salvation was in danger and was very troubled. St Martin guarded himself against having any further communion with Ithacius or his supporters, believing it had caused the loss of his own power to heal and cure.

Martin confessed in tears to Severus and his friends, saying that he felt a diminution of his power on account of the evil of that communion in which he had taken part through necessity, going against the instincts of his own heart and conscience.[37] Martin lived for sixteen more years after this incident but he avoided diocesan bishops for the rest of his life and refused to attend another church synod. Severus says, 'Never again did he attend a synod and he kept carefully aloof from all assemblies of bishops'.[38] For a monk to do this was not unusual, but for a monk who was a bishop to do this was a sign of real conflict between early forms of monasticism and the emerging hierarchy of the church.[39]

Severus met Martin on several occasions and describes how St Martin washed his feet and spoke great wisdom. He held deep respect for Martin as a person and the genuine holiness that permeated St Martin's approach to Christianity and the spiritual life. Severus tells us that he saw in Martin the model of religious life which revealed a profound and genuinely Christlike spirituality. His language reflects the educated, formal rhetorical style of his day, so unlike the Latin of St Patrick, but what Severus records about St Martin and the brief five-year period when Maximus was Emperor from 383–388 CE is very significant. Severus was a very articulate spokesperson for events taking place around him, exhibiting a remarkable courage and independence of mind considering the dangers of the times. He chose not to be silent about this.

St Martin's holiness was centred in the heart from which it 'shone forth in compassion and light', compared with those who opposed him. Severus tells us that the way Martin was treated by the bishops also affected him, because of his close association with Martin. This is why Severus had to make arrangements for a delay in publishing a Life of Martin until after his death. The price of such controversial publicity in the church at that time was simply too great. Death was now a real possibility for those accused of heresy, including any supporters. Severus viewed this development as a form of wickedness within the church.[40]

In a response that is remarkably similar to St Patrick's approach to those 'seniors' in the church with whom he was in conflict, Severus chose not to name names. He provides insights into events taking place in the late fourth and early fifth centuries which involved people with whom St Patrick and his family may have been associated and events with which they were probably familiar. This author knew the kind of Christianity adopted and practised by St Martin and his followers, which he witnessed personally.

If Patrick spent four years with St Martin or joined the community shortly after Martin's death, this is the kind of Christianity St Patrick would have known and practised during his mission in Ireland.[41] From the way St Martin's approach to Christianity is described, we can detect many similarities with the writings of St Patrick. This includes the practice of asceticism through spiritual exercises and fasting leading to self-induced dreams and visions.[42]

At the heart of St Martin's approach to the Christian life, as with St Patrick, we find the voluntary renunciation of personal property and material wealth. In his own writings, St Patrick is very anxious to defend himself against any accusations of simony. He refused material gifts or payments that were offered to him personally, although financial resources were used to foster good relations with the Irish chieftains, since this would guarantee him safe passage when he needed to make a journey in the course of his ministry in Ireland. Sincerity of faith and 'purity of heart' is the essential component of St Patrick's approach to the gospel and how Christian discipleship could be practised.

Many of St Patrick's converts were women who lived in continence, keeping to some kind of 'monastic' vows but sharing communion in the context of pastoral and evangelistic mission with outreach to villages. This resonates strongly with the kind of monasticism adhered to by Martin, who was following the example of St Antony and the Desert Tradition of Egypt.[43]

If St Patrick was born in 384 or 385 CE, taken captive in 400 CE and escaped from Ireland in 407 CE, his religious training could have taken place from 407–427 CE. If so, perhaps he returned to Ireland before the traditional date, 432 CE. A pioneering mission by an early 'monastic' community linked to St Martin but based in Brittany could have taken place before 431 CE when Palladius was sent as a bishop 'to the Irish believing in Christ' as part of the first official Roman mission. If Patrick's mission had begun before 431 CE, then it was unlikely to have been commissioned by Rome. If a pioneering mission had been sent to Ireland from monastic groups linked to St Martin of Tours' foundations in Brittany, let's say in the early 420s, then this may have been the cause, at least in part, of initiatives taken by Rome when Germanus was sent to Britain in 428 CE and Palladius was sent to Ireland in 431 CE.

The approach to Christian discipleship taken by St Martin and St Patrick is very different to the lifestyle adopted by some of the other clergy in the church, who preferred to embrace the comforts of an overt material lifestyle which accompanied their privileged social status.[44] If there is any truth in those records which associate St Patrick and his family with Martin, Conan and Maximus then we have grounds to suspect that St Patrick's life and mission may also have been embroiled in these events and conflicts which surrounded these enigmatic personalities.[45]

In a detailed study of St Martin, Mary Caroline Watt suggests that St Martin was almost condemned to death as a Priscillianist and that he died a schismatic. She says Martin's 'repugnance and dislike for honours paid to the hierarchy of the church' led him to spend the last years of his life apart from the emerging diocesan structures.[46] Donaldson writes about the powerful, formative influence of Celtic monks on early English Christianity, acknowledging that historians are only just beginning to understand that 'the key to it all is undoubtedly St Martin'.[47] The same applies to early Christianity in Ireland, Wales, Scotland, Brittany and Germany where Martin's memory is still greatly honoured.

The origins of Christianity in these places is linked to St Patrick, St David, St Illtud, St Ninian and St Killian, all of whom are said to have been associated directly or indirectly with Martin of Tours. St Martin's influence on the formation of early monasticism in Ireland and elsewhere in the west has yet to be fully appreciated.

In relation to uncertainties regarding the Easter Cycle introduced by St Patrick, it is reasonable to suggest this may have been the eighty-four-year Paschal table compiled by Sulpitius Severus which came into Ireland in the early fifth century. It was present on Iona in the mid-sixth century and was used as a basis for the Iona Chronicle.[48]

Could it be that St Patrick's position was affected by his links to St Martin and those groups that Martin chose to support, as well as St Martin's aversion to and detachment from an increasingly powerful diocesan hierarchy within the church, which was influenced by and supportive of the writings of St Augustine and St Jerome?[49] From the evidence presented to us by Severus it seems reasonable to suggest that St Patrick's spiritual formation was linked to St Martin's community.

Nothing Severus said about St Martin's approach to monasticism is incompatible with the ethos and values which give such character to St Patrick's own writings. It is, therefore, reasonable to suggest that it is far more likely that St Patrick was associated with an early monastic form of Christian community linked to St Martin rather than any formal training under St Germanus. This is a matter of great significance in relation to St Patrick's real identity and the true nature of the religious teachings that characterised his mission.

---

*Notes*

1. Sulpicius Severus, 'Life of St Martin' in *The Nicene and Post Nicene Fathers*, xi, eds Philip Schaff and Henry Wace (New York, 1894), ch. xxiv.

2. Deric records that St Patrick's mother, Conchessa, was St Martin's niece. Martin's sister, her mother, was born in Pannonia. In Gaul she married Ochimus, Conchessa's father. See Gilles Deric, *Histoire Ecclésiastique de Bretagne*, ii (Paris, 1778), p. 148.

3. Severus, 'Life of St Martin', ch. xxvi, p. 16 ff.

4. Severus, 'Life of St Martin', ch. x, p. 9. Severus said, 'As long as I live and retain my senses, I will ever celebrate the monks of Egypt.' See 'Dialogues' in *The Nicene and Post Nicene Fathers*, xi, eds Philip Schaff and Henry Wace (New York, 1894), i, ch. xxvi, p. 36.

5. Severus, 'Life of St Martin', ch. xxvi, p. 16. A favourite disciple of St Martin's, called St Victor, was sent by Martin to St Paulinus of Nola; Martin and Victor together persuaded Paulinus to withdraw from the world. Could this be the person called 'Victor' who appeared to St Patrick in his dream? See John O'Hanlon, *Lives of the Irish Saints* (Dublin, 1875), p. 502.

6. Severus, 'Life of St Martin', ch. x, p. 8 ff. Similar limestone caves occupied by monks at the time of St Martin can be seen near Candes Martin, where St Martin died. His death is portrayed on a beautiful stained-glass window in a chapel dedicated to him in the local parish church.

7. 'A few persons, however, among these some of the bishops, who had been summoned to appoint a chief priest, were impiously offering resistance (to Martin's election as bishop) asserting that Martin's person was contemptible, that he was unworthy of the episcopate, that he was a man despicable in countenance, that his clothing was mean and his hair disgusting.' Severus, 'Life of St Martin', ch. ix, p. 8.

8. Severus, 'Life of St Martin', ch. xxvii, p. 17.

9. Severus, 'Life of St Martin', p. 3.

10. Severus is said to have also incurred charges of heresy because he embraced Pelagian opinions.

11. Severus, 'Life of St Martin', ch. xx, p. 13. *Emphasis added.

12. Severus, 'Life of St Martin', ch. xxvii, p. 17.

13. This person was a Celt from Gaul. Severus was from Aquitania. See Severus, 'Dialogues', iv, p. 25 ff.

14. 'We had our dwelling close to the river as Sulpitius has already described', Severus, 'Dialogues', iii, ch. x, p. 50.

15. Severus, 'Dialogues', i, ch. viii, p. 27 ff.

16. See Gerald Bonner, *St Augustine of Hippo: Life and Controversies* (Norwich, 2002), p. 89.

17. Severus, 'Dialogues', ch. ix, p. 28.

18. Jerome, *Jerome, Comm. on Jeremiah*, ch. Ezekiel.

19. St Augustine's 205th Letter.

20. Severus, Letter 2, ch. xv in Schaff and Wace, p. 65, n. 1.

21. Severus, Letter 2, ch. xvii, xix in Schaff and Wace, p. 66, 67.

22. 'Written on your hearts.' C 11; 'turn sincerely with all your heart.' C 19, 'troubled in heart.' C 23; 'sincerity of heart.' C 48; 'the unseen honour which is believed in with the heart.' C 54; 'exultation of heart.' C 60.

23. Severus, 'Life of St Martin', ch. xxii, p. 14.

24. Severus, 'Life of St Martin', ch. xxiv, p. 16.

25. See William Reeves, *The Culdees of the British Islands* (Dublin, 1864; fasc. edn, Llanerch, 1994), p. 74 ff.

26. Severus, 'Dialogues', ii, ch. v, p. 40 ff.

27. 'How Martin acted towards the Emperor Maximus.' Severus, 'Life of St Martin', ch. xx, p. 13 ff.

28. The Latin phrase *regni necessitatem* meaning 'a sovereign requirement', 'sovereign necessities' or 'requirements of the kingship' probably refers to the Imperial responsibilities associated with 'divinely appointed' kingship. See Schaff and Wace, p. 13, n. 1.

29. Severus, 'Dialogues', ii, ch. vi, p. 43. Although Severus describes the rebellion as 'illegal' he places it in the context of a civil war.

30. Severus, 'Life of St Martin', ch. xx, p. 13.

31. This story is reminiscent of Saint Aidan's conduct in Northumbria with King Oswald, at the Royal Palace in Bamburgh.

32. Severus, 'Dialogues', ii, ch. vi, p. 43. Welsh tradition holds that after the death of Maximus, Helen returned to Wales where she was an influential figure in the development of monasticism. The early saints in Wales including St David, St Illtud and St Non practised a form of Celtic monasticism which shows great kinship with St Martin.

33. Severus writes that 'Priscillian did not deny he had given himself up to lewd doctrines, that he had been accustomed to hold by night, gatherings of vile women, and to pray in a state of nudity.' Severus, 'Sacred History', Book II, Schaff and Wace, p. 121.

34. The Latin phrase used by Severus *ultra Britannias*, 'beyond the Britains', can possibly be interpreted again as including Brittany. If so, this provides another example of a reliable contemporary historical witness that Brittany was known as 'Britain' at the time of St Patrick's birth. See Severus, 'Sacred History', Book II, ch. li, Schaff and Wace, p. 121 ff.; also 'Dialogues', iii, ch. xi, p. 50 ff.

35. It is interesting to note that Severus mentions 'the two Spains'. The civil wars raging at this time may have caused divisions within Britain, Gaul and Spain. St Patrick applies a plural designation to Gaul: *Galliis* – the 'two Gauls'; and perhaps also to Britain: *in Britanniis* – the two 'Britains'.

36. Severus, 'Dialogues', iii, ch. xii, p. 51.

37. Severus, 'Dialogues', iii, ch. xii, p. 51 ff.

38. This helps to date St Martin's death. If he lived for sixteen years after this event, which took place between 385 and 389 CE, Martin died between 401 and 405 CE, perhaps during the time that St Patrick was held in captivity in Ireland.

39. Gregory of Tours tells us that St Martin had persuaded Maximus against the war which he was planning in Spain in an attempt to wipe out the heretics, 'considering it sufficient for them to be expelled from the Catholic churches and from Catholic communion.' According to Gregory of Tours, St Martin died in the village of Candes, aged eighty one years. See Gregory of Tours, *History of the Franks*, trans. Lewis Thorpe (London, 1974), p. 594.

40. Severus is using very strong language to describe these bishops when he speaks of the 'evil communion' of Ithacius.

41. If St Martin died in 405 CE and Patrick was a member of Martin's community from 407 to 411, then Patrick would not have met Martin personally but may have arrived at the monastery very soon after his death, when these political and ecclesiastical issues were increasingly significant within the Church.

42. Nora Chadwick, *Age of the Saints in the Celtic Church* (Durham, 1960; facs. edn, Llanerch, 2006), p. 27. See notes 1, 2.

43. Dr Lanigan said the most consistent accounts bring St Patrick to the monastery of St Martin. Mabillon said the monastic institution was introduced into Ireland by St Patrick who was following the discipline of St Martin – *in Hiberniam per S. Patricium, S Martini disciplunom.* See Moore, Thomas, *History of Ireland* (New York, 1835), iii, p. 220.

44. The stark contrast between alternative lifestyles can be clearly seen by comparing Patrick's *Confession*, or the way Severus describes St Martin, with the Letters of Sidonius Apollinaris, c.450 CE who gives a graphic description of his opulent lifestyle as Bishop of Clermont Ferrand, treasuring classical social values. Sidonius was a close friend and associate of St Germanus. See O. M. Dalton, trans., *Sidonius Apollinaris, Letters* (London, 1915).

45. Politics must have played a huge part in the development of the church at this time. Severus tells us that in Rome and Gaul there were 'powerful bishops' strongly supportive of the deposed Emperor, Valentinian.

46. Mary Caroline Watt, *St Martin of Tours* (London, 1928).

47. Christopher Donaldson, *Martin of Tours: The Shaping of Celtic Spirituality* (Norwich, 1997), p. xi.

48. See Daniel McCarthy, 'The Status of Pre-Patrician Irish Annals', *Peritia*, 12 (1998). Severus died in 423 CE.

49. Deric identifies the very distinctive character of religious communities and solitaries in Brittany. See Deric, *Histoire Ecclésiastique de Bretagne*, p. 280 ff.

# CHAPTER SEVENTEEN

# Barefoot Hermits

Only those who risk going too far can
Possibly find out how far there is to go.[1]

According to some of the ancient Lives of St Patrick published by John Colgan, after St Patrick left St Martin's community at Tours he spent several years undertaking spiritual formation and religious training with a group of 'barefoot hermits' who were resident in the 'isles of the Tyrrhene Sea'. The geographical location of these islands has never been securely identified but they play an important part in several of the ancient accounts given for this period in St Patrick's life. A sense of confusion and contradiction is compounded by the fact that these 'islands' could refer to actual islands, early forms of monastic settlement, or both. The Latin word *insula* applied not only to islands but also to groups of hermits living in remote places such as islands or forests, especially in Gaul.

Modern geography locates the Tyrrhenian Sea in the Mediterranean, between the south-east coast of France and north-west coast of Italy, extending towards Sicily. Some of the ancient writers appear to have assumed this was its location.[2] Other references exist, which suggest it was located adjacent to the Bay of Mont St Michel, off the north-west coast of Brittany. If so, this region was not only the place where St Patrick lived and from which he was taken captive, it may have been associated with much of his religious training and spiritual formation. Like Nemthor and Armoric Letha, the Tyrrhene Sea is not mentioned directly by St Patrick in his own writings but several references are preserved in the ancient secondary sources which provide clues to identify its true location. Unravelling the various threads of tradition calls for great patience and perseverance. If these 'islands' can be identified, a little more of the truth as to where St Patrick was trained and commissioned for the mission to Ireland can be established.

When considering these accounts it is important to remember that many of the statements made about St Patrick are written as hagiography and, therefore, cannot be taken as a reliable historical witness. Some trustworthy material was passed on which may provide clues to the truth. The challenge is to try and separate the threads of historical possibility from the tangled web of hagiography and tradition.

*Muirchú*

According to Muirchú's narrative, when Patrick was thirty years old he went to Rome to honour the 'the head, certainly of all the churches in the world', in preparation for his mission to Ireland. Pope Celestine held office from 422 to 432 CE. Muirchú describes how St Patrick travelled from Britain to Gaul by ship, journeyed overland through Europe and was about to cross the Alps to go to Rome when he met St Germanus, the bishop of Auxerre. He records that St Patrick spent a considerable time under the guidance of St Germanus – some said thirty or forty years – learning 'obedience, wisdom and charity'. Then Victor (an angel or spiritual mentor who had appeared to St Patrick in frequent visions) told Patrick that the time had come for him to go to Ireland to preach the gospel.

Muirchú describes how steps were taken to prepare for this journey. St Germanus arranged for an older man, a priest called Segitus, to travel with St Patrick as a companion because he (Patrick) 'was not yet ordained in the Episcopal grade by the holy lord Germanus'.[3]

When news reached St Germanus that Palladius had died, Patrick changed direction and went towards 'a certain wondrous man, the highest bishop, Amathorex by name, dwelling in a neighbouring place' and according to Muirchú it was he, not Germanus, who ordained Patrick a bishop. The identity of Amathorex is uncertain. He was probably a Gallic bishop. Etymology suggests that he may have been a local king or associated with a royal family, as well as being a bishop.[4] His name is possibly derived from the prefix *Amator* and the suffix *rex*, which means 'chieftain' or 'king'.[5] The bishop in Auxerre before Germanus was called Amator. He fled Auxerre in 418 CE, after an altercation with St Germanus. One of the earliest sources to mention Amator is Nennius, who records that Patrick's original name was Maun but Amator renamed him Patrick.[6]

After being ordained as a priest and bishop by Amathorex, 'according to the order of Melchizedek', Patrick travelled to Ireland to begin his mission. In Muirchú's account St Patrick never made it as far as Rome and there is no mention of St Patrick being ordained by Pope Celestine. Muirchú locates all St Patrick's ecclesiastical training with Germanus in Auxerre and his ordination by the mysterious Amathorex at an unspecified location on the continent.[7]

St Germanus (380–448 CE) was born from one of the noblest families in Gaul. His grandfather had been Prefect in Gaul. He was educated in the schools of Arles and Lyons then went to Rome to study law. Having developed a successful legal practice in Rome, his professional talents and the reputation of his family brought him in contact with the imperial court. The Emperor sent him back to Gaul, appointing him as one of the six dukes, entrusted with the government of the Gallic provinces with a residence in Auxerre.[8]

Germanus loved hunting and for this reason is said to have incurred the displeasure of St Amator, who was still the bishop in Auxerre at that time. St Germanus used to hang the heads of all the animals he killed on a tree sacred to local people as a place of worship. Amator challenged him about this behaviour, which led to conflict between them.

One day when Germanus was out of town, Amator cut the tree down and burned the trophies. Fearing for his life because Germanus wanted to kill him, Amator fled but was determined to convert Germanus to a more spiritual way of life and tonsure him as a monk. Amator is said to have received permission to do this from the Prefect in Gaul and returned to Auxerre to fulfil his ambitions. When Germanus arrived inside the church, Amator locked the doors and tonsured Germanus apparently against his will, telling him to live as one destined to be his successor. After that, Amator appears to have disappeared from history, like Patrick and Pelagius.[9] Legend records that he fled to Brittany, to be a hermit. If Amathorex can be identified with Amator of Auxerre, this presents an intriguing possibility that he may have lived in the 'isles of the Tyrrhene Sea'. If so, he could have been the one who ordained Patrick.

*Tirechán*

In Tirechán's narrative, which is preserved alongside Muirchú's *Life of St Patrick* in the *Book of Armagh*, we find the following account, which includes a tradition not found in Muirchú. Tirechán describes how St Patrick escaped from slavery in Ireland when he was twenty-two years old. Then he spent seven years walking and travelling by water 'through Gaul and all of Italy and in the islands of the Tyrrhenian Sea'.[10] Bishop Ultan had informed Tirechán (his pupil) that St Patrick 'spent thirty years on one of these islands, which is called Aralensis'. It has been suggested that this name refers to Lerins or Arles, both located in the south-east corner of Roman Gaul, based on a belief that the Tyrrhene Sea was part of the Mediterranean between what is now Italy and France, where the famous monastery of Lerins was established by St Honoratus around 400 CE. This is where modern geography locates the Tyrrhenian Sea but, as we shall see, this was not always the case.

*St Fiacc's Hymn*

*Fiacc's Hymn* also appears to locate these islands in the Mediterranean. After Patrick escaped from slavery in Ireland:

> He went all over Albion,
> Great God, it was a marvel of a course
> Till he left himself with Germanus in the south,
> In the southern part of Letha

In the isles of the Tyrrhene Sea he fasted,
Therein he ponders.
He read the canon with Germanus,
That is what books declare.[11]

This hymn is thought to be one of the earliest documents relating to St Patrick after Patrick's own writings but even here the geographical references are uncertain and misleading. The locations of both Letha and the Tyrrhene Sea appear to be misunderstood. Fiacc identifies Letha with St Germanus in Auxerre. The difficulty is that Auxerre is about a hundred and fifty kilometres or ninety-two miles south of Paris in the centre of Gaul and a long way from Letha or 'the southern part of Letha' which is most likely a reference to Armoric Letha, on the coast of Brittany.[12]

According to *Fiacc's Hymn*, after Patrick had completed his religious formation with St Germanus he then went to the 'isles of the Tyrrhene Sea' where he fasted for an extended time of spiritual reflection. Muirchú and Tirechán both mention the Tyrrhene Sea, but do not identify it. St Fiacc appears to locate it in the Mediterranean Sea between southern Gaul and Italy. There was obviously considerable confusion about the true location of these places. This was picked up by later writers.

### The Scholiast

When the Scholiast added notes to *St Fiacc's Hymn*, probably in the ninth century, he attempted to correct or clarify these geographical statements. The Scholiast knew that Germanus was based in Gaul, but unfortunately he appears to have assumed Letha was in the south of Italy. Uncertainty about the location of these places was, therefore, compounded further when he says:

> 'Letha' that is *Latium*, which is also called Italy, so named because Saturn fleeing from Jupiter *latuit* there. Howbeit Germanus was in the Gauls, as Bede says, *Letavians* therefore, in latitudine, in the south part of Gaul by the Tyrrhene Sea.[13]

The first mistake is evident when the Scholiast identifies Letha with Latium or Italy. Letha, or Armoric Letha, was a coastal region in north-west Brittany. A second error occurs when he identifies the 'isles of the Tyrrhene Sea' as *Fiacc's Hymn* appears to have done, in 'the southern part of Gaul'. These are errors and uncertainties that have affected later writers.[14]

Just as the significance of Aleth in relation to St Patrick's home at Bannavem Tiburniae appears to have been lost or forgotten, so the meaning of 'Letha' and the 'isles of the Tyrrhene Sea' appear to have been lost to historical memory in relation to St Patrick's biography. At the same time, curious fragments of a forgotten geography have been preserved, trapped inside the tangled web of tradition.[15]

The Scholiast repeats the claim that Patrick trained under St Germanus, who advised him to go to Rome so that Pope Celestine could confer orders upon him. Suddenly, the plot thickens considerably, showing how creative, contrived and confusing hagiography can be. According to the Scholiast, St Patrick went to Rome but Pope Celestine refused to ordain him because he had already sent Palladius as a bishop to Ireland.[16] After being 'rejected' by the Pope, St Patrick went to these mysterious 'islands of the Tyrrhene Sea'. The account given here is complicated and extremely jumbled but if we follow the various threads of tradition a little further, something closer to the truth slowly begins to emerge. The Scholiast continues:

> So Patrick went to the Islands of the Tyrrhene Sea after Pope Celestine's refusal [to grant him holy orders] and there he found The Staff of Jesus [*Baccail Jesu*] on the island called Alanensis … Mount Arnon.[17]

The *Baccail Jesu* or 'Staff of Jesus' is said to have been a staff given to St Patrick as a symbol of his authority to preach the gospel and be an apostle in Ireland, perhaps akin to a bishop's staff or crosier. We will consider its significance later in this chapter.

According to the Scholiast, after receiving the sacred Staff of Jesus on Mount Arnon in the 'islands of the Tyrrhene Sea', St Patrick went again to St Germanus who sent him back to Pope Celestine but things were different this time.[18] The Pope had recently learned that Palladius had died suddenly in Britain, so he ordained St Patrick to take his place, an event traditionally dated to 432 CE, the year after Palladius went to Ireland. In this account, Amathorex is conveniently brought to Rome for St Patrick's ordination:

> Patrick was ordained in the presence of Celestinus [Pope Celestine] and Theodosius the Younger [Emperor of Rome] king of the World. Amatorex, Bishop of Auxerre was the one that conferred orders upon [Patrick]. Celestine was only alive for a week after he ordained Patrick.[19]

In another account, St Patrick is said to have spent thirty years with St Germanus. After leaving Auxerre, Patrick 'went upon the Tyrrhene Sea' until he came to an island where he received the sacred Staff of Jesus from two hermits living there. Patrick then went to an unnamed archbishop who ordained him bishop.[20]

As the story unfolds it gets even more complicated, when angels get involved. After news had reached them in Rome that Palladius had died (after less than a year in Ireland) the papal authorities ordered St Patrick to go to Ireland. Angels told St Patrick to go to Ireland promptly, but St Patrick refused to go, until he had spoken directly with Jesus Christ:

So the angel brought him to *Armoric Letha, to the city named Capua, on Mount Arnon, by the shore of the Tyrrhene Sea* and there the Lord spoke to him as he had spoken to Moses on Mt Sinai.[21]

It is the geographical reference in this version of the story that is very significant. Here, Mount Arnon and the Tyrrhenian Sea are both given the same geographical location, which is nowhere near Auxerre, Italy or the south-east of France. Mount Arnon and the Tyrrhene Sea are both identified with Armoric Letha. This leaves absolutely no doubt that as far as this document is concerned the Tyrrhene Sea was located off the north-west coast of Brittany. Mount Arnon is described as being located 'by the shore of the Tyrrhene Sea' and if so, this allows for a possibility that it could be a reference to Mont St Michel.

### Colgan's Third and Fourth Lives

In the *Third Life* published by Colgan, another version of the story records that after having first been with St Germanus and then spending four years with St Martin at Tours, the angel told St Patrick to go to Mount Arnon in Armoric Letha. This mountain is described as 'a big rock in the Tyrrhene Sea' near a city called 'Capua'. The Latin description *ad Montem Arnon in Airmairch Letha super petram Maris Tyrreni* can be rendered into English as 'St Patrick was told to go to Mount Arnon in Armoric Letha; a big rock beside the Tyrrhene Sea'.[22]

Once again, the Tyrrhene Sea is very clearly identified with the coast of Brittany. The description given in this passage also strongly suggests that Mount Arnon can be identified with Mont St Michel. In the Latin phrase *supra petram Maris Tyrreni*, which describes Mount Arnon, *supra petram* means 'a high or pinnacled rock'. Since this was in Armoric Letha, Mont St Michel matches this description perfectly.[23] The identification of Mount 'Arnon' or 'Hernon' with Mont St Michel appears to be confirmed by another manuscript copy of Colgan's *Third Life* which uses a slightly different phrase, *montem Arnon in Armairc Lete super ripam maris Tyrreni*. This translates as 'Mount Arnon in Armoric Letha a large (rock) beside the shore'.[24] The description aptly applies to Mont St Michel, which is very close to the shoreline. The *Fourth Life* of St Patrick published by John Colgan also identifies the Tyrrhene Sea with Brittany. The author locates it 'beside' Armoric Letha.[25]

Although they appear in the secondary sources and cannot be taken as first-hand historical evidence, these geographical references have provided important clues to help identify where St Patrick's religious training and ordination took place.

As this document continues the story, St Patrick sails through the Tyrrhene Sea where he receives the Staff of Jesus from two hermits living there. Then St Patrick speaks to God on a mountain and is told to go to Ireland. In what appears to be an act of irreverence and disobedience, at least in relation to what he had just been told by God, Patrick instead goes first to Rome. This time he is well received by the Pope, who gives him relics of saints before sending him to Ireland. As with Muirchú's account, nothing is said about St Patrick's ordination in Rome.[26]

## Probus

At an earlier stage it was suggested that the true location of St Patrick's homeland was known to Probus, who identified it with a coastal region in north-west Brittany. If this author proved to be reliable in relation to the location of Bannavem Tiburniae, can he also be trusted as to where St Patrick was trained and ordained? Probus includes an intriguing account that is very different to those we have encountered so far. He describes how, when St Patrick returned to his homeland after escaping from slavery in Ireland, he did not go to Rome or St Germanus in Auxerre as other accounts suggest. Instead, St Patrick went immediately for religious training to the community of St Martin of Tours, based in those famous limestone caves at Marmoutier on the banks of the River Loire. This is where he spent the next four years. Probus records that St Patrick was trained within Martin's community and that he was tonsured there. It was here that St Patrick was first ordained in holy orders and learned about doctrine and the lectionary.[27]

When St Patrick left the community of St Martin, Probus records that he spent the next eight years on an island with 'the people of God' who are described as a community of 'barefoot hermits'.[28] Then Patrick went to another group of solitaries, living on an adjacent island which is described as being 'between the mountain and the sea'.[29] According to Probus, it was after being on this island for several years that Episcopal orders were conferred on St Patrick by a bishop called 'Saint Senior'. This name strongly suggests a local connection with Brittany. Breton historians record the first bishops established in Brittany during the settlement under Maximus in 383 CE were called 'Senior' or 'Seigneur'. This title is still applied to senior clerics and the nobility in France. In his *Confession*, Patrick refers to the religious leaders who were involved with his ordination as 'seniors'.[30]

Probus provides geographical clues to identify where St Patrick was ordained as a bishop. St Senior was based on 'Mount Hermon', a mountain 'on the right side of the ocean' known as 'the city with seven walls'.[31] He describes how St Patrick had to climb steeply up this mountain so that he could speak with God. The geographical descriptions given are significant, especially the use of the Latin word *ascende*, which means to ascend, or climb up steeply.[32] This is almost certainly another reference to Mont St Michel. It also matches the description Nennius gives for Mons Jovis, one of the landmarks that designated the boundaries of Armoric Letha in which this mountain is described as *super verticem* or 'rising almost vertically'.[33]

Mont St Michel is a precipitous, pyramid-shaped rock which ascends very dramatically, almost 'vertically' from the sea. It was once an island, close to the shoreline but is now joined to the mainland by a causeway. Mont St Michel was probably one of the most famous of all the 'islands in the Tyrrhene Sea'. Probus records that St Patrick was ordained as a bishop there. The reference to 'seven walls' is significant. Those who have visited Mont St Michel, which is now a world heritage site, will be familiar with the steep climb to the church on the summit. Several walls have been built over the centuries, primarily as retaining walls for buildings and paths, also for safe access, helping to separate the religious or monastic areas above from the more secular activities taking place below. Models on display today for visitors to the Abbey, attempt to show the development of structures on this rocky island over the centuries. This confirms the existence of several ancient walls. At Mont St Michel, the retaining walls are intersected by a path which directs pilgrims towards the summit, known as the Merveille. It is certainly possible that there were seven walls on Mont St Michel at some stage, if not at the time of St Patrick then perhaps by the time Probus was writing in the ninth century.

In a detailed study of the history of Mont St Michel, French author Louis Blondel records that a College of Druidesses, in the Gallic, pre-Roman period, was established on the rock now called Mont St Michel. It was a sanctuary to the Celtic God of fire and the Sun Belenos. After the Romans occupied Gaul, it became a sanctuary for the Roman god Jupiter. The holy mountain then became known as Mont Jou or Mont Jovis, which appears to have been the name familiar to Nennius. After the fall of the Roman Empire, the mount became known locally as 'Mont Tumba'. Blondel describes an early Christian religious community on Mont St Michel or 'Mount Tumba', founded by St Paterne and St Pair, the first apostles of Neustria, in the fifth century. They established a monastery called The Monastery of the Two Tombs.[34] The identity of the person or persons buried there is uncertain.[35]

In 705 CE St Aubert, the Bishop of Avranches, built a new church on the rock dedicated to the Archangel Michael. Custody fell to the expanding monastic order of the Benedictines. Since that time, this sacred mount has been known as Mont St Michel.

If 'Mount Hermon', as mentioned by Probus, can be identified with Mont St Michel, we may be coming very close to the truth as to where St Patrick received spiritual training and was ordained as a bishop for Ireland, despite the obvious confusion and misleading statements in the ancient sources. Considering all these curious references, it certainly appears possible that St Patrick may have belonged to a spiritual community who practised asceticism on certain islands off the coast of Brittany in the vicinity of Dol. These islands and early 'monastic' communities were known to ancient writers as the 'isles of the Tyrrhene Sea'.[36]

From a historical point of view, can we be confident that we have identified the location of the Tyrrhene Sea correctly?

In Julius Honorius' *Cosmographia*, the 'Mare Tyrrhenum' is part of the 'Oceanis Occidentalis', the Western Sea, which associates it with the coast of Brittany.[37] One reference in an ancient Irish source identifies the Tyrrhene Sea closely with the Iccian Sea, which we know refers the stretch of water between Ireland, south-west Britain and Brittany. In this passage, the reference to the Archangel Michael suggests a possible link with Mont St Michel. It confirms that some of the early Irish writers understood the Tyrrhene Sea to be located off the coast of Brittany.[38]

Scholars have wrestled with these enigmatic and elusive geographical descriptions concerning St Patrick and some accepted the identification with Mont St Michel.[39] In his masterful *Ecclesiastical History of Ireland*, published in 1823, Dr John Lanigan suggested that the geographical descriptions mentioned above refer to Mont St Michel.[40]

When J. H. Todd published a detailed and controversial study of St Patrick in 1864, he also recognised the significance of these descriptions. He said these legends 'preserve curious fragments of a forgotten geography, which lead to the suspicion of their possible authenticity'. Unfortunately, Todd was unable to disentangle the various threads of tradition and geographical clues that may have allowed him to identify these places with greater certainty.[41] Having accepted these descriptions applied very aptly to Mont St Michel, Todd was concerned that he could find no record of this place ever being called 'Mount Hermon', 'Arnon' or 'Morion'. He identified the Tyrrhene Sea with the Mediterranean, although Todd placed a question mark over this, accepting the uncertainty.[42]

In fact, Todd's scholarly eye had penetrated deeply into all these confused and contradictory accounts about the location of St Patrick's religious and spiritual training far enough for him to suggest that confusion had arisen because two different stories had been woven together, one relating to the ordination of Palladius and the other to the ordination of St Patrick 'on the south side of the ocean' at an island 'on the Sea of Armorica' (ar-muir-Letha). Todd accepted this was obviously a reference to the coast of Brittany. In making these remarks about Palladius and Patrick, Todd shows he had anticipated O'Rahilly's theory of the Two Patricks.

This had serious implications for the church's understanding of St Patrick's biography. Places and people integral to the life of Palladius (St Germanus, Pope Celestine, the church of Auxerre, Arles, Lerin, Capua, Italy and Rome) appear to have been transferred to St Patrick by many of the ancient writers when they attempted to establish a clear and perhaps more acceptable framework for St Patrick's biography. If we remove these from the list of places associated with St Patrick, we are left with St Martin of Tours, the isles of the Tyrrhene Sea, a community of 'barefoot hermits', Armoric Letha, Mount 'Hermon' or 'Arnon' (Mont St Michel), the city of seven walls, Amathorex and St Senior. Since there is no historical record of Palladius being associated with any of these places, it would seem reasonable to suggest these references belong to material that applies to St Patrick. They probably reflect the truth about where St Patrick received his religious training and where he was ordained and commissioned for the mission to Ireland.

We can only be grateful to the ancient writers and scribes who faithfully compiled or copied these ancient manuscripts down through the centuries. Although these sources cannot be viewed as primary historical evidence they have preserved certain names, geographical descriptions and traditions without which the truth about St Patrick's origins and the place where he is most likely to have been ordained and received religious formation, might never have been identified.

If the ancient manuscripts collected and published by John Colgan and his colleagues at Louvain had not survived, it would not have been possible to make comparisons between them and thereby glimpse patterns, which have allowed us to separate history from hagiography and put some of the more complex and difficult pieces of the puzzle of St Patrick together. Such is the beauty of manuscript transmission. Sometimes scribes intervened and made certain changes but they also retained some of the old names and traditions which have been passed down to us faithfully through many centuries. Without these references, the truth about St Patrick may have been lost forever.

### The Staff of Jesus

Some of the ancient legends attached to St Patrick are intriguing and very mysterious. The following account describes a remarkable experience Patrick is said to have had during his time in the 'isles of the Tyrrhene Sea' when he met a holy couple who were living together on one of the islands. They gave St Patrick the sacred staff, known in Ireland as the *Baccail Isu* (Staff of Jesus).

> When Patrick went to sea nine was his number. And it is then that he came to the island and he saw the new house and the young married couple inside. In front of the house he saw a decrepit old woman on her hands. 'What is wrong with this old woman?' Patrick asked. 'Great is her feebleness,' the young man replied, 'She is my grand-daughter but if you could see her mother, she is even more feeble.' 'How did that come to pass?' said Patrick. 'Not hard to answer' said the young man.

'We have been here since the time of Christ, who came here and dwelled amongst us. We made a feast for him. He blessed our house and us but that blessing did not come upon our children. Because of his blessing, we shall abide here without aging or decay until the Day of Judgement'. The young man said to Patrick 'Your coming to us has been foretold for a long time. God left us with knowledge and understanding that you would be the one to come and that you would preach to the Gaels [Irish]. He left this token with us that is His staff, and said it was to be given to you.' 'I will not take it', said Patrick, 'unless Christ himself gives me his staff.'

St Patrick stayed three days and three nights with them and then went to Mount Hermon in the neighbourhood of the island. And there the Lord appeared to him and told him to go and preach to the Gael and gave him the Staff of Jesus. He said that it would be a helper to him in every danger and in every unequal conflict in which he should be … St Patrick asked that three promises should be given to him if he went to preach the gospel in Ireland.

Firstly, that he [Patrick] would be at Christ's right hand in the kingdom of heaven, secondly that Patrick alone would be judge of the Irish at the End of Days and thirdly, he should be given as much gold and silver as nine companions could carry to support and further St Patrick's mission in Ireland.[43]

However much detail may have been embellished by myth and storytelling, it is possible that when St Patrick came to Ireland as an apostle, he carried a staff as a sign of the authority given to him to preach the gospel in Ireland. The existence of such a staff has been recorded from an early date. The famous 'Staff of Jesus' was a relic closely associated with St Patrick and the church in Armagh. It was preserved for many centuries in Ireland, first in the monastery at Armagh and later in Christ Church Cathedral, Dublin, where it survived until the Reformation, at which time it appears to have been burned or destroyed. Another tradition claims it may have survived.

In a recent history of the Cathedral, Milne records an alternative possibility that St Patrick's Staff was smuggled away and kept secretly by a community of Catholic religious sisters at an unnamed location in County Meath, where it is said to have been seen on at least one occasion, having been brought out of hiding for a special religious ceremony.[44] The *Baccail Jesu* is one of three famous relics associated with St Patrick, together with St Patrick's Bell which is preserved in the National Museum in Kildare Street, Dublin and a sacred book, thought to be the *Book of Armagh*, preserved at Trinity College, Dublin. The rediscovery or reappearance of this sacred relic would be a miracle. St Patrick's

Staff was one of Ireland's greatest national treasures, as priceless as the Book of Kells.

If there is any truth in the intriguing legend that surrounds this famous staff, Ireland and the early Irish church retained possession for many centuries of one of the most unique and priceless of all the holy relics of Christianity. It was not just a special staff that may have been carried by St Patrick as a sign of his authority as an apostle in Ireland; according to tradition, this was the very staff that had once been carried in the sacred hands of Jesus Christ himself. No other cleric in history, apart from St Patrick and those who inherited his legacy, was given the privilege of bearing such a unique responsibility.

The closest we come to knowing what this relic was like is to view the splendid display of crosiers or abbots' staffs preserved at the National Museum in Kildare Street, Dublin. These include the original crosiers of St Columba of Iona and St Ciaran of Clonmacnoise, among those of many other early Irish saints. They are wooden staffs encased in metal and covered with ornate decoration and precious stones.

### Summary

Hagiographers were determined from an early date to link St Patrick's spiritual formation to St Germanus in Auxerre and his ordination and commission to be an apostle in Ireland, to Pope Celestine and the authorities of the church in Rome. There was clearly a strong desire and need to honour Rome and the Papacy, in accounts which appear somewhat uncomfortably beside other records and traditions where there is no reference to Rome. St Patrick and his mission to Ireland had to be seen to be sponsored by the Papal authorities if he was going to be regarded as an apostle with legitimate religious authority, an important issue at the time these later documents were compiled.

In documents related to St Patrick, the evidence strongly suggests that the 'isles of the Tyrrhene Sea' must have been located off the north-west coast of Brittany, in what is now the Bay of Mont St Michel. This helps to clarify the place where St Patrick received spiritual formation and was prepared for his mission to Ireland. Some of the ancient sources appear to have located the Tyrrhene Sea in the Mediterranean as is the case with modern geography. This misconception led to great confusion and uncertainty in relation to St Patrick's biography.[45] Many references in the ancient Lives of St Patrick and in other sources, clearly link the 'isles of the Tyrrhene Sea' with Armoric Letha, a region on the coast of Brittany.

In his own writings, St Patrick does not tell us the name of the person or persons who commissioned him for the ministry in Ireland or which church or religious group supported his mission. His spiritual friends appear to have been based in Gaul; he describes how he longed to visit his family *in Britanniis* and then proceed into the Gauls (*Galliis*) to visit them. If these religious colleagues were based on the Loire, at Martin's Community, this would not be incompatible with what is recorded in Patrick's *Confession*.

Trying to disentangle conflicting threads of tradition has not been easy and is fraught with difficulties because we are almost entirely dependent on later secondary sources, which cannot be used as historical evidence. The fact is, we simply do not have enough reliable information to make any final judgement.

From the references available, it would seem reasonable to suggest that St Patrick is more likely to have been trained within an early form of Christian monastic community of the kind associated with Martin and other hermits who lived on the 'isles of the Tyrrhene Sea' near Mont St Michel than elsewhere. This is most likely to have been the place where St Patrick was ordained as a bishop and commissioned for the mission in Ireland. The chart 'A Possible Chronology For Saint Patrick' (p. 11) presents a suggested chronology based on the possibility that St Patrick was born in Brittany in 385 CE.

This chronology is based on a combination of Breton accounts with Bury's proposed date for St Patrick's birth, M. de Gerville's claim that St Patrick was born in Brittany, with details of religious training and spiritual formation according to Probus. This is only a tentative framework; as with so many aspects of St Patrick's biography, nothing is ever certain.

---

*Notes*

1. T. S. Eliot.

2. The uncertainty which surrounds its true location is compounded by another story related to St Martin, suggesting that the Tyrrhene Sea was in the Mediterranean east of Italy. When expelled from Milan, Martin is said to have sought shelter as a hermit on the island then called Gallinaria, now the Isola d'Albenga 'in the Tyrrhenian Sea'. In 361 CE he returned to Tours with Hilary at Ligugé. L. Clugnet, 'St Martin of Tours' in *The Catholic Encyclopedia* (New York, 1910), *New Advent* [website] <http://www.newadvent.org/cathen/09732b.htm>

3. David Howlett, *Muirchú Moccu Mactheni's 'Vita Sancti Patricii'* (Dublin, 2006), p. 55.

4. The ordination as it is described appears to have been characteristic of Celtic customs which required only one bishop to be present. Rome required at least three for episcopal orders to be conferred.

5. A copy of the *Historia Brittonum of Nennius*, by Mark the Anchorite, records that St Patrick was ordained at twenty five years of age by 'King Mattheus' – probably another reference to the elusive Amathorex.

6. 'Maun', 'Mawn' or 'Mawr' is a name found in Wales and Brittany. It may signify an ancient noble lineage, perhaps related to a concept of the sacredness of the land.

7. If Muirchú knew who 'Amathorex' was or where he was based, he does not mention it.

8. *The Catholic Encyclopedia* (New York, 1910), *New Advent* [website] <http://www.newadvent.org/cathen/>

9. Patrick's ordination by Amator may reflect confusion between the lives of Patrick and Palladius who was ordained as a deacon in Auxerre when Amator was bishop there. See J. H. Todd, *St Patrick, Apostle of Ireland* (Dublin, 1864), p. 315 ff.

10. In the *Book of Armagh*, a fragment preserved as a 'Saying of St Patrick' again mentions the Tyrrhenian Sea. Patrick is alleged to have said, 'I had the fear of God to guide me on my journey through Gaul and Italy and in the islands of the Tyrrhenian Sea.' LA Fol. 9, r. 32–43. See Ludwig Bieler, *The Patrician Texts in the Book of Armagh* (Dublin, 2004), p. 104. De Paor suggested this possibly referred to the monastic island of Lerins that was closely connected with the Metropolitan Church at Arles and Episcopal promotions in the late fifth century. See, Liam de Paor, *St Patrick's World* (Dublin, 1993), p. 202.

11. 'Albion' or 'Alba' was an ancient name for Scotland. *Fiacc's Hymn*, trans. Whitley Stokes, *Tripartite Life of St Patrick* (London, 1887), p. 405.

12. The ancient writers confused 'Letha' and 'Latium'. Hence 'the southern part of Letha' was interpreted to mean the south of Italy (Latium). Letha and Rome thus became confused. Stokes translated 'Roim Letha' as 'Rome of Latium'. See *Tripartite Life*, i, p. xliv, sec. 101, n. 2 and ii, p. 417.

13. See Notes on *Fiacc's Hymn* in Stokes, *Tripartite Life*, ii, p. 418, 419. *FLH*, p. 36

14. Bieler, *PTBA*, p. 125.

15. Todd calls these references 'curious fragments of forgotten geography, which lead to the suspicion of their possible authenticity'. Todd, *St Patrick, Apostle of Ireland*, p. 310 ff. See especially p. 335.

16. According to Prosper's *Chronicle*, Palladius had been sent to Ireland by Pope Celestine in 431 CE, as the first bishop 'to the Irish believing in Christ'. See Liam de Paor, *St Patrick's World*, p. 72 ff.

17. The island of 'Alenensis' has been seen as another form for Alanensis or Arlenensis and taken as a reference to Arles or Lerins, but this is not certain and the identity of 'Mount Arnon' is even less clear.

18. The Scholiast says St Patrick was sixty years old at the time, which shows how ridiculous this whole story is, except the reference to the Tyrrhene Sea, which appears in a more credible context elsewhere.

19. Stokes, *Tripartite Life*, p. 421.

20. Stokes, *Tripartite Life*, p. 445.

21. Stokes, *Tripartite Life*, p. 447. *Emphasis added.

22. Latin *supra*: above, high up; *petra*: rock. See Bieler, *FLL*, p. 132.

23. 'Mount Arnon', 'Hernon' or 'Hermon' are possibly names taken from the bible. Bieler noted that they are found together in Deut 3:8. See Bieler, ed., *Four Latin Lives of St Patrick* (Dublin, 1971), p. 222. Heremon was also the name of an Irish High King, who according to legend married Temar, a Jewish princess in the lineage of King David.

24. *Ad ripam* means 'by the shore (stream or river)'. *Ripa*: river, stream, bank, river. This comes from *arripare*, to 'touch the shore', in the sense of coming ashore after a long voyage.

25. In this document, the Tyrrhene Sea is located adjacent to Armorica *terram quae Armorica dicitur iuxta mare Tyrrenum possideret*. 'Vita Quarta', Bieler, *FLL*, p. 51 and Todd, *St Patrick, Apostle of Ireland*, p. 323 ff.

26. Bieler, *FLL*, p. 77. Todd suggests this was a clear example of interpolation. The writer had two different accounts and incorporated both without realising their inconsistency. See Todd, *St Patrick, Apostle of Ireland*, p. 324.

27. *Et fugiens inde peruenit ad Martinum episcopum Turonis et quattuor annis mansit cum eo et tonso capite ordinatus est ab eo in clericum et tenuit lectionem et doctrinam ab eo.* Probus, *Liber* I: 14; Bieler, *FLL*, p. 195. Various dates have been recorded for St Martin's death. Some say 397, others 402 and even 411 CE.

28. *Eremitas et solitarios nudis pedibus.* Probus, *Liber* I:15, Bieler, p. 195.

29. *Vade ad illos qui sunt in insula inter montes et mare.* Probus, *Liber* I:16, Bieler, FLL, p. 195. A similar geographical description in the *Tripartite Life* is more geographically specific and locates this place in the Tyrrhene Sea. *Quodam tempore dum esset S Patricius in Mari Tyrrheno venit ad locum, in quo errant tres alij Patricii. Erant enim hi in quodam solitario specu inter montem et mare.* See Stokes, *Tripartite Life*, i, p. 27.

30. *Senioribus meis.* C 26, Bieler, *Clavis Patricii II: Libri Epistolarum Sancti Patricii Episcopi* (Dublin, 1993), p. 72. Dr Lanigan notes (from Martiniere) that hermits were resident on Mont St Michel and surrounding islands, long before a church dedicated to St Michael was built by St Aubert, the Bishop of Avranches around 705 CE. John Lanigan, *Ecclesiastical History of Ireland*, 4 vols (Dublin, 1822; 2nd edn, Dublin, 1829), p. 166 ff.

31. *Vade ad sanctum Seniorum episcopum qui est in Monte Hermon in dextro latere maris oceani, et uallata est ciuitas eius septem muris.* Probus, *Liber* I, pp. 17–25. John Colgan, *Trias Thaumaturga*, ed. Eamonn De Burca (Dublin, 1977), pp. 48–9; Stokes, *Tripartite Life*, i, p. cxxxvii ff. See Bieler, *FLL*, p. 196. Jocelyn calls it 'Mount Moriah' or 'Morion' which is again located near the 'Tyrrhene Sea'. Stokes, *Tripartite Life*, p. cxxxix: Lanigan identified Mount Hermon with Mont St Michel, which is in the south of the ocean. He also suggested this name might derive from the Celtic words 'her' great and 'maen' rock although in the Bible, Hermon is given as another name for Mount Sion. See Lanigan, *Ecclesiastical History of Ireland*, p. 165 ff.

32. *Rursu angelus Domini apparuit sancto Patricio dicens, 'Vade ad sanctum seniorem episcopum, qui est in monte Hermon.' … in dextro latere maris oceani, et uallata est ciuitas eius septem muris … ascende cacumen montis Hermon.* Probus 18:15, Bieler, *FLL*, p. 196.

33. See Dr Lanigan, *Ecclesiastical History of Ireland*, p. 109, n. 129.

34. Louis Blondel, *Notice Historique du Mont-St-Michel, de Tombelaine et d'Avrenches* (Avrenches, 1823), p. 7.

35. Nennius's description of the 'cumulum' or perhaps 'tumulum' Occidentale, suggests it may have been the mythic burial ground for the setting sun in the West as Newgrange in Ireland is the mythical 'resurrection' ground of the rising sun in the East, at the winter solstice. The island adjacent to Mont St Michel is called Tombelaine (Tombe-Elaine) or Helen's Tomb. This name could be connected to St Helena, the Mother of Constantine, or perhaps Helen or Ellen, wife of Magnus Maximus.

36. Here I must disagree with Todd who suggested St Patrick's ordination by St Senior on Mount Hermon was another fragment of the life of Palladius. Todd was uncertain about the location of the Tyrrhene Sea and as a result may have underestimated the significance for St Patrick, of references to Armoric Letha. He noted that Mount Hermon, Arnon, Morion, as it is variously called, is described as being on 'the south side of the ocean', 'ar muir Letha', 'on the Sea of Letha', 'on a rock in the Tyrrhene Sea', in 'the city of Capua' or 'near the city of Capua' saying it was not easy to guess what place was intended, but 'we should understand by the ocean the Mediterranean'. See Todd, *St Patrick, Apostle of Ireland*, p. 336 ff. The location is far more likely to have been off the north-west coast of Brittany.

37. 'The Western Ocean (Mare Occidentale) is in another part called the Tyrrenian Sea which designates the Turonian Sea at the mouth of the Loire opposite the country inhabited by the Turones or, as now denominated, the people of Turaine, whose capital, Tours, was a great city

even in the time of the Romans.' *Life of St Patrick*, (Paris, 1870), p. 13. 'Tyrrhene' may therefore be connected to Tours, the ancient capital of the Tourones.

38. 'The sons of Muirchú of Connaught made this hymn to [the archangel] Michael to save themselves from a tempest on the Iccian Sea or to save themselves from famine on 'the island of the Tyrrhene Sea' *(tempestate Mare Icht no ara soerad de fame in insola Maris Tyrreni)* There is also mention of Mont Jovis 'montis Iouis' which Stokes mistakenly identifies with the Alps (St Bernard's Pass). Mont St Michel would seem more appropriate as the context of this passage relates to the Tyrrhene Sea. See Stokes, *Tripartite Life*, i, p. cvi; Louis Blondel, *Notice Historique du Mont-St-Michel, de Tombelaine et d'Avrenches* (Avrenches, 1823).

39. Dr Lanigan suggested the 'city of seven walls' most likely referred to Mont St Michel. At first he wondered if it may have referred to Aleth or St Malo, but he could find no reference to fortifications there which would match the description given. See Lanigan, *Ecclesiastical History of Ireland*, p. 165 f.: Bieler rejected the suggestion of Mont St Michel and suggested Mt Hernon was in the Bay of Naples. See Bieler, *FLL*, p. 222.

40. He accepted that St Patrick was trained in Rome. See Lanigan, p. 166. Also Todd, p. 337.

41. Todd understood that 'Letha' or 'Letavia' frequently signifies Armorica but is sometimes used for Latium. He said 'the confusion here is inextricable' and this is reflected in Todd's comment that 'Ar Muir Letha' refers to the Mediterranean. See Todd, *Patrick, Apostle of Ireland*, p. 337, n. 1.

42. Todd said, 'It must be admitted that this description applies very well to Mont St Michel'. See Todd, *Patrick, Apostle of Ireland*, p. 338, n. 1.

43. See Stokes, *Tripartite Life*, p. 446 ff.

44. See Kenneth Milne, *Christ Church Cathedral: A History* (Dublin, 2000), p. 164.

45. Stokes suggested the island in the 'Tyrrhene Sea' was a reference to the monastery of Lerins and therefore locates it in the Mediterranean. See *Tripartite Life*, i, p. cxxxiv.

# CHAPTER EIGHTEEN

# Saint Patrick's Family

Was it without God or according to the flesh that I came to Ireland? Who compelled me? I was bound by the spirit not to see any of my family. Can it be held against me that I have deep spiritual compassion for those who once took me captive and devastated the male and female servants of my father's house? I was born free according to the flesh, my father was a Decurion. I sold my nobility for the sake of others and I have no regrets and am not ashamed of this.[1]

As far as possible during the course of this enquiry, a determined effort has been made to explore the uncertainties that surround St Patrick from a balanced historical perspective. Much of what has been written about Patrick takes the form of legend and stories passed on through the centuries in 'secondary sources' that cannot be viewed as reliable historical information. At the same time, these sources have preserved treasures of truth, including geographical references that have helped to solve part of the jigsaw puzzle of St Patrick.

If the established tradition has been in error with regard to the location of St Patrick's homeland and other places mentioned in his *Confession* and if we have been 'misled' as to where St Patrick received his religious training and the real identity of those who sponsored the mission to Ireland, could it also be possible that we have not been told the truth about other aspects of St Patrick's life and real identity?

Breton historians record intriguing and detailed information about St Patrick's family, which links them even more directly to Brittany. They claim that St Patrick's father, Calpurnius, was a 'Scottish' prince and that two of Patrick's sisters were founding members of an independent monarchy in Brittany at the time of the settlement in 385 CE.

Apart from accounts given by early Breton historians, genealogical tables are the only resource we have to pursue these matters further. These are well attested from around the ninth century but uncertain before that, so they cannot be taken as reliable historical evidence but like the ancient Lives of St Patrick they may have preserved some of the missing pieces in the puzzle.

In their account of the settlement under Maximus, Breton authors include some intriguing personal information about St Patrick's family. This begins with Conan, an elusive historical figure who can perhaps be identified with the Welsh 'Cynan', the son (or nephew) of Eudes (Eudav Hen), a leading member of the nobility in Britain at the close of the fourth century.[2] Welsh tradition preserves the 'legend' that Magnus Maximus married Helen or Ellen, the daughter of Eudes who was Conan's father (or uncle).[3] This was understood to have been an arranged marriage, by which Maximus was invited to become part of the royal family in Britain because of their imperial ambitions.[4] After Maximus launched the rebellion and entered Gaul with the legions under his command, Conan is said to have been appointed Duke of the Armorican Tract and appointed as the first 'king' of Brittany as part of a new monarchy.

Breton historians record the close family ties that are said to have existed between Conan and St Patrick's father, Calpurnius. Both came from noble families in Albany (Scotland) and were related as cousins. If there is any truth in this claim, then St Patrick's family were closely related to the Emperor, Magnus Maximus. In a section of his *Histoire de Bretagne* entitled 'Calpurnius goes to Armorica' Dom Morice records the following story:

> Calpurnius, the father of St Patrick, was a powerful lord in Albania (Scotland). In Gaul he had married one of St. Martin's nieces, named Conchèse. He was also the cousin of Conis or Conan, to whom Maximus had given part of Armorica [Brittany]. Since Conan was a widower he remarried with Darerca, Calpurnius's daughter, who was St Patrick's sister.
>
> Through this marriage Calpurnius inherited land in the territory of the Diablintes[5] close to the sea but he barely had time to enjoy this as he was murdered in 388 by pirates from Hibernia [Ireland].[6]

M. Deric also records that Conan married Darerca and that Calpurnius had an estate 'close to the sea' in the territory of the Diablintes near Aleth, where Château Bonaban is now located.[7]

In a detailed historical study of the Château and nearby village of Gouesnière, Joseph Viel records the opinion of various authors that Bonaban dates back to the late Roman period. He includes the following statement about the settlement in Brittany in 385 CE which suggests that Calpurnius came to Brittany with an established noble pedigree and some impressive resources:

> Calpurnius, a little prince of Scotland and cousin of Conan [Meriadec] was one of these exiles. He had a large family, slaves, a whole nation [or following]. Conan received him magnificently [in Brittany], married his daughter, the beautiful Darerca and gave him a large and fertile territory, located near the sea, in the country of the Diablintes or Aleth that a few authors, including M. de Gerville, believe to be Bonaban.[8]

A number of early Breton historians record that Calpurnius and Conan were cousins and that both were members of an ancient Scots-British royal family. Similar claims are recorded in Britain. The *Legend of John of Tinmouth* describes Calpurnius as one of the chief Lords of Scotland as does as the *Aberdeen Breviary*. This suggests that St Patrick's father may have had a royal pedigree.[9]

An ancient established tradition has always linked Patrick's family to Strathclyde. This still forms part of the Scottish historical record and has to be accounted for. Could St Patrick's father, Calpurnius, have been a 'Scottish' prince? The country we now call Scotland was not known by that name at the time of St Patrick. 'Scotti' was a name originally applied by the Romans to the Irish, including those who had settled in northern Britain. 'Alba' was an ancient name for Scotland.

At the time of St Patrick, Strathclyde can best be described as a kingdom occupied by various tribes of the ancient Britons who were Welsh. It was located close to the northern boundary of Roman influence between Valencia and the Pictish kingdoms of Caledonia. This was Dalriada, an ancient kingdom of the Scots or Irish. It included lands on both sides of the Irish Sea. Dalriada existed in the north-east of Ireland around Antrim and in the Highlands and Islands in Western Scotland (Argyll). The capital of the kingdom of Strathclyde was the heavily fortified Rock of Dumbarton (Dun Briton, the fort of the Britons). It separated the Britons to the south from the Scots-Irish of Dalriada, in the north.

According to the ancient Lives of St Patrick, Calpurnius also had family ties in Gaul. Irish and Breton sources record that St Patrick's mother, Conchessa, was 'of the Franks'. They claim she was also a close relative of St Martin of Tours.[10]

> Now Patrick's kin was the Britons of Dumbarton. Calpurn was his father's name, an arch presbyter was he. Otid was the name of his grandfather ... Conchessa was his mother's name. She was the daughter of Ochbas, of France was her kin ... she was a sister of St Martin.[11]

This suggests that Patrick's family were Britons from Strathclyde on his father's side and Franks from Gaul through Conchessa.

If Calpurnius was from Strathclyde, then most likely he would have been related to some branch of the early kings of Wales or Scotland, perhaps even those who had intermarried with the Irish who settled from an early date on the north bank of the Clyde, near Dumbarton. The most significant royal families in this region are the early kings of Strathclyde and Scots Dalriada.[12]

There is no direct reference to Calpurnius in any of the genealogical charts currently available but some records are worth exploring further, because they suggest a possible connection to a particular Scottish lineage. The first clue is the name itself. Calpurnius is a Latin name, well known in the late Roman period. St Patrick's father may have belonged to that group of the ancient

Britons who had been Romanised. This does not discount the possibility that his name had Gaelic origins. This would be the case, for example, if 'Calpurnius' was a Latinised version of 'Calpurn' or 'Calpin', as recorded in many of the ancient documents related to St Patrick.

In the Highlands and Islands of Scotland, St Patrick was remembered as Patrick McAlpin.[13] In Gaelic, Patrick's name appears as Padraig M'Alpin (pronunciation: Pawrig). 'Mac', or the abbreviated 'Mc', means 'son of' and, therefore, he was remembered as Patrick 'Mac Calpurn' (son of Calpurn), which became Patrick McAlpin when anglicised. Patrick is frequently called Patrick McAlpin in the ancient poems of Ireland.[14] This suggests that his father may have been associated with the McAlpins in the minds of local people. The Alpins or McAlpins represent one of the most important royal families in Scotland. Most of the kings of Scotland down to the twelfth century came from the McAlpin dynasty.[15] If Calpurnius was a 'Scottish' prince as Breton historians claim and his family was based in Strathclyde, this is the lineage he is most likely to have been related to.

Another clue which suggests that Calpurnius may have been related to progenitors of the McAlpins is the name of St Patrick's sister, Darerca. Dar-erca is a Gaelic name carrying a particular meaning that suggests a possible royal pedigree. The prefix *Dar* means 'oak' in Irish and Scots Gaelic. The suffix *Erca* suggests a link to Erc, the high king of Ireland from whom the kings of Scots Dalriada and the McAlpins are descended. As the table on page 231 shows, King Erc or 'Eirca' was the royal progenitor of the McAlpins. Darerca is a Scottish name of feminine gender that means 'the daughter of Erc' or 'daughter from the oak of Erc'. Names always carried special significance for indigenous people including the Celts, as they still do.

St Patrick's sister was born several generations before Erc became the high king of Ireland around 480 CE, but her name allows for the possibility that she was 'from the lineage of Erc'. This ancient royal family is symbolised by the oak tree. If Darerca's name was chosen to honour her father's relatives or ancestors, the lineage of 'Erc' was important to him. She may have been given this name by her parents to acknowledge the ancient ancestors of Calpurnius (who may have been Irish) and the significance of her own place in this pedigree.[16]

The table is a simplified version of an original chart compiled by Laurence Gardner, who was Presidential Attaché to the European Council of Princes and Jacobi Historiographer Royale. It shows only the main line of descent, as this appears relevant to the uncertainties that surround the origins of St Patrick.[17]

Such genealogical connections cannot be verified historically owing to the lack of reliable records but names are usually chosen for a purpose, especially in royal families. If St Patrick's father, Calpurnius, was linked to the ancient Irish dynasty associated with King Erc of Dalriada, then genealogical records

# THE KINGS OF SCOTS DAL RIADA

### ERC of Dal n'Araide
(Dal Riata) Ireland

| I | I | I |
|---|---|---|
| Fergus Mor | Loarn | Aengus |
| d. 501 CE | Kingdom of N. Argyll | Kingdom of Islay |
| Kingdom of Alba | | |

I

Domangart
(501–608 CE)

I

Gabran
(537–559 CE)

I

Aedhan mac Gabran
(574–608 CE)
Progenitor of the McAlpins
Anointed by St Columba of Iona on the 'Stone of Destiny' in 574 CE.

for the kings of Scots Dalriada may provide further clues to shed light on uncertainties that surround his family origins. At this point, the genealogical tables reveal some interesting surprises. The kings of Scots Dalriada trace their lineage directly from King Coroticus of Strathclyde.

Coroticus was a British king or 'warlord' who was in conflict with St Patrick. In his *Letter to Coroticus*, St Patrick chastised the King for acts of violence which had been perpetrated against some of Patrick's recent converts. St Patrick threatened to excommunicate him if he did not make redress and return those who had been taken captive. The identity of Coroticus (450–470 CE) is no longer disputed. His lineage is confirmed by established genealogical records including those compiled by the Directory of Royal Genealogical Data at the University of Hull and the Magoo Centre.[18] Coroticus (Welsh: Ceredig or Ceretic) was the ruler of Strathclyde from about 450–470 CE. In a genealogy attached to Nennius's *Historia Brittonum* in the Harleian MS, he is called

'Gwledig' (Guletic) which means 'a ruler' in Welsh. This was a title not simply related to Roman military rank but also a royal pedigree. Magnus Maximus (recorded in Welsh traditions as Maxim Gwledig) is probably the best known holder of this title. Coroticus was the founder of a famous dynasty that ruled Strathclyde down to the eighth century.[19] Coroticus may have held the title 'Dux Britanniarum'. This was a noble title given to British kings when the island was under Roman occupation. It continued in use for a time after the legions left Britain in 406 CE, when certain British warlords came to prominence as local leaders. Coroticus was one of these.

Even though he was king of Strathclyde as we have already noted, it would be wrong to think of him as 'Scottish' since at that time this applied to the Irish (the original 'Scotti'). As far as we know, the country we now call Scotland was not known by that name before the tenth century. Coroticus probably belonged to a tribe of the ancient Britons who were Welsh or Cornish although it is also possible that he may have been related to the Irish who had settled around Strathclyde. At the time of St Patrick, the kingdom of Strathclyde extended from the River Derwent in Cumberland in the South, to the Firth of Clyde in the North. The River Clyde separated the Britons to the south from the Scots (Irish) of Dalriada in the North. Its population came from two British peoples (as opposed to Anglo-Saxons, Picts or Scots/Irish). These were the Cymric or Welsh to the south while the northern part of the kingdom was occupied by the Damnonii who belonged to the Cornish. The capital of this kingdom was the heavily fortified rock on the Clyde, called by the Britons 'Alcluid' and known as Dumbarton (Dun Briton) the 'Fort of the Britons'.

When Britain was administered by the Romans, Hadrian's Wall provided the most stable line of defence against the marauding Picts and Scots (Irish). Security disintegrated rapidly and Britain lost all her defensive capability following the rebellion of Maximus when the legions under his command crossed to Gaul.[20] This was a period of social disorder and lawlessness especially in northern Britain. Strathclyde was beyond Hadrian's Wall and vulnerable to attack. Breton historians record that St Patrick's family moved from there to Brittany at this time. In light of the deteriorating security situation, this would have been a sensible decision, especially for a young family.

As a decurion, a position that held significant military responsibilities, Calpurnius would have been well informed about the broader political situation and if he was closely related to Conan and Maximus, as the early Breton historians claim, then he may even have been privy to plans for the new settlement in Brittany. In genealogical tables for the kings of Strathclyde, Coroticus holds a very prominent position. He was a direct descendant of Confer of Strathclyde.[21]

The McAlpins trace their lineage back to Aedhan mac Gabhran (574–608 CE), who was the first king of Scots Dalriada and the table below shows that Aedhan was a descendant of Coroticus.

## STRATHCLYDE AND THE GWYR Y GOGLEDD

| I | I |
|---|---|
| KING COROTICUS<br>of Strathclyde<br>Ruled c.450–470 CE<br>(Welsh: Ceredig) | COEL HEN GODEBOG<br>of Rheded<br>Born c.380 CE<br>Seat at Carlisle. Married Ystralfael,<br>daughter of Conan and Darerca |

From these two royal houses descend …

| I | I |
|---|---|
| King Aedhan of Dalriada<br>(574–578 CE)<br>Anointed by St Columba | Ywain (Owain)<br>Lord of Llwyfenydd |
| I | I |
| King Arthur (son of Aedhan)<br>(d. 693 CE)<br>Ard Ri (High King)<br>and Guletic | Comte de Leon d'Acqs<br>(d. 513 CE)<br>Married Alienor, daughter of<br>King Buidic I of the Bretons |

If Calpurnius belonged to the noble lineage of King Erc of Dalriada from whom the McAlpins trace their origins, this suggests that St Patrick and King Coroticus of Strathclyde were related, having belonged to rival or 'dislocated' branches of the same noble lineage.

If so, then there may have been underlying reasons for the conflict between them which has not been recorded. This cannot be verified historically, but even the possibility that it could be true would have significant implications

for St Patrick's biography. It is one of the reasons why these genealogical tables
are so intriguing and potentially significant for the study of St Patrick. In his
*Letter to Coroticus* St Patrick more or less told King Coroticus that he would
be damned forever if he did not make redress for his evil actions and seek forgiveness from God.[22] We can only imagine how this letter was received. A

## SCOTS IMPERIAL DESCENT

### Lleiffer Mawr (King Lucius) – *Gladys*
### c.180 CE

| Caradawc (Caratacus) | *St Helena (Elaine)* | Cunedd |
|---|---|---|
| | Married Constantius I | |
| Eudes (Eudaf) | Constantine I | Confer of |
| | (The Great) 312–337 CE | Strathclyde |
| *Elen (Orienne)* | *Helen of Hosts* | |
| Married to Magnus Maximus | | |
| Emperor of the West (383–388 CE) | Cinhil, etc. | |
| | *Gratiana* | |
| | Married Tudwall of Galloway | |

| *Severa* | Coroticus of Strathclyde |
|---|---|
| Vortigern 418–464 CE | (Ceretic Guletic) 420–450 CE |

Descent to Aedhan mac Gabhran, 574 CE
and the Kings of Scots Dalriada

British king and his soldiers and supporters would react strongly to being challenged so publically in this way, especially from a bishop in Ireland. This letter probably placed St Patrick's life in even greater danger.

The chart on page 234 that claims to be a record of 'Scots Imperial Descent' is a simplified version of Gardner's original. It reveals a possible link in the lineage between the ancient kings of Strathclyde and Scots Dalriada, Eudes, Maximus and the House of Constantine.

These charts are controversial and many of Gardner's claims would not be accepted by some historians. Genealogical tables can be unreliable and are usually controversial. They were and still are prone to manipulation, to enhance the claims of certain royal families and even to support a particular political, ecclesiastical or military agenda. At the same time, the lives of many of the historical figures who appear in his charts have already been well documented. The significance of these charts is that they include various figures directly or indirectly associated with St Patrick in a variety of sources, which is surprising and perhaps more than coincidental.[23]

In the following chart (p. 236) for the House of Wales and Brittany, members of St Patrick's family are directly recorded. The chart is another greatly simplified and revised version of Gardner's original, showing only key figures in the main line of descent. This includes Eudes, Helen, Conan and Maximus as descendants of Constantine. It also presents a link to the early kings of Brittany, showing Conan as the first king.

One of the most striking aspects of this chart is that it records that Conan married Darerca, who Breton historians identify as St Patrick's sister. On Gardner's chart she is named as the 'grand-niece' of St Martin of Tours, which concurs with claims found in the ancient Lives of St Patrick, that St Patrick's mother, Conchessa, was St Martin's niece. This chart shows a line of descent for the early kings of Brittany from Conan and Darerca to Urbien and then Solomon and Aldron. Breton historians identify both Urbien and Ystrafael as the children of Conan and Darerca.[24] If these personal family details are reliable, then they were St Patrick's nephew and niece.

There is some discrepancy in the initial line of succession but this is understandable, considering the lack of reliable documents from the fifth century. Some Breton authors say Urbien was also called Grallon and they date his rule from 405 CE, others place it later around 435–446 CE. Some accounts place Salomon's rule before that of Grallon.

In the genealogical chart included on page 238, we have given the line of succession for the early kings of Brittany, according to Bertrand d'Argentré's *Abrégé de l'Histoire de Bretagne*, published in Paris in 1695. The royal status of St Patrick's family is clearly apparent from this list. The same basic claims can be found in the writings of Dom Morice and Pièrre Le Baud, amongst others.

# THE HOUSE OF WALES AND BRITTANY

*St Helena* — Constantine Chlorus

---

| | |
|---|---|
| I | I |
| Caradawc | Constantine (The Great) |
| I | I |
| Eudes (Eudaf) | Magnus Maximus |
| | Married Ellen, daughter of Eudes. |
| I | |
| Cardawc I | |
| I | |

Conan

Conan Meriadec (Cynan)
Duke of the Armorican Frontiers
First king of the Bretons, d. 421
Married St Darerca,
grand-niece of Martin of Tours.*

---

| I | | I |
|---|---|---|
| *Istrafael* | | Urbien |

| I | I | I |
|---|---|---|
| Cunedda | Gwawl (Grallon) | Solomon I |
| | | King of the Bretons, |
| I | Married Patrick's sister Tigris or | Son of Urbien |
| | D'Agris, Breton sources say. | |
| KINGS OF | | I |
| STRATHCLYDE | | Aldron (Aldroneus) |
| | | Married the sister of Germanus of Auxerre, says Gardner. |
| | | I |
| | | Budic I |
| | | King of the Bretons |

*According to Breton historians, Darerca was St Patrick's sister. Conan and Calpurnius were cousins. The ancient Lives of St Patrick record that St Patrick's mother, Conchessa, was St Martin's niece. If so, then Patrick's sister Darerca would have been St Martin's grand-niece.

When this table is compared with Gardner's chart for the House of Wales and Brittany, it suggests that members of St Patrick's family came from a significant noble lineage with an ancient Scots-Welsh pedigree that played a central part in the foundation of a monarchy in Brittany following the settlement that took place at the time of the rebellion of Magnus Maximus in 385 CE.

In relation to uncertainties that surround the origins of St Patrick, it is significant that Breton authors record that when Grallon succeeded to the throne after the death of Conan he married St Patrick's sister, Tigris. M. Deric describes Tigris as 'the sister of Queen Darerca'.[25] He believed that her name confirms that she was of high noble birth and belonged to a very illustrious family.

According to these authors, members of St Patrick's family were senior founding members of the early Breton aristocracy. The dates given for all these marriages are consistent and plausible from a chronological point of view.

Unlike claims made towards the end of the seventh century by Muirchú and the ancient Lives of St Patrick, Breton historians provide some interesting historical and linguistic evidence to support their claims. M. Deric insists that the name 'Tigris' or 'D'Agris' confirms the high birth of her father, Calpurnius. It derives from the Gaelic name for house – *tigh* or *tig* – and king – *ri* or *ris*. D'Agris comes from *d'ag*, which means race, and *ri* or *ris*, a royal house. If so, the name of St Patrick's sister may not be from the Latin *tigris* (which means 'a little tiger') but Gaelic, meaning 'an issue from a royal house' or 'from the House of Kings.'[26]

A list of names for St Patrick's sisters was recorded in some of the ancient manuscripts published by Colgan in 1647. These documents include various accounts of the members of St Patrick's family, giving names for St Patrick's sisters and a brother called Senan.[27] Darerca and Tigris are mentioned in these lists consistent with those recorded by Breton historians. What we do not find in the ancient Lives of St Patrick published by Colgan or in the *Book of Armagh*, is any prevailing reference to the marriages between Conan and Darerca or Grallon and Tigris. Nor do we find any record of the alleged family ties between Calpurnius, Conan and Maximus. These family details appear to have been recorded only in Breton sources, with one significant exception. There is one reference in the *Tripartite Life of St Patrick* that concurs with the essential substance of these accounts. It describes how, when St Patrick came across the sea from the land of 'Bretan' (Brittany) to Ireland, he travelled with clerics who were 'sons of Conis and Darerca, St Patrick's sister, as the households of their churches say, and that is not to be denied.'[28] This reference shows that the Irish church was aware of Conan's existence and his marriage to Patrick's sister, Darerca.

# THE EARLY KINGS OF BRITTANY

I. Conan (383 CE)

Married St Patrick's sister, Darerca

I

II. Grallon (388 CE)

Married St Patrick's sister, D'Agris or Tegreda

I

III. Salomon (405 CE)

Son of Grallon

I

IV. Audren (412 CE)

Son of Salomon, 'fils aine'

I

V. Budic (415–487 CE)

Son of Audren

I

VI. Hoel I 'Le Grand' (487 CE)

I

VII. Riothem

I

VIII. Hoel II (d. 560)

---

| | |
|---|---|
| I | I |
| Rivallon | Hoel III (594 CE) |
| Married a daughter of Hoel II | Son of Hoel II |

I

Alain (560–594 CE)

I

Salomon II (640 CE)

Son of Hoel III

I

Alain 'Le Long' (660–690 CE)

Nephew of Salomon II

Source: Bertrand d'Argentré, *Abrégé de l'Histoire de Bretagne* (Paris, 1965).

These are remarkable claims but are they trustworthy? The origins of Brittany and its relations with the kings of France is a complex and controversial subject. It is clouded by issues which have greatly influenced the views of individual historians. Conflicting historical accounts are linked to complex political and ecclesiastical issues concerning the so-called Merovingian Conspiracy and the origins of the French kings, not least in terms of the relationship with Britain and Rome before the foundation of the Carolingian Empire. There was obviously a battle going on for control of Brittany and the line of succession is understandably controversial.[29] These disputes are reflected in contradictory claims that can be found in various genealogical tables and they have significant implications in relation to understanding the truth about St Patrick.

M. Daru and other Breton authors suggest that two alternative lines of succession have survived for the early kings of Brittany. One can be traced through Conan to Salomon and Alain, and the other through Rivallon. In one, St Patrick's family plays a very prominent part. In the other, they are excluded. M. Daru says the role of Conan and Darerca in the line of succession has been erased from many historical records as a result of efforts by the Church to establish itself more securely in Gaul in the centuries which followed the collapse of the western Empire. Following d'Argentré, he claims that in Brittany there are two sovereign lines, one stemming from Conan and another through Rivallon.[30] In his opinion, the true line of succession was preserved through Conan, despite being erased in chronicles compiled by the Church. M. Daru is convinced that the names of Conan and Salomon retain the ancient language and, therefore, an authentic lineage. The same applies to St Patrick's two sisters, Darerca and Tigris. This view is shared by a number of early Breton historians, but rejected by others, who deny the existence of Conan and his role in the foundation of a monarchy in Brittany.

The origins of such discrepancies are of importance in resolving uncertainties about St Patrick's story as they involve significant claims with regard to members of his immediate family. One of the sensitive political issues is whether the British occupied this region as refugees or conquerors. Vertot claims that the ancient Britons did not settle in Brittany until their arrival as refugees in the sixth century but his work has been criticized for distorting historical facts to show the original dependence of the Bretons on the French kings.[31]

Arthur de La Borderie joined the ranks of French historians who said Conan's existence was a fable.[32] This includes Cornette, who promulgated the view that the legend of Conan was invented to serve the political ambitions of later Dukes in Brittany who were searching for a legitimate reason to free themselves from the king of France, by claiming the Breton kings were an independent sovereign lineage.[33] Tourault said the existence of Conan and those who descended from him was all part of a legend created by the Bretons for ideological and political motives.[34] It is possible that the exact opposite may be true in this case. The exclusion of Conan could have been politically motivated, to show that the Bretons were always dependent on the Franks and, therefore, held no sovereign claim to independence from France. Removing any clear record of Conan's identity and his position in Brittany may have helped to secure the political and ideological ambitions of France and Rome and remove any legitimate claim that he and Maximus and the British royals may have had to this particular region or to any further imperial advancement.

There is huge historical uncertainty and no shortage of political and ecclesiastical intrigue and controversy attached to this period of history.[35] M. Daru notes that the same authors who argue against the independence of the Bretons also question the existence of Conan and dispute claims that he was established by Maximus as the first king of Brittany, thus denying any of his successors a place within the Breton aristocracy.[36] Most of the early Breton historians take a radically different view. They record that Maximus landed forces at the mouth of the River Rance, using the Roman port of Aleth, located close to the estate at Bannavem Tiburniae that was owned by Patrick's father, Calpurnius.[37] Dom Morice claims that they landed in Brittany, as does Barbier.[38] The historical truth surrounding these events is crucial to rediscovering the truth about St Patrick and the significance of his family as founding members of the Breton aristocracy.

Many of the accounts recorded by local Breton historians who were writing before the so called 'era of modern scholarship' are viewed as historically unreliable by contemporary Breton scholars, who continue to wrestle with the facts concerning the origins of Brittany. Uncertainties yet to be resolved centre on a lack of reliable sources from the fifth century and complexities linked to the historical relationship between Britain and France, the claims of certain royal families and the influence of the Church.

M. André Yves Bourgès, who is a well-respected authority in Brittany today, advises that we should be very wary of claims made by the early Breton historians concerning Conan and Maximus and the details given about St Patrick's family. Breton authors appear to have been dependent on Geoffrey of Monmouth for information about Conan and many of the details about St Patrick and his family can be found in the writings of M. Jacques Gallet, whose views influenced others.[39] These claims may have arisen in the context of Breton historiography in the seventeenth, eighteenth and nineteenth centuries, when Breton authors are said to have come under pressure to provide 'evidence' to support a particular ducal ideology. At the same time, it is important to remember that the origins of Brittany or 'proto-Bretagne' remains cloaked with uncertainty. The complex nature of historic relations between the Bretons and the Franks, not to mention the growing influence of the diocesan Church in the aftermath of the fall of Rome, suggests that the truth as to what took place in Brittany at this time may have been lost. This may have affected records concerning St Patrick and the significance of his family.[40]

This is what makes the claims recorded by many of early Breton historians doubly intriguing. They are convinced that members of St Patrick's family belonged to an authentic noble lineage from which the kings of France are descended. These claims are impossible to verify because of the lack of trustworthy historical records. Genealogical tables cannot be taken as a reliable source for historical information. The origins of the kings of France are especially uncertain but the detailed personal information about St Patrick's family which has been recorded in Brittany could be authentic and should not be dismissed as a legend. The presence of so many connections in the genealogical tables is intriguing and worthy of being the subject of further enquiry by those suitably qualified for the task. The complex nature of political and ideological factors suggests that we should remain cautious.

Could it be true that St Patrick belonged to a significant royal family? According to a variety of old Breton, Irish and British sources, five members of St Patrick's immediate family are recognised as having noble status. This includes Calpurnius, who is identified as a Welsh or 'Scottish' prince and cousin to Conan, a close relation of the Emperor, Maximus. *St Fiacc's Hymn* records that St Patrick was 'heir to his father's nobility'.[41] St Patrick's sister Darerca is said to have married Conan when he was crowned as the first king of Brittany in 383 CE. Another sister of St Patrick called 'Tigris' became an important member of this royal household when she married Grallon, who succeeded to the throne of his father and become the second king in Brittany. According to the *Tripartite Life*, a third sister called Cinnemon was remembered in Ireland as 'Royal Cinne'.

Finally, there is St Patrick himself. In his *Letter to Coroticus*, St Patrick tells us that he 'sold his nobility' for the sake of others.[42] This strongly suggests that he may have renounced his royal entitlements when he committed himself to the religious life and became an apostle in Ireland. The Latin phrase given in the earliest manuscript is *vendidi enim nobilitatem meam*. *Vendidi* is the first person singular of the Latin verb *vendo* (to sell) written in the past tense, meaning 'I sold'. *Nobilitatem* comes from *nobilitas* or *nobilitatis*, which means nobility or royal pedigree. An appropriate translation of his words would be, 'I sold my nobility (my royal title) for the sake of others'. If so, St Patrick's royal status would be confirmed. Members of his own immediate family such as his sisters Darerca and Tigris would never have held such high status without the existence of a proven pedigree. St Patrick's writings, therefore, provide the best evidence of all to confirm that his family was of noble status.

There is so much about St Patrick's life that remains uncertain. Many of the claims that have been made about him are impossible to verify because of a lack of reliable historical evidence. That is what makes the study of St Patrick so interesting. There is so much about him that remains a mystery, not least because we have so little information about events taking place at the time of St Patrick in the fifth century.

St Augustine once said, 'we should not believe anything on a dubious point, lest in favour to our error we conceive a prejudice against something that truth hereafter will reveal'. If there is any truth in the claims recorded by the early Breton historians concerning the royal status of St Patrick's family, it not only strengthens the case for locating Patrick's homeland in Brittany, it surely confirms it.

---

*Notes*

1. LC 10.

2. Deric describes Conan as a Scottish prince, *un Prince d'Albanie ou Ecosse.* See Gilles Deric, *Histoire Ecclésiastique de Bretagne*, ii (Paris, 1778), p. 138.

3. Welsh tradition holds that Cynan (Meriadog) led a large army of Britons over to Gaul. This is recorded in the Welsh Triads as one of the *tair cyuordwy* or three emigrations that left Britain and never returned. See Robert Williams, *Enwogion Cymru: A Biographical Dictionary of Eminent Welshmen*, p. 216.

4. For an excellent article on Helen and Maximus and the events which surround them, especially in Brittany, see *Lives of the Queens of England Before the Norman Conquest*, ch. 8, 'Helena'.

5. The Diablintes was a Celtic tribe that inhabited a coastal region between St Malo and Mont St Michel.

6. P. H. Morice, *Histoire de Bretagne*, (Paris, 1744), translated by Francine Bernier, i, p. 8.

7. *Conan espousa Darerca, le beau père eut un etablissement dans le territoire des Diablintes d'Alet, assez pres de la mer.* Deric, *Histoire Ecclesiastique de Bretagne*, p. 193 (see n. 3).

8. Joseph Viel, *La Gouesnière et Bonaban* (Dinan, 1912), pp 114–119, trans. Francine Bernier.

9. *Patricius Hiberensium apostolos expatre Calphurnio de Scottorum nobili familia ortus.* Macnab, Duncan, *Archaeological Dissertation on the Birthplace of St Patrick* (Dublin, 1865).

10. Morice claims that St Patrick was taken captive in 388, escaped in 395 CE and travelled to 'the Gauls' where he went into solitude with community of St Martin, his grand-uncle, from whom he received a monastic tonsure. *Patrice recourvre la liberte vers l'an 395 & repassa dans les Gaules. Il se retira d'abord aupres de saint Martin, son grond uncle, qui lui donner la tonsure monachale.* This implies that Patrick was born in 372 CE. It suggests that the lands were inherited around 385 CE. See Morice, *Histoire*, p 8.

11. 'Lebar Brecc Homily' in Whitley Stokes, *Tripartite Life of St Patrick* (London, 1887), ii, p. 433.

12. For information on the kingdom of Strathclyde, see W. F. Skene, *Celtic Scotland* (Edinburgh, 1886), p. 237.

13. 'St Patrick or Patrick M'Alpain as he was designated by the Highlanders.' See Dugald Mitchell, *History of the Highlands and Gaelic Scotland* (Paisley, 1900), p. 36. Also 'Patrick son of Alpurn' (Mac Alpurn), Stokes, Trip. Life, p. 561.

14. See *Transactions of the Royal Irish Academy*, Dublin 1787, p. 80 (n. c) and p. 104. Also, 'Patrick, son of Alpurn' (Old Irish, *Patraic maicc Alpuirn*' in the Lebear Brecc, Stokes, *Tripartite Life*, p. 552; 'Calpurn's son (*mac Calpuirn*) was meek, was great' Stokes, p. 551; 'Patrick, son of Calpurn (*mac Calpuirn*), Stokes, *Tripartite Life*, p. 427.

15. This includes: Alpin (736–740 CE); Alpin, King of Scots (839–841); Kenneth I (844–859); Donald I (859–863); Constantine I (863–877); Constantine II (900–942); Constantine III (995–997); Duncan I (1034–1040); Macbeth (1040–1057). Malcolm III (1058–1093 CE) was the last representative of the royal line of McAlpins. The origins of this clan go back to Aedhan mac Ghabran who was anointed as King of Scots Dalriada by St Columba of Iona in 574 CE. This is the first record we have in Western Europe of the anointing of a king by a Christian cleric.

16. Erc was king of Irish Dál Riata until 474 CE. He was the father of Fergus Mór, one of two sons including Loann Macc Ercc or Macc Ercae. The surname Macc Ercae may have come from the maternal side, as there is mention of a legendary mother called Erca. In Irish mythology Eochaid is named as 'son of Erc', son of Rinnal, of the Fir Bolg.

17. For the original charts see Laurence Gardner, *Bloodline of the Holy Grail* (NY, 2006).

18. Brian Tompsett, Dept. Computer Science, University of Hull: *Directory of Royal Genealogical Data*: B.C.Tompsett@dcs.hull.ac.uk see also http://www.magoo.com/hugh/scotskings.html. For information concerning the identity of Coroticus see T. M. Charles-Edwards, *Early Christian Ireland* (Cambridge, 2000), p. 227 ff.

19. Skene, *Celtic Scotland*, p. 184.

20. Hadrian's Wall extended between the Solway Firth (Carlisle) and Tynemouth (Newcastle). Maximus led a successful military campaign against the Picts, before he left for Gaul. During that campaign, the Romans may have been able to protect an area further to the north possibly as far as the Antonine Wall, which extended between the Firth of Forth and the Clyde estuary (Strathclyde). This was an earthen rampart built in 138 CE when Antonius succeeded Hadrian. See Skene, *Celtic Scotland*, p. 59 ff., p. 97.

21. According to Gardner's chart for the kings of Strathclyde, King Coroticus (Welsh: *Ceredig Guletic*, c.450–470 CE) was a direct descendent of Confer, the progenitor of the Strathclyde dynasty, born c.282 CE. See Gardner, *Bloodline of the Holy Grail*, p. 358.

22. LC 19.

23. For the original charts see Laurence Gardner, *Bloodline of the Holy Grail*, pp 342 ff. For a more detailed study of the significance of these charts in relation to St Patrick's royal pedigree, see Marcus Losack, *St Patrick and the Bloodline of the Grail: the Untold Story of St Patrick's Royal Family* (Annamoe, Wicklow, 2012).

24. Ystrafael is recorded as the daughter of Conan Meriadec. She married Coel Hen Godebog of Regged, a Welsh prince born c.380 CE whose seat was at Carlisle. See Charts for the House of Wales and Brittany, Gardner, *Bloodline of the Holy Grail*, p. 342 ff.

25. *Il avoit epouse Tigris ou Agris, soeur de la Reine, Darerca.* Deric, *Histoire Ecclésiastique de Bretagne*, ii, p. 263.

26. *Le nom de Tigris confirme ce que nous avons dit ci devant de la haute naissance de Calpurnius son pere.* Tigris: *tigh* (maison, house) and *de ris* (Roi, king); d'Agris: *d'ag* (race) and *ris, roi* (issue of a royal house 'issue de maison royale'). See Deric, *Histoire Ecclésiastique de Bretagne*, p. 263, n. (b).

27. Liaman and Cinnemon are given as the names of two other sisters. See Deric, *Histoire Ecclésiastique de Bretagne*, p. 149.

28. Stokes, *Tripartite Life*, i, p. 83.

29. Deric identifies Rivallon as a child from Conan's first marriage to Ursula, not from his second marriage, to St Patrick's sister, Darerca. See Deric, *Histoire Ecclésiastique de Bretagne*, p. 240–5.

30. *Duo in Britannia Armorica reges, unus e Conani, alter e Rivallonis prosapia.* Daru, *Histoire de Bretagne* (Paris, 1826), i, p. 94, n. 1.

31. See John O'Hanlon, *Lives of the Irish Saints* (Dublin, 1875), iii, p. 447, n. 174.

32. See *Liste des Souverains de Bretagne*, http:/fr.wikipedia.org.

33. *La légende de Conan a perduré car elle servait les ambitions politiques des derniers Ducs au moment où ceux-ci cherchaient à légitimer leur pouvoir et s'émanciper de leur suzerain le roi de France.* See Liste des Souverains de Bretagne, http:/fr.wikipedia.org.

34. Tourault insists there were no kings in Brittany before 840 CE. *Des motifs politiques et idéologiques expliquent un tel travestissement – les Bretons, en lutte permanente contre les rois de France, ont toujours eu besoin de s'assurer une position avantageuse: En réalité la Bretagne ne s'est constituée en royaume que vers 840.* Philippe Tourault, *Les Rois de Bretagne IVème–XIXème Siècle* (Paris, 2005).

35. Lobineau's genealogical charts do record the name of Conan but no personal details are given to help identify him. Lobineau dates Rivallon's presence in Brittany to 458 CE, as part of the first major settlement of the ancient Britons which in his opinion, led to a change in name from Armorica to Bretagne. G. A. Lobineau, *Histoire de Bretagne* (Paris, 1707), p. 6 ff.

36. *Les auteurs qui on ecrit contra l'independence des Bretons, vont jusqu'a contester l'existence de Conan et des rois qui lui succederent'.* Daru, *Histoire*, p. 42, 43, see n. 1.

37. M. Daru, *Histoire de Bretagne*, p. 42 ff.

38. *Les vents favourables, l'avand conduit a l'embouchure de la rivierre de Rence.* P. H. Morice, *Histoire*, p. 6. See also C. Barbier, *Les Ducs de Bretagne* (Rouen, 1859), p. 16.

39. This author provides a fascinating study of the origins of Brittany in which he quotes as many ancient sources as were available to him then, to document the settlement under Maximus and the role of Conan. He includes a number of detailed claims related to members of St Patrick's family as founding members of the Breton royal family. See Jacques Gallet, *Dissertation sur L'Origins Des Bretons in Histoire des Ducs de Bretagne*, i (Paris, 1739).

40. This is a complex subject that relates to the so called 'Merovingian Conspiracy' and an alliance between the Roman Church and the Franks that led to the establishment of the Carolingian Empire. The Merovingian kings were associated with a 'Messianic' lineage, linked to the family of Jesus and Israel's King David. The Church is accused of seeking to destroy any record of this lineage, and its claim to an alternative religious authority. See Marcus Losack, *St Patrick and the Bloodline of the Grail: the Untold Story of St Patrick's Royal Family* (Annamoe, Wicklow, 2012).

41. *St Fiacc's Hymn*, which is considered to be one of the earliest documents related to St Patrick, suggests that Calpurnius may have been of noble birth: *Succat ejus notnen in Tribubus dictum, Quis ejus Pater sit notum:* 'When captured by an Irish band, He took their Isle for fatherland; Succat by Christian birth his name, Heir to a father's noble fame'. St Fiacc's *Hymn*, v 2.

42. LC 10.

CHAPTER NINETEEN

# *Conclusions*

History is an amazing presence.
It's the place where vanished time gathers.[1]

The fifth century is known as the 'lost century', full of intrigue and mystery because so few documents have survived from the period. The truth about St Patrick's place of origins and the real identity of those who supported his mission to Ireland were lost to historical memory in the centuries after his death. Fortunately, Patrick wrote two letters which survived from the fifth century. Without them, we would have been left completely in the dark. These letters provide the only reliable, historical evidence about his life and they hold the essential clues that can help solve the mystery of his true identity. In his *Confession*, Patrick mentions five key geographical references related to his place of origin and significant events in his life. Unfortunately, it is impossible to clearly identify these locations solely from the information given in St Patrick's own writings.

Despite these uncertainties, stories about St Patrick were passed on through the centuries and in the closing decades of the seventh century the Church in Armagh commissioned a scribe called Muirchú to write the first official 'biography' of St Patrick. Muirchú's narrative was influenced by an ecclesiastical and political agenda affecting the Irish Church in general and the Church in Armagh in particular at this time. Until then, St Patrick was historically anonymous in as much as there is no evidence to show his life was honoured by the Irish Church or that St Patrick was held in any special veneration, a fact that suggests that he may have been outcast and almost forgotten.

Thanks to the Monastery of Armagh, this situation changed dramatically. Muirchú was given responsibility for 'cleaning up the file' and providing all the necessary details so that any uncertainty that may have existed about St Patrick could be removed. St Patrick was now elevated to a position of authority and honoured as Ireland's patron saint and founding apostle. He was presented as Ireland's champion of Catholic orthodoxy, having been sent by Rome.

In the medieval period, Irish hagiographers functioned as ecclesiastical spin doctors and were capable of masterful fabrication. St Patrick's 'resurrection' in the ecclesiastical record helped to resolve internal civil and religious conflicts, increasing Armagh's influence as the mother house of the *Patricii Paruchia* – a growing federation of monasteries claiming St Patrick as their founder.

Muirchú had access to a copy of St Patrick's *Confession* but much of what he said about Patrick was hagiographical. Muirchú's narrative was in many ways fabricated and through it the 'Legend' of St Patrick was born. In relation to Patrick's place of origins, Muirchú made certain statements which have shaped our image and understanding of St Patrick for more than a thousand years. He claimed to know that St Patrick came from Britain, that Patrick's homeland was in Britain and that Bannavem Tiburniae, the place from which St Patrick was taken captive, was 'without doubt' also in Britain.

Muirchú was a genius. The Church in Armagh expected him to resolve existing uncertainties. To achieve this, Muirchú created a 'map' and used descriptive geography to locate Patrick's homeland in Britain. Muirchú appears to have been faithful to the text of St Patrick's *Confession* by retaining 'Britanniis' as the name for St Patrick's homeland but in his narrative this name was carefully and deliberately applied to the island of Britain exclusively. Muirchú may have brought order to St Patrick's story at the end of the seventh century but he achieved this by creating an illusion or 'delusion', hoping to resolve matters of dispute within Ireland and between Ireland, Britain and Rome. In that sense, it is not unreasonable to suggest that Muirchú 'cast a spell' around St Patrick's story. Irish druids had been masters of the art of delusion and casting spells by magic, before they became Christians; Muirchú's narrative shows how effective Christians could be at maintaining that tradition, weaving their own special form of hagiographical 'magic', introducing ecclesiastical influences that quickly became revered, replacing older traditions. Many of those who wrote after him accepted Muirchú's authority and built upon his account, a process which helped to develop an established tradition that St Patrick came from Britain. The spell that was cast was so strong that it has bound the popular image and understanding of St Patrick to the present day.

Despite Muirchú's best efforts, uncertainties about St Patrick's place of origins and true identity refused to disappear. Other Lives of St Patrick were compiled after the seventh century. Some of these included material that must have survived in a written or oral form and that predated Muirchú. Alternative accounts existed concerning St Patrick and various scribes over the centuries tried to make sense out of these conflicting stories. Many of these documents emphasised St Patrick's connections with Brittany, claiming that before he was sold into slavery in Ireland, Patrick was taken captive from a region called 'Armoric Letha', which can be identified as a coastal region of Armorica, now called Brittany. One of the ancient authors, Probus, claimed to know 'without doubt' that St Patrick's homeland was in Brittany, that he was born there and also that Bannavem Tiburniae, the place from which St Patrick was taken captive, was located 'close beside the Western Sea' on the north-west coast of Brittany which at the time Probus was writing formed part of the Frankish province of Neustria.

When John Colgan published seven of these ancient Lives of St Patrick in 1647, this became a major resource for the study of St Patrick. Without these documents we may never have known that such alternative accounts existed. Muirchú had not been able to monopolise the material. Despite the fact they are essentially hagiographies, these manuscripts are priceless because they have preserved some of the missing pieces in the jigsaw puzzle of St Patrick. Although certain geographical references mentioned in these later sources are not found in St Patrick's writings, they are of crucial importance to determine the truth about his place of origins.

We must give thanks to the scribes who faithfully transcribed these ancient names down through the centuries, despite the fact that they, like us, may not have fully understood their meaning or their precise geographical location. These scribes recognised the uncertainties about St Patrick's life held within the ancient sources and attempted to clarify them, and in so doing ensured they were passed on. Preserved within their documents are important clues that hold the keys to establishing the truth, by comparing all the ancient manuscripts in light of other historical evidence.

Much of the confusion surrounding St Patrick's origins centres on the meaning of the Latin name 'Britanniis' which Patrick used to describe his homeland. Muirchú decided that it meant Britain but others suggested that St Patrick came from a region called 'Britain' on the continent. The names for 'Britain' and 'Brittany' (Bretagne) were very similar and could easily have been confused. In 1647, when John Colgan was preparing these ancient manuscripts for publication, he was aware of contradictory claims in the ancient sources. Colgan admitted that, 'because the cited authors speak in general terms, there is controversy as to which Britain or what part of Britain St Patrick was born.'[2] This is a clear indication that St Patrick's place of origins had remained uncertain despite what Muirchú had said.

Even though he was conscious of the confusion and contradictory accounts in the ancient sources, Colgan concluded his 'Inquiry into the Birthplace and Family of St Patrick' by stating categorically that St Patrick had come from Britain. The references to Brittany were discounted. Colgan ridiculed Probus, saying he was 'not sufficiently skilled in Patrician matters and the location of places'.[3] The document attributed to Probus includes some ancient material which appears to be authentic. It can be considered as one of the ancient sources that has preserved authentic information about St Patrick's place of origins. This information concurs with other references preserved in some of the ancient Lives of St Patrick published by Colgan that identify the place where St Patrick was taken captive as 'Armoric Letha'. This can be identified without doubt with the coastal region of north-west Brittany. The name 'Armoric Letha' strongly suggests a connection with the Roman port city of Aleth, which was strongly fortified in the closing decades of the fourth century, as well as with the *Laeti* in Brittany.

The significance of Aleth as a major port and Roman military base or *tiburnia* for the Legion of Mars is well documented. It was an important base for the Roman navy before the legions in Gaul were withdrawn to protect the Empire from increasing attacks from the Barbarians. It was also an important centre for local political and military administration during the rebellion of Maximus in 383 CE. Calpurnius could have been employed here as a Decurion, supporting those soldiers who remained loyal to Maximus.

Breton historians identify the lands given to St Patrick's father, Calpurnius, within a specific part of this coast, between Aleth, Dol and Mont St Michel. This region was previously in the territory of a local Celtic tribe called the Diablintes and was known to the ancient writers by various names, including Letha, Armoric Letha and Lethania Britannia. This is precisely where Château Bonaban is located and suggests that local traditions about St Patrick could be true.

The evidence itself and clues that have been gleaned from a variety of sources have allowed a clearer and more composite picture to emerge concerning St Patrick. This supports the case for a radical new theory of origins. All the key geographical references relating to St Patrick's place of origins that are found in his own writings can now be identified within a specific geographical area on the coast of north-west Brittany, between the Roman port at Aleth and Mont St Michel. Identifying them all within this region is not incompatible with the geographical descriptions given by St Patrick in his own writings and nothing exists in those writings to contradict any of these proposals.

Hopefully St Patrick's *Confession* can be even more fully understood and appreciated if it is accepted that some of the uncertainties which have surrounded him for more than fifteen centuries may now be resolved. The evidence that is now available to support the case for Brittany far outweighs any that can be provided for Britain. This is true to such an extent that we must now view the established tradition, that St Patrick came from Britain and that Bannavem Taburniae was also located in Britain, as unsafe and, therefore, unacceptable. Future translations of St Patrick's *Confession* will need to be revised on the basis that his use of the Latin name 'Britanniis' did not refer to the island of Britain exclusively and there is now more than sufficient evidence to suggest that it refers to Brittany.

Although the evidence to locate St Patrick's homeland in Brittany is compelling and local traditions recorded at Château Bonaban are, therefore, possibly authentic and trustworthy, absolute or final verification will only be possible following a supervised archaeological excavation. There are now compelling reasons for this to be done.

Celtic axes have been found in the local area and significant remains from the late Roman period are already well documented, including the network of local Gallo-Roman roads and military installations at the Roman port of Aleth (St Malo). Roman remains were discovered in the basement of the château during renovations that took place in 1859, according to a local historical study published in 1912 by Joseph Viel. This author recorded details of some intriguing conversations and meetings he had with a clergyman called Rev. A. Boutlou on July 8th, 1911. Fr Boutlou was originally from the Côtes du Nord but had moved to the United States forty years previously.[4] Returning to Brittany to see the country where he had spent his youth, he asked Joseph Viel to be his guide in the local commune at Bonaban.

Fr Boutlou informed Joseph Viel that in 1859 his (Boutlou's) father had been hired as a painter to help with restoration work that was taking place at the château. During these restorations he found several pieces of Roman mortar stuck to fragments of bricks. He was convinced that these remains, based on their appearance, must have been part of a Roman bathhouse or swimming pool. During the late Roman period, only the wealthiest and most privileged had such facilities in their own private homes. Could this bathhouse have once belonged to St Patrick's father, Calpurnius?

Joseph Viel was sure that excavations could reveal more remains that would easily demonstrate the antiquity of Bonaban. Following M. de Gerville, who had been the first to make this claim in 1848, he was also convinced that this was the true location of the estate owned by St Patrick's father, Calpurnius:

> Calpurnius is likely to have stayed at Bonaban. Roman coins found near the château support that assumption. Celtic axes discovered on the edge of Bois-Renou have proved that the site is ancient. You only need to study the topography of the area to become aware that the granite hill where many Châteaux de Bonaban, were built over time was in the past a blue chip strategic point.[5]

Aerial photograph of Château de Bonaban. Note the lake in the foreground and the elevated nature of this ancient, walled site which was surrounded by water until the introduction of land drainage schemes in the eighteenth century. A local tradition claims the first building on this site dated to the late Roman period and was the home of St Patrick's father, Calpurnius, being the place where Patrick was taken captive.

Examination of this ancient site in relation to the surrounding countryside had convinced him that local traditions recorded about St Patrick were true and that the description given in Patrick's *Confession* concerning his abduction by pirates relates perfectly to the local topography and proximity to the coast. Joseph Viel suggested that an archaeological excavation could reveal something of great significance and that any stone, bronze, cement or brick discovered would reveal the truth. He concluded his study of the local area by reflecting on the fact that the true meaning of the stories and legends attached to many of these ancient sites is to be found underground, not in books.[6] Hopefully this can inspire someone with the necessary contacts and resources to plan a supervised archaeological excavation of the site.

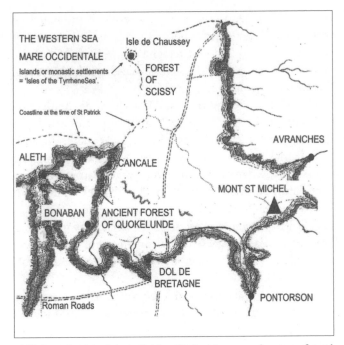

St Patrick's homeland *in Britanniis* identified with a coastal region of north-west Brittany, between Aleth, Dol and Mont St Michel, with proposed location of Bannavem Tiburniae (on or close to the site of Château Bonaban) and the Wood of Foclut (La Forêt de Quokelunde) close beside the Western Sea (Mare Occidentale). This map shows the coastline today and the coastline at the time of St Patrick, before an inundation of the sea caused the Forests of Quokelunde and Scissy to become submerged.

## Where was St Patrick born?

Attempts to identify the place where St Patrick was born and establish a chronology for his life are fraught with difficulties because these matters are not easily verified. This is an important aspect of St Patrick's story that deserves to be addressed, accepting that any proposals will be tentative, as there are so many diverse and conflicting accounts. There is an established tradition, preserved in the Scottish historical record, that St Patrick was born near Strathclyde.

The author of *St Fiacc's Hymn* said he was born at Nemthor which the Scholiast identified with Strathclyde. Many early Breton historians record that St Patrick was born in 372 CE and that he moved to Brittany with his family as part of the settlement that took place at the time of the rebellion of Magnus Maximus from 383–388 CE. This implies that St Patrick was born in the region we now call Scotland and that he was around ten or twelve years old when he arrived in Brittany. M. Daru says that as a result of the marriage between Conan and Darerca, Calpurnius inherited lands in the territory of the Diablintes, between Aleth and Dol-de-Bretagne. These lands included the coastal area covered by the Forest of Quokelunde and the higher ground where Château Bonaban is now located.

According to M. Daru, Calpurnius and Conchessa did not live long enough to enjoy their inheritance. He describes how Irish pirates attacked the family estate in 389 CE, when St Patrick was abducted and taken to Ireland to be sold into slavery. St Patrick's mother and father were both killed during the slaughter that took place. If these dates are correct, it places St Patrick's birth in Scotland in 372 CE, the family's move to Brittany in 383–385 CE and the attack on Bannavem Tiburniae, when St Patrick was taken captive, to 389 CE. According to this schedule, St Patrick would have escaped from slavery in Ireland in 395 or 396 CE. These are the dates suggested by the majority of Breton historians who recorded personal information about St Patrick and the migration of his family from Strathclyde to Brittany.

These writings have so far appeared to be trustworthy concerning the location of Bannavem Tiburniae. Can we also trust their record that Patrick was born in Scotland in 372 CE? This is not straight forward, because not all Breton authors agree that St Patrick was born in northern Britain. M. de Gerville, who was the first to identify Château Bonaban with St Patrick's 'Bannavem Tiburniae', claims that Patrick was born on his father's estate in Brittany. Robidue recorded the statement that follows after his own historical enquiries and it is worth reading again, since it brings us full circle to the first time we encountered these local traditions in Brittany:

> Scottish historians hold Dumbarton to be the birthplace of St Patrick. M. de Gerville identified Bannavem Tiburniae, the geographical designation given in Latin in St Patrick's *Confession* as Bonaban and the place of his birth. He believed this to be so without doubt, a view shared with unanimity by all Breton historians, except Lobineau.[7]

Having given credit to M. de Gerville, Robidue continues his account, concerning a well documented local tradition which is widely accepted by the majority of ancient Breton historians.

> It was in 388 AD, when the Roman general Magnus Maximus withdrew his legions from Britain, that St Patrick's family moved here from Scotland. Maximus was hoping to become Emperor and came to Brittany with many soldiers under his command.
>
> As Britain was left without protection, St Patrick's father, Calpurnius, who was a Scottish Prince, also came here with his family. He was cousin to Conan-Meriadec, the legendary king of Wales, who gave him a large fertile estate on lands next to the sea. Local tradition claims it was from

here St Patrick was taken captive to Ireland, when pirates attacked the family estate at Bonaban.[8]

Robidue is right in saying that the majority of his fellow Breton historians at that time identified the place from which St Patrick was taken captive as being in Brittany and that the family had migrated to Brittany as part of the settlement at the time of Maximus from 383–388 CE but he is not presenting an accurate assessment of their claims in relation to where St Patrick was born. Most of the accounts given by the Breton historians clearly assume that St Patrick was born in Scotland.

M. de Gerville actually presents a very different claim when he says St Patrick was born at his father's estate in Brittany. Can we trust claims that St Patrick was born in Scotland or have the older Breton historians themselves placed too much trust in the established tradition concerning St Patrick's birth, even though they accept that he was taken captive from Brittany? If Patrick was born in 372 or 373 CE, was taken captive in 389 CE, escaped from slavery in Ireland in 395 or 396 CE, as many of these authors claim, and he then spent about twenty years in spiritual formation and training before returning to Ireland to begin his mission, such a chronology would date his return to Ireland as an apostle in 415 or 416 CE.

M. Daru says that following Conan's death in 421 CE Darerca went to Ireland to help her brother, St Patrick, in his mission, which implies that Patrick had begun his mission before 421 CE. Daru's chronology, therefore, suggests that St Patrick returned to Ireland as an apostle several years earlier than the traditional date of 432 CE that appears in the Irish annals. This raises difficulties in relation to the traditional dates given for St Patrick's mission to Ireland and also his death. If St Patrick came back to Ireland as an apostle in 432 CE, as the established tradition claims, then according to M. Daru's chronology, he would have been almost sixty years old, which seems unlikely. Alternatively, if St Patrick was born in 384 or 385 CE, was taken captive in 400 CE and escaped from Ireland in 407 CE, as Bury suggested, this would allow for the possibility that Patrick returned to Ireland as an apostle in 427 or 428 CE.[9]

Most of the Breton historians writing before the nineteenth century who provide a detailed account of Patrick's family situation in Brittany appear to rely on the ancient Lives of Saint Patrick published by John Colgan, for their information about St Patrick's place of birth. Many of these writers accept the established tradition that St Patrick was born in Scotland and, therefore, make no attempt to identify Nemthor, the name which probably holds the key to the truth as to where St Patrick was born. If St Patrick was born in Nemthor, as many of the ancient manuscripts claim, then as far as most of these Breton historians are concerned, Nemthor must have existed in Scotland because their chronology implies that St Patrick was born in Scotland.

The truth as to where Patrick was born is impossible to establish with certainty. In his *Confession*, St Patrick tells us the name of his homeland and the place from which he was taken captive, but he does not tell us where he was born. Attempts to rediscover the truth are not made easy because there are conflicting accounts in the ancient Lives of St Patrick published by Colgan and accounts recorded by Breton historians.

In light of the uncertainties, are there any more clues in the ancient sources which can help shed light on this important historical matter?

*St Fiacc's Hymn*, which is one of the earliest documents relating to St Patrick, records that he was born at Nemthor.[10] At an earlier stage, claims concerning its location and etymological arguments which could help to identify a specific place were examined. Some of the ancient writers understood 'Nemthor' as referring to a 'heavenly tower' or 'lighthouse' and modern authors have used this argument to identify the place of St Patrick's birth as Strathclyde in Scotland or Boulogne in France on the basis that a Roman tower or lighthouse existed in these places.[11] This is not sufficient evidence. The same etymological arguments could apply Mont St Michel (the Holy 'tor' or High Place) or the Roman tower and 'lighthouse' at Aleth that guided ships into the Roman port. Could Nemthor have existed in Brittany?

Some writers have suggested the claim that St Patrick was 'born' in Nemthor might not refer to his physical birth, but rather the place where he was 'spiritually born', when he was tonsured or became committed to the religious life. Villemarque and Hoey were convinced it refers to 'Holy Tours' (*Naem-Tour*), the place where St Martin built his monastery. This seems to be a reasonable interpretation. If so, then Nemthor could be a reference to Tours, since many of the ancient documents claim that Patrick was trained and tonsured within St Martin's community. The possibility that Conchessa was St Martin's niece adds to the mystery that surrounds the location of this place, since she may have gone to give birth to St Patrick in a place that was safe because of family relationships. The location of Nemthor will probably always be uncertain and controversial so all we can do is weigh up the balance of probabilities from the existing references.[12]

Unlike other geographical references that have been considered during the course of this enquiry, there is probably not sufficient evidence to identify the precise location of Nemthor but if we trust the account given by Probus, it is more likely to have been in Brittany rather than Scotland or elsewhere in Britain. Probus identifies Brittany as St Patrick's homeland and the location of Bannavem Tiburniae. He says it was the place where he was born and suffered 'the misfortunes of his youth' and that St Patrick was already resident there when Irish pirates attacked his father's estate, before he was taken captive and sold into slavery. Probus writes about St Patrick's place of origins as if he was seeking to correct alternative records, especially the account written by Muirchú which had claimed to know 'without doubt' that St Patrick had been taken captive and grown up in Britain. Probus presents a very different scenario. He states clearly that St Patrick was already resident in his homeland (Brittany) when the attack took place. When he locates this region in Armorica there can be no doubt about this.[13]

There are intriguing similarities and differences between the Breton accounts and those preserved in the ancient Lives of St Patrick about the circumstances which led to St Patrick being taken into captivity. These may provide clues as to when and where St Patrick was born.

If Calpurnius came from Strathclyde, as seems probable from what is recorded in Scottish and Breton historical records, the family may have lived for a time in Scotland before they migrated to Brittany. From a historical point of view, it is most likely this migration took place around 385 CE, as the Breton historians claim. Once Maximus launched his rebellion and the Roman legions left Britain it would have been impossible for St Patrick's family to remain in Scotland.

The date when St Patrick was born is, therefore, relevant to the question as to where he was born. If Patrick was born between 383 and 385 CE, he could have been born in Scotland then travelled to Brittany with his family when he was an infant or young child. He would still have grown up knowing Brittany as his homeland until the age of sixteen when he was taken captive. On the other hand, if the family moved to Brittany sometime between 383 and 385 CE and St Patrick was born in 384 or 385 CE he may have been born in Brittany, perhaps on his father's estate at Bannavem Tiburniae, as M. de Gerville has proposed, or possibly with the support of his mother's side of the family at Tours, if this is the true meaning of 'Nemthor'.[14] Without the discovery of authentic historical records we will probably never know exactly when or where St Patrick was born. Unfortunately, the Romans did not issue birth certificates. But it would make a very boring end to this enquiry if we sat on the fence.

A personal opinion can, therefore, be offered, not based on any reliable historical evidence, but linked to another possible clue in the secondary sources. The documents published by Colgan in 1647 contain several versions of a story which claims that St Patrick's family were only visiting their relations in Armorica, or Brittany, at the time Patrick was taken captive. None of these documents say the family had migrated from Scotland to Brittany and were resident there, as the Breton historians claim. What is common to both sources, however, is that St Patrick was taken captive from Brittany. The differences are in some ways understandable.[15]

In some accounts, the family members who made the journey from Strathclyde to Brittany are listed. Most versions identify the travellers as St Patrick, his father, Calpurnius, and mother, Conchessa, five sisters including Lupait, Tigris, Liaman, Darerca and Cinnemon and a brother called Senan. Breton historians record an identical list of names (in French) and most, like M. Deric, claim the children were all born before Calpurnius left Strathclyde. In their description of the voyage, all the family members listed above travelled together to Brittany as part of the settlement under Maximus in 383–385 CE.

One version of the family's journey from Scotland to Brittany presents an intriguing difference in personal detail. This concerns the list of family members who are said to have travelled with Calpurnius and Conchessa when the family boarded the ship for Brittany. The same basic story can be found in various ancient sources, but this account is unique in one significant respect. Patrick was not included by name in the list of travellers. This version of the story appears in notes added to *St Fiacc's Hymn* by the Scholiast, as recounted by John Colgan after he had analysed and compared all the various manuscripts at Louvain in 1647. The following passage can be found in the Appendix of Colgan's *Trias Thaumaturga*, in his reflections 'Concerning the Homeland and Family of St Patrick':

> In the second place, I quote from the Scholiast to St. Fiechin [*Fiacc's Hymn*, n. 5] where he says, 'This was the reason for the slavery of St Patrick. His father Calpurnius, and mother Conchessa, daughter of Ocmusius and his five sisters, Lupita, Tigris, Liemania and Darerca and the name of the fifth, Cinnemon and his brother Senan, all travelled together from Alcludensian Britain [Strathclyde] across the Iccian Sea in a southerly direction, for the sake of business, to Lethanian Armorica, alias Lethecan Britain: because in that place was a certain relative of theirs, *and because the mother of the expected offspring, that is to say, Conchessa*, was from France and a close relative of St Martin.[16]

At the beginning of the story, the author tells us the names of those family members who travelled by ship from Strathclyde to Armoric Letha. Calpurnius and Conchessa are listed on board. Five of St Patrick's sisters are named including Lupita, Tigris, Liaman, Darerca, Cinnemon and a brother called Senan. The one person who is not listed directly as one of the travellers is St Patrick. The passage above appears to be claiming that when the family made the journey by ship from Scotland to Brittany, Conchessa was pregnant.[17]

Could St Patrick have been the child in her womb? If so, and if there is any truth in this story, this allows for the possibility that St Patrick may have been conceived in Scotland, but born in Brittany. If Patrick was conceived at Strathclyde (which was a Welsh kingdom at that time) let's say in late 384 CE and the family migrated to Brittany early in 385, St Patrick could have been born in Brittany in 385 CE.

In either case, if he was conceived in Scotland and born in Brittany or moved to Brittany when he was an infant, Patrick would have grown up knowing Brittany as his homeland.

When Colgan examined the ancient manuscripts in 1647 he admitted that there were contradictory accounts as to where St Patrick was born. Colgan acknowledged an ancient tradition shared by a number of ancient Irish authors that St Patrick was born on the continent in a region known as 'Britannia Armorica'.[18]

A possibility that St Patrick was conceived in Scotland and that when the family boarded that ship to seek their fortunes in Brittany, Conchessa carried within her womb a child that would grow to become Ireland's patron saint and founding apostle adds to the sense of adventure which eventually characterised his whole life.

It would add yet another interesting dimension to the mystery and significance of the ancient site where Château Bonaban is now located, since this may not simply have been the place from which St Patrick was taken captive, but also perhaps, the place where he was born, or grew up as a young child. If so, then the château can rightly claim to be located in a significant, ancient historical site which deserves to be honoured and recognised as a sacred place of pilgrimage.

The deep sea of legend surrounding St Patrick is one in which storms of controversy have always gathered and no doubt will continue to do so. At an earlier stage in this enquiry, we reflected on the power of maps to change and shape our world view. The same basic principle applies with regard to history. The way history has been recorded has affected our understanding not only of the past but also of ourselves, the roots of our heritage and religious identity.

After the ancient Britons were crushed by the Anglo-Saxons between 450 and 550 CE many fled to Ireland, Brittany and remote parts of Wales; the places where Celtic Christianity was strong and survived longest. Churches in these regions were targeted by Rome for supporting the teachings of Pelagius and maintaining Jewish traditions. Before that, the presence of early monastic traditions such as those pioneered by St Martin of Tours, was strong. The years following the death of Maximus and Martin witnessed the increasing influence of Jerome and Augustine in the Church. Those associated with Irish or Gallic monasticism were increasingly suspect and marginalized. Severus records that for the last sixteen years of his life, after the Priscillian controversy, St Martin avoided the company of the diocesan bishops and refused to attend Church synods. This was the time of the real St Patrick, not the 'virtual' St Patrick of later legends and tradition.

Tensions and differences between the monks of St Martin and diocesan clergy continued, long after Martin's death. Martin was a very popular figure, especially among the people in Gaul and the Church recognised this when his body was interred in Tours Cathedral and his shrine became an important focus of pilgrimage. However, this did not take place until the Council of Tours in 461 CE, more than fifty years after St Martin's death. Those intervening years were crucial, for they witnessed a dramatic increase in the authority and influence of the Roman Church in Gaul. St Germanus and Pope Celestine were key players at this stage in history, who acted to safeguard the interests of Rome. They were both very loyal supporters of the teachings of St Augustine.

If St Patrick's family had migrated to Brittany and was closely related to Conan and Maximus and if Patrick had received spiritual formation and training at first with St Martin and then with a marginalized religious group in Brittany, then it is not unreasonable to suggest that St Patrick and his family may have come into conflict with these emerging diocesan authorities and their political allies. How closely St Patrick may or may not have been associated with those who were being marginalised or declared 'heretical' by the Church in the fifth century has yet to be fully determined.

What did St Patrick really look like? What ecclesiastical garments did he wear? How did he dress? What form of tonsure or 'hair style' did he adopt, if any? What kind of Christianity did he teach and bring to Ireland? These are all important questions because they have significance not only for knowing the truth about St Patrick but also for understanding the truth about ourselves, our heritage and history, all of which forms an essential part of our own sense of identity.

This period is not called the Dark Ages in Europe without reason. There are very few lights to guide us along this particular stretch of the highway of history. There is so much about St Patrick's story that is uncertain and will always remain a mystery but this should not prevent us from searching for the truth. St Patrick's life and our lives, his story and our story, are inextricably intertwined.

In his *Confession*, St Patrick writes as though he had already parted company with the Church in Brittany or Gaul that had originally supported him and some of the 'seniors' of that church had now parted company with him. His decision not to leave Ireland to defend himself further against the charges made against him suggests that he was determined to follow what he understood to be the guidance of God and his own conscience in relation to his calling and mission. St Patrick made this decision based on a deep sense of personal ethics and a spiritual calling that came to him directly from God. He chose to remain in Ireland for the rest of his life, to continue with the ministry he believed God had entrusted to him, completely committed to those he had been called to serve.

One of the many uncertainties about St Patrick's life concerns the circumstances in which he died. When he wrote the *Confession* he was sound of mind, but gives the impression he knew death was close at hand. We will probably never know how or why he died, whether from old age and natural causes, or for some other reason.

In the circumstances prevailing at that time, taking into account the serious nature of his conflict with Coroticus and the rejection by 'seniors' which may have involved accusations of financial irregularity and perhaps even heresy, it is possible that St Patrick may have died a martyr's death. It is so difficult for us to imagine what life was like for him in the fifth century, the beginning of the Dark Ages in Europe, yet there is something deeply mysterious and enduring about his story, which captures the imagination and touches the heart.

For St Patrick, Christian faith was a real adventure that required complete commitment and total disclosure of the heart before God, with renunciation of personal glory, wealth and social status and a willingness to face great dangers in a country where the old religion was strong and violence was common.

St Patrick was the great adventurer, a pioneering apostle in Ireland, beyond the known boundaries of the civilized world. He was prepared to boldly go where none had gone before and encouraged others to follow him and risk all for the promise of salvation. Patrick holds such a special place in the hearts and minds of so many people not only because he was Ireland's great apostle but because he was the last of the apostles, taking the Gospel to the ends of the earth at the very beginning of those Dark Ages when Europe was in great turmoil following the collapse of the Roman Empire.

Novelist and religious poet D.H. Lawrence catches the sense of adventure which characterized St Patrick's approach to the spiritual life and was so typical of those like him who embraced Christian faith as if it was the greatest adventure of all time. His words catch something of the spirit of those days and perhaps also a part of the reality of our own times when he says:

When Rome collapsed, Europe was a dark ruin. Wolves howled in the deserted streets. Then those whose souls were still alive withdrew together and gradually built monasteries and convents, little communities of quiet labor and courage. Helpless, yet never overcome in a world flooded with devastation. These alone kept the human spirit from disintegration, from going quite dark, in the Dark Ages. These men and women made the Church, which made Europe...

The flood of barbarism rose and covered Europe from end to end. But bless your life there was Noah in the Ark with all the animals. There was young Christianity. There were the lonely, fortified monasteries, little arks floating and keeping the adventure afloat. There is no break in the great adventure in human consciousness. Throughout the howlingest deluge, a few brave souls were steering the Ark under the rainbow...

If I had lived in the year 400, pray God, I should have been one of them.

I would have been a true and passionate Christian, the Adventurer. But now I live in 1934…and the Christian adventure is dead. We must all begin afresh on a new adventure towards God.[19]

St Patrick's life epitomized the best of Christian discipleship, at a time when Christianity was still considered to be an adventure. Of all that we can say about St Patrick and thank him for, one thing never to be denied is that he was essentially an honest, courageous and deeply spiritual person who sacrificed much in the service of others. During the course of his life, Patrick experienced great dangers and difficulties, but destiny now carried him to the threshold of Heaven. St Patrick is one of the greatest of the great saints and deserves to be remembered for who he really was. Whatever trauma he may have carried from the past, Patrick had found peace in his own heart and with God.

As the days of his mortal life drew to a close, St Patrick knew he was moving inexorably closer to the paradise he so strongly believed in and deeply longed for, clearly sensing God's presence, anticipating glory and fully prepared for death. His faith was so complete, he knew in his heart the adventure would continue. St Patrick strongly believed death was not the end; it was just the beginning of an even greater adventure and more mysterious journey. When he chose those final words that end his *Confession*, Patrick knew he was entering that mystic, sacred place, the proverbial 'thin place' where earth and heaven seem to meet and there is a sense that God is not far away. He could sense he was standing on the edge of a glory that is not of this world. However much he might have wanted to hold on, St Patrick understood the time had come to let go. And even though there is so much more of St Patrick's story that has yet to be told, the time has come for us to let go too.

May the Blessing of God and St Patrick always be with you.

---

*Notes*

1. John O'Donohue, *Anam Cara: Spiritual Wisdom from the Celtic World* (Great Britain, 1997).

2. When Colgan published *Trias Thaumaturga* in 1647, he accepted that there was a constant tradition amongst the inhabitants of Gaul that Patrick was a native of 'Armorican Britain' and he says this was endorsed by several Irish sources. John Colgan, *Trias Thaumaturga*, ed. Eamonn De Burca (Dublin, 1977), app. v., p. 2. *Emphasis added.

3. *Probus vero non (s)atis peritus rerum Patricianarum & locorum probatur.* App. v: 'Concerning the Homeland and Family of St Patrick'. See Colgan, *Trias Thau.*, p. 220.

4. Joseph Viel describes Rev. Boutlou as a 'minister of the Reformed religion' but this is not accurate. Rev. Fr Adeodatus Boutlou was born in France in 1850 and died in Baltimore, Va., USA in 1921. He is buried in Holy Cross cemetery, Fairmont, Marion County in West Virginia.

He was a Roman Catholic priest in the diocese of Rennes who left for the diocese of Wheeling (USA) on 9 December 1876. <www.heritagepursuit.com/UOhio1890P225.htm>

5. Joseph Viel, p.118: Translated by Christophe Saint-Eloi.

6. English translations are by Francine Bernier and Christophe Saint-Eloi.

7. *Les archaeographes ecossaise font naitre Saint Patrice aux portes de Dumbarton – M. de Gerville traduit 'Bonvenna de Tiburniae', designation géographique prise dans les Confessions du saint, par 'Bonaban', et place la son berceau. Il s'appuie, sans doute, sur le témoignage a peu prés unanime des historiens Breton, moins Lobineau.* Bertrand Robidue, *Histoire et Panorama d'un Beau Pays* (Rennes, 1953), p. 56.

8. Robidue, *Histoire*, p. 54 ff.

9. Coincidentally and perhaps significantly, St Germanus was sent to Britain to combat the teachings of Pelagius shortly afterwards in 429 CE. It is possible that the visit of Germanus to Britain and the appointment of Palladius to Ireland in 431 CE may have been in part a response by Rome and the diocesan authorities of the Church, to initiatives being taken by more marginalised monastic groups in Brittany, which had followed the teachings of St Martin and to which St Patrick belonged.

10. *St Fiacc's Hymn* begins by saying Patrick was born in 'Nemthor', which suggests this matter was of importance to the author, perhaps reflecting an authentic early tradition. See Whitley Stokes, *Tripartite Life of St Patrick* (London, 1887), p. 405.

11. No satisfactory evidence has ever been presented to locate 'Nemthor' anywhere in Britain.

12. An ancient tradition that St Patrick was born in France appears to have also been preserved in Colgan's *Fourth Life*, which refers to St Patrick's birth not in relation to Strathclyde in Scotland but in 'a more distant country'. Don Philip Sullivan Beare, who published a work on St Patrick in 1621, supported this view as did Dr Keating and Dr Lanigan. See Quarta Vita, John O'Hanlon, *Lives of the Irish Saints* (Dublin, 1875), p. 449, n. 186.

13. *In ciuitate eorum Arimuric.* See Bieler, ed., *Four Latin Lives of St Patrick* (Dublin, 1971), p. 195. Canon Flemming translates this as 'in their own sea-side city' on the basis that Caesar said all the towns on the sea coast of Armorica were called 'Armoricae'. He quotes Camden, *Britannica* (Abridged, London, 1701), i, p. 13. See William Flemming, *Boulogne-sur-Mer* (London, 1907), p. 68 ff.

14. Some of the ancient sources record that St Patrick was nurtured as a child by his mother's sister. It is likely she was living in Gaul, because that is where Conchessa's side of the family was resident possibly somewhere close to her uncle, St Martin.

15. The earliest accounts probably emerged from oral traditions and whenever they were recorded, it is to be expected that ancient authors would explain the various stories in circulation from their own perspective. Muirchú's narrative was influential and documents compiled in Ireland or Britain were bound to show variations to other records which may have been preserved in Brittany. This makes it even more remarkable that such detailed, complementary records survived, concerning the family's close associations with Brittany. Those who compiled Lives of St Patrick after Muirchú and who may have had access to other traditions which claimed that St Patrick was taken captive from a region on the continent had to find ways to reconcile conflicting accounts.

16. Colgan, *Trias. Thau*, p. 220. Translated by John Luce. *Emphasis added.

17. The Latin phrase recorded by Colgan is *& mater etiam praedictae prolis, nempe Conchessa*, which can be translated 'the mother of the expected offspring, namely Conchessa'. A few paragraphs later, Colgan records another version of the story, in which again St Patrick is not

listed as one of those who travelled with the family from Scotland to Brittany. The Latin phrase used to describe Conchessa's condition is *mater praedicta prolis, nempe Conchessa.* Colgan, *Trias. Thau,* p. 220. The precise meaning of both expressions is not easy to interpret, but suggests she was pregnant.

18. *In Britannia Armorica regione Gallia natum esse, vetus est tradition incolrum istius terra, cui & nonnuli suffraganta Hiberni, qui id eruere conantur:* 'That he was born in Brittany (Britannia) of the Armorican region of Gaul, is an ancient tradition of the inhabitants of that land; to which view also a number of Irish authors add their vote, who have tried to work this out from certain ancient records of their own country.' Colgan, *Trias Thau.,* p. 220. Translated by John Luce.

19. D. H. Lawrence, *Letters,* 1934.

# Bibliography

d'Argentré, Bertrand, *Histoire de Bretagne* (Paris, 1618).

— *Abrégé de l'Histoire de Bretagne* (Paris, 1695).

Barbour, Philippe, *Cadogan Guide to Brittany* (London, 2008).

Le Baud, Pierre, *Histoire de Bretagne* (Paris, 1638).

Bede, *History of the English Church and People*, trans. Leo Sherley-Price (USA, 1980).

Bieler, Ludwig, *The Patrician Texts in the Book of Armagh* (Dublin, 2004).

— ed., *Four Latin Lives of St Patrick* (Dublin, 1971).

— *The Life and Legend of St Patrick* (Dublin, 1949).

— *The Works of St Patrick* (New York, 1952).

— 'The Problem of Silva Focluti', *Irish Historical Studies*, 3/12 (1943).

— *Clavis Patricii II: Libri Epistolarum Sancti Patricii Episcopi* (Dublin, 1993).

Binchy, D. A., 'Patrick and his Biographers', *Studia Hibernica*, 2 (1962).

Bizeul, *Memoire sur les Origins du Mont-St-Michel* (Paris, 1844).

Blanchet, A. 'Fouille du mur de l'ancienne ville Alet', *Bulletin Archéologique du Comité des travaux historique et scientifiques*, 25 (1908).

Blondel, Louis, *Notice Historique du Mont-St-Michel, de Tombelaine et d'Avrenches* (Avrenches, 1823).

Bonner, Gerald, *St Augustine of Hippo: Life and Controversies* (Norwich, 2002).

Brenot, C., 'Les monnaies romaines des fouille d'Alet', *Les Dossiers du centre regional d'archeologie d'Alet*, 2 (1974).

— 'Monnaies d'Alet', *Annales de Bretagne*, 76/1 (1969).

Bury, J. B., *The Life of St Patrick, His Place in History* (London, 1905).

Cahill, Thomas, *How the Irish Saved Civilization* (New York, 1995).

Camden, *Britannica* (Abridged, London, 1701).

Carew, Mairead, *Tara and the Ark of the Covenant* (Dublin, 2003).

Carney, James, *Studies in Irish Literature and History* (Dublin, 1979).

de Paor, Liam, *St Patrick's World* (Dublin, 1993).

de Paor, Marie, *Patrick: The Pilgrim Apostle of Ireland* (Dublin, 1998).

McCarthy, Dan, *The Irish Annals: Their Genesis and History* (Dublin, 2008).

McCarthy, Pádraig, trans., *My Name is Patrick: St Patrick's Confessio* (Dublin, 2011).

Chadwick, Nora, *Age of the Saints in the Celtic Church* (Durham, 1960; facs. edn, Llanerch, 2006).

Charles-Edwards, T. M., *Early Christian Ireland* (Cambridge, 2000).

Chèvremont, Alexandre, *Les Mouvements du Sol sur les Côtes Occidentales de la France*, ed. E. Leroux (Paris, 1882).

Colgan, John, *Trias Thaumaturga*, ed. Eamonn De Burca (Dublin, 1977).

Commission Histoire de Skol Vreizh, *L'Histoire de la Bretagne et des Payes Celtique* (Morlaix, 1966).

Conneely, Daniel, *The Letters of St Patrick* (Maynooth, 1993).

Cope, Julian, *The Megalithic European* (London, 2004).

Cosgrave, B., ed., *The Life of Bishop Wilfrid by Eddius Stephanus* (Cambridge, 1985).

Ó Cróinín, Dáibhí, ed., *A New History of Ireland* (Oxford, 2005).

Cunningham, Bernadette, *The Annals of the Four Masters: Irish history, kingship and society in the early seventeenth century* (Dublin, 2010)

Cusack, M. F., *Life of St Patrick, Apostle of Ireland* (London, 1877).

Daru, P. A., *Histoire de Bretagne*, i (Paris, 1826).

Davies, Oliver, ed., *Celtic Spirituality* (New York, 1999).

Deric, Gilles, *Histoire Ecclésiastique de Bretagne*, ii (Paris, 1778).
— *Memoires Relatifs a L'Histoire de France* (Paris, 1835).

Desfontaines, Pierre François Guyot, *Histoire des Ducs de Bretagne*, i (Paris, 1739).

Desroches, Jean-Jacques, *Histoire du Mont St Michel*, i (Caen, 1838).

Doremet, Jacques, *L'Antiquité d'Aleth* (La Cane de Montfort, 1628).
— *De Antiquité de la Ville et cité d'Aleth, ou Quidalet*, ed. Thomas de Querci (St Malo, 1894; Slatkine Reprints, 1971).

Errman, Bart D., *Misquoting Jesus: The Story Behind Who Changed the Bible and Why* (New York, 2005).

Flemming, William, *Boulogne-sur-Mer* (London, 1907).

Anon., trans., 'St Fiacc's Hymn', *Ecclesiastical Record* (1868), O'Curry MS, Catholic University.

Geoffrey of Monmouth, 'History of the Kings of Britain', in *Six Old English Chronicles*, trans. J.A. Giles and Aaron Thompson, (1848).

de Gerville, Charles, *Lettres sur la communication entre les Deux Bretagnes* (Valognes, 1844).

Gibbon, Edward, *Decline and Fall of the Roman Empire*, 8 vols (London, 1862).

Giles, J. A., *Six Old English Chronicles* (London, 1868).

Gregory of Tours, *History of the Franks*, trans. Lewis Thorpe (London, 1974).

Hanson, R. P. C., *St Patrick His Origins and Career* (Oxford, 1997).

Heather, Peter, *The Fall of the Roman Empire* (London, 2005).

Henry, René, *Au Péril de la Mer* (Paris, 2006).

Howlett, David, *Muirchú Moccu Mactheni's 'Vita Sancti Patricii'* (Dublin, 2006).

Kenney, James, *The Sources for the Early History of Ireland: Ecclesiastical* (Dublin, 1997).

Langouet, L., 'La Forêt du Scissy et La marée de 709, Légende ou Réalité?' *Dossiers du Centre Régional d'Archéologie d'Alet*, 24 (1996).

— *Alet Ville Ancienne* (Rennes, 1973).

— 'L'Histoire d'Alet', *Dossiers du Centre Régional d'Archéologie d'Alet*, 2 (1974).

Lanigan, John, *Ecclesiastical History of Ireland*, 4 vols (Dublin, 1822; 2nd edn, Dublin, 1829).

Lappenberg, Johann Martin, *A History of England under the Anglo-Saxon Kings*, i, trans. Benjamin Thorpe (London, 1865).

Lobineau, G. A., *Histoire de Bretagne*, 2 vols (Paris, 1707).

MacDari, Conor, *The Bible: an Irish Book* (London, 2005).

Macnab, Duncan, *Archaeological Dissertation on the Birthplace of St Patrick* (Dublin, 1865).

MacNeill, Eoin, *Saint Patrick, Apostle of Ireland* (London, 1934).

— 'Silua Focluti', *Proceedings of the Royal Irish Academy, Section C: Archaeology, Celtic Studies, History, Linguistics, Literature*, 36 (1923).

Manet, Gilles, *De L'etat Ancien et De L'etat Actuel dans La Baie de Mont Saint Michel* (St Malo, 1829).

— 'Memoires Sur Les Origins du Mont St Michel', *Memoires de la Societé Royale des Antiq. De France*, 17 (1844).

Maury, Alfred, *Memoires de la Societe Nationale des Antiquaires*, 7/17.

— 'Observations sur Les Origins du Mont St Michel et en particulier sur l'existence de la Forêt de Scissy', *Memoires de la Societe Royale des Antiq. De France*, 17 (1844).

Milne, Kenneth, *Christ Church Cathedral: A History* (Dublin, 2000).

Mitchell, Dugald, *History of the Highlands and Gaelic Scotland* (Paisley, 1900).

Mohrman, Christine, *The Latin of St Patrick* (Dublin, 1961).

Molloy, Dara, *The Globalisation of God* (Inismor, Aran Islands, 2009).

Moore, Thomas, *History of Ireland* (New York, 1835).

Morice, P. H., *Histoire de Bretagne*, 2 vols (Paris, 1742–6).

— *Memoires Pour Server de Preuves a l'Histoire de Bretagne*, 3 vols (Paris, 1742–6).

Nennius, 'History of the Britons: Historia Brittonum' in *Six Old English Chronicles*, ed. J. A. Giles (London, 1858).

O'Donnell, James, *The Ruin of the Roman Empire* (US, 2009).

O'Flaherty, Roderic, *Oxygia* (Dublin, 1775).

O'Hanlon, John, *Lives of the Irish Saints* (Dublin, 1875).

O'Leary, James, ed., *Ancient Lives of Saint Patrick* (New York, 1880), *Project Gutenberg* [ebook] <http://www.gutenberg.org/files/18482/18482-h/18482-h.htm> published online 1 June 2006.

O'Loughlin, Thomas, *Discovering St Patrick* (London, 2005).

— *St Patrick: the Man and His Works* (London, 1999).

O'Neill, Patrick, 'The Identification of Foclut', *Journal of the Galway Archaeological and Historical Society*, 22/4 (1947).

O'Rahilly, Thomas, *The Two Patricks* (Dublin, 1942; repr. 1981).

Origine Gallo-Romaine de l'Eveche d'Alet, *Annals de la Societe d'Histoire et Archéologie de Saint Malo* 95, 1974.

Palgrave, Francis, *History of Normandy and Britain* (London, 1861).

Anon., *Life of St Patrick*, (Paris, 1870).

Poslan, M., *Cambridge Economic History of Europe* (Cambridge, 1966).

Pfister, J. G., 'Stray Leaves from the Journey of a Traveller in Search of Ancient Coins', *The Numismatic Chronicle and Journal of the Numismatic Society*, xix (London, 1857).

Probus, 'Life of St Patrick: Vita Auctore Probo' in *Four Latin Lives of St Patrick*, trans. Ludwig Bieler (Dublin, 1971).

'Histoire de Bretagne', *Foreign Quarterly Review*, xii, London, 1827.

Reeves, William, *The Culdees of the British Islands* (Dublin, 1864). Facsimile reprinted by Llanerch Publishers, Somerset, 1994.

Rio, Joseph, *Myths Fondateurs de la Bretagne, Aux Origins de la Celtomania* (Rennes, 2000).

Robidue, Bertrand, *Histoire et Panorama d'un Beau Pays* (Rennes, 1953).

De Roujoux, P. G. *Histoire des Rois et des Ducs de Bretagne* (Paris, 1828).

Rouze, Michel, *La Forêt de Quokelunde* (Paris, 1953).

Ruault, L'Abbé, *Abrégé de l'Histoire des Solitaires de Scissy* (St Malo, 1734).

de Saint-Pair, Guillaume, *Le Roman du Mont-Saint-Michel* (Caen, 1856).

Sulpicius Severus, 'Life of St Martin' in *The Nicene and Post Nicene Fathers*, xi, eds Philip Schaff and Henry Wace (New York, 1894).

— 'Dialogues' in *The Nicene and Post Nicene Fathers*, xi, eds Philip Schaff and Henry Wace (New York, 1894).

Skene, W. F., *Celtic Scotland* (Edinburgh, 1886).

Stephanus, Eddius, *Life of Wilfrid*, trans. J. F. Webb (London, 1986).

Stokes, Whitley, *Tripartite Life of St Patrick* (London, 1887).

— Anon., *Anecdota Oxoniensia* (Oxford, 1890), facs. edn trans. Whitley Stokes, as *Lives of the Saints from the Book of Lismore* (Somerset, 1990).

Sullivan, William, *Historical Causes and Effects from the Fall of the Roman Empire 476 to the Reformation 1517* (Boston, 1838).

Taylor, Jeremy, *Dreamwork* (New York, 1983).

Thierry, Augustin, *History of the Norman Conquest* (London, 1847).

Thomas, Charles, *Christianity in Roman Britain to AD 500* (Berkeley and Los Angeles,1981).

Thompson, E.A., 'Procopius on Brittia and Britannia', *The Classical Quarterly*, New Series, 30/2 (1980).

Todd, J. H., *St Patrick, Apostle of Ireland* (Dublin, 1864).

Tourault, Philippe, *Les Rois de Bretagne IVème–XIXème Siècle* (Paris, 2005).

de Saint-Luc, P. Toussaint, 'Histoire de Conan' in *Dissertation Historique sur L'Origins des Bretons*, i (Paris, 1739).

de Saint-Pair, Guillaume, *Le Roman du Mont-Saint-Michel* (Caen, 1856).

Trébutien, Guillaume-Stanislas, *Le Mont St Michel au Peril de la Mer* (Caen, 1841).

Tukner, J.H., 'An Inquiry as to the Birthplace of St Patrick', *Archaeologica Scottica*, v (1890).

Turner, Sharon, *The History of the Anglo-Saxons* (London, 1852).

Ussher, James, *A Discourse on the Religion Anciently Professed by the Irish and the British* (London, 1631).

Vermaat, Robert, *Procopius of Caesare*, Vortigern Studies [website] <http://www.vortigernstudies.org.uk/artsou/procop.htm>

de Vere, Nicholas and Tracy Twyman, *The Dragon Legacy: A Secret History and of Ancient Bloodline* (San Diego, 2004).

Villemarque, *La Legende Celtique* (Paris, 1864).

Wallace, J. M., *Chronicle of Fredegar* (Oxford, 1960).

Wenzler, Claude, *Genealogies of the Kings of France* (Rennes, 2010).

William of Malmesbury, *The Kings before the Norman Conquest*, trans. Joseph Stevenson (Somerset, 1989).

— *The Antiquities of Glastonbury*, trans. Frank Lomax (Somerset, 1992).

Williams, Hugh, trans., *Two Lives of Gildas by a monk of Ruys and Caradoc of Llancarfan* (Cymmrodorion Series, 1899; facs. edn Llanerch, 1990).

Kaiser, Ward and Denis Wood, *Seeing through Maps: the Power of Images to Shape our World View* (Massachusetts, 2001).

Woods, Richard, *The Spirituality of the Celtic Saints* (New York, 2000).

White, N. J., *Translation of the Latin Writings of St Patrick* (London, 1918).

Wylie, J. A., *History of the Scottish Nation* (London, 1887).

Zimmer, Heinrich, *The Celtic Church in Britain and Ireland* (London, 1902).

## CHARTS

Chart of Roman Roads, *Statistique Monumentale du Department du pas De Calais* (Commission des Antiquities, 1840).

## ANNALS

*Annals of Ulster (AU)*, trans. Sean Mac Airt and Gearoid Mac Niocaill, Dublin Institute for Advanced Studies (Dublin,1983).

*Annals of Tigernach*, trans. Whitley Stokes, i, *Revue Celtique* 16 (1895); facsimile edition published by Llanerch, 1993.

*Annals of Ireland by the Four Masters*, 7 vols, de Burca (Dublin, 1990).

*Annals of Inisfallen*, trans. Sean Mac Airt (Dublin 1944 [1951]), Celt: The Corpus of Electronic Texts (UCC) [website] <http://www.ucc.ie/celt/published/T100004/index.html>

# Index